INTERNATIONAL
RADIO BROADCASTING

INTERNATIONAL RADIO BROADCASTING

The Limits of the Limitless Medium

Donald R. Browne

PRAEGER SPECIAL STUDIES • PRAEGER SCIENTIFIC

Library of Congress Cataloging in Publication Data

Browne, Donald R.
  International radio broadcasting.

  Bibliography: p.
  Includes index.
  1. International broadcasting.   2. Radio
broadcasting.   3. Radio in propaganda.
I. Title.
HE8697.P6B76   384.54   81-22707
ISBN 0-03-059619-X   AACR2

Published in 1982 by Praeger Publishers
CBS Educational and Professional Publishing
a Division of CBS Inc.
521 Fifth Avenue, New York, New York 10175, U.S.A.

© 1982 by Praeger Publishers

23456789   145   987654321

Printed in the United States of America

PREFACE

Certain subjects seem to be more "faddish" than others, interest in them waxing and waning for a host of reasons. International radio broadcasting is a member of this oft-distinguished company. It has received extensive lay and scholarly attention during three major periods of time: in the course of and just after World War II, during the late 1950s and early 1960s, and again in the early to mid-1970s. War or threat of war has been one apparent factor, but so have public debates on the subject of whether international broadcasting is worth the money spent on it. Accordingly, many of the books and articles written during those periods tend to examine international broadcasting in those lights.

While we may be approaching another "war or threat of war" period as I write this preface, I hope that I have managed to avoid the sometimes unacknowledged and even unrecognized (by themselves) tendencies of various writers to view international broadcasting through wartime or economy-time glasses. I have sought to draw on my nearly 25 years of exploration of international broadcasting, and on articles, books and reports dating back to the 1920s, to provide an historical treatment of this subject that would avoid those narrower perspectives and would consider how and why international broadcasting has evolved and what its effects have been, or may have been.

Although the individual chapters of the book should speak for themselves, writing them has given me a stronger conviction than ever that international radio broadcasting has been and remains a significant form of international communication. One cannot, it is true, point to specific instances of how it has ended or averted war, although it appears to have played some role in starting several conflicts and in foreshortening a few. In fact, as with mass media in general, it is very difficult to pinpoint any specific effects of this form of communication. But as the chapters unfold the story, it should become evident that the cause of promoting better understanding among nations and peoples has been served, albeit to varying degrees, by international broadcasting. There are also plenty of instances in which international broadcasting has been employed to sow discord or foment rebellion; whether for good or evil purposes is a matter of individual judgement.

My central thesis is that international radio broadcasting, despite its glamor and its widespread adoption, functions within some rather severe limitations, principally

political, cultural, technical and economic. Some of those
limitations can be and have been overcome, but lack of well-
defined objectives and strategies and insufficient attention
to assessment of possible effects of broadcasts have made
the task more difficult. I have developed my thesis primarily through an examination of the history of international
broadcasting, and a selective history, at that: I do not
mention every international station that has ever existed,
and I present relatively few in any detail. My documentation
varies a good deal, usually because of availability of sources.
It is richest for the Western stations and thinnest for the
Third World stations, while the Communist stations are covered
to a considerable extent through Western sources. Still, I
feel that the variety of stations is wide enough to provide
you with a reasonably comprehensive picture of international
radio broadcasting.

My main intention in writing this book is to help you to
understand better the reasons for the birth and growth of
international stations in particular and international radio
in general, the sorts of internal and external pressures that
bear upon stations, the sorts of messages they broadcast, and
the types of listeners they reach. I have attempted to balance
my experiences as scholar and practitioner (the latter including service as a Voice of America correspondent in Tunisia
in the early 1960s) in preparing an account of a fascinating
but misunderstood and perhaps oversold medium of international
communication. I have provided extensive footnotes and a
selective bibliography as aids to any wishing to pursue
further studies. I hope there will be many who do. To para-
phrase the Biblical parable, in this particular scholarly
vineyard, the laborers are few!

A final word of advice: the majority of you who read
this book will most likely live in industrially developed,
"democratic" societies. One of the clearest indications we
have from audience research in international broadcasting is
that listening to international radio is far from widespread
in such societies. As you make your own assessments of the
importance of this medium of communication, you might consider what international broadcasting could mean to listeners
in developing and/or "non-democratic" nations, where the flow
of information is restricted by monetary, political or physical
factors. It is in those settings that international radio
might be expected to display most clearly such value as it
possesses. Unfortunately, it is in those settings that we
know least about its impact.

I wish to acknowledge the assistance of several people
who read portions of the manuscript for this book: Sydney
Head, Glenn Hauser, Kim Andrew Elliott, Bernard Bumpus,
Gerard Mansell, Anita Mallinckrodt, Fred Collins, Hugh Olds,
Peter Janicki, Bert Steinkamp, Errol Hodge and Carmino

Leicester. I also wish to thank the BBC Monitoring Service for granting me permission to make reference to items appearing in their <u>World Broadcasting Information</u> and <u>Summary of World Broadcasts</u>. And finally, I wish to thank the University of Minnesota Office of International Programs, McMillan Fund and Department of Speech Communication, the Fulbright-Hays program and the NATO Fellowship program for their financial assistance.

Work on the manuscript was completed in fall 1981. However, much of the material on broadcast hours and languages, budgets and numbers of listener letters portrays situations as they were in 1980 and as they were reported in yearbooks and annual handbook appearing in 1981.

Note: Script excerpts, unless otherwise identified, are transcribed from my own monitoring of broadcasts.

CONTENTS

INTERNATIONAL
RADIO BROADCASTING

1

THE PROCESS OF
INTERNATIONAL BROADCASTING

When Guglielmo Marconi carried out his experiments with the transmission of information through radio waves, he often did so with a touch of drama. The most dramatic of those early experiments was the 1901 transmission of a signal from southwestern England and its reception in Newfoundland. That might be called the first international broadcast, except that there was nothing very broad about it: only one receiver was capable of picking it up, and the message was in telegraphic code. But it was a very graphic demonstration of the power of radio waves to carry messages throughout the world, and to do so instantaneously.

Although there were further experiments with the same sort of wireless telegraphy that Marconi had used, and although others soon devised ways of getting radio waves to carry voices and music, over 20 years were to pass before nations attempted to communicate with each other's citizens through radio broadcasting,[1] and over 25 years before any of them established an ongoing radio station for that purpose. Yet by the early 1930s political figures such as Germany's Josef Goebbels were to speak of international broadcasting as a "limitless medium," and to see it as a powerful instrument of international diplomacy, persuasion, and even coercion.

International radio broadcasting enjoyed an almost meteoric rise during the late 1930s and World War II, and, after pausing just after the war, another rapid climb during the 1950s and 1960s. While that growth has levelled off during the past decade, it is evident that few nations, with the major exception of most of those in Latin America, intend to be without it. Some are prepared to spend $100 million a year or more on it; a few spend just as much to keep their citizens from receiving it. Its limits may be more evident now than they were some 50 years ago, but international broadcasting still carries with it some of that aura of limitlessness. It can travel everywhere (with enough power),

it can speak to literate and illiterate alike, and it can use
the persuasive power of the human voice.

The growth of international radio was as diverse as it
was rapid, and by the late 1930s international broadcasting
was being employed by national governments, religious
organizations, commercial advertisers, domestic broadcasters
and even educators to bring their various messages to
listeners abroad. That same diversity exists today, and
seems likely to continue for some time to come, as new
stations come on the air almost every year with the support
of governments, religious groups and advertisers. In a world
that is increasingly television-minded, international radio
still seems to play a prominent role as an instrument of
international communication.

International television is increasing in importance,
too, but I say very little about it in this book, simply
because there's plenty to say about international radio.
Nor does international television work in the same "direct-
from-broadcaster-to-audience" manner. Direct broadcasts
from satellites to home receivers (DBS) are already possible,
but very few television viewers can afford the necessary
receiving apparatus, and no television station as yet treats
viewers with DBS home receivers as its primary audience.
Within the next few decades, however, and despite some
tremendous financial, legal, technical and socio-psychological
problems, that form of international television will grow.[2]
There is also a very lively trade in television program
distribution among nations, in the form of the rental and
free provision of series and individual programs. However,
most of those programs are made for domestic audiences,
rather than for viewers abroad. The United States, Great
Britain and West Germany are especially active in such
international distribution, which itself has been criticized
as perhaps the worst form of "media imperialism"--the
instiller of alien and often harmful ideas and values in the
minds of Third World (developing nations) viewers.[3] (Several
Third World nations, such as Egypt and Mexico, are also
major exporters of television programs). International
television already merits book-length treatment; when that
book appears, I would be surprised if many of the issues I
cover in the present book do not reappear.

As you'll see in the succeeding chapters, international
radio stations, however different their goals, have certain
concerns in common. All must create or obtain programing
material appropriate to their purposes, all must select the
best means of transmitting their broadcasts, all must operate
within the (admittedly loose) framework of international
regulations, all must procure financial support, and all
must realize that their purposes for broadcasting entail both
limitations and opportunities. The present chapter treats

each of those concerns in a more or less general fashion, so
that, when you read later about the activities of specific
international radio stations, you may consider those activities within the overall context of restrictions and possibilities faced by all who seek to use this "limitless
medium".

There are two terms of reference that occur throughout
this book, and that should be defined before going any
further. One of them forms part of its title. "International radio broadcasting" has been used by some authors
to refer to any broadcast picked up outside the borders of
the originating country. I employ the term in a more restricted manner, to include only the purposeful attempts on
the part of stations in one country to reach listeners in
other countries. I also refer to international broadcasting
organizations as stations, even though they may include many
separate (but interrelated) broadcast services in many
different languages. To someone listening to BBC's Swahili
service, she or he may be unaware of the 39 other language
services broadcast by the station; for her or him, the
Swahili service is the BBC, but that does not make the other
services any less a part of the BBC, or change the fact that
all of the services are under some measure of central control.

BROADCASTS AND BROADCASTERS

Given the fact that international radio stations have
anywhere from two or three to 60 or more language services,
and that they may be on the air for 10 to 100 hours a day or
more, the preparation of program materials is bound to be
akin to life on a treadmill for most of them. Some ease
their burdens by retransmitting large amounts of material
from the domestic radio services; others do so by rebroadcasting original (station-produced) programs two, three or
more. times during the day. Still others devote large amounts
of broadcast time to pre-recorded music. When all is said
and done, however, there is a great deal of original material
on the international airwaves each day. I discuss specific
programs in the chapters on the individual stations, and
undertake here a more general consideration of formats and
styles, production practices, language services and the
broadcasters themselves.

Formats and Styles

Although international broadcasting is associated most
often with informational broadcasting, that information can

appear through a wide variety of formats: newscasts, talks,
interviews, press reviews, documentaries and many others
(see Appendix A). Few international stations lack news
coverage of domestic and world events, but many informational
programs also attempt to portray the economic, scientific,
educational, religious and cultural life of the broadcasting
nation. In that case, the formats already listed may be
joined by dramas, music, live broadcasts of religious
services and sports events, etc. In short, most of the
formats used in international radio will be familiar to anyone who regularly listens to public radio in the United
States or to non-commercial radio in most other parts of the
world. There is even a certain amount of educational broadcasting on some international stations, in that several of
them offer lessons in their nations' major language(s).

Most international broadcasters place heavy emphasis on
contests, music request shows, listener mailbags (for
answering listeners' questions), DX programs (for long
distance listener hobbyists), and brief announcements asking
for listener reaction to programing. Most international
radio stations probably spend more time soliciting listener
feedback than do their domestic counterparts, because that
feedback can be used for several purposes: to produce
evidence to show others that there <u>are</u> listeners out there;
to learn more about quality of reception of the broadcast
signal; to gain more concrete impressions of listener
opinion on programing; to assure listeners that the station
--and by implication its governmental, religious or commercial sponsor--is both friendly and receptive.

It's an open question as to whether there is any such
thing as "pure entertainment" in international broadcasting.
Most stations which program large amounts of music claim to
do so because it will tell listeners something about the
culture of the broadcasting nation or organization. Some
stations also program music from the listeners' own
countries, to show listeners that the station and its sponsor
respect other cultures. (It helps that music is relatively
inexpensive to program, and is less likely to arouse the
suspicion or hostility of a listener, who in turn may be led
gradually to other, more "meaty" fare).[4] International
commercial radio stations concern themselves with music that
will attract listeners in sufficient numbers to interest
advertisers, and do not bother themselves overmuch about the
images the music will evoke in the minds of listeners, but
such stations are few.

Program formats vary from station to station, but
almost all stations offer news, music and listeners' mailbag
programs. Most also offer features on life within the
broadcasting nation. Some offer press reviews (summaries of
major stories and editorials from the domestic press),
language lessons and DX programs. A few have special

programs on business and industry and on tourism, designed to "sell" the nation's tourist attractions and business products. Very few international stations prepare documentaries or dramas, partly because they are time-consuming and expensive to produce and partly because the more elaborate sound patterns of such productions cannot be received all that clearly over short wave. Most programing is done in 10-, 15- and 30-minute blocks, in a firmly fixed schedule, although the more loosely-structured "magazine" formats (mixtures of music, news, features, etc.) seem to be more and more common. Most of the individual language services are on the air for 30 minutes to two hours at a time, often with repeat broadcasts later in the day. Music usually accounts for anywhere from 10 to 50 per cent of a station's schedule, except for international commercial stations, where it may go to 80 or 90 per cent, and for clandestine stations or stations with brief (30 minutes or less per day) language services, where there may be no music at all.

A listener hearing most international stations for the first time probably will be struck by their heavy concentration on talk and by their relative formality. Certainly anyone accustomed to the disk jockey-hosted programs of U.S., Canadian, British and French radio, or to the sometimes rather informal delivery of the news by newsreaders on many of those same stations, will find international radio a bit more staid, on the whole. For some international stations, this is a necessity: the news and certain features must be translated or directly read from governmentally-approved copy, which is often formal and even turgid. For others, the formality seems to be a reflection of domestic radio style: there are many national radio services which strongly discourage informal scripting and delivery, and, since many international stations are linked administratively with national services, they follow suit, regardless of the tastes and styles of the countries and listeners they seek to reach.

Most international broadcasting seems to assume a fairly high level of language comprehension on the part of listeners. Only one station, so far as I know, broadcasts in a simplified form of a language (VOA, in special English, which employs a 1,200-word vocabulary and a delivery rate of 90 words per minute). Several stations broadcast some news and other material in slow-speed delivery, but this appears to be done to allow listeners to take dictation, rather than as an aid to comprehension. (Such listeners may then use the broadcast material in their own newsletters, leaflets, handbills, etc.) The few research studies that have been directed at assessing the degree to which listeners actually comprehend international broadcasts are discussed in Chapter 12.

Many of the larger international stations, and some of
the smaller ones, employ writers and announcers who are
citizens or former citizens of other countries, and who speak
and write the languages of those countries fluently and
correctly. Some of those individuals have already had
journalistic experience, and bring their old habits with them
when they come to work for the station. Those old habits
will probably include formal style and the assumption that
the average audience member is capable of comprehending
fairly complex sentence structures and vocabulary--one more
factor which helps to account for the "sound" of much international broadcasting.

As I have already noted, some stations have moved
toward greater informality during the 1960s and 1970s. The
Voice of America introduced its "Breakfast Show" in 1963;
U.S. listeners who tuned it in probably found it much like
NBC's weekend "Monitor": a mixture of brief newscasts,
features, interviews and music, presided over by "informal"
hosts and hostesses. There was nothing quite like it in
international broadcasting at the time, but several stations
have added similar shows to their schedules since then, and
many stations use disc jockeys, as well, some of whom have
developed considerable followings among their listeners.
There is some evidence that informality is appreciated by
some listeners, although others seem to prefer a more
formal, "dignified" approach.[5]

Production Practices

As I stated in the preface, I do not intend to examine
in any detail the process of program production in international stations. However, there are a few aspects of that
process which are worth mentioning here, because they will
help to explain why stations sometimes encounter difficulties in terms of broadcasting incorrect or misleading
information or utilizing almost incomprehensible styles of
writing and delivery.

Different stations follow different practices, but most
function with a central news room which prepares newscasts
for translation and delivery by the various language services. Some stations permit their language services wide
latitude in the editing and translation of the centrally-
prepared newscast, while others (BBC and VOA in particular)
do not. Some stations also prepare many or even all of their
talks and features centrally; again, some of those stations
allow various measures of creative freedom and selectivity
to their language divisions, while others insist upon strict
adherence to the centrally-prepared text.

A few stations, most notably BBC, have taken care to
establish close working relationships between the central
news room and the language services, so that problems
encountered by writers and announcers in the language
divisions can be discussed with the news room personnel who
originally prepared the material. Many stations I have
visited are indifferent to such a possible need, and a few
seem absolutely hostile to the idea. The results of the
latter may be lack of initiative, indifferent performance
and inaccurate or overly "bookish" translations of copy.

Most international stations attempt to be reasonably
up to date with at least some of the news. If the procedure
I have just described fails to work smoothly, the result can
be delays in the broadcast of some items and hastily and
often sloppily-prepared translations of others. But because
few stations have systematic and frequent checkbacks on
their broadcast output, many of them fail to detect errors
unless they are really colossal, and many never may come to
realize that their highly formal and sometimes cliché-ridden
or even antique styles of writing and delivery may be costing
them many listeners.

Language Services

Very few international radio stations broadcast in one
language only; most broadcast in anywhere from three or four
to 30 or more languages. Yet, although there are hundreds
of languages spoken around the world, those chosen for
broadcast by international stations number little more than
a hundred. Most of the choices are logical enough: the
national languages of one's own country, the major world
languages.* But why does BBC choose to broadcast in Norwegian, while VOA does not? Why does Deutsche Welle
initiate a Farsi (Iranian) service, Radio Cairo a Wolof
(West Africa) service, Radio Moscow a service in Quechua
(South American Indian)?[6]

A look at the dates of initiation of language services,
coupled with an examination of Keesing's Contemporary
Archives or the World Almanac, will answer some questions.
World crises often cause nations to respond by directing
international broadcasts to audiences living in or near
crisis areas, if they are not served already. Initiation
of a language service by one nation may cause opposing
nations to broadcast in the same language, so as not to be
outflanked. Establishment or resumption of diplomatic
relations between two nations may produce a like response,
although it may also cause certain language services to be
dropped, if their content was hostile. The desire to
strengthen trade relations may see new language services

---

*See Appendix C

introduced. A country which plays host to exile groups, as
Great Britain, the USSR and the United States did during
World War II, as the latter two continue to do, and as
Egypt and Tanzania have done in Africa, Cuba in Latin
America, and the Peoples' Republic of China in Asia, may
provide international broadcast facilities for those groups.
Even the presence of sizeable and/or politically powerful
immigrant communities can help lead to the development of
new language services, as for example the Armenian community
in the United States showed in the late 1940s and early
1950s,[7] when it encouraged the development of an Armenian
service on VOA.

New language services frequently are suggested through
embassies, whether of the broadcasting nation or of the
potential receiving nation. Creation of a language service
can be a symbol of strong diplomatic and/or trade relations,
as I have noted above, and embassies are among the strongest
advocates of such a step, since it reflects credit on them.
The initiation of a Persian (Farsi) service by West Germany's
Deutsche Welle in 1962 apparently was suggested by the
Iranian embassy in Bonn as a useful symbol of West German
interest in Iran.[8]

Even when there are several good reasons to develop a
new language service, other factors may prevent it from
materializing. Chief among them is the shortage of qualified personnel--not only announcers and writers, but also
supervisors. It is possible to recruit staff from other
countries, but it is costly, and if a station broadcasts
much ideological material, it may not be easy to find staff
with compatible ideological viewpoints. Supervisors may be
even more difficult to find; ideally, they should be citizens
of the broadcasting nation, so that they will (in theory)
better insure that broadcast content is in line with national
policy. However, many nations have very few citizens able
to understand the more exotic languages, especially those in
which subtle vocal inflections make all the difference in
the meaning of a word or phrase. Furthermore, those few
individuals who have the necessary command of the language
may be in heavy demand by foreign ministries or by
businesses, where rewards of greater prestige and/or higher
pay may make international broadcasting work relatively
unattractive.

There is also the matter of start-up time. It usually
takes several months to prepare a new language service. For
example, it took BBC about six months to develop its Pushto
service (for Afghanistan) in 1981. If the new service is in
response to a crisis, and if the crisis is likely to be
short-lived, there isn't much sense in trying to develop it,
although stations have been known to put new services on the
air hurriedly and take their chances with polish and accuracy
of broadcasts.

Whatever reasons govern choice of languages, one thing
is clear: most international stations have added very few
to their schedules over the past ten years, perhaps because
of the difficulties I have just mentioned. (See Appendix
B). On the other hand, very few international stations have
dropped language services either, and when they have,
budgetary restrictions appear to have been the major cause.

The International Broadcaster
and the Audience

Throughout most of this book, I treat international
broadcasting as an institution, and pay relatively little
attention to the persons who operate it. Yet it is
important to remember that it is individuals who gather
information, write scripts, read copy, edit tapes, operate
equipment, conduct research and supervise. I will suggest
in this chapter that those individuals have little influence
over the policies about which they often broadcast, but it
is incontestable that individuals can have a great deal to
do with correctness of word choice, precision of translation,
clarity of reading, creation of atmosphere (of warmth,
seriousness, etc.) and a host of other elements that can
enhance or detract from the persuasive value of the message.
There have been times when some international radio
stations have been staffed by dedicated "propaganda
warriors", especially during World War II and the early years
of the "Cold War". Still, in my own interviews with over
300 individuals from some 30 stations and running from 1957
to the present, I have met only three or four who appeared
to fit the "dedicated propaganda warrior" mold and they had
had their initial experiences with international radio during
World War II or early in the "Cold War". The vast majority
of those I have met, including production staff, supervisory staff, administrators, engineers and researchers,
could have been working for a domestic broadcasting station
or a non-broadcast enterprise just as easily.
Most of them, it is true, were and are interested in,
if not fascinated by, the process and problems of communicating with other people in other places. Most of them have
above-average interest in international relations. Few of
them are chauvinistic. Most are good enough at what they
do to be employable elsewhere. However, they have not
entered the field of international broadcasting because they
see themselves engaged in a desparate struggle between conflicting ideologies, nor do they spend hours concocting
plans for propaganda coups or polishing each and every word
of each and every script so that it will be as persuasive
as possible to every listener.

For one thing, there simply isn't enough time. Most international broadcasting operations are understaffed in comparison with their domestic counterparts. Concocting plans and polishing words require time, and most of the staff find themselves with their hands full meeting daily deadlines, especially for newscasts and commentaries. For another, most of them are just a bit cynical about ideological hair-splitting, so that they would be ill-suited for the role of zealous ideologue. And for a third, most of them are wise enough to know that with all the word-polishing in the world, many listeners will hear what they want to hear rather than what broadcasters actually say.

If international broadcasters have one characteristic that has surprised me, it is that few of them seem willing (or able?) to think about their target audiences in concrete, human terms. Few can describe typical listeners in terms of the problems that they as broadcasters might face in reaching those listeners. A number of them have even told me that "listeners are pretty much the same all over the world," which is much like saying that music is a universal language.

There are two categories of international broadcasting staff that do seem more able to think of listeners in concrete terms: personnel who have lived in a given foreign country for an extended period of time, whether as reporters, embassy personnel, students or something else; and personnel who were born and brought up in another country. The former often serve as heads of language services for international stations, the latter as writers and announcers. But even they tend to think in terms of people they have known, or people who write to the station, when describing typical listeners. If their circles of acquaintance have been wide enough, or if letters come from a broad cross-section of listeners (which they rarely do), and if their knowledge is recent enough, that description might be quite accurate. However, that description is just as likely to be based on personal acquaintance of 10 or more years ago, or a mere handful of letters.

There is a further potential problem with these two categories of staff: their primary loyalties may lie with the country to which they broadcast, rather than to the broadcasting nation or organization that employs them. It is perfectly possible for a German, an American or an Egyptian who has worked in another country for an extended period of time to develop a strong feeling of attachment and even loyalty to it, to the point where its interests and policies become paramount. Personnel who were born and brought up as citizens of one country and later became citizens elsewhere may remain true to their birthplaces, although it is not unknown for some of them to reject their

own homelands. Those who come to work at an international
station in another country for two or three years--and this
is a common practice for recruiting announcers and writers
in the more exotic language services for many stations--will
almost certainly owe their primary loyalties to their native
lands.

The perfect international broadcaster probably would be
someone who has a strong but not unquestioning sense of
loyalty to the nation or organization on behalf of which the
station broadcasts; a sensitivity to other nations and other
cultures, based in part on extended residency abroad; an
ability to visualize the physical and psychological contexts
within which people listen to international broadcasting;
and possession of the requisite skills in writing, announcing,
production, research, administration, etc. While some of the
people I have met come fairly close to meeting that
description, others seem to think of their work as "just a
job", albeit more interesting than certain other occupations
they might consider.

Many international broadcasters seek to reach more than
one audience because they have more than one purpose. A few
are able to provide separate broadcast services for their
different audiences, but most provide a mixture of programs,
each element of which will have greater or lesser appeal to
any one listener. Still, most broadcasters seem to make
certain general assumptions about listeners: that they have
some interest in or curiosity about the broadcasting nation
or organization, that they take international radio listening
seriously enough to pay fairly close attention to a broadcast
for more than a few minutes, that they are above their
country's average levels of education and income, and that
they listen to more than one international station. The
first two assumptions probably do not apply to the audiences
for international commercial stations, and the second and
third may not apply to audiences for all of the international
religious stations, but they all should fit the great
majority of international services.

Given those assumptions, the formal style and relatively
complex sentence structure and vocabulary used by most
stations appears to be justified--up to a point. If a broadcaster seeks opinion leaders who will hear programs and then
pass information and impressions from them along to others,
that stylistic approach should work. If the broadcaster
wishes to reach a mass audience directly, probably it would
not. Listeners who are only mildly curious about the
originating nation or organization might find such an
approach uninviting. Listeners who are somewhat suspicious
of or hostile toward the nation or organization might find
further confirmation of their initial impressions, although
informality could also arouse suspicion if listeners feel

that the broadcaster is "trying to lull my suspicions by
sounding friendly." And if listeners were to sense that a
station was catering to one audience in particular, through
use of "in-group" references or assumptions of a great deal
of prior knowledge about a subject, it could also result in
a sense of disinterest or alienation.[9]

Most international broadcasters attempt to make their
programs sound authoritative and well informed, yet not too
opinionated, to have them serve a variety of interests, and
to come across in a human and friendly manner. As you will
see in the chapters to come, there are many approaches to
achieving a satisfactory mixture of programing, but there is
no formula for the perfect mix.[10] For example, various VOA
and BBC listener panels (see Chapter 12) indicate that
listeners tend to distrust stations which sound as if there
is only one correct way to look at world events, but a true
believer in a nation or cause would not welcome signs of
vacillation, weakness or lack of conviction by a station
representing that nation or cause.[11] In short, as in so
much else in life, it's impossible to please everyone!

TRANSMITTING THE SIGNAL

Transmission and Retransmission

When we think of broadcasting, most of us think of
signals sent from a given location and directly received by
the audience. Most international broadcasting functions in
just that way in what are called direct broadcasts--that is,
direct from station to listener. Some international broadcasters use relay stations to boost signal strength. BBC,
VOA, Deutsche Welle, Radio Moscow and others follow that
practice, although it can be costly in financial and diplomatic terms, as you'll see later in the book.

There are three other means of getting the message
through to listeners, and again, several international
broadcasters employ one or more of them. All, however,
suffer from one common drawback: they turn control of the
broadcast material over to someone other than the broadcaster.

Retransmission of Relayed Signals

During the 1940s and 1950s, a number of international
radio stations, VOA and BBC among them, broadcast programs
to domestic radio stations in other countries, e.g. Sierra
Leone and South Korea, for immediate or slightly delayed

rebroadcast by those stations. Most programs so relayed were
newscasts, where immediacy was all-important, and where the
domestic station might not be capable of originating a
comprehensive newscast of its own. Such an arrangement depended on the good will of the receiving country and/or
station, which could mean that, should relations between
transmitting and retransmitting nation go sour, the rebroadcast would be halted just when it was most needed. For
that reason and others--one being that it implies that
something is lacking in the domestic station's news service--
it is little practiced by most stations now, although BBC
still has direct rebroadcast arrangements with some three
dozen countries.

Retransmission of Pre-recorded Materials and Scripts

Many international stations operate transcription
services which make disc and tape recordings (and sometimes
scripts) available to the domestic radio stations of other
countries. Some of that material already will have been
broadcast on the originating station, but some of it, music
in particular, is material especially prepared for use by
other stations. The tapes and discs usually are sent by
air mail, but because of the likelihood of numerous delays
en route, most of them are entertainment programs, "soft"
(non-topical) features, and weekly roundups of editorial
opinion. The originating station has no control over when
or in what form the pre-recorded material is finally used,
if it is rebroadcast at all.[12] Nevertheless, BBC, Deutsche
Welle, Radio Moscow, Radio Nederland, Swiss Radio International, VOA and others give considerable emphasis to local
placement, as it is usually called; BBC's Transcription
Services supplied material to stations in over 100 countries
in 1980.*

Monitoring Services

Although even less predictable than the two forms of
rebroadcasting already mentioned, monitoring services do
constitute a form of retransmission, and even rebroadcast;
some international broadcasting stations probably reach a
larger audience through monitoring service reports than they
do by direct broadcasts. Almost every major nation in the
world operates a monitoring service, as do many smaller
countries. Their job is to comb the airwaves, listening for
politically significant broadcasts from domestic and international services in other countries.[13] Some monitoring
services are highly sophisticated technologically, broadly
multilingual and worldwide in scope, while others concentrate on the broadcasts of their immediate neighbors and

---

*Cuts in the BBC External Services budget in October 1981
 will almost certainly reduce the size of the Transcription
 Services.

deal in a handful of languages. The BBC Monitoring Service
and the U.S. Foreign Broadcast Information Service (FBIS)
have a partnership arrangement which allows each to concentrate on different areas of the world and then share their
respective data.[14]
     Given the magnitude of the task--there are tens of
thousands of radio stations around the world, many broadcasting over several frequencies and in a host of languages
for most hours of the day and night--no monitoring service
can hope to cover all of the broadcast output of any one
station. Daily monitoring reports are intended primarily
for use by foreign policy decision-makers. Therefore,
informational broadcasts such as news, commentaries, interviews and major speeches or proclamations are the central
object of the monitors' attention. Furthermore, the services operate under general guidelines on what to look for,
so that the monitors themselves do not transcribe everything
they hear. Few items from any given newscast will be transcribed for the daily reports, and many commentaries are
passed over, while "cultural" broadcasts almost never appear
in the daily reports.
     Monitoring service reports form an excellent way for
many nations or revolutionary groups to bring their messages
to the attention of foreign policy decision-makers, but they
have other uses, too. Domestic and international broadcasting stations sometimes use monitoring service material
in their own newscasts. BBC's External Services use information gathered by the BBC Monitoring Service in almost every
newscast--the newsroom receives a continuous computerized
feed from the Monitoring Service--and that information also
is the chief source of material for the External Services'
weekly program "Listening Post".   And, while there are no
guarantees that one's station will be monitored on any given
day or at any given hour, chances are good that, if the
station represents a liberation movement, political opposition group or nation temporarily or continuously prominent
in world politics, it will be picked up. In fact, for many
of the opposition groups and liberation movements, this is
one of the very few means of bringing their causes to the
attention of the outside world, and I have long had the
impression that reaching the monitoring services themselves
was the primary purpose of many clandestine (unauthorized)
stations over which those organizations often broadcast.

          The Frequency Spectrum and Technological Control

     Works by Head, Foster and others contain explanations
of how radio waves are transmitted, and the reader may refer

to them.[15] But the various portions of the frequency spectrum have their own particular strengths and limitations
where international broadcasting is concerned, as follows:

Low Frequency (including long wave, 30 to 300 kHz)

     This has the advantage of carrying signals roughly
equal distances regardless of time of day or night, but
requires considerable transmitter power to do so; most LW
transmitters are 500, 1,000 or 2,000 kW. Furthermore, few
frequencies are available for broadcast use, and those only
in Europe, North Africa and the USSR (including Mongolia).
Most of the world has no long wave broadcast services, and,
for all practical purposes, long wave stations have little
importance in international broadcasting, although the two
major European commercial international stations, Radio
Luxembourg and Radio Monte Carlo, have powerful and popular
long wave services.

Medium Frequency (including medium wave) 300 to 3000 kHz)

     This is the portion of the frequency spectrum that most
listeners in most parts of the world associate with domestic
radio broadcasting, although a number of international
stations have medium wave services, too. Unlike long wave,
time of day has a considerable effect on medium wave transmission: with equal amounts of power, a medium wave signal
will travel considerably further at night than it does
during the day, and daytime range is usually restricted to a
few hundred miles unless hundreds of thousands of watts are
used. That factor alone limits its use for international
broadcasting, but there is another problem: because medium
wave frequencies are so heavily used for domestic purposes,
there is little room for international broadcasting, and
relatively few nations will use the scarce medium wave
frequencies for anything but their own domestic broadcast
communication.

High Frequency (including short wave, 3,000 to 30,000 kHz)

     Although most international broadcast activity falls
within this portion of the frequency spectrum,[16] other
services such as amateur (two-way) communication also
function there, and short wave broadcasting is more or less
confined to 11 specific sections of the spectrum, three of
them for tropical broadcasting (within the tropics) only.
     Short wave transmissions function through sky waves,
but, with the right combination of power and atmospheric
conditions, they can travel great distances irrespective of
time of day. It is not unusual for a North American
listener with a medium-quality receiver to be able to pick

up shortwave broadcasts from an African country to listeners
in Europe, or vice versa, even though it is nighttime in
Europe or Africa and daytime in the U.S. or Canada. But
signal interference is a major problem on shortwave, and
listeners must accustom themselves to fading signals and
various kinds of noise, as well as overlapping station
signals caused by increasing overcrowding of the SW broadcast bands. The same conditions make shortwave less suitable
than LW, MW and FM for music broadcasts.

Very High Frequency (including FM, 30 to 300 MHz)

FM operates by line-of-sight transmission. It has a
limited radius, and since that radius is rarely more than
75 miles (120 km), FM is generally impractical for international broadcasting. When it can be used (as between
East and West Germany), it has the advantages of superior
signal quality and relatively high resistance to jamming.

Satellite Transmission

Although satellites are far more commonly associated
with television broadcasting than with radio, they do
transmit audio material, and do have a place in international radio broadcasting, since several nations (e.g.
Great Britain, West Germany, The Netherlands, The Soviet
Union and the U.S.) use them to send broadcast signals
to their own overseas relay transmitters. However, the
average person is unlikely to be willing to spend the
thousands of dollars currently required to purchase the
necessary receiving and conversion equipment; international
broadcasts beamed to and from satellites are in the Super
High Frequency portion of the spectrum--3,000 to 30,000 MHz--
and are converted to MW or SW at the point of reception.
Technical developments may very well lead to low cost reception antennas and converters in the future, but it seems
doubtful that international radio broadcasting will enjoy
a very high priority in the assignment of frequency spectrum
space in the SHF range.

Jamming

Just as many nations have been anxious to communicate
their viewpoint to others, so have many nations been anxious
to keep those viewpoints from reaching their citizens. The
first evidence of deliberate broadcast interference, or
jamming, that I have discovered (but see footnote 1) goes
back to the dawn of international radio broadcasting: in
March 1923, a German station began broadcasting programs
protesting French occupation of the Ruhr, and a French

station broadcast on the same frequency, trying to overpower
the German station with its own programs and with noise.
Within a few days, the German station discontinued operations.[17] Over the next 15 or so years, there were further
instances of jamming, most of them as limited in scope and
as short-lived as the first one had been, although the
Spanish Civil War in the mid to late 1930s saw more protracted jamming activity carried out by both sides.

With the outbreak of World War II in 1939, jamming came
into prominence. Germany blocked, or attempted to block,
BBC broadcasts in 17 European languages, including German,
and treated broadcasts from the other allied powers in like
manner. Great Britain and the United States did not jam,
but the Soviet Union did, as well as France, before it fell
to the Nazis in 1940. (The French at one point considered
jamming German broadcasts to be more important than broadcasting their own international programs!)[18]

Jamming ceased when World War II ended in 1945, but the
coming of the Cold War in the late 1940s brought about its
renewal, particularly on the part of the Soviet Union and
Eastern European nations. As Cold War tensions have waxed
and waned, jamming has risen and fallen, but has never
totally disappeared. The Soviet Union jammed Radio Liberation (Liberty) from its first day of broadcast in 1953 to
the present, and the Israeli international service has
received much the same treatment from the USSR, as have
broadcasts from China since the early 1960s. Soviet jamming of the Voice of America, BBC and Deutsche Welle has
come and gone and come again (most recently reintroduced at
the time of the Polish crisis in the summer of 1980), as
East-West relations have improved and soured.[19] Some of
the Eastern European countries have dropped the practice
altogether: Romania in 1963, Hungary in 1964. They found it
expensive, not very efficient, and possibly even more
attention-inducing in terms of attracting listeners who
could tell that their governments didn't want them to hear
something, which made them all the more determined to hear
it! Others appear to be utilizing it more sparingly than
they once did.

Non-Communist countries have practiced jamming, too,
although generally for brief periods and in connection with
a specific incident or situation. Following its Unilateral
Declaration of Independence, Rhodesia (now Zimbabwe) jammed
a British transmitter operating from nearby Bechuanaland
(Botswana) between 1965 and 1968. France jammed the Voice
of Free Algeria (from the outlawed FLN) in the late 1950s
and early 1960s, jamming some of its own broadcasts (as
relayed by Radio Tunis) in the process. Great Britain
jammed Greek broadcasts to Cyprus (urging Cypriot "union"
with Greece) in 1956. Chile jammed many "leftist"

(including Radio Sweden) and "communist" stations following
the military takeover of the government in 1973. Egypt has
jammed broadcasts from "hostile" sources for the past 25
years or so, though not continuously.[20]

Jamming is simply the transmission of noise or program
material on the same frequency as an incoming broadcast
signal; to be effective it requires an array of transmitters
to block those signals. Low power city-based jamming transmitters, usually located in police stations or military
headquarters, can be very effective over a limited radius,
but overpowering an incoming signal for a large geographical
area requires very powerful jammers. Various U.S. estimates
have held that the Soviet Union operates between 2,000 and
3,000 jamming transmitters, at a cost of several hundred
million dollars a year.

Furthermore, several devices make it possible to overcome most jamming efforts. Saturation broadcasting, in
which an international station amasses a good share of its
transmitting power and broadcast frequencies and focuses
them on a single nation or area, will overcome much jamming. It is not simple to arrange, since it involves
redirecting some transmitters from their normal targets,
which also deprives some listeners of their usual broadcasts, but it can be a graphic demonstration of one nation's
disapproval of another's actions. VOA used saturation
broadcasting in 1961, in an effort to make Soviet listeners
aware of the USSR's resumption of nuclear testing.[21]

An international station also can "cuddle", which is to
broadcast just next to a frequency used for domestic broadcasting in the target country. If that country jams the
incoming signal, it jams its own as well. Since most
countries which practice jamming on a regular basis are
perfectly willing to jam their own stations, anyway, the
practice is not very effective. Shifting frequencies
quickly or broadcasting at unscheduled times can help evade
jamming, although modern jamming equipment can lock in on
changed frequencies in less than a minute, but such changes
usually involve unauthorized use of frequencies and are
difficult for the listeners themselves to follow.

Despite its inefficiency, despite the fact that it has
been condemned by various nations speaking at the United
Nations,[22] and despite the likelihood that it provokes more
curiosity than it stills, the practice of jamming seems
destined to continue, simply because some nations cannot
stand the thought of "hostile" propaganda reaching their
citizens.

Other Technological Forms of Control

Given the inefficiency and expense of jamming, it is
not surprising that governments have looked for other

mechanisms which would limit access to unwanted broadcasts.
Perhaps the most common of these is the marketing of radio
sets which are incapable of receiving broadcasts from abroad.
The Volksempfanger, or People's Radio Receiver, was developed
in Nazi Germany to provide the mass public with inexpensive
radio sets. But the receiver was cheap in part because it
could be tuned to one or two German stations only. The
Soviet Union developed wired radio before World War II,
again because it made radio available to people at low cost,
but also because it limited access to international broadcasts. A wired radio system works in much the same manner
as does cable television. Signals are received or originated
at a central location in a town or city, and are then transmitted by wire to individual sets.[23] More recently, some
nations have pushed the development of FM for one or more of
the domestic broadcast services. Technical quality of
transmissions, scarcity of MW frequencies, and problems of
atmospheric interference with MW and SW transmissions are
three major reasons for that action. However, the Republic
of South Africa appears to have supported FM service for
the Black "homelands" within South Africa in part because
it would prevent listener access to international broadcasting; most international broadcasters are too far distant
to make effective use of FM in reaching the "homelands".

THE REGULATION OF INTERNATIONAL BROADCASTING

Anyone accustomed to the orderly regulation of business
enterprises, technological systems or anything else is in
for a rude awakening where the regulation of international
radio is concerned. It is not very orderly, despite valiant
attempts to make it more so. Furthermore, regulation
itself takes place in two interrelated yet separate spheres:
technical and programatic. Neither appears to be particularly amenable to order, again for separate but sometimes interrelated reasons.

International Regulation--Technical

If radio waves behaved in a perfectly predictable manner
and if all broadcast stations had evolved at the same time
and at the same rate all around the world, there might be a
chance that there would exist a well-ordered international
regulatory system. Unfortunately, radio waves are not
perfectly predictable and broadcast systems have not grown
at the same rate; so, while we have an international

regulatory system, it doesn't work very well. The basic
problems are these: there is very little space provided in
the overall frequency spectrum for domestic or international
broadcasting, and more nations than ever wishing to use that
space. International broadcasting in particular suffers
from those two problems, partly because most of the spectrum
space in long and medium wave broadcast bands was taken up
by domestic broadcasting before international broadcasting
had come on the scene, relegating the latter to short wave.
(As I have noted earlier, LW and MW are not perfectly suitable for international broadcasting, either). The development of FM broadcasting helped alleviate some of the pressure
on domestic radio, but was of almost no help to international.
The fact that long distance transmission is less predictable
than short distance transmission hasn't helped either.

Broadcasters have met together in regional and international conferences from the mid-1920s to the present,
attempting to cope with the twin problems of interference
and overcrowding of the spectrum. Perhaps the most significant of those efforts, because they are truly worldwide,
have been the various attempts made through the International Telecommunication Union (ITU), a United Nations
agency, to utilize the frequency spectrum in a fair and
rational manner. The ITU goes back to 1865. In the period
from 1947 to the present, it has held dozens of conferences
on broadcasting and frequency assignments and has also
developed a frequency registration list through its own
International Frequency Registration Board (IFRB).[24]

Once the members of the ITU had agreed upon the uses to
which each portion of the spectrum would be put, they were
then expected to register the various electronic services in
territories under their control (nations, colonies, protectorates) with the IFRB. It became apparent almost
immediately that there were far more entries to the
registration list than there was spectrum space available.
Some nations registered only services already in existence,
while others also registered planned-for services. The
IFRB's early attempts at published lists were rejected by a
few nations (e.g. Albania, The USSR) and taken exception to
by still others. In a move that acknowledged the unpre-
dictability of radio transmissions, the IFRB did allow a new
service that looked as if it would interfere with an existing one (the IFRB has generally followed a "right of prior
occupancy," or "first come, first served" priority system
for registration) to use that frequency until there was
evidence of interference; if there was none after six years,
the new service would be duly registered as a "legal" co-
user of that frequency.

The IFRB attempts to minimize interference in other
ways, too, by experimenting with alternate methods of

transmission and reception, and by notifying nations whose
frequency requests are likely to cause interference how they
could avoid interference by shifting to a neighboring
frequency, redirecting transmitting antennae, reducing power,
changing time of transmission, etc. Those suggestions have
been followed in some cases, but demand has continued to
outstrip supply, and more and more nations have taken the
law into their own hands chiefly by authorizing transmissions in portions of the frequency spectrum not intended
for those particular services, and therefore in violation of
agreements reached through the ITU. Some 43 nations,
including the USSR, Great Britain, Israel, The Vatican, and
the Peoples' Republic of China, conduct "out-of-band" (outside authorized portions of the spectrum) international
broadcasting, not all of which, however, are illegal in the
eyes of the ITU.[25]

What may have caused even more difficulty is the
"superpower race", where various international broadcasters
have replaced their 100 kilowatt (kW) transmitters that were
the 1950s norm with 200, 250, 500 and even 1,000 kW transmitters. In 1961, there were 16 shortwave transmitters of
200 kW or more, in 1972 there were 185, and in 1981 there
were 325.[26] The practical effect of this superpower contest
has been to make international broadcasting more expensive
for those who wish to stay in the game, but it has not
reduced the number of players. Instead, it seems to have
made those who can't afford to raise or meet the ante even
more aware of their weakened position, and more determined
to find redress through the ITU.

Most of those disadvantaged nations have come from the
developing world, and suffer from the inability to invest
the enormous sums of money (usually "hard" currency, which
is particularly difficult for them to obtain) required to
stay in the contest. A 200 kW shortwave transmitter will
probably cost over one million dollars for the equipment
and its installation. And if nations can afford the price,
there may be insufficient space within the frequency
spectrum to accommodate their proposed services. Most of
those frequencies were allocated when the Western and
Communist nations held the balance of power in the ITU.
However, the coming of independence for so many African,
Caribbean and Pacific nations in the 1960s and 1970s caused
the ranks of the ITU, as an agency of the United Nations, to
swell considerably. The 1959 ITU Geneva Conference was
attended by 96 delegates; 154 delegations attended the ITU's
1979 World Administrative Radio Conference (WARC). Given
the "one nation, one vote" principle followed by the United
Nations and its agencies, the balance of power within the
ITU swung toward the developing countries. They campaigned
for more and better frequency allocations, as well as

assistance from the developed nations, at WARC 79. They met
with some success, although most of the really difficult
decisions have been postponed to 1984 or 1986, when the ITU
will hold two further WARCs to reallocate uses of the High
Frequency (shortwave) portion of the spectrum. Some, including IFRB member Abderrazak Berrada, wonder whether there
is a sufficient spirit of compromise among nations to lead
to a satisfactory outcome.[27]

Spirit of compromise is the fundamental question. Few
nations seem ready to reduce or eliminate international
broadcasting, while many wish to expand. No nation appears
ready to part with frequencies assigned for that purpose,
while more and more seem ready to invest in even more powerful facilities, including such poverty-stricken countries
as Bangladesh. Broadcasters, regulators and scholars with
whom I have discussed these problems at various international conferences over the past several years have felt
that matters could become much worse during the 1980s, with
marked increases in out-of-band broadcasting, more interference between signals as a result of increased transmitter
power, and possibly a total collapse of the present frequency allocation system.

Such a collapse is possible because, as with international law in general, the "law" of frequency allocation
is enforcable only if the ITU members wish to abide by it.
Should one country interfere with transmissions from another,
the ITU can state which country it feels has the right to
use that frequency, and can tell the offending country how
it can make adjustments which would eliminate the cause of
interference, but it cannot fine or otherwise penalize a
country for refusing to adjust. If both countries would
agree to abide by its decision, the matter can be brought
before the International Court of Justice (World Court), but
no such case has ever arisen. A country which refuses to
abide by an ITU notification to vacate a frequency runs the
risk that, if the tables are turned at some future date, ITU
members will not be very sympathetic to it. That has
brought some otherwise recalcitrant countries into line,
because most nations realize that international law rests
first and foremost on international cooperation, on "give
and take".

                International Regulation--Programing

Compared with the international regulation of broadcast
content, the international regulation of frequency usage
seems almost simple. Whereas the latter involves items that
can be assigned numbers--frequencies, amounts of power,

times of day, directions of antennae--the former involves a
semantic jungle. How can one define the broadcasting of
truth, slander, lies, incitement to revolution, etc., in an
objective manner? Yet various international bodies, chief
among them the League of Nations and the United Nations, have
attempted to do so, perhaps most notably (and most ironically
given the fact that it was approved just before World War II)
in the League's International Convention Concerning the Use
of Broadcasting in the Cause of Peace, which came into force
in April 1938. The Convention, despite its positive title,
chiefly deals with prevention of harmful broadcasts; Article
2 is a good example of its tone:

> The high contracting parties mutually undertake
> to ensure that transmissions from stations within
> their respective territories shall not constitute
> an incitement either to war against another high
> contracting party or to acts likely to lead thereto.[28]

Quite aside from the massive problem of determining
whether a given broadcast constitutes an incitement to war,
provided one could even monitor each and every minute of
broadcasting, there is the further problem of whether the
truth of a statement justifies its appearance on a broadcast,
as well as the already-cited problem of enforcement. As
international communications scholar L. John Martin notes:

> In modern psychological warfare, truth is
> the weapon more often than not. It is through the
> choice of the truth that states deliver their most
> stinging darts. Many disputes are bound to arise
> when states feel they have the law on their side.
> And should these come to arbitration, the treaty
> prescribes no penalties for infringements. What,
> therefore, does a state stand to gain through
> litigation?[29]

And as if that were not enough, there are the non-
signatory nations to consider: the League Convention was
not signed by Germany or Italy, which were making "bel-
ligerant" use of broadcasting at the very time the
Convention was being discussed and signed. The worst
offender is often least amenable to international law.
Subsequent attempts to deal with international broadcast content have run into the same problems. When the
United Nations and two of its committees condemned jamming
in 1950, the Communist countries represented at the U.N.
defended the practice by stating that they were protecting
their citizens from psychological warfare; the Polish
delegate claimed that "each country had . . . the sovereign
right to defend itself against this form of aggression, just

as it had the right to prevent opium smuggling, the sale of
pornographic literature or the traffic in persons. . . ."[30]
VOA, BBC and other Western international broadcasters may
well have regarded their program content as "The Truth" or
even THE truth, but that made no difference, since the
Communist countries simply refused to abide by the U.N.
resolution, and continued to jam as they pleased.

The U.N. debate over jamming in 1950 had been preceded
by a Universal Declaration of Human Rights (1948), in which
it was stated that:

> Everyone has the right to freedom of opinion
> and expression; this right includes freedom to
> hold opinions without interference and to seek,
> receive and import information and ideas through
> any media regardless of frontiers. (Article 19)[31]

That article had been cited by some of the delegations speaking to the 1950 resolution on jamming as one of the major
reasons why jamming was illegal. This became known as the
"free flow of information" argument, and it has reappeared
often in the more than 30 years since its passage. In 1950,
the Council of Europe passed the European Convention for the
Protection of Human Rights and Fundamental Freedoms;
Article 10 of that Convention reiterated Article 19 of the
U.N. Declaration (1948), but added a clause stating that
exercise of those freedoms may be subject to restrictions
"necessary in a democratic society"; included among those
possible restrictions were "the protection of health and
morals". In 1966, the U.N. General Assembly adopted a
Covenant on Civil and Political Rights, in which Article 19
stated that:

> 1) Everyone shall have the right to hold opinions
> without interference.
>
> 2) Everyone shall have the right to freedom of
> expression; this right shall include freedom to
> seek, receive and impart information and ideas
> of all kinds, regardless of frontiers, either
> orally, in writing or in print, in the form of
> art, or through the media of his choice.[32]

But paragraph three of Article 19 stated that the first two
paragraphs may be subject to "special restrictions", including "respect for the rights or reputations of others"
and "protection of national security or of public order or
of public health or morals."[33] Such special restrictions
became part of the concept of "national sovereignty":
the right of a nation to restrict the flow of information
from outside its borders.

Throughout most of the earlier discussions and debates over the free flow of information, the United States had come out strongly in favor of a virtually unrestricted flow, and had received the support of most of its Western European allies and many other countries. As the United Nations began in the late 1960s to discuss the regulation of direct broadcasting of television signals from satellites to home receivers, many of the developing nations (by now in the majority in the United Nations) feared that free flow of information as conveyed through satellites would be even more of a one-way flow from developed nations to developing ones than was the flow of information through existing modes of transmission--and, in their opinion, the present flow was already heavily in favor of the developed nations. U.N. General Assembly Resolution 2916 (1972) stated that "the introduction of direct television broadcasting by means of satellites could raise significant problems connected with the need to ensure the free flow of communications on a basis of strict respect for the sovereign rights of States" (italics mine).[34] The United States delegation did not feel that the resolution placed sufficiently positive emphasis on free flow of information principle. For that and other reasons, it opposed the resolution. However, support for the U.S. position, strong at first, evaporated in the face of Third World and Communist arguments, and the final vote was 102 in favor, 1 against (the U.S.), and 7 abstentions.

In 1975, 35 heads of state from Eastern and Western Europe and North America gathered in Helsinki to sign an agreement reached by their respective delegations at the Conference on Security and Cooperation in Europe (CSCE). Much of the agreement dealt with military security, technical cooperation and related fields, but "Basket III" covered the flow of information between East and West. Where international broadcasting was concerned, its most relevant provision was this:

> The participating states note the expansion
> in the dissemination of information broadcast by
> radio, and express the hope for the continuation
> of this process, so as to meet the interest of
> mutual understanding among people and the aims
> set forth by this Conference.[35]

To most of the Western nations represented at CSCE, the "Basket III" accords represented a reaffirmation of the "free flow of information" principle; to the Communist nations, the goals of national sovereignty and mutual non-interference in internal affairs placed limits on that flow. The U.S. delegation attempted to include within the "Basket III" provisions explicit references to the cessation of jamming, but the Soviet Union would not agree.[36]

The most recent manifestation of international "agreement" involving the "free flow of information" has been the
New International Information Order (NIIO), developed during
the 1970s principally by Third World and Communist nations
working through UNESCO. No formal agreement has yet
emerged, although the Mac Bride Commission Report (1979)[37]
is regarded by many UNESCO members as a blueprint for one.
However, it is clear that this highly controversial issue,
involving as it does such sensitive matters as the licensing
of foreign correspondents by governments and the "prevention
of attacks on indigenous cultural values by foreign media",
as well as better balance in the flow of information between
East and West, North and South, would have profound implications for international broadcasting,[38] especially for
those stations which undertake to report and comment on
developments outside of their respective countries, as not
all of them do.

During the post-World War II era, then, there have been
two conflicting concepts of international communication:
free flow of information and national sovereignty. Each has
had its particular champions, but many nations have sought
to amalgamate parts of both concepts, although national
sovereignty appears to be winning more adherents at the
present. The practical problems associated with employing
either concept, or some amalgam of both, as basis for the
regulation of international broadcasting are those noted in
connection with the 1938 League Convention: lack of precise
or mutually acceptable definition of terms, lack of meaningful enforcement mechanisms. "Regulation" through international organizations seemingly is no more effective now
than it was then, and disputes over the right to jam or
otherwise restrict access to international broadcasting, or
the right to control what is said about one country by the
media of another, are certain to continue for some time to
come.

On a more modest scale, nations often engage in bilateral or multilateral treaties and agreements affecting
international broadcasting, usually within the broader
context of overall communication policies or the conduct of
diplomacy. The North American Regional Broadcast Agreement
(NARBA) covers medium wave (AM) frequency assignments for
Canada, the United States, Mexico, Cuba and the Bahamas,
while numerous bilateral treaties between the USSR and other
countries include pledges to "mutually refrain from interference in each other's internal affairs", which is usually
defined as including broadcast communication. Again, such
arrangements depend upon mutual good will, and it would not
surprise anyone familiar with U.S.-Cuban relations over the
past two decades to discover that there have been complaints

from U.S. radio station owners about Cuban "abuses" of the
terms of the NARBA, to the point where the U.S. stations
have encountered signal interference.[39]
    Finally, nations unable to protect themselves from what
they consider harmful international broadcasting through
international, regional or bilateral agreements may resort
to municipal (domestic) law to do so. The Nazi government
in Germany before and during World War II made listening to
foreign broadcasts from hostile powers a crime. Many Eastern
European governments, especially during the 1950s, made it a
crime to discuss with others the "hostile" foreign broadcasts
one had heard.[40] As with every other method of controlling
access to foreign broadcasts, legal penalties are less than
totally effective, and may even heighten listeners' desires
to hear what is forbidden.

FINANCING AND CONTROL

    Aside from the few international commercial radio
stations, international broadcasters do not raise their own
revenues, but must depend on others for their financial
support. Some international stations receive money as a
specific allocation from the national legislature, as do
BBC's External Service, VOA, Radio Free Europe, Radio Liberty
and Deutsche Welle, but more often the money is part of the
annual budgetary appropriation for the national broadcasting
system of which the international service is so often a
part. That money may have come from general tax revenues or
from license fees assessed on all listeners and viewers in a
given country. International religious stations--the
Christian ones, at any rate--receive money through direct
contributions from listeners, general contributions to
churches or religious organizations which in turn make money
available to the stations, and sale of air time to specific
groups wishing to present their religious messages over the
stations' facilities.
    Any system of financing raises the question of control.
The old adage "whoever pays the piper calls the tune" may
not be universally applicable, but it applies often enough
to be worth considering, although its specific influence
may be subtle. In international commercial radio, for
example, the control exercised by advertisers in a direct
sense may be negligible, since no one advertiser furnishes
very much of a station's revenue. However, the station is
unlikely to risk offending advertisers in general by carrying many news items or features that reflect negatively on
the free enterprise system, and it probably will place a
higher priority on entertaining its audiences than it does

on informing them. An international religious station that
sells air time to other religious groups will seek to make
its overall schedule attractive to those groups, so that they
think of the station as an appropriate "home" for their
particular programs.

More direct control should be in evidence where legislative bodies make annual appropriations, but control exercised by parliaments, congresses and other elected bodies is
more likely to be sporadic. Most of those bodies have the
power to hold special hearings on international broadcasting
whenever they wish, but few have chosen to do so. Instead,
they rely chiefly on hearings held in connection with annual
budgetary appropriations, and much of their attention seems
to be focused on reviewing proposals for new or expanded
activities, or, in times of budgetary stringency, on possible
cuts. Few hearings pass without questions regarding evidence
of effectiveness, and in hearings held in the British Parliament or the U.S. Congress there will almost certainly be
questions regarding the effectiveness of BBC and VOA, Radio
Free Europe and Radio Liberty in reaching Communist countries.
From the evidence I have gathered through interviews and
through examination of legislative hearings in the United
States, Great Britain, Canada, India and Australia, few
legislators appear to have much understanding of international radio broadcasting, and legislative bodies do not
appear to exert much direct influence on broadcast policies.

Heads of state (presidents, prime ministers, etc.)
sometimes appoint directors of international broadcasting
services, and occasionally make pronouncements about the
great value of those services to the cause of international
understanding. On rare occasions a head of state "lobbies"
on behalf of international broadcasting, usually to
strengthen broadcasts to a specific area, as U.S. Presidents
Carter and Reagan both did early in their administrations
with respect to Communist countries. Otherwise, there is
little evidence of financial involvement or control from
this quarter. They may exercise control in more indirect
ways, through ministries of foreign affairs or national
broadcasting organizations (provided the international
service is part of the national structure), but even that is
likely to be rare. Most heads of state exhibit little continuing interest in international broadcasting, although
several Third World leaders such as Egypt's Nasser have
been exceptions to that general rule.

National broadcasting organizations themselves exercise
a sort of control over international services that are part
of the national broadcasting system. Although that control
has little to do with policy, it has a great deal to do with
growth: when a national broadcasting system finds itself
faced with rising costs and too little revenue to meet them,

it will sometimes "rob Peter to pay Paul" and stint the international service, which usually is smaller than the national
services. It can be cut or "frozen" without producing a
public outcry, since few members of the general public in
any country know much or care much about the international
service. For example, the galloping costs associated with
television in Japan, as well as TV's galloping popularity,
have meant that NHK, the national public broadcasting service
of which Radio Japan (the international service) is a part,
has put the bulk of its budgetary increases into TV, and
Radio Japan has grown little over the last 20 years.

Foreign ministries rarely finance international stations
although a show of support from them can sometimes help a
station win larger appropriations for itself. They do,
however, take a lively interest in the broadcasts of those
stations when the stations have carried material that upsets
a foreign government to the point of protesting the "offending" broadcast through diplomatic channels. If the foreign
ministry is high in the governmental pecking order, as it
often is, and if the international service is low in that
order, as it almost always is, the latter may comply with
the wishes of the former, regardless of how it feels about
the accuracy or justice of the broadcast itself.

Finally, the public, which pays for most international
broadcasting in one way or another, seems in relative
ignorance of most of those services which it supports.
Some stations, notably BBC, Radio Canada International and
Radio Nederland, have tried to increase public knowledge
of their activities, in the apparent hope that there might
be some public pressure on parliaments not to cut the
budgets of international stations. However, there are no
signs that this effort translates into any sort of public
impact on the control of those stations.

For the most part, then, international stations are not
subject to continuing control on the part of "outsiders",
whether they help to finance the stations or not. Outside
control generally is sporadic, where it exists at all. The
"insiders", particularly those administering the stations,
almost certainly will be sensitive to the wishes of those
in positions of power. They may even be political appointees,
members of the ruling party, etc., which will better insure
that the stations broadcast in accordance with the government's overall policies and desires. If stations are not
directly controlled by those involved in foreign policy
decision-making, and many are not, it may be because many
foreign policy decision-makers do not appear to consider
international broadcasting to be all that important in the
conduct of foreign relations.

PURPOSES

The system of financing and sources of control for an
international station often will have a great influence on
its purposes. With nearly 150 international radio stations
around the world, there is bound to be a wide range of
purposes, especially when stations are financed by such a
wide range of institutions, governmental, public service,
religious, military, etc. Succeeding chapters will show how
stations have implemented various purposes; the list that
follows introduces them.

Instrument of Foreign Policy

Writing about Radio Free Europe, political scientist
Robert Holt referred to the station as a "nonofficial
instrument of [U.S.] foreign policy."[41] In a conference on
international public diplomacy held at Tufts University in
1967, international broadcasting was called an "instrument
of public diplomacy."[42] There are no precise definitions
for either of these concepts, but they imply that international broadcasting does have a role in the conduct of
diplomacy, and, therefore, a role in foreign policy.

One may examine foreign policy from a variety of perspectives, but all would include two elements: policy
making and policy execution. There is very little evidence
that international radio broadcasting plays any role in
policy making. As I have pointed out earlier in this
chapter, most international stations have no direct administrative links with the chief foreign policy-making
bodies: ministries of foreign affairs or defense, executive
offices, etc. It is rare that station administrators consult with or are consulted by policy makers,[43] although
those administrators may receive briefings on foreign
policy.

Policy execution offers little more evidence of influence by broadcasters. If an international station seeks
to present its nation's domestic and foreign policies to
the rest of the world (and not all stations do), it may
encounter difficulties in learning just what that policy
is, since the various policy makers might not be in agreement among themselves, or might not have grasped the
"public diplomacy" implications of what they had agreed
upon. Even when policy is unanimously agreed upon and
perfectly clear to its makers, which is something of a
rarity, there probably will be several bodies which convey
that message internationally. An international radio

station will be one of many potential policy "executors": the domestic press, wire services, motion pictures, television, exhibits, even other international radio stations (a few countries, as you will see, operate more than one).

If the various policy executors are under different administrative units, getting them coordinated may not be easy. The United States faced that problem during World War II, when the Office of War Information, which was the "parent" organization for the Voice of America at the time, attempted to coordinate its own information activities with those of several other governmental departments, chiefly the armed services, the State Department and the Office of Secret Services. The effort was largely unsuccessful; OWI was not regarded by the other departments as having very high standing within the governmental hierarchy.[44] Similar attempts were made during the 1950s, first through the Psychological Strategy Board, then through the Operations Coordinating Board, but they, too, failed; most of the departments involved had no desire to cooperate, had little respect for the information agency in charge of coordinating their efforts, and saw little evidence that their departmental heads and, above all, the President, cared whether they worked in harmony or not.[45]

One respect in which many stations often do reflect foreign policy is through decisions about specific languages to be used and amounts of broadcast time to be devoted to each one. This appears most clearly in the activities of the Communist stations, BBC and VOA, but also appears in the broadcasts of certain other stations, such as Radio Cairo, Deutsche Welle and Radio Korea (South Korea). The major world "hot spots" of the past 15 years--Czechoslovakia in 1968, Pakistan and India in 1971, Chile in 1973, Iran in 1979-80, Afghanistan in 1980-81, Poland in 1980-81--have seen a number of international broadcasters reacting by increasing transmission time in the appropriate language services and/or by adding or restoring such services.

I have already suggested that there are many different reasons--some connected with foreign policy, others not-- for the appearance of new language services on international broadcast schedules.[46] In most "non-crisis" cases, broadcast hours for those services will increase or decrease slightly or remain the same from year to year. But if a broadcasting nation is deeply concerned about specific events taking place in another country, it may react by dramatically increasing broadcast hours and/or broadcast frequencies for certain language services, to the point where either or both may be doubled or tripled for the duration of the "crisis". Once the crisis is over, hours and frequencies usually return to "normal", and the service may even disappear altogether.

It is next to impossible to determine the effectiveness
of "crisis" broadcasting, since surveys rarely are possible
within the target area.[47] Certainly such intensification
will make it easier for listeners to receive the broadcasts,
and the sheer magnitude of the increase will make it clear to
the government of the target nation and to governments of
other nations directly involved in the crisis that the
broadcasting nation feels strongly about the situation. The
listeners themselves may appreciate the added attention;[48]
conversely, they may feel "used", because "Country A only
takes an interest in us when there's trouble here."

Certain stations serve as instruments of foreign policy
by conveying official or semi-official statements from their
governments. The statements may take the form of proclamations, reports, major policy addresses, etc., and may be
carried in full or in part. Most statements are couched in
such formal terms that they are uninteresting to listen to
and difficult to comprehend; stations generally are obliged
to broadcast them in their official form, even if that makes
for poor broadcast copy. Since 1978, VOA has carried a
commentary in which the official U.S. viewpoint on various
issues appears as a three- or four-minute message written by
the broadcasters themselves (members of VOA's News and
Current Affairs staff), but even it sounds quite stiff and
formal.

Mirror of Society

Most international stations claim to present a picture
of the national life of their countries. Their charters or
broadcast laws may make that mission explicit. Some
stations fulfill the mission by rebroadcasting portions of
the domestic service: Radio France International, Radio
Denmark and stations in some of the smaller Arab nations
rely heavily and even exclusively on this source of programing. Others use special newscasts, such as BBC's "News
About Britain", original features, talks, interviews and,
more rarely, dramas and documentaries, to serve the purpose.
In almost every case, the arts provide a major component of
the schedule, ranging from folk to classical, and embracing
music, drama and the visual arts. Other facets of national
life may fare less well: religion, for example, may be a
prominent item for some stations, but largely or altogether
absent on others. Economic life is quite apt to be prominently covered through news reports on strikes and negotiations (though many stations suppress such coverage), the
condition of the stock market, if the country has one, and
the general state of the economy.

Many stations present "portraits" of their individual citizens, as on Radio Japan's "One in a Hundred Million." Such programs serve to "humanize" the broadcasting nation, particularly where a wide variety of occupations and ways of life is displayed. However, little is broadcast about those who are alienated from society, unemployed, abjectly poor, or frustrated in their attempts to change society. The vast majority of international stations say little about social problems of any kind within their societies, although often their domestic media counterparts follow a similar practice.

For most international stations, the mirror held up to society is highly selective, and many elements and facets remain largely unreflected. It is hardly surprising that international stations should wish to place the accent on the positive, especially given the interest of many members of parliaments and congresses in having them do so. Still, it is interesting that those stations which come out on top on the few occasions where surveys have asked listeners to rate stations for their relative credibility should be the stations which do carry a certain measure of negative material about their own countries.

Symbolic Presence

A number of countries seem to have introduced international broadcasting as a symbol of their newly independent status, somewhat akin to the introduction of a national airline. The country may have little idea of what it wishes to do with the station, but will find a way to fill transmission hours and staff language services all the same, even though the drain on national resources in the form of initial investment and continuing operating costs may be considerable; few international stations cost less than several million dollars a year to operate, which can account for a significant share of the budget of a small developing nation.

Many stations now on the air were developed under circumstances and for purposes that no longer exist, notably during World War II, when combating enemy propaganda, displaying solidarity with one's allies, reaching one's captive countrywomen and men from bases abroad, etc., were important. However, of the many stations that were developed for those purposes, very few have gone out of existence (Ireland is one), aside from clandestine stations. Why do they live on? Again, the reason may have to do with their value as symbols of "internationally involved" nations. If a nation ceases its international broadcasting, that might be interpreted as a sign that it has little of interest to say to the rest of the world, or that it cares little about world opinion.

Few nations are likely to regard themselves in that light, or
to wish others to do so.

There is also the possibility that stations live on
because their staff members like their jobs and manage to
convince their budgetary masters of the wisdom of keeping
the station on the air, even if there is little specific
evidence of listeners or of the value of the broadcast
service to the nation; after all, they may argue, doesn't
every (self-respecting and/or "important") nation have an
international service? Many stations are helped in that
respect by their modest size: the savings that would result
from their abolition might have little impact on the national
budget. Besides, station supporters can always argue that,
once the stations are dismantled, it will be very difficult
to reassemble a trained staff and reclaim relinquished
frequencies should the nation ever wish to resume international broadcasting.

Converter and Sustainer

Most international broadcasters hope to persuade
listeners to accept at least some of the viewpoints and
policies, and possibly beliefs, of the originating country
or organization, but not many strive for outright conversion. Those that do are apt to be supported by fundamentalist Christian groups, whose essential message is
acceptance of Jesus Christ as one's savior. Some of the
Communist stations present broadcasts which make an explicit
case for the superiority of Communism as a socio-economic
system, but ordinarily the case is not presented in terms
of "accept it, and be saved; reject it, and be damned," as
it sometimes is over Christian stations.

On the other hand, sustenance of the faithful appears
frequently as an element in international broadcast programing, taking such forms as the presentation of scripture
or dogma, such as readings from the Bible or the Koran,
presentation of the resolutions of the 26th Congress of the
Communist Party of the USSR, excerpts from Chairman Mao
Zedong's "Little Red Book", etc. There is also news of
special interest to the "faithful", for example Radio
Vatican's news about the Catholic world or American Forces
Radio and Television Services (AFRTS) news for military
personnel, as well as programs featuring messages of thanks
from those sustained by the station's broadcasts.

Coercer and Intimidator

International broadcasting was used to coerce and
intimidate long before World War II started; in fact, some
of the earliest recorded uses of the medium were for that
purpose. However, World War II saw a far greater use of
coercion and intimidation through international radio, as
most of the major participants employed it to one or both
of those ends.

Coercion and intimidation continue to appear as elements in international broadcasting, although seldom as
blatantly as during World War II. They appear most frequently in clandestine broadcasts, in which governments and
leaders sometimes are threatened with annihilation unless
they alter their behaviors or even leave office. The
effectiveness of such broadcasts appears to depend upon
whether listeners perceive them as backed by force. German
broadcasts just before and in the early years of World War
II probably carried some weight with listeners because the
Germans were able to demonstrate their willingness and
ability to carry out their broadcast threats. The lack of
German follow-through later on in the war did not stop the
threats from being broadcast, but there is some evidence to
suggest that listeners stopped taking those threats
seriously.[49]

Educator

Few international stations have been established in
order to educate listeners in any formal manner; indeed,
Walter Lemmon's W1XAL, which often broadcast "home study"
courses between 1935 and 1952, seems to have been the only
such station (see pp. 93, 151). However, many international
stations broadcast language lessons, through which one can
study Chinese, Arabic, Russian, Dutch, Japanese, English
and other languages by radio, often with the aid of texts
supplied free of charge. The lessons often educate in
another way: the dialogue and monologue situations may contain ideological material. Certainly that material is over-
whelmingly positive: the people portrayed in the situations
are friendly, helpful, intelligent, and have manageable
problems. The unemployed, the malcontented, the dull-witted,
do not appear, and rarely does anyone speak in anger!

Entertainer

I have already expressed my doubts about the existence of "pure entertainment" on international broadcasts. However, there is no doubt that much international programing is meant to entertain first and foremost, even if its basic purpose is to attract listeners to stay tuned for informational programing or to induce them to have a favorable image of the broadcasting nation. Musical request programs are particularly useful as generators of listener mail, while certain hosts and hostesses of music shows come to personify the station, as VOA's "Music USA" host Willis Conover seemed to do for Eastern European listeners in the 1950s: he received tumultuous welcomes from jazz fans when he visited their countries.

Much entertainment programing falls into the "mirror of society" category, especially light and serious drama, quiz shows (few but BBC offer them), and those music shows where hosts and hostesses talk about the music and the artists, slip in details about the broadcasting nation, etc. But much of the music played over international stations has no such "accompaniment", and may be presented with no identification whatsoever. In that case, stations may be offering something as close to "pure entertainment" as is possible, although it's likely that the programers themselves think of the music as filler to be inserted between informational broadcasts, which helps to account for the fact that music presented in that manner may be halted abruptly when the next informational program is scheduled to go on the air.

Seller of Goods and Services

By the end of the 1920s, radio broadcasting in the United States had become clearly identified with advertising, which was its major form of financial support. The late 1920s also saw some of the first specific uses of international broadcasting for advertising, as various stations in France and serving French listeners began to carry occasional ads placed by British firms over specific programs intended for British listeners. From that time to the present, international commercial stations have always been around, although never in large numbers. Today they can be found on almost every continent. They are remarkably similar, in that their programing mainstay is popular music, whether Indian film music as broadcast by Sri Lanka's commercial service, African (and European) popular music, as

broadcast by Africa No. One in Gabon, Arabic popular music as
broadcast by Radio Monte Carlo-Cyprus, or disco as broadcast
by Radio Luxembourg. Most of them also are quite profitable.
   Most of these stations thrive because they are able to
present something that is not available, or insufficiently
available, to listeners over their domestic services. A few,
such as Radio Monte Carlo-Cyprus, add to their attraction by
providing relatively unbiased and timely newscasts.[50] None
spends a great deal of time attempting to project the life
and governmental policies of its host country, and the commentaries, interviews, news analyses and press roundups that
appear regularly on so many international stations are
largely absent on the schedules of commercial stations.
   A few international stations attempt to "sell" their
country's tourist attractions, as do Radio Japan and BBC.
Others inform listeners of new products manufactured by
domestic firms but available for export, as do BBC, VOA and
Deutsche Welle. Still others, the Christian stations in
particular, sell or allow others to sell books and other
materials related to Bible studies, etc. In the broadest
sense, almost all international stations could be said to
act as sellers of ideas, although some go about it more
consciously than do others.

BARRIERS TO EFFECTIVE INTERNATIONAL BROADCASTING--
SOME FINAL CONSIDERATIONS

   As I have already suggested, there are several reasons
why messages sent and messages received do not always cor-
respond, and there is a vast body of literature on that
subject. There are also several reasons why people do not
choose to expose themselves to certain messages or certain
media of communication. It is not my purpose in this book
to present and discuss those reasons in any detail, the more
so because, where international broadcasting is concerned,
so few of them have been studied on a scientific basis.
However, before you read about the development and activities
of various international broadcast stations, it might be
helpful for you to think about two barriers to effective
international communication faced by all stations, large and
small, secular and religious, capitalist, Communist and
politically neutral.

Physical Barriers

   Several factors come into play here, including transmission quality, operation of radio receiver, wording and

delivery of broadcast material, time of broadcast and duration of broadcast. As I stated earlier in the chapter, most
international broadcasting is done on short wave, which is
subject to a good deal of signal interference and fading.
There are many ways for a listener to minimize the effects
of that interference: a high-quality receiver, a carefully-
strung receiving antenna, skill in manipulating the dial,
all will help, but they require money, patience and a bit of
ingenuity. The broadcaster can help, too, by broadcasting
on more than one frequency, by delivering spoken material at
a slightly slower-than-normal rate, by avoiding complicated
phraseology in copy, by building in a certain amount of
redundancy, and by using transmitters located fairly close
to the audience or by turning to local placement of tapes
and discs. A careful study of best times of day or night
to reach specific audiences should increase a station's
effectiveness, and broadcasting in a specific language for
30 minutes or an hour, rather than 10 or 15 minutes, also
will improve a listener's chances of receiving the station.
Again, however, those steps take time, money and effort,
and a certain amount of sensitivity to the difficulties
faced by the listener. If international broadcasters have
had much of their work experience in domestic broadcasting,
and many have, it may be difficult for them to visualize
how different things may be for an international listener.

Psychological Barriers

Even if all of the physical barriers to effective communication could be overcome, there are several psychological barriers to face. Listeners may have stereotyped
notions about the broadcasting nation or organization,
and may refuse to open their ears to the station at all, or
may attribute much of what is broadcast to hidden motives.
Those suspicions may be fed by one or more of the listener's
peer groups, or by the listener's own closed-mindedness.[51]
Listeners may lack curiosity about other countries, whether
because of chauvinism, mental laziness or fatalism.
Listeners may consider international broadcast listening a
secondary activity--something they might do if it's timed so
as not to conflict with more important matters. More receptive listeners can be discouraged, if not angered, when
information provided to them by the station turns out to be
incorrect, and their chagrin will be all the greater if they
have conveyed that incorrect information to others.
Here, too, there are certain steps a station can take
to minimize these problems. Accuracy of information is
paramount, but honesty about one's own shortcomings may be

just as important in overcoming listener resistance. The use
of "side attacks" (see footnote 4) may help, too. Paying
some attention to the history, culture and current events
of the listener's own country may serve to awaken curiosity
about another country or organization that has the good
sense to recognize the merits of one's native land. Emphasizing cooperation between the listener's country and the
broadcasting nation and celebrating certain "universal"
elements (all people work and play; here's how we do it)
may dispel a certain amount of hostility.

As you will see when reading about the specific practices of different stations, some international broadcasters take some of these potential barriers into account
some of the time. Others pay little attention to barriers,
seeming to trust in providence or to assume that everything
is as clear and understandable to the listener thousands of
miles away as it is to the producer in the studio. The
perfect international broadcast may be unattainable, but
many represent far less than perfection, perhaps because
their makers are unable or unwilling to think in terms of
barriers.

As this chapter closes, you may wonder why any country
or organization bothers to engage in international radio
broadcasting when so many negative factors seem to surround
the activity. While some countries and organizations might
be hard pressed to tell you why they do, aside from stating
"Because we always have," most could give you more concrete
reasons, many of them based on past, present and/or
projected successes in achieving various goals. You may
judge for yourself whether the reasons seem sound after you
have read the next several chapters; I reach a few tentative
conclusions in the final one.

                              NOTES

    1. In 1917-1918, both President Woodrow Wilson, with
his "Ten Points for Peace," and the new Soviet government,
with messages about its victories and policies, communi-
cated those messages through radio, but in telegraphic
form. Guback and Hill note Lenin's acknowledgement of some
of those early successes, which included at attempt at
jamming by the Germans! Thomas Guback and Steven Hill,
"The Beginnings of Soviet Broadcasting and the Role of
V.I. Lenin," Journalism Monographs (December 1972):5.

    2. See my article, "International Television--
Problems and Prospects," Journal of Communication 17
(September 1967):198-210, for a consideration of some of
these problems. Costs of direct reception equipment have

dropped considerably, but the other factors--legal, technical and psychological--seem to me to be as important as
ever. I have examined further aspects of international
television in "The American Image Overseas--the Impact of
U.S. Television Abroad," Journalism Quarterly 45 (Summer
1968):307-316, and in "International Television Programming:
If People Could Have It, Would They Watch It?", ERIC Document ED 097 705 (March 1975). K.E. Degnan, et al., "Direct
Broadcast Satellites: Policies, Prospects and Potential
Competition," Washington, D.C., U.S. Department of Commerce,
National Telecommunications and Information Administration,
Report NTIA-SP-81-11 (March 1981), provides a thorough
analysis of economic factors in DBS transmission and
reception.

     3. Several authors have written about "media imperial-
ism". Perhaps the most important works are Herbert
Schiller, Mass Communications and American Empire (New York:
Augustus Kelley, 1969); Herbert Schiller, Communication and
Cultural Domination (White Plains: M.E. Sharpe, 1976); Alan
Wells, Picture Tube Imperialism? (Maryknoll: Orbis Books,
1972); Armand Mattelart, Multinational Corporations and the
Control of Culture (Atlantic Highlands: Humanities Press,
1979); Luis Ramiro Beltran and Elizabeth Fox de Cardona,
Comunicacion Dominada: Estados Unidos en los Medios de
America Latina (Mexico: Editorial Nueva Imagen, ILET, 1980);
Jeremy Tunstall, The Media are American: Anglo-American
Media in the World (New York: Columbia University Press,
1977); and Kaarle Nordenstreng and Herbert Schiller, eds.,
National Sovereignty and International Communication: A
Reader (Norwood: Ablex Publishing, 1979). Most of these
books are extremely critical of the United States, and very
few even begin to consider the possibility of Japanese,
Mexican or Soviet "media imperialism" through television,
even though each country is a fairly active exporter of
television programing.

     4. Irving Janis and Brewster Smith, "Effects of Edu-
cation and Persuasion on National and International Images,"
Herbert C. Kelman, International Behavior (New York: Holt,
Rinehart and Winston, 1965):213-214, have discussed the idea
of "side attacks". Music would be a good example of a
"side attack", because it does not attack the most deeply
held beliefs of listeners, and thus is more likely to be
received with lessened resistance.

     5. Several small-scale surveys conducted by Kim
Andrew Elliott suggest that some listeners, especially DXers,
appreciate at least occasional informality. See his An
Alternative Strategy for International Radio Broadcasting,
unpublished Ph.D. dissertation, University of Minnesota,
1979, passim, and his survey of listening preferences of
readers of the publication Review of International Broadcasting, done in 1981 and published in the September 1981

issue of <u>RIB</u>. The Voice of America 1975-1978 listener panel
research project, cited in Chapter 12, also indicated some
preference for informality in wording and delivery, although
several panelists stated that they did not think it appropriate where news and commentary were concerned.

6. See Richard Wood, "Language Choice in Transnational
Radio Broadcasting," <u>Journal of Communication</u> 29 (Spring
1979):112-123, for further treatment of this subject.

7. Jack Nargil, "The Voice of America as an Instrument
of American Foreign Policy: A Case Study of the Armenian
Service," unpublished M.A. Thesis, The George Washington
University, May 1976, particularly pp. 55-66 and Appendix
III.

8. <u>Deutsche Welle 1953-1966</u> (Koln: Deutsche Welle,
1966), p. 87. Pressure from Turkestani exile groups is also
cited as a reason for the commencement of the service.

9. See also L. John Martin, "The Moving Target:
General Trends in Audience Composition," in <u>Propaganda and
Communication in World History, Vol. III: A Pluralizing
World in Formation</u>, ed. Harold Lasswell, <u>et al</u>. (Honolulu:
University of Hawaii Press, 1980), Chapter 8, especially
pp. 274-290. Douglas Boyd, "A Q Analysis of Mass Media
Usage by Egyptian Elite Groups," <u>Journalism Quarterly</u> 55
(Autumn 1978):501-507, offers interesting insight regarding
national and international media preferences by different
sorts of people.

10. See Elliott, <u>An Alternative Strategy</u>, for extensive consideration of an "ideal" program mix.

11. There are differing opinions as to whether it is
better in terms of persuasive strategy for an international
broadcaster to attempt to present more than one side of an
argument. Kelman, <u>International Behavior</u>, contains a number
of chapters in which various authors discuss the "one-sided
versus the multi-sided" question. The only study I have
seen in which listeners were asked about their preferences
was "The Differential Approach and Communications Appeal
Among East Europeans," (Study II), Munich: Radio Free Europe,
Audience and Public Opinion Research Department, March 1975.
In that study, East European visitors to Western Europe were
shown differing versions of the coverage of one event and
asked to state their preferences and the reasons for those
preferences. There was a range of treatments, including
highly positive, highly negative and mixed. Those surveyed
indicated preferences for the negative and mixed approaches
(the story concerned general elections in East Europe), but
the variety of reasons given for those preferences was wide
enough and the sample frame itself sufficiently non-random,
that it is not possible to reach any very firm conclusions
in light of the results of the survey.

12. My own experience as Radio-Television Officer for

the U.S. Information Service in Tunisia from 1960 to 1963
was that Radio Tunis probably used less than half of the
materials placed with it by the Voice of America, even
though most of the materials had been requested by Radio
Tunis itself. In that case, it is probable that the
ultimate unsuitability of the material, most of which had
been ordered on the strength of catalogue descriptions, was
the major reason for its non-use. I have visited a number
of stations in developing countries where it is evident that
international broadcast tapes are ordered in part because
they can be erased and reused by the stations.

13. See Julian Hale, Radio Power (Philadelphia:
Temple University Press, 1975), Chapter 14 for a fuller
description of monitoring services. One of the few indications we have of the "effectiveness" of monitoring service
reports as retransmitters of information comes from World
War II Germany. Josef Goebbels, angered at the "rumors"
that were being spread by "responsible" government officials
who read the German monitoring service reports, tried (with
little success) to severely restrict circulation of the
reports. Willi A. Boelcke, ed., The Secret Conferences of
Dr. Goebbels (London: Weidenfeld and Nicolson, 1967),
p. 162, p. 169, pp. 205-207; Louis A. Lochner, ed., The
Goebbels Diaries (Garden City: Doubleday, 1948), p. 10.

14. The Daily Monitoring Reports produced by both
services are subscribed to by many university and other
public libraries, and are a useful, but neither random nor
complete indication of themes and styles in national and
international broadcast services. My article "The Media of
the Arab World and Matters of Style," Middle East Review 12
(Summer 1980):11-19, offers a consideration of styles of
expression as revealed through monitoring service reports.

15. Sydney Head, Broadcasting in America, 3rd edition,
(Boston: Houghton-Mifflin, 1976), Chapters 2 and 3; Eugene
Foster, Understanding Broadcasting (Reading: Addison-Wesley,
1978), Chapter 2.

16. This is partly because, by the time international
broadcasting began to develop, the medium wave portion of
the spectrum was already quite full in Europe and the
Americas. The superior long-distance transmission characteristics of short wave also made it especially suitable for
international communication.

17. "German Station Broadcasting Ruhr News and Music
is Drowned Out by Eiffel Tower," New York Times, March 6,
1923, p. 1. Germany did not have a national broadcasting
service at this time; the "Ruhr station" was created for the
purpose of reaching Germans in the Ruhr, and possibly other
European listeners. It ceased broadcasting by March 9.

18. Asa Briggs, The History of Broadcasting in the
United Kingdom, Volume 3: The War of Words (New York: Oxford
University Press, 1970), p. 173.

19. See Maury Lisann, Broadcasting to the Soviet Union
(New York: Praeger, 1975), passim, for a detailed study of
patterns in Soviet jamming of Western broadcasts.
20. The British and U.S. foreign broadcast monitoring
services have released reports on jamming activities from
time to time. Hale, Radio, Chapter 12, provides a summary
of jamming activities.
21. Saturation broadcasting was also used in broadcasts to Cuba and Latin America on the occasion of the
Cuban missile crisis in 1962, but more to insure that the
U.S. message got through (and perhaps to display the seriousness with which the U.S. viewed the situation) than to overcome what little jamming there may have been. On that
occasion, several U.S. commercial broadcasters made their
facilities available to VOA, in order to increase the level
of medium wave saturation. See Thomas Sorensen, The Word
War (New York: Harper and Row, 1968), pp. 200-201. Sorensen
mentions the 1961 saturation broadcasts on pp. 147-148.
22. L. John Martin, International Propaganda: Its
Legal and Diplomatic Control (Minneapolis: University of
Minnesota Press, 1958), pp. 86-87.
23. The wired radio system backfired on the Russians
during World War II, when the Germans conquered much of the
western USSR and took control of the wired services there,
leaving most listeners there without access to broadcasts
from the unconquered portion of the USSR.
24. The best overall source on the earlier history of
the ITU remains George Codding, The International Telecommunications Union (Leiden: E.J. Brill, 1952). A more
succinct and slightly updated version appears in George
Codding, Broadcasting Without Barriers (Paris: UNESCO, 1959),
Chapter 6. Delbert D. Smith, International Telecommunication Control (Leyden: A.W. Sijthoff, 1969), pp. 21-35, is
also useful. The IFRB was established in 1947, but the
International Broadcasting Union had developed a frequency
registration list in 1926.
25. Estimates on numbers of nations furnished by Roger
Legge, International Frequency Management Service, Etlan,
Virginia, in letter to author, July 19, 1981. Not all are
in violation of IFRB assignments, due to various loopholes
and grandfathering arrangements, and the ITU does "permit"
out-of-band broadcasting if it does not actually interfere
with other services. If interference does arise, the
service that can show that it is entitled to operate in that
portion of the spectrum has the "right" to the use of that
frequency.
26. Ibid.
27. Informal remarks made by Berrada following his
presentation of a formal statement at the 1981 Annual Conference of the International Institute of Communications,

Strasbourg, France, September 9, 1981. There are many
analyses of what happened at WARC 79, and a number of conflicting interpretations. A concise and generally neutral
account can be found in Willi Menzel, "Broadcasting After
the World Administrative Radio Conference (WARC), Geneva,
1979," World Radio TV Handbook 1981 35 (Hvidovre, Denmark:
J.M. Frost and Billboard, A.G., 1981), pp. 34-41. A rather
more optimistic Canadian view of WARC 79 appears in Brian
Segal, "The 1979 World Administrative Radio Conference:
International Negotiations and Canadian Telecommunications
Policy," Ottawa: Department of Communications, Government
of Canada, 1980.
    28. Cited in L. John Martin, International Propa-
ganda, p. 81. Martin provides a detailed description of the
Convention and its weaknesses, pp. 80-82.
    29. Ibid., p. 82.
    30. New York Times, December 15, 1950, p. 22, cited
in Ibid., p. 86.
    31. U.N. General Assembly, Official Records, Third
Session (I), Resolutions, p. 7, cited in Delbert Smith,
Telecommunications, p. 11.
    32. Human Rights Covenants, Annex to U.N. General
Assembly Resolution 2200 (XXI) adopted December 16, 1966
(A/Res/2200/(XXI)), cited in Ibid., p. 15.
    33. Ibid., p. 16.
    34. U.N. General Assembly Resolution 2916, November 9,
1972, cited in Benno Signitzer, Regulation of Direct Broadcasting From Satellites: The UN Involvement (New York:
Praeger, 1976), p. 95. Signitzer quotes from a wide variety
of delegation presentations on this subject; see pp. 46-48.
    35. David Abshire, International Broadcasting: A New
Dimension of Western Diplomacy (Beverly Hills: Sage, 1976),
p. 11. Abshire's account of CSCE is very much from the U.S.
official point of view; for a more neutral assessment, see
United States Advisory Commission on International Education
and Cultural Affairs, "The Effects of the Conference on
Security and Cooperation in Europe on the Cultural Relations
of the United States and eastern Europe," Washington: U.S.
Government Printing Office, Executive communication 2276,
1976. For a Soviet viewpoint, see Sh. Senakoyev, "A New
Milestone in European History," International Affairs (Moscow, October 1975), pp. 3-14. Gerhard Wettig, Broadcasting
and Detente (New York: St. Martin's Press, 1977), describes
campaigns conducted by Eastern European nations against
broadcasts coming from West Germany, particularly during
1968-1976, then relates the campaigns to the Helsinki agreement. The nature of the campaigns is not particularly well-
documented, and the author is strongly pro-Western.
    36. Abshire, Ibid.
    37. The full title of the Commission is International

Commission for the Study of Communication Problems. Its
report is contained in Sean Mac Bride, et al., Many Voices,
One World: World Communication for Society Today and
Tomorrow (Paris: UNESCO, 1980). Several books have appeared
on NWIO; perhaps the most useful, albeit from a variety of
perspectives, are Thomas L. McPhail, Electronic Colonialism:
The Future of International Broadcasting and Communication
(Beverly Hills: Sage, 1981); Johnathat F. Gunter, The United
States and the Debate on the World "Information Order"
(Washington, D.C., 1979); Colin Legum and John Cornwell, A
Free and Balanced Flow (Lexington: D.C. Heath, 1978); and
Oldrich Bures, ed., Towards a New World Information Order
(Prague: International Organization of Journalists, no date).
There is a useful summary of the history of the NWIO debate
in Robert L. Stevenson and Richard Cole, "Foreign News and
the New World Information Debate," U.S. International
Communication Agency, Washington, D.C.,Office of Research,
Report R-10-80 (July 1, 1980).
    38. Those implications could range from assisting
developing countries in improving their own international
broadcasting, technically and programmatically, to taking
frequencies away from some international broadcasters and
reassigning them to others. International broadcast
services which regularly report from other countries through
their own correspondents and stringers might find the
activities of those individuals curtailed or redirected by
other countries, and the reporting done by the major wire
services, upon which almost all international broadcasters
rely, would be affected similarly. Although I do not intend
to pass judgement on the strengths and weaknesses of the
NWIO, I can state that the major Western international
broadcasters' coverage of events in the Third World
(developing nations) and, to a large extent, the Communist
world, does provide a heavy concentration on disasters and
problems, at least in general service newscasts. (Some of
the stations have special newscasts for certain parts of
the world, e.g. BBC's "African News", where coverage of that
particular area is more diversified). Stevenson and Cole,
Foreign News, p. 17, contend that Western media treat their
own societies in much the same manner as they treat Third
World countries--rather critically.
    39. Ernest Holsendolph, "House Panel Told U.S. and Cuba
Face a Radio War," New York Times, June 7, 1981, p. 8.
    40. However, there were cases in the Peoples' Republic
of China well into the 1960s where listeners caught in the
act of listening to "hostile" foreign broadcasts were
sentenced to undergo "thought reform". Here, apparently,
the act of listening itself was judged sufficient reason
for quasi-legal action. See "Hear No Evil," China News
Service, Hong Kong, Report No. 301, December 18, 1969.

41. Robert Holt, Radio Free Europe (Minneapolis: University of Minnesota Press, 1958), Chapter 9.

42. Robert Delaney and John Gibson, eds., American Public Diplomacy: The Perspective of Fifty Years (Medford: The Lincoln Filene Center for Citizenship and Public Affairs, Tufts University, 1967).

43. Many stations receive daily or less frequent guidances and/or briefings from ministries of foreign affairs, state departments, etc., but these involve little consultation. Furthermore, stations are not necessarily required to broadcast in line with those guidances or briefings, and many do not.

44. James Warburg, Unwritten Treaty (New York: Harcourt and Brace, 1946), Chapter 8, mentions some of the difficulties involved in coordination of activities, but his bias against the Director of OWI is apparent. Alan Winkler, The Politics of Propaganda: The Office of War Information, 1942-1945 (New Haven: Yale University Press, 1978), notes some of the specific problems of coordination as they stemmed from personality differences among the major figures involved; see especially pp. 43-51.

45. Murray Dyer, The Weapon on the Wall (Baltimore: Johns Hopkins Press, 1959), Chapter 5. The Operations Coordinating Board was abolished in 1961.

46. A ministry of foreign affairs may or may not initiate a request for expansion of introduction of a language service in a "crisis" situation. The British Foreign Office asked BBC to expand its Portuguese service during a time of political unrest in Portugal in the mid-1970s. BBC had been requesting Foreign Office permission to introduce a Pushto service for Afghanistan for a number of years, but was not granted permission to do so until early 1981. Interview, Austen Kark, Deputy Managing Director, BBC External Services, London, September 15, 1981.

47. A survey conducted by Radio Free Europe of over a thousand travelers from the Eastern European nations to Western Europe during the period August-November 1980, indicated that there had been a sharp increase in listening to Western radio stations by those individuals, apparently because of the crisis in Poland. See "Listening to Western Broadcasts in East Europe, 1979 to 1980," Munich: Radio Free Europe, Audience and Opinion Research, January 1981.

48. Although it does not deal specifically with the effect of international broadcasting, W. Phillips Davison's article "Political Significance of Recognition via Mass Media--an Illustration from the Berlin Blockade," Public Opinion Quarterly 20 (Spring 1956):327-333, does offer some interesting thoughts on the prominence felt by people involved in a crisis which they know to be commanding world attention. It is also possible that some international

stations are listened to by the "general public" <u>only</u> during
times of crisis in the broadcasting nation itself.

49.   Asa Briggs, III, pp. 231-237.

50.   A listener panel conducted by the U.S. Information
Agency in Kuwait in 1975-1978 (see Chapter 12) found several
participants claiming that they listened to Radio Monte
Carlo in part because its newscasts were up-to-date, brief,
direct and accurate. In my own residence in Lebanon during
1973-1974, several of my Lebanese and other Arab acquaintances spoke of their respect for RMC's newscasts.

51.   An excellent introductory work on the subject is
Milton Rokeach's <u>The Open and Closed Mind</u> (New York: Basic
Books, 1960). Herbert Kelman, ed., <u>International Behavior</u>
(New York: Holt, Rinehart and Winston, 1965), applies some
of these considerations to international communication; see
especially Chapters 5-8.

2

THE GROWTH OF
INTERNATIONAL RADIO

Every medium of communication has a history--several
histories, perhaps, if technology, managerial practices,
modes of financing and content are treated as separate
subjects. International radio has all of these histories
and more. The broad chronological history I present here
should help to establish who came on the scene, when, with
what sort of broadcast service, and why.

In the first two decades of this century, there was a
good deal of experimentation with radio transmission.
Because an early object of such transmission was to achieve
distance--the major goal being to communicate with and
between ships at sea--it was inevitable that signals
originating in one country would be heard in another. But
those signals weren't intended to reach foreign listeners
in order to convince them of the sterling qualities of the
broadcasting country, or to persuade them of the bad
qualities of their own governments. Even if they had been,
it is highly doubtful that they would have had many listeners, since most of the signals were in code. Even when
U.S. President Woodrow Wilson's Fourteen Points of Peace
were "broadcast" late in World War I, they were designed
to be picked up by governmental receiving stations, and
were thus transmitted in code. The general public would
have had virtually no access to Wilson's message, the more
so because most nations directly engaged in the war had
placed restrictions or even outright bans on the operation
of amateur radio receivers.

During the early 1920s, most of the industrialized
nations established radio services, but none of these--not
even that of the Soviet Union--was intended for listeners
abroad. The Soviet Union did employ radio as part of a
propaganda campaign against Romania in 1926, but that was a
short-lived effort.[1] The first "permanent" (more or less
continuous) broadcast service for listeners overseas appears
to have been established by Holland in 1927. It was in

Dutch, and was directed to Dutch citizens serving in
Holland's then far-flung colonial empire. It consisted
largely of Dutch domestic radio broadcasts, and thus served
as something of a "home away from home" touch for Dutch
citizens in the Netherlands, East Indies, Dutch Guiana, etc.
Because of the broadcast content and the language generally
employed, it is doubtful that many listeners who were not
Dutch citizens or expatriates listened to this service.[2]
Just the same, it was an important first step, because many
nations in years to come were to establish similar services
for their citizens, commonwealth colleagues and/or expatriates overseas: Germany in 1929, France in 1931, Great
Britain in 1932, Japan in 1934. Few nations engaged in
international broadcasting have failed to devote at least a
few hours a week to such a service, and even today several
nations, the Soviet Union among them, feature broadcasts
for their foreign service staff, sailors and military personnel abroad.

     Those "colonial service" stations also led to the
development of other types of international broadcast
services, as it became apparent that some of them were
attracting listeners who were not citizens or expatriates
of the broadcasting nation. In many cases, members of this
secondary audience wrote to the stations expressing their
interest in these programs and asking for at least some
broadcast fare tailored to listeners with a less intimate
knowledge of the country. Usually, they were told that the
station wasn't really intended for them; if they cared to
tune in, well and good, but they'd have to manage to follow
along as best they could. The coming of World War II saw
many stations changing their attitudes in this respect, but
there are still many traces of "colonial service" broadcasting in the program schedules of many international radio
stations. It's difficult otherwise to account for BBC's
broadcasts of summaries of local football and cricket
matches, for example--or Deutsche Welle's heavy concentration on German language broadcasts.

     Thus, one early form of international broadcasting re-
mains with us today, even if the colonies and territories
which generally gave rise to it have now largely disappeared. But a second early form, which appeared at about
the same time, has been a far more consistent and important
element in international broadcasting from its birth to
the present day. There is no convenient title for it,
but "politically ideological" might do as well as any. It
made one false start, or possibly two, if one counts the
short-lived Soviet broadcasts to Romania in 1926. The
Soviets were its originators, and it came about in about 1927
the Tenth Anniversary of the Bolshevik Revolution. Many
foreign guests visited Moscow for the festivities, and the
Soviet broadcasting authorities arranged for them to

broadcast back to their respective homelands in their own
languages. When the anniversary celebration ended, so did
the broadcasts, but the experience seems to have encouraged
the Soviet Union to set up a permanent "politically ideological" broadcast service, which it did in 1929.[3] Soon, it
was broadcasting in several languages, including many of the
European tongues and Mandarin (Kuoyu). The majority of
those early broadcasts appear to have been explanations of
what had been created in the USSR by the Revolution, and
programs dealt with such subjects as "Life in a Moscow Boot
Factory," Russian folk music, etc. Attacks on other nations
and ideologies rarely appeared on Radio Moscow at this time,[4]
but that changed rapidly after 1933, when Hitler came to
power in Germany.

Soviet attacks on Nazi Germany drew predictable responses from the latter. This served to launch politically
ideological international broadcasting in a major way. Italy
followed suit in 1935, attacking British Mideast policies in
its Arabic broadcasts to the Middle East from Radio Bari.
Japan began to employ radio in its war with China during the
late 1930s. And when the BBC's Empire Service first began
to use a language other than English in its broadcast
schedule, that language was Arabic: the British had decided
that they must respond to Radio Bari's attacks. Thus,
despite the efforts of the League of Nations (which had
established its own international radio service in 1932) to
prevent the use of radio for hostile purposes, the so-called
"war on the short waves" was joined.[5] Colonial service
broadcasting continued, but now frequently took the form of
attempting to persuade expatriates to aid the homeland in
one way or another: by acting as advocates, by sending
money "home", even by engaging in espionage.

Another type of ideological broadcasting made its
appearance in the early 1930s. Religious organizations,
tempted by the prospect of speaking to believers, unbelievers and the uncommitted throughout the world, began to
establish international broadcast services. Vatican Radio
commenced in February 1931, with an inaugural blessing by
the Pope. HCJB--the ititials mean "Heralding Christ Jesus'
Blessings"--came on the air in December 1931 from Quito,
Ecuador, where it had been set up by an American-based
Protestant missionary organization.[6] Ensuing decades have
seen such broadcasting organizations spread to all five
continents (assuming Oceania to be a continent). While
Christianity is the dominant international religious broadcasting power, Egypt's "Voice of the Holy Koran" and
similar stations in Libya and Saudi Arabia could be considered the Islamic equivalent. There are also many
international broadcasting services which include religious
programs as one part of their overall schedules, although

the religions of South and Southeast Asia and the Far East
appear rarely, even as subjects of individual broadcasts.[7]
     Whether one could consider advertising as a form of
ideological broadcasting is an open question. In any case,
international commercial radio stations have not been common. But they did make their debut quite early in the
history of international broadcasting, and a handful of such
stations remain in existence today. Radio Luxembourg began
broadcasting its mixture of popular music, news and commercials to other European countries in 1933, but even it
had been preceded in a minor way by several French stations,
among them Radio Paris, Radio Toulouse and Radio Normandie,
which broadcast occasional sponsored programs (mainly light
entertainment) from France to England starting in 1925.[8]
Several American stations, among them General Electric's
experimental shortwave station, rebroadcast their U.S.
programs to Latin America and Europe as early as 1923, although advertising directed specifically to foreign listeners
was not allowed on those services until 1941. Radio Monte
Carlo began to broadcast to France and other European
countries in 1943.[9] Ceylon (Sri Lanka) established a com-
mercially-supported broadcasting service for India's
southern area in 1950.[10] A group of French businessmen set
up Europe Number One to broadcast from the Saar to France
in 1955. In more recent years, Radio Monte Carlo has
established a branch operation on Cyprus, to broadcast in
French and Arabic to the Middle East, and several international commercial stations have sprouted up in various
parts of Europe, Africa and the Middle East.[11] Two international commercial services connected with U.S. domestic
radio stations in New Orleans and Miami were slated to go on
the air in 1982--the latest in a long line of U.S. international commercial stations.
     And finally, there is a category of international
broadcast service which falls under the title "clandestine".
A clandestine service often pretends to come from within
the country it serves, while actually coming from someplace
else, often hundreds and even thousands of miles away. Some
who write on the subject of international broadcasting
expand the category to include any unauthorized station which
broadcasts programs in the name of an exile or "opposition"
group.[12] Clandestine stations were in existence at least as
early as the Spanish Civil War.[13] The longest-lived clandestine station, Radio Free Spain, came into being just
after the Spanish Civil War and continued to broadcast
until the mid-1970s, operating largely from the Soviet Union
and Romania.
     World War II saw a tremendous increase in the number
of clandestine stations. No major power was without at
least a few of them, and their goals included everything

from inducing dissension in the military ranks to encouraging
desertion from combat duty to causing panic buying or even
flight from the cities on the part of the civilian population.[14]Some of the stations lasted a few weeks, others a
month or two, and a few for several years, but virtually all
of them disappeared at the end of World War II. Shortly
thereafter, new clandestine stations began to appear, most
of them operating from within the Soviet Union, Eastern
Europe, and, somewhat later, the Peoples' Republic of China,
North Vietnam and North Korea. Those stations attacked
governments in Greece, Turkey, Iran, Malaysia, Thailand,
West Germany and several other countries. During the 1956
Suez Canal crisis, Great Britain operated such a station
from Cyprus, in order to reach listeners in the Middle East.
Clandestine operations were also quite prominent during the
Vietnam War, and political tensions within and among Third
World nations often are accompanied by their presence.

By the outbreak of World War II, then, the five basic
categories of international broadcast station that to this
day make up the field were all in place: colonial,
political-ideological, religious, commercial and clandestine.
And if one were to claim that clandestine really should be
considered as a form of political-ideological, I would not
argue the point; while certain of the stations may have
devoted at least some broadcast time to religion or culture,
it is done within a political framework.

What we find after World War II is basically a repe-
tition of already well-established categories, albeit with
certain refinements appropriate to the ensuing decades.
World War II had seen an enormous growth in international
broadcasting, but, since most of this expansion was tied to
the war effort, one might expect that it would have disappeared with the end of the war. In fact, some stations
did disappear--Germany and Japan lost their international
services, and didn't regain them until several years later--
while others, the BBC and VOA among them, were cut back
somewhat. The Soviet Union reduced Radio Moscow's broadcast
schedule, but at the same time actually expanded its international broadcast activities, chiefly by the expedient of
setting up or resurrecting international broadcast services
in the various Eastern European nations. Through them, it
coordinated a broadcast campaign that attacked the American
role in aiding Western Europe and supported international
communism. Radio Warsaw, Radio Budapest, Radio Sofia and
several others, including international stations operated
through various of the Soviet republics (Lithuania,
Azerbaijan), grew out of that situation, and, among other
things, caused the U.S. Congress to reconsider the wisdom
of abolishing the Voice of America.[15]

This Soviet action drew a further reaction from the

United States, which itself set up a number of highly specialized international broadcast services to reach Eastern Europe, the Soviet Union and the Peoples' Republic of China from transmitters located in West Germany, Spain, Portugal, Taiwan, The Philippines and South Korea. Those operations--Radio Free Europe, Radio Liberation (later to be called Radio Liberty) and Radio Free Asia--were established in the 1950s. The first two operate to this day; Radio Free Asia was abolished in 1955. The U.S. Government also converted a broadcast service it had set up for listeners in West Berlin: with the advent of the Berlin Blockade in 1948, Radio in the American Sector of Berlin, or RIAS, began to turn more and more of its attention to reaching audiences in East Berlin and East Germany. None of those U.S. operations called specific attention to their American origins or financial support, in contrast with VOA, but neither did they pretend to be set up within the countries they were attempting to reach. Thus, they weren't clandestine operations, but they weren't officially-sponsored stations, either. In the "color-coding" sometimes used to describe the various types of international broadcasting stations, they would be grey, as contrasted with black (clandestine) or white (official).16

The United States also encouraged the reestablishment of international broadcast operations in West Germany and Japan in the early 1950s, to strengthen further the Western radio voice. During the decade, the Soviet Union, the Eastern European nations and the Peoples' Republic of China doubled and redoubled their hours of international broadcasting; China, in fact, went from a handful of hours in 1949 to nearly 700 hours per week by the end of 1960. The Soviet Union developed a second major international broadcast service in 1964, but by this time the "enemy" lay both to the east and to the west, and the new station, Radio Peace and Progress, divided its time between attacks on the Peoples' Republic of China and its followers and the various capitalist nations of the West. Peace and Progress employed considerably stronger language than did Radio Moscow, supposedly because it was functioning as a nonofficial voice of the Soviet Union; in fact, the station is operated as part of Radio Moscow, utilizing the same transmitters, frequencies and, in some cases, announcers.

Thus, the radio "war" that began in the 1930s (discounting earlier skirmishes) never really let up after World War II; it simply embraced new friends and foes. And, as had been the case with the League of Nations in the 1930s, the United Nations sought to establish ground rules for more peaceful uses of international radio. But it became clear through U.N. debates on the "free flow of information" in the late 1940s and early 1950s that many nations were

unwilling to forego broadcasts that other nations deemed
hostile; nor were nations which indulged in jamming broadcasts from abroad interested in ceasing the practice.
Communist and Capitalist definitions of what was "true" or
"accurate" were worlds apart.

Whether international broadcasting would have disappeared if there had not been a cold war is a debatable
issue. Some nations probably still would have seen it as in
their interests to carry out such activities, although it's
doubtful that they would have done so on such a grand scale.
There were still colonial empires and commonwealths to
serve, although even by the late 1940s they were beginning
to crumble: Holland lost most of its empire when Indonesia
became independent then; Great Britain lost a sizeable chunk
of the British Empire when India and Pakistan did likewise.
But Radio Nederland and BBC both continued to broadcast, as
did the French, Spanish, Portuguese and Belgian international services after their countries' empires had
diminished or dissolved.

In fact, as the old colonies and protectorates became
independent nations, they, too, wanted to reach the rest of
the world, or selected portions of it, with their own
international services. One of these--Radio Cairo--became
very prominent in very short order. Colonel Gamal Abdel
Nasser saw radio as a means of speeding up decolonization in
Africa and the Middle East, and Radio Cairo soon assumed a
place among the leading international broadcasting stations
in terms of weekly hours of broadcasting, not to mention
notoriety. It functioned as the official voice of Egypt,
but also operated separate services to broadcast the Holy
Koran, to support various independence and liberation movements (Palestinian, Algerian, Kenyan), and to attack Israel.
Radio Ghana was established in 1961, in large part to further Ghanaian President Kwame Nkrumah's program of Pan-
Africanism. Nigeria, the Ivory Coast, Senegal, Tanzania,
Zaire and several other African nations added their own
international services during the 1960s, as did many nations
in the Middle East and Asia. India in particular has
developed one of the largest international broadcast services of all the Third World nations; even in the early
1950s, All-India Radio's Overseas Service was broadcasting
in English, Indonesian, Kuoyu (Mandarin), Cantonese, Arabic,
Persian and several of the languages of India's more immediate neighbors, and using 100 kilowatt transmitters to
do so.

Israel set up its own international broadcast service
in 1950, well before Radio Cairo had been established,
largely to reach out to the diaspora--the Jewish community
throughout the world. This remains one of its chief missions
but answering its Arab critics is almost as important in its

list of activities, and a separate station for Arabic
language broadcasts was created in 1958.[17]

It was not always easy for developing nations to
establish international broadcast operations. Frequently
these were founded on a tide wave of revolutionary, post-
independence zeal, but day-to-day practicalities soon began
to assert themselves: transmitters had to be maintained,
reasonably professional staff had to be recruited. If that
was a problem for Egypt, and it was, one can only imagine
the difficulties faced by a smaller, poorer nation such as
Ghana, or its West African neighbor, Guinea, which set up
an international broadcast service (primarily for West
Africa) in 1959. As Guinea discovered, it was one thing to
announce the initiation of the Voice of the Revolution, but
another to sustain it. Recruitment of staff qualified to
write and speak foreign languages, even English, posed a
major problem, and much of the station's early effort was
quite amateurish in both content and delivery.[18]

Those problems were largely unknown to Latin American
countries, for the simple reason that very few of them
had international broadcast services--a situation that per-
sists to this day. Mexico, Brazil, Uruguay, Venezuela,
Nicaragua, Guatemala, and Argentina all have modest operations, and the other nations have none at all, unless one
includes Ecuador-based HCJB in the list.[19] Whether this is
due to a possible lack of interest among Latin American
nations in communicating their views internationally, whether
political instability might be a factor, or whether the
largely commercial orientation of Latin American domestic
broadcasting acts to discourage the creation of international broadcast stations, is hard to say; the fact
remains that Latin America remains relatively inactive in
terms of originating international radio broadcasts.

The one major exception to this rule--and it is a
Caribbean exception--is Cuba, whose Radio Havana Cuba is
one of the world's most powerful and sophisticated international stations. Founded in 1961, shortly after Fidel
Castro's rise to power, and given considerahle Soviet
technical and monetary support, Radio Havana soon became a
major element in Cuba's program of "exporting revolution",
as its broadcasts called attention to various inadequacies
and faults of governments throughout the Americas. The
station seeks to reach listeners not only in Spanish,
Portuguese and English, but also in Latin American Indian
and "native" languages such as Guarani, Creole and Quechua.
In overall power and scope, it easily surpasses any other
international station broadcasting from Latin America or
the Caribbean.

The United States also chose to respond to this new
broadcast rival, just as it had responded to increased

Soviet broadcast activities in Eastern Europe and Asia some
ten years earlier. Through the Central Intelligence Agency,
it set up Radio Swan (later to be called Radio Americas),
whose principal aim was to support liberation groups in
Castro's Cuba. In fact, Radio Swan's inauguration actually
predated the formal inauguration of Radio Havana, although
international broadcasts began to emanate from Cuba as early
as 1959. Radio Swan came on the air in 1960, and, as with
Radio Free Europe, Radio Liberty and other CIA operations,
there was no indication that the CIA was involved with the
station. Instead, it was given a commercial "cover", pre-
tending to exist as a vehicle for commercial advertising.
It disappeared sometime in the mid-1960s.[20]

All during the 1950s and 1960s, religious stations were
gaining in strength and numbers. The pioneers in the field,
HCJB and Vatican Radio, were joined by Trans World Radio,
the Far East Broadcasting Company, ELWA in Liberia, Radio
Veritas and others, most of them established by American
evangelist groups. Trans World Radio has grown to the
point where it now broadcasts in several dozen languages
from transmitters on every continent except North America.
HCJB broadcasts more than 400 hours of programing per week.
By any measure, several of the international religious
broadcasters must be reckoned with as major forces in international broadcasting.

The growth of international broadcasting, then, has
been phenomenal, but it has not been steady. There have
been spurts of activity, but lulls as well. We now seem to
be experiencing a lull: many clandestine radio services
went off the air during the early to mid-1970s, a few
nations have dropped or severely curtailed their international broadcast services (Ireland, Denmark and France,
for example), and very few of the existing stations are
adding more language services or expanding their hours of
transmission (see Appendix B). Some stations--notably Radio
Nederland and Canada's RCI--were hit by large budget cuts in
the late 1970s, and the BBC was threatened with budget cuts
throughout the 1970s and on into the early 1980s. However,
the general state of international radio broadcasting is
healthy. Most stations are able to hold their own or even
expand slightly, and many are replacing old transmitters
with new and far more powerful models. One or two international stations (most of them from commercial and religious
organizations and developing nations) come on the air each
year. Government officials, members of parliament, and
listeners continue for the most part to speak favorably of
international broadcasting.

This overview of the history of the medium should have
revealed one other thing: that much of the development of
international broadcasting has been on a reactive basis.

The primary example of this is the United States and the
Soviet Union and their respective allies, which have
established or redirected many of their international broadcast services to cope with actions taken by the "other
party", as well as to take advantage of or to counteract a
favorable or unfavorable political development in some
other nation.

International broadcast organizations generally seem to
be unaware of, if not indifferent to, the historical
development of international radio, and particularly to the
past and present programing practices of their rivals,
friends and enemies alike. Perhaps the failures and successes of the past simply cannot be replicated at present,
but no international broadcast station appears to have made
any comprehensive studies to determine what could be learned
from the past or present experiences of others.[21] The past
generally is seen as having little or no practical importance. Yet, as we shall see in later chapters, certain
general and specific assumptions about what "works" and
what doesn't seem to be shared by a number of broadcasters,
and several of those assumptions have their roots in practices of the late 1930s and World War II.

NOTES

1. A 1974 Radio Moscow broadcast advanced the claim
that "foreign" languages were broadcast by the Soviet Union
as early as 1923, but these appear to have been short-lived
efforts, such as the one in 1926 for British miners. See
BBC Monitoring Service, Radio Moscow in English for South
and Southeast Asia, 1100 GMT, May 7, 1974, Monitoring
Service Report SU/4596. See also "Moscow Reds Now Use Radio
to Address British Miners," The New York Times, October 21,
1926, p. 1. Radio Moscow staff member Viktor Kuprianov
states that there was external broadcasting from the USSR in
German in 1920, but I consider it most likely that this was
done in code. See Viktor Kuprianov, "Supplement from
Moscow," Journal of Broadcasting 4 (Fall 1960):336-338. The
Franco-German radio "war" mentioned in footnote 11, Chapter
1, may or may not have been truly international.

2. From early on, however, the Dutch international
service did carry one weekly program in several languages,
or, rather, hosted by a gentleman capable of speaking
several languages. This was Eddie Starz's "Happy Station,"
a weekly medley of music, small talk and greetings to
listeners who had written to the station. Starz served as
host for the program for over 35 years, gaining the affec-
tion of a large number of listeners for the personal touches

he brought to what was at the time a largely impersonal
medium of communication.

3. See Willi Boelcke, Die Macht des Radios (Frankfurt:
Verlag Ullstein, 1977), p. 31.

4. However, Soviet radio attacks on the German government were reported as early as 1930. See "Soviet Radio
Talks Resented in Berlin," The New York Times, July 11, 1930,
p. 10.

5. Harwood Childs and John Whitton, eds., Propaganda
by Short Wave (Princeton: Princeton University Press, 1942),
p. 5, mention brief radio wars between Germany and Poland
and Germany and France in the 1920s, but provide no details.
The same authors also provide considerable coverage of the
radio wars of the 1930s, as do the following sources: Willi
Boelcke, Radio; Asa Briggs, The History of Broadcasting in
the United Kingdom, II: The Golden Age of Wireless (New
York: Oxford University Press, 1965); Henry Delfiner,
Vienna Broadcasts to Slovakia (Boulder: East European Quar-
terly, 1974), East European Monographs No. 7; Thomas Grandin,
The Political Use of the Radio (Geneva: Geneva Research
Center, 1939); Arno Huth, Radio Heute und Morgen (Zurich:
Europa Verlag, 1944); Morgen die Ganze Welt (Koln: Deutsche
Welle, 1970); Charles Rolo, Radio Goes to War (New York:
G. Putnam, 1942).

For League of Nations activities during this period,
see Broadcasting and Peace (Paris: International Institute
of Intellectual Cooperation, 1933); and L. John Martin,
International Propaganda: Its Legal and Diplomatic Control
(Minneapolis: University of Minnesota Press, 1958).

6. See Clarence Jones, Radio--The New Missionary
(Chicago: Moody Press, 1946). Several religious groups,
American in particular, had placed programs on stations in
other countries in the 1920s, paying for the air time they
used.

7. However, Radio Veritas, a Catholic Church-run
international broadcast station located near Manila, has for
several years now followed a policy of presenting regular
broadcasts about non-Christian religions and even "pagan"
legends (e.g., Philippine creation myths). Its approach
seems to be one of cultivating a genuine understanding and
appreciation of other religions, and it has received considerable praise for its efforts. See Review of International Broadcasting, Issue 7 (September 1977), page 5
and Issue 10 (December 1977), page 11.

8. See Briggs, II, pp. 339-369, for a discussion of
the activities of these stations. Most of the English-
language programing material was at first prepared in
England itself, and was broadcast sporadically, but it
became more and more frequent in the 1930s.

9. See Leonard Slater, "Radio Monte Carlo," Newsweek
33 (January 3, 1953):40. Boelcke, Radio, provides a
detailed account of Radio Monte Carlo's activities in World
War II, when the station was to all intents and purposes
controlled by the Italians and Germans. Although RMC was
founded in 1943 as an international commercial radio station,
it appears that it derived very little, if any, revenue from
the sales of air time, and it was almost totally supported
by the Germans and Italians, who saw it as a useful propaganda weapon (Boelcke, pp. 196-206).

10. See "Reaching India by Radio," Business Week
(August 8, 1953):104-107.

11. There are many more stations that could be considered both international, in that they broadcast from one
country to reach listeners in other countries, and
advertiser-supported. This list would include Radio Vallee
des Andorres (Andorra to France), Radio Swaziland (Swaziland
to the Republic of South Africa), the Middle East Service
(Egypt to the Middle East), and others recently departed,
such as Radio Lourenço Marques (Mozambique to the Republic
of South Africa).

12. See Larry Magne, "Clandestine Broadcasting 1975,"
in World Radio TV Handbook 1976 (Hvidovre, Denmark: Frost,
1976), pp. 55-70. See also Boelcke, Radio, especially
Chapters 8-10, for a review of various clandestine broadcast
activities throughout the world; Reimund Schnabel, Missbrauchte Mikrofone (Vienna: Europa Verlag, 1967), for
documentation on Nazi clandestine activities; Sefton Delmer,
Black Boomerang (New York: Viking Press, 1962) and Charles
Cruikshank, The Fourth Arm (London: Davis-Poynter, 1977),
for accounts of largely British clandestine efforts; and
Daniel Lerner, Psychological Warfare Against Nazi Germany
(Cambridge: MIT Press, 1971) and Ellis Zacharias, Secret
Missions (New York: G.P. Putnam's Sons, 1946), for details
on American activities. It is readily evident from these
various accounts regarding coordination between American,
British and French officials in charge of clandestine
broadcasting that there were many disagreements over both
policy and procedure, and that the effectiveness of these
efforts was often doubtful, when it was discernable at all.
Cruikshank is especially informative in this regard; see
Chapters 2, 3 and 9. See Wallace Carroll, Persuade or
Perish (Boston: Houghton-Mifflin, 1948), pp. 366-367, for a
description of one of the few scientifically-based studies
on the effectiveness of Allied broadcasting to Axis soldiers.

13. See Childs and Whitton, Propaganda, pp. 26-27,
and Rolo, Radio, p. 50. It is also possible, but not
certain, that the Soviet Union established a clandestine
station to broadcast to Czechoslovakia in 1931; see "Red's
Secret Station is Hunted in Czechoslovakia," The New York
Times, March 19, 1931, p. 11.

14. World War II saw the publication of a number of
books and articles on how individual listeners should
analyze enemy broadcast propaganda. A scholarly approach
to the subject is taken by Edrita Fried, in Childs and
Whitton, Propaganda, pp. 261-301, while Mathew Gordon, News
is a Weapon (New York: Knopf, 1942) and W.A. Sinclair, The
Voice of the Nazi (London: Collins, 1941), are somewhat more
emotional and "popular" in their approach to the subject.
     Aside from Boelcke, Radio, there are no works that
provide a reasonably complete picture of radio's role in
World War II. Various books help to fill in details from
various perspectives; these would include Childs and Whit-
ton, Propaganda; Rolo, Radio; Briggs, II, and Asa Briggs,
The History of Broadcasting in the United Kingdom, III:
The War of Words (New York: Oxford University Press, 1970);
Julian Hale, Radio Power (Philadelphia: Temple University
Press, 1975); Harold Ettlinger, The Axis on the Air (In-
dianapolis: Bobbs-Merrill, 1943); Harold N. Graves, Jr.,
War on the Short Waves (New York: The Foreign Policy
Association, 1941); Ernest Kris and Hans Speier, German
Radio Propaganda (London: Oxford University Press, 1944);
L.D. Meo, Japan's Radio War on Australia, 1941-1945 (Mel-
bourne: Melbourne University Press, 1968); Tangye Lean,
Voices in the Darkness (London: Secker and Warburg, 1943);
Carl Brinitzer, Hier Spricht London (Hamburg: Hoffman und
Campe, 1969); Jeremy Bennett, British Broadcasting and the
Danish Resistance Movement, 1940-1945 (Cambridge: Cambridge
University Press, 1966).
     15. The post-World II activities of the major inter-
national broadcast stations will be covered in detail in
subsequent chapters. No general history of international
broadcasting during this period is available, although
Boelcke, Ibid., and Hale, Ibid., are of some assistance.
     The Soviet propaganda "threat" brought forth a fresh
spate of works on propaganda analysis, some of them
scholarly, e.g., John Clews, Communist Propaganda Techniques (New York: Praeger, 1964), some of them "popular",
e.g., Oliver Carlson, Handbook on Propaganda (Los Angeles:
Foundation for Social Research, 1953); and D. Lincoln
Harter and John Sullivan, Propaganda Handbook (Philadelphia:
Twentieth Century Publishing, 1953).
     16. See David Wise and Thomas Ross, CIA: The In-
visible Government (New York: Random House, 1964), for a
brief treatment of several CIA radio activities.
     17. Mordecai Avida, "Broadcasting in Israel," Middle
Eastern Affairs 3 (November 1952):321-328; Seth King, "New
Israel Radio Speaks to Arabs," The New York Times, February
22, 1958, p. 1.
     18. I was in Guinea soon after the Voice of the
Revolution was inaugurated (1959), and monitored several

English and French language broadcasts from the station.
While a few of the announcers were quite professional, most
were not. Hesitations, mispronounciations and incorrect
phrasing were common, and were further compounded by almost
unreadable scripts, which frequently included sentences a
paragraph long. Brief accounts of international broadcasting
to and within Africa, Asia and the Arab world are contained
in my articles in Sydney Head, ed., Broadcasting in Africa
(Philadelphia: Temple University Press, 1974), pp. 175-200;
John Lent, ed., Broadcasting in Asia and the Pacific
(Philadelphia: Temple University Press, 1978), pp. 318-337;
and in Douglas Boyd, Broadcasting in the Arab World (Philadelphia: Temple University Press, 1982), Part 3.

19. However, Argentina in the early 1950s had an
impressive international radio service, with several hours
per day in English, Spanish and Portuguese, an hour a day
in French, German, Italian and Swedish, and 50 and 100
kilowatt transmitters. World Radio Handbook (Hvidovre,
Denmark: Frost, 1952), pp. 93-94. The service continues
today, but it has changed little since its debut.

20. Wise and Ross, CIA. It may have "resurfaced" in
the mid-1970s; see pp. 150.

21. Comparative studies of newscast content have been
undertaken by BBC, Deutsche Welle, VOA, Radio Free Europe,
Radio Liberty and a few other international broadcasters,
but these contain little or no reference to past practices
where newscasts are concerned, and are typically confined
to the examination of a sample week or treatment of a single
event. To my knowledge, there have been no comparative
analyses of "non-news" programing.

3

WORLD WAR II

What happened to and within international broadcasting during World War II had a tremendous impact on the growth and future directions of the field. Many nations inaugurated international stations then, still others expanded existing stations. Programatic and technological experiments, some of them based on domestic radio practices, led to changes that we take for granted today. Much of what international radio now is stems from what it became during World War II. The five categories of wartime broadcast practice that I examine in this chapter--clandestine stations, themes, personalities, program formats and strategies--figure among the most profound and lasting of those changes.

CLANDESTINE STATIONS

Perhaps the most sensational and colorful of World War II uses of international broadcasting was clandestine broadcasting, where stations either did not announce their identity or location, or pretended to be broadcasting from within an "enemy" nation. The Soviet Union may have initiated this practice vis-a-vis Czechoslovakia in 1931, although that is unproven.[1] It was employed during the Spanish Civil War, quite possibly with German and Soviet assistance to the two combattants. But it reached its full flower in World War II, as Germany established clandestine stations to help soften up opposition, military and civilian alike, in most of the countries of Europe.[2]

The Soviet Union, Great Britain, the United States, Italy and Japan were not far behind, and, as the war drew on, the numbers of these stations grew rapidly. Some were short-lived, while others operated for a year or two.[3] Some were highly specialized, intended for submarine crews or factory workers, while others catered to a more diversified audience.

The resourcefulness needed to operate such stations has been
well documented by the manager of several of them, the
Englishman Sefton Delmer. To catch the listener's attention
with these stations at all was no mean feat, since they had
to commandeer whatever broadcast frequencies they could and
come on the air with no prior publicity.[4] In order to overcome those handicaps, many clandestine stations employed
frequencies as close as possible to those used by major
domestic stations in the target region, so that listeners
might be more apt to discover them while attempting to tune
in the domestic station.

It was also necessary to maintain certain fictions
through careful planning and execution. If they were to
pass as stations run by opposition groups within the country,
the clandestine stations could not be on the air for long
periods of time; otherwise, they would surely be "discovered" by national authorities. There also would have to
be occasional irregularities in broadcast schedules, as the
station sought to "avoid" detection by national authorities.
Announcers and writers for the station would have to play
their roles to perfection, with appropriate accents and
styles of wording and delivery. This was something of a
problem for Germany, since the sheer number and variety of
German clandestine stations--at one time there were four of
them broadcasting to the British civilian population alone,
one "Christian", one "Scottish", one "peace movement", one
"workers"--made it difficult to find the necessary talent.
(Prisoner-of-war camps became one of the more popular recruiting grounds for both sides).

German clandestine stations reached beyond Europe in
the early years of the war, as the Balkans fell under German
rule. Belgarde and Athens became transmission sites for
clandestine stations aimed at Allied soldiers and sailors in
the Mediterranean and at civilian listeners in North Africa
and the Middle East. Captured transmission equipment in
Holland served for a clandestine service for India on which
the Germans used as many as eight Indian languages to reach
Indian listeners with anti-British messages, frequently
broadcast by Nazi sympathizer Chandra Bos. Japan and Italy
also operated clandestine stations for India. The Allied
nations did not operate as great a variety of clandestine
stations, and concentrated their attention more heavily on
listeners in the Axis armed forces.

Given the variety of languages and locales these stations
were designed to cover, there is no typical example to offer
of how they carried out their mission. However, Gustave
Siegfried Eins, which purported to come from within Germany
and to be run by a dissident officers' group, but which
actually came from within Great Britain, bears many of the
hallmarks of the genre. First, it was believable that such

a station could have existed, because some of the German
officers were known to be dissatisfied with the conduct of
the war. Furthermore, they would have had access to radio
equipment, and would have had a better opportunity to use it
in more or less unmolested fashion than would most civilians.
The station's creator, Sefton Delmer, was well acquainted
with the Nazi and German military mentalities, and knew the
styles of wording (a liberal amount of swearing, condemnatory references to Jews, etc.) that would be appropriate to
officers running such a station. He also knew that gossip
would be welcome, provided it did not stretch the truth too
much. He recruited his announcers and writers from among
Germans available in Great Britain, and coached them himself
until he was satisfied that they were able to write and
speak like the German officers they were supposed to be.
As a final touch of authenticity, the station's first broadcast contained a reference to a "previous broadcast," which
it was hoped, would cause the official German monitoring
stations to wonder whether they had missed something!

The station's main announcer was a "no-nonsense" type
called simply "Der Chef" (the chief). In the station's
first broadcast (1941) he dealt with the desertion of
Rudolf Hess, a high-ranking Nazi official:

> First, let's get this straight. This fellow
> is by no means the worst of the lot. He was a
> good comrade of ours in the days of the Free
> Corps. But like the rest of this clique of
> cranks, megalomaniacs, string-pullers and par-
> lour Bolsheviks who call themselves our leaders,
> he simply has no nerves for a crisis. As soon
> as he learns a little of the darker side of
> developments that lie ahead, what happens? He
> loses his head completely, packs himself a
> satchel full of hormone pills and a white flag,
> and flies off to throw himself and us on the
> mercy of that flat-footed bastard of a drunken
> old Jew, Churchill. And he overlooks completely
> that he is the bearer of the Reich's most
> precious secrets. All of which the damn
> British will now suck out of him as easily as
> if he was a bottle of Berlin white beer.[5]

Hess's hypochondria was a common item of gossip, and
the intended audience would have appreciated the reference
to Berlin white beer, since white beer is light in alcohol,
and is often drunk in large swallows to quench thirst. And,
while "parlour Bolsheviks" (a favorite term of German
officers for high-ranking "anti-military" civilians) and
others were condemned, the Führer (Hitler) was referred to

in favorable terms only; any faults that might have been
attributed to him were "really" the work of his advisors.

The success of any clandestine station also depended
quite heavily on the quality and recency of intelligence
information being fed to it. If a station claimed to
operate from within another country, it had to sound well
informed and up to date. Timing also was important. For
example, if intelligence reports from within Germany indicated that German officers were beginning to gossip among
themselves about the sexual behavior of German civilian
government officials, that might be the best time to release
one or two specific bits of information on the subject,
whether real or fabricated.[6] Although few surveys were conducted on listening to clandestine stations during World War
II, such anecdotal information as is available indicates
that accurate (or seemingly accurate), specific, recent
information delivered at the right psychological moment was
quite likely to be believed, even if the listener did not
necessarily accept the bogus identity of the station.
Clandestine and "grey" (unidentified as to place of origin)
stations ever since have attempted to follow the same path.

Toward the end of the war, it became more and more
difficult to keep track of the activities of clandestine
stations; many of them were being deployed in highly tactical situations, and appeared and disappeared as military
fortunes shifted. During the first two months of 1945, the
Nazis put six or seven new clandestine stations on the air,
one for the U.S. army, one for the U.S., British and French
armies, one for the French army, two for the Russian army,
one for Polish armed forces on the Western front, and one
for Italian partisans. One of the stations for Soviet
troops imitated the announcing style of BBC, but talked
pessimistically about the Soviet prospects for success on
the Eastern front in such terms as "We pray to God that the
Red Army may not find its grave in Berlin." The station for
Allied troops featured a voice shouting slogans (usually
repeated three times) such as "German and Soviet troops are
destroying civilization, culture and Europe."[7]

While most clandestine stations were operated with considerable resourcefulness, they won only grudging support
from many military commanders and civilian government
officials, who often considered them unethical if not a
sheer waste of time and energy. But they had their devoted
champions, too: Winston Churchill reportedly was "fascinated" by the prospect of using a specially-built 500 kW
transmitter, nicknamed "Aspidistra", to broadcast over
German radio frequencies and cause panic among the German
civilian population by issuing false evacuation orders.
Neither skeptics nor champions could cite anything more than
anecdotal information in support of their cases, since few

had any further evidence to offer.[8] Since the end of World
War II, dozens of clandestine stations have come and gone.
Most have sounded much like their World War II counterparts:
announcers with bogus titles, "interrupted" broadcasts,
occasional use of off-color language (an announcer on one of
the anti-Ayatollah Khomeini stations told his Iranian
listeners that they should be aware that the station was
sometimes heavily jammed, and that the jamming sounded like
"Khomeini's farts"). And most have no more proof of success
or failure than did their predecessors.

THEMES

     The Germans discovered even before the war that it could
be effective to hammer upon certain themes, such as the evil
influence of the Jews in Slovakia.[9] Radio Moscow had cele-
brated the strength and promise of "the world's first
socialist state" in broadcast after broadcast from its first
day of transmission in 1929. But many international broadcasters seem to have avoided any sort of "thematic" approach
during the 1930s, whether consciously or unconsciously.
     World War II changed this situation radically. Hence-
forth, international radio was regarded commonly as an
"instrument" in a "propaganda arsenal", and was often
accorded highly specific tasks.[10] These might range from
supporting the work of exile governments (provided the
government was of a political persuasion congenial to its
host) to encouraging listeners to commit acts of sabotage.
Some of the stations were highly tactical, and were on the
air only long enough to support specific military operations
(e.g., encouraging citizens to flee from a given city,
thus making it more difficult for military traffic to move).
Most, however, broadcast throughout the war, and with such
consistency that the messages they conveyed may be cate-
gorized according to theme.
     There has been no comprehensive analysis of World War
II broadcasts in general, or even for one nation, for the
entire period of the war. However, a number of individual
analyses,[11] most of them conducted in the early and middle
years of the war, serve as a reasonably firm basis for conclusions about prevalent themes. Those analyses and my own
examination of tapes and partial transcripts of late World
War II broadcasts from Germany, Italy and the USSR have led
me to identify certain of the themes that seem to have been
employed throughout the war.[12] They include:

     We have the strength to win.
     Your friends (both allies and fellow citizens)
     really aren't.

If you think it's rough now, just wait.
Your leaders are misleading you.
The world we're struggling to create will be a
better world.

"We Have the Strength to Win"

Any combattant in a war would like to convince its own
people, its allies and its enemies of its strength. The
difficulty is that events at any one moment may contradict
that contention. It is also difficult to convince enemies
or even skeptics to listen to it, since it is usually the
last thing they want to hear!
For the Italians, Germans and Japanese, it was quite
easy to sustain this theme up to the middle of the war,
simply by announcing fresh victories. (The Germans sometimes had so many at once that they withheld announcing some
of them in order to save them for future use!) The Russians,
British and Americans had a harder time of it during this
period, but leaned heavily on the aspect of the theme that
stressed the willingness of military and civilians alike to
sacrifice until victory was theirs.
By the midpoint of the war, with the successful Allied
invasion of North Africa and the Russian counterattacks on
the Eastern front (1943), matters looked far less promising
for Germany and Italy, and each began to resort to the
technique the Allies had employed earlier: our will to
fight remains strong, and the people themselves are our
greatest strength. This is how Rome handled it:

A less resilient people than the Italians
would perhaps have lost faith and hope. It would
be futile to believe that the Italians after
the events in Tunisia have lost confidence and
faith in final victory. On the contrary, the
more the war approaches their homeland, the more
the Italians are firmly determined to resist
and fight until final victory.[13]

Earlier in the war, the British had put forth the same
sort of message, at times couching it in "typical" BBC
understatement:

"Please pass the marmalade," said the
little old lady. I was having breakfast in a
small hotel in an English south coast town a
few hours ago. At this moment the air raid
sirens began to wail, and the man at my elbow

looked up at the clock. "A little ahead of
himself this morning," he remarked. "They
were three minutes ahead of their schedule
yesterday." I drank my coffee and tried not
to gulp it. No one around me budged. "Would
you please pass the marmalade?" said the little
old lady again, more firmly this time as the
warbling siren died away.[14]

By the end of the war, the situation was almost completely reversed from what it had been several years
earlier, although Germany continued to claim the ability and
will to resist, if only in such broad statements as "Germany
. . . is a force that grows."[15] For its part, Great
Britain was generally inclined to play the "strength" theme
with some restraint, especially where military power was
concerned. Shortly before D-Day, BBC Director General
William Haley cautioned against "gloating" in BBC broadcasts to Germany or anywhere else:

> . . . the BBC's policy regarding the bombing
> of Germany is that it is a scientific operation,
> not to be stunted, to be gloated over, or to be
> dealt with in any other way than the most ob-
> jective factual reporting arising from the
> communiques and from material obtained from Air
> Headquarters or Bomber Stations.[16]

Whether Haley was aware of it or not, there is the contention in psychological warfare that it is particularly
effective to deliver a message of strength, and military
strength in particular, in the most straightforward, un-
excited manner possible. Confidence in one's own capabilities thus manifests itself as "Here is our latest feat of
strength, but there's nothing very surprising about it;
it simply fits a pattern that we've been telling you about
all along, and it will continue."

"Your Friends Really Aren't"

The technique of dividing and conquering is ancient,
but its age did not prevent it from serving as a major
theme in World War II broadcasts. It was used by the Nazis
in their 1939-1940 broadcasts to France, and probably
found many sympathetic listeners who had little faith in the
capabilities of their government or military leaders and
little trust in the English. The Russians used this theme
frequently in their broadcasts to various parts of Central

and Eastern Europe, including Germany; here, the dominant
"line" was that the Eastern European "allies" couldn't get
along with one another and/or were unreliable fighters.
Sometimes the broadcasts were aimed at soldiers, sometimes
at civilians; the following samples are quite typical:

> Soldiers, for whom are you fighting? For
> whom are you allowing yourselves to be butchered?
> For the capitalists in Holland, France and
> England?
> German radio to the Dutch army, May 11, 1940[17]

> Flemings, Soldiers! In the Belgian state
> you have always been citizens of inferior
> status. In the Belgian Army you are treated
> in the same way as the French and English
> treat their black colonial troops, as
> cannon fodder and nothing more.
> German radio to Flemish soldiers, May 13, 1940[18]

> Hitler prides himself on his Allies, and
> Goebbels boasts about them every day. But
> at close range it looks different. The
> Rumanian radio denies the Hungarians achieved
> any victories. . . . For more than three weeks
> the Slovaks have issued no war communiques
> because there simply aren't any Slovak troops
> fighting.
> Radio Moscow to Germany, 1942(?)[19]

In one respect, this was and is the most sure-fire of
all themes, since it appeals to that element within most of
us which cannot wholly accept the help of allies, perhaps
because their motives are not as "pure" or their abilities
as great as ours.

"If You Think It's Rough Now, Just Wait"

Out-and-out intimidation is another time-honored element
of wartime propaganda. In World War II, it was used in a
variety of circumstances, sometimes just before the deployment of a new weapon (e.g. the German V-1 rocket bomb),
sometimes in the midst of a military campaign, sometimes
just after a major defeat, as a way of saying "We'll strike

back." This technique usually featured a good deal of innuendo or suggestion, rather than specific detail, and was
designed to get the listener to imagine even greater horrors
than she or he had yet experienced. The following BBC
German service broadcast, which was preceded by the ticking
of a clock, illustrates one way in which this theme was
presented:

Do you hear the clock ticking?
Do you hear your own clock in your house ticking
the seconds?
One, two, three . . . six, seven.
Every seven seconds a German soldier dies in
Russia.
According to reports, over a million Germans
have fallen in the first four months of the
Russian field campaign.
Every week 80,000.
Every hour 500.
For what? For blighted earth?
For whom? For Adolf Hitler?
For what? Power?
Every seven seconds . . . hour after hour
. . . day and night . . . day and night
every seven seconds.
Is it your son? Your husband? Your brother?
Every seven seconds . . . shot . . .
drowned . . . frozen.
How much longer?
Every seven seconds.
For what? For what?[20]

As the tide of war turned against the Germans, their
broadcasters developed the "mystery weapon" angle. When the
V-1 rocket bomb attacks were launched against Great Britain
in June of 1944, it was after a long (too long, in
Goebbels' opinion--he had expected the weapon to be launched
six months earlier)[21] propaganda campaign that had been
initiated to encourage the German public and discourage
Germany's enemies. One of Goebbels' staff members had
suggested that the symbol "V" be used because it would
stand for retaliation (Vergeltung), and that there be
reference to a series of such weapons--V-2, V-3, etc.--
yet to be developed, in order to heighten anticipation and
anxiety.[22] Such a reference appears in this October 25,
1944 broadcast excerpt (Berlin to North America):

And here is a point that cannot be too
seriously borne in mind by the parents of those
soldiers. . . namely, the V-1 is only a mild
foretaste of that havoc which will be wrought
when V-2, V-3 and further new weapons from
Germany's mystery arsenal are brought into play.
And they will be, at the exactly timed moment
chosen by the German high command.[23]

The chief difficulty with "worse yet to come" broadcasts is that the threat must be perceived as real, and
that usually depends on the circumstances of the war itself.
When the Germans were amassing victory upon victory in the
first few years of World War II, it was easy for listeners
to conceive of terrors yet to come. When a terror campaign
was carried on for several months with no appearance of the
specific weapon of destruction, or when the weapon turned
out to be less destructive than promised, however, the
propagandists faced a difficult choice; as noted by one of
Nazi propagandist Lord Haw-Haw's biographers:

[The technique of terror messages] neces-
sitated constant assertions that something nasty
was going to happen to the enemy very soon. Over
a short period this plan may work, but when even
the most nervous listener noticed that he was
still alive, still eating, and that his Prime
Minister had after all not fled to Canada, the
Goebbels organization was faced with the choice
of changing its policy or pulling even more
hideous faces.[24]

"Your Leaders Are Misleading You"

This could be considered as a variation of the "Your
friends really aren't" theme, but it appears to have been
used often and widely enough during World War II to warrant
separate consideration. The basic intent was to get the
larger public to lose faith in the nation's leadership,
especially political leaders. Condemnation of leaders
appeared in several different forms. One was historical
comparison:

Do you still remember the prominence given
by the Nazis to certain financial scandals in
pre-Hitlerite Germany? Bribery and corruption
have become the normal standard of behavior in
Germany under the Nazis and are no longer the
exception but the rule. Some bacon and butter

will today secure a privileged position in the
ranks of apartment seekers. In exchange for
razor blades and a safety razor the manu-
facturer now secures leave for his son from
the front.
Radio Moscow to Germany[25]

Another was sarcasm:

These leaders speak of equal sacrifices
for all. It makes me want to laugh! Has
Goebbels told you of his castle, his country
house, and a 50-room mansion in Berlin? And
Goering too needs Lebensraum--a hunting place,
a large Berlin mansion and a summer resort at
Dach. The eight years of the Nazi regime
have been fat years for the Nazi leaders but
lean ones for the German people.
BBC to Germany, 1941[26]

Some broadcasts exploited class differences:

Sir Ernie Bevin . . . [Bevin was Minister
of Labour at the time] Just think of the
bloody rat sitting in his office, drawing
his dough and telling us that we ought to work
84 blinking hours a week.
Workers' Challenge, a German clandestine station,
to England[27]

Others belittled political leaders for their lack of
qualifications. Australia's leaders supposedly were:

. . . men trained in grocers' shops and in
small factories to be the parliamentary
leaders of the people. To mismanage one's
affairs hopelessly and become bankrupt in a
little shop is the best qualification to
become prime minister in an Australian
Labor government. . . . Poor Australia!
Australia's own politicians are none too
clean, and Australia's political leaders
are as silly and inefficient as could be
imagined . . .
Radio Batavia, a Japanese station, to Australia, 1943[28]

Such broadcasts may have succeeded in increasing the
level of listener discontent, but there was also the risk
that they might strengthen the listener's resolve to support
his or her leaders, since enemy attacks on those leaders
could be a sign that the leaders must be quite effective

in order to warrant such attacks! The power of this appeal
was almost certainly lessened when the enemy could not
offer a suitable alternative. For example, Nazi broadcasts
to Russian listeners blamed the Soviet leadership for much
of the country's sorry plight early in World War II, but the
cruel and contemptuous treatment received by Russians at the
hands of the invading German army hardly gave those listeners much faith that German leadership would be any improvement.

"The World We're Struggling to Create
Will Be A Better World"

Some international broadcasters offered visions of the
future. Although some of the visions consisted simply of
variations on "Won't it be good to stop the senseless shed-
ding of blood?", others looked ahead in philosophical and
practical terms to a "new world":

> Our victory will not bring about the sub-
> jection of an entire continent or foreign
> domination based on a foundation of racial
> hatred and inequality. Our victory will bring
> peace, peace and cooperation, a victory in
> which the German people, too, can take part,
> if they--together with us--turn against the
> men who today, in the name of Germany, trample
> under all of Europe and set it in chains.
> BBC to Germany, July 1942[29]

> . . . life is progressive by nature. It cannot
> be stopped. Attempts to interrupt natural
> evolution by force lead to explosions. The
> world is ripe for a new order. . . because
> historical evolution has reached this point
> when transitions cannot be avoided. And
> Germany stands among the nations that realize
> the necessity of this transition.
> Germany to North America, December 1940[30]

> Do his own work, and get his own pro-
> visions. That is what the Axis is askin' for.
> There were plenty of Italians down there in
> Africa working their farms. Houses were
> improvin'. . . . Now what I believe, war or
> no war, not waitin' till the war ends, or even
> putting it second to any military contingency,
> I believe that every social reform put thru

in the Axis countries ought to be DEFENDED.
I believe the American people ought to defend
those social measures.
Ezra Pound over Rome Radio to North America, May 1943[31]

Listen to the drone of our planes! It is
the roar of liberation, the spectacle of roused
Asia, stretching out mighty arms to recover her
birthright. China, you are one of us!
Radio Tokyo to China, probably 1941[32]

Give us an equal and fair chance together
with all the other members of the sisterhood of
nations. In the British Empire, South Africa
will compete with your wool, Canada with your
wheat, New Zealand with your mutton. But here
with us you would have a monopolistic market,
if your conditions are reasonable.
Japan to Australia, December 1942[33]

It seems likely that the broadcasters dwelled on themes
because they reflected the beliefs of leaders, and indeed
nations, in the respective countries. Whether individual
members of radio staffs believed in them or not, or even
thought they might make effective propaganda, may have been
immaterial.[34] However, as Lucy Meo's examination of Japan's
World War II broadcasts makes abundantly clear, certain of
these themes were at times juxtaposed in such a way as to
seem ludicrous to any halfway intelligent listener: reasoned
appeals to join in the Greater East Asia Co-Prosperity
Sphere were preceded or followed by condemnation of Australia's "anti-Asian" immigration policy and threats of what
would happen to the country when Japan took it over.[35]
There were other sorts of contradictions, too: a station in
one country could sometimes find itself in the position of
calling upon others to do or look forward to something that
its own citizens would or could not do, or to which they
could not look forward.[36] For example, BBC appeals to
German workers sometimes spoke of those workers as "building
a new and better order" to replace Hitler's New Order, yet
Great Britain at that time hardly represented the model of
a workers' state, and German radio had stressed that point
to its own citizens time and again.
    While "thematic" broadcasting began well before World
War II, it became far more prevalent during the war, and has
continued ever since. In fact, four of the five themes
covered just above are still present in the broadcasts of
most of the major international radio stations, although the
specific approaches taken to each are somewhat different.
For example, "We have the strength to win" is more likely

to be couched in economic, rather than military, terms. "If you think things are rough now, just wait" is more likely to be in the form of references to another nation's internal problems and the likelihood that they are bound to become much worse (e.g. the Communist stations broadcasting about rising unemployment and industrial strife in the capitalist nations).

There is the implication in thematic broadcasting that it is conducted in a calculated, formulaic way. There were many instances during World War II where that was so, as Joseph Goebbels' diaries clearly indicate.[37] There were many instances, however, where the stressing of certain themes is likely to have arisen far more accidentally. For example, if a nation achieved a protracted string of military victories, it could sound to some listeners as if the theme "We have the strength to win" were being stressed, when it might have been only a matter of routinely reporting the day's news. If, however, the same nation was to have withheld reports of victories so as to be sure to have some to report the next day or the next week, or if reports of battles which that nation had lost were turned into reports of tactical victories (e.g. "luring the enemy into a trap")[38] then we are dealing with a conscientiously-developed theme. It is this particular aspect of international broadcasting in World War II that is most notable as a change from previous practices and as a change which has continued to manifest itself up to the present.

PERSONALITIES

On the basis of the little evidence we possess regarding the effectiveness of international broadcasts in World War II, it is likely that "personality" was a greater factor than were "themes".[39] These two elements were, in fact, sometimes combined: Rear Admiral Ellis Zacharias' broadcasts from the United States to Japan in 1945 made use of Admiral Zacharias' ability to speak in a manner that would be perceived by the Japanese as straightforward, honorable, and concerned about their sensitivities, and combined this with the theme that there was a way for the Japanese to surrender unconditionally but honorably.[40] Certain broadcast personalities seem to have identified themselves with certain themes, as well. William Joyce (Lord Haw-Haw) voiced the theme of "decadent, class-ridden England" over German radio throughout the war, apparently because he believed it himself.[41] Ezra Pound's broadcasts on Rome Radio harped on the economic policy shortcomings of the United States, apparently because he believed in the superiority of his own economic philosophy.[42]

As was the case with themes and clandestine operations, personality had appeared as an element in pre-World War II international broadcasting. One broadcast personality, Eddie Starz, could probably claim the title of "longest running" international broadcast personality. He began his weekly multilingual "Happy Station" broadcasts from Holland in 1928, and continued them, except for the war years, until his retirement in 1969. Few emulated his example, however, until the early years of World War II, when individuals such as Ferdonnet, Obrecht, Joyce and Pound began to broadcast for Germany and Italy. We have few details on how most of them actually became broadcast personalities, but, if William Joyce (Lord Haw-Haw) is typical, the process must have been quite accidental: he did poorly on his audition, and was hired by the Germans reluctantly, in part because there was so little English-speaking talent available in Berlin at the time. His German supervisors apparently did not think of him as a "personality" for the first several months he was on the air, and he was not the first Lord Haw-Haw, although he replaced the original "Lord" (Norman Baillie-Stewart) in less than a year. Even the personality of Lord Haw-Haw seems to have developed haphazardly.[43]

However, the Germans were certainly devoted to the concept of personality broadcasting, even if they had few apparent plans for its development or usage. A wide range of personalities was broadcasting for the Deutschlandsender by 1940, and others were added in succeeding years. They included for the North American service alone "Paul Revere" (a "patriot" warning Americans against British treachery), Donald Day (a former Chicago newspaper correspondent), O.K. (Otto Koischwitz, a former professor of German at Hunter College), Constance Drexel ("A Philadelphia socialite and heiress"), Fred Kaltenbach (a "plain-talking, common-sense Iowan"), and many more. Italy had Ezra Pound, Japan had "Tokyo Rose" and "Mopy Dick", as well as "Orphan Annie", but those two Axis nations never had the array of personalities featured by the Germans. Most of the personality broadcasters were individuals sympathetic or even devoted to the Axis cause, but still citizens of the countries to which they broadcast, although a few were prisoners of war who, for various reasons, decided to collaborate with their captors. Very rarely had any of them had previous broadcast experience.[44]

Personalities were less prominent in foreign radio broadcasts undertaken by the Allies, but a few stood out. The British had their "V for Victory" campaign in 1941, which, although it was begun by a Belgian, Victor de Lavelaye, achieved greater fame through the efforts of a fictional personality on the BBC's English service. A BBC staff member, Donald Ritchie, took upon himself the title

"Colonel Britton", and, in addition to further establishing
the "V for Victory" slogan, extended the campaign to "advocate 'gentle' disruptive activities in Europe."[45] Listener
response to the personality of "Colonel Britton" was favorable, as it was for another fictional colonel, "Colonel
Stevens," who broadcast over the BBC's Italian service.[46]
    Lindley Fraser was a noted personality who spoke in his
own name on the BBC's German service. He relied heavily on
wit and humor, but above all on a sense of authority, to
get his points across to his listeners, and his BBC German
service colleague Carl Brinitzer called him "the best-
known [British] name in Germany after Winston Churchill"
in World War II.[47] Rear Admiral Ellis Zacharias, mentioned
above, became a recognized personality to Japanese listeners in very short order--he made a total of 14 broadcasts--
but the United States developed other personalities over a
longer period of time. Two of these were fictional:
"Commander Norden", who broadcast to German submarines, and
"Peter Arnold", who broadcast to the German infantry.[48]
And, just as the Germans and Italians had secured the
services of some noted literary figures, e.g. Ezra Pound,
for their foreign broadcasts, the United States and Great
Britain utilized German novelist Thomas Mann on several
occasions.
    Axis and Allied stations alike employed personality
broadcasters to reach each other's soldiers and sailors,
although the practice was far more common among the Axis
nations. Both used male and female personalities, but the
female personalities attracted far more attention, largely
because of their alleged seductive approaches. "Axis
Sally" for the Germans and "Tokyo Rose" for the Japanese
became quite famous for their supposed ability to evoke
nostalgia, jealousy or suspicion in the minds of their
listeners. Both sets of women (several individuals took on
those roles) did have warm, pleasant voices, and both could
be quite informal, at least by radio standards of the time.
They must have been something of a relief from much of the
broadcast fare available to front-line soldiers or sailors
at sea, but it is just as likely that part of their attrac-
tiveness could be found in their frequent and unintention-
ally amusing mixtures of formality and informality:

        Nature must have a reason for keeping love
    right on hand, don't you think so, boys? As I
    was in my teens, the doctor wanted me to give up
    smoking. "It's very unhealthy," he said. "So
    is kissing," I replied, "but we don't stop it,
    all the same." Oh-oh! Oh, no, boys, love is
    just around the corner. (Followed by song,
    "Love is Just Around the Corner").
    Axis Sally, Berlin to Allied soldiers, July 1944[49]

> Hello, you fighting orphans in the Pacific.
> How's tricks? This is [next few words unintel-
> ligible] back on the air strictly under U.N.
> orders. Reception OK? Well, it better be,
> because this is all-request night, and I've
> got a pretty nice program for my favorite
> little family, wandering in the Pacific
> Islands. The first request is made by none
> other than "The Boss", and guess what? He
> wants Bonnie Baker and "My Resistance is
> Low." Well! What taste you have, sir, she
> said. (Followed by music)
> Tokyo Rose, Tokyo to U.S. sailors, August 1944[50]

The styles of wording and speaking employed by most
personality broadcasters were quite distinctive, and often
exhibited a mixture of formality and informality. Ezra
Pound frequently dropped his terminal "g" (e.g. "This is
Ezra Pound speakin'"), which made him sound almost folksy,
until the listener encountered a statement such as this:

> In any case, secret agreements between an
> usurious nature-faker, whether in or out of the
> White House, are illegal, and a [word unintel-
> ligible] government which presents these secret
> pledges to its people as if they were acts of
> the United States of America participates, and
> naturally has participated, in the swindle.
> Ezra Pound, Rome to United States, February 1942[51]

William Joyce frequently pounded the table for emphasis,
often pronounced Germany as JARmany, and more than once came
before the microphone in an intoxicated state, but he spoke
with unmistakable conviction, perhaps never more so than in
his final broadcast:

> I speak now personally. I want to talk to
> you of what I know, and what I feel. I have
> always hoped and believed that, in the last
> resort, there would be an alliance, a combine,
> an understanding, between England and Germany.
> Well, at the moment, that seems impossible.
> Good . . . if it cannot be, then I can only
> say that the whole of my work has been in vain.
> Lord Haw-Haw, Berlin to England, April 30, 1945[52]

Joyce and his colleagues also were fond of a loftily
sarcastic style, as demonstrated in this October 25, 1944
broadcast by "Paul Revere," dealing with Allied attempts to
belittle the importance of the V-1 rocket bomb:

The second line of the Brit propaganda
defense was a branding of the new weapon as
"unsportsmanlike, unfair, contrary to the
humane ethics of Anglo-American war direction!" It was pointed out that the murder by
night conducted by the Royal Air Force is
performed by gallant crews of pilots and
technicians who risk their own precious lives by
dropping thousands of tons of explosives and
incendiary bombs on sleeping citizens. The
hypocrisy involved in this formulation is too
raw for European consumption, and, indeed,
caused dark, bitter laughter throughout the
continent. I can well imagine that it also
produced a moral disgust among my compatriots
in America, particularly that element of the
American population which is aware of the
essential Jewishness of this war and its
leaders. No uncontaminated Anglo-Saxon mind
would be capable of bringing forth so whining
and pusillanimous a protest.
Paul Revere, Berlin to North America[53]

The relative success or failure of personality broadcasts is difficult to assess, because so few studies of
listener reaction to it were undertaken during World War II.
The BBC conducted surveys early in the war through which
it sought to assess the impact of Lord Haw-Haw's broadcasts;
the surveys showed that he was widely listened to at first,
partly as a novelty, partly for comic relief, but partly
because he did touch some responsive notes: mistrust of
government leaders, fear of Communism, anti-semitism,
respect for the seeming power of Germany.[54] The FBI under-
took an investigation of the effects of Ezra Pound's broadcasts to the United States, but found that relatively few
listeners had heard him.[55] A certain amount of anecdotal
evidence turned up in studies of Axis prisoner-of-war
listening habits before they became prisoners. This is very
little evidence upon which to base any firm conclusions.
What it seems to indicate is that listeners may be willing
to accept the enemy viewpoint as long as the enemy is
enjoying success. That viewpoint appears to be even more
palatable if it is delivered by a personality with whom the
listeners can identify. The more colorful personalities
also seem to have succeeded in getting their messages talked
about; listeners would convey them to non-listeners, sometimes in distorted terms. Highly specific details about
life in the listener's country or, better yet, immediate
surroundings, seem to have been especially impressive, and
sometimes caused listeners to attribute degrees of specifi-
city and accuracy to those messages that they never contained.

The personality broadcasters of World War II have some
rough equivalents at present, although a few seem as colorful as Lord Haw-Haw or Tokyo Rose.[56] There are personalities of one sort or another on most international radio
stations, hosting music shows, answering listener letters,
presenting commentaries. If they are on the air long
enough, they often gain a considerable personal following.
This should not be surprising, since radio is well suited
to convey a highly personal sense of communication. In
order to succeed, however, it seems necessary for such
broadcasters to develop distinctive styles, as have Joe
Adamov of Radio Moscow, Anatol Goldberg of BBC, Yvonne
Barclay and Willis Conover of VOA, Tom Meijer of Radio
Nederland, and, for a time, Ahmed Said of Radio Cairo's
Voice of the Arabs. And, while it is probably stretching
the point to suggest that these present-day personalities
owe a debt to their World War II predecessors (Adamov in
fact began broadcasting for Radio Moscow early in the war),
it was those predecessors who established personality
broadcasting as a major element in international radio.

PROGRAM FORMATS

Up until World War II, most international broadcast
program schedules were quite limited: news, commentaries,
features, music, press roundups, written and read in a
manner that reflected the predominantly formal style of
domestic broadcasts.[57] During World War II, those program
formats and approaches continued to form the bulk of each
station's schedule. However, as I have just noted, personalities began to play a major role in international
broadcasting at that time, and, as they did, program formats
were created or adapted for them. Broadcasts of recorded
music,[58] for example, now acquired hosts and hostesses who
used the time between records to extol the virtues of the
broadcasting nation, or to sow doubt in the minds of their
listeners concerning the cause for which they were fighting, or to play upon discomforts and dangers:[59]

Well, you boys of the AEF (Allied Forces),
don't you think it would be nice to live a little
more in the past? The world of the trenches
isn't much fun, is it, at the present time, with
. . . pilotless bombers floating around your
heads. I don't suppose that these times are
exactly your idea of something pleasurable . . .
if the war would go backwards, like going off
to Palm Beach, back to the good old days when

the orchestras first began to play "Jada".
Well, it's quite a long time ago, but we just got
a brand new recording: "JaDa, JaDa, Jada Jada
Jing Jing Jing" (followed by musical selection).
Axis Sally, Berlin to Western European front,
July 27, 1944[60]

"Skits", or minature dialogues, which had occurred in
the context of comedy or variety shows on some domestic
radio services, now became program elements in their own
right on some international stations. BBC's German service
had a "Frau Warnicke" who delivered various opinions on
current events in Germany from the perspective of a Berlin
housewife. The following excerpt is based on the German
newspaper practice of printing "In Proud Mourning" after
death announcements for German soldiers:

Well, I know that Luwise Spindler certainly
isn't proud that her Heinz was torn to pieces
by a grenade, and the Kutemeiers over there
aren't very proud, either, that their young
one was drowned someplace or other in the North
Sea.[61]

German radio devised "dialogues" among Americans,
between Germans and Americans, Canadians and Americans, etc.
Monologues sometimes took the form of "telephone conversations" (e.g. between a "switchboard operator" for the
"Pittsburgh Tribune" and various callers) or the reading
of letters from friends. The usual style in these broadcasts was colloquial, or something that was supposed to pass
for it:

Jim: If Germany hadn't been ready to save
       Europe from the Red aggression, those
       Bolshevists would have walked right
       in and mowed us down.
Johnny: Gosh, yes, that was a close call all
       right for Europe![62]

At times, the broadcasts were in dialects, and sought
to perpetuate certain stereotypes, e.g. of cowardice among
American Black soldiers:

Smitty: Oh, oh, here come de boss! Ah, wah,
       an' it look lak de man got de dynamite
       right under his arm!
Sam: Wo, wo, wo! Smitty, you talk to de man.
       Ah's gwine be right behind you all de
       time.

```
Officer:   Hello, there, boys.  I've got a job
           here that I want you boys to do.
Smitty:    Yyyyyyyy You's talkin' to de wrong
           man, boss.  Ah, ah, ah mean, what do
           you wan' us, what do you wan' me to do?
Officer:   Well, I want you to take this bunch
           of dynamite . . .
Smitty:    Bunch???
Officer:   Yeah, this bunch of dynamite.  And I
           want you to blow up the river bed
           down at the end of the valley.  Now
           here, you take this and see what you
           can do.
Smitty:    Wa, wa, what is dis, pointin' dat ting
           right at mah head.
Sam:       Quit shakin' lak that, boy, quit
           shakin'.  You liable to drop de ting.
Radio Tokyo to U.S. Military in the Pacific,
August 12, 1945[63]
```

Certain broadcasters employed the device of "answering"
speeches from political leaders in enemy nations, or inter-
rupting news broadcasts from enemy stations with comments
of their own. Although the Russians were more famous for
the latter (see page 225) than were the other major
broadcast powers, the Germans, British and, less often,
Americans, employed both of these techniques. Deutschlandsender's Fred Kaltenbach "answered" a recording of
President Roosevelt's "Fireside Chat" of May 27, 1941:

```
Roosevelt:    Every dollar of material we send
              helps to keep the dictators away
              from our hemisphere.
Kaltenbach:   Why this needless concern, Mr.
              President?  Adolf Hitler is a
              poor sailor.  He hates the sea.
              I am sure he would never under-
              take a boat trip so far from home.
Roosevelt:    Germany would literally parcel
              out the world.
Kaltenbach:   Now come, now come, Mr. President.
              You know as well as I do that
              Adolf Hitler is not in the real
              estate business.[64]
```

Stations developed or reworked other types of entertainment for the purpose of conveying propaganda. BBC took
the formula of the domestic quiz program and developed a
German language version of it. Questions came from listeners
in Sweden, Switzerland, and occasionally Austria or Germany.[65]

In its spontaneity and "group" approach, this program fore-
shadowed Radio Moscow's "Moscow Mailbag" (pp. 228-229).
However, not all broadcasters felt that entertainment was a
universally effective propaganda device. Noel Newsome, then
Chief Editor of BBC's European News Service, sent a memo to
Hugh Carleton Greene of BBC's German service in which he
indicated that "on their home radio the Germans will be
hearing the grim story of the Generals' trial in the Peoples'
Court [on charges stemming from the July 1944 "bomb plot"
against Hitler] ; they should not get jokes when they tune
in to London."[66]

Once again, we have little beside anecdotal evidence to
tell us whether these new or revised broadcast formats had
specific positive or negative effects on listeners. They
certainly contributed a good deal to the "de-formalization"
of international broadcasting, and many of them live on
today: several stations (e.g. BBC and VOA) have used
satirical skits, during the 1950s Cold War period in particular; and popular music programs still serve for some
stations as vehicles for the transmission of political
propaganda.[67]

RADIO AS A STRATEGIC WEAPON

While international radio certainly had served strategic
purposes before World War II, the war saw a dramatic increase in that usage of the medium. And, since listener
research was either impossible or unimportant for most
international stations engaged in this sort of strategic
warfare, most of them developed their own "theories"
or ground rules for "warfare" by radio.

Broadly speaking, international radio in World War II
operated under two types of strategy: offensive and
defensive. They were not mutually exclusive--in fact, most
large stations practiced both--but one usually predominated
in any given station at any one time. In an offensive
strategy, the themes stressed were generally those of
attack: one's own readiness and ability to carry it out and
the weakness of one's enemies in attempting to resist it.
In a defensive strategy, the emphasis was generally on
refuting the enemy's charges by calling attention to their
errors or falseness. Daniel Katz, analyzing BBC broadcasts
to North America early in World War II, made no secret of
the fact that he thought a defensive strategy (then employed,
he contended, by BBC's North American service) weak:

As a rule it is a mistake to let one's
opponent define the points of difference in the

dispute, but it is even more of a mistake to
defend the role he has assigned you than to
attack and expose the role he has assigned
himself. In defending oneself the charges of
the opponent are publicized explicitly or
implicitly and through positive suggestion
receive a certain acceptance. Even if one
succeeds in clearing himself, the emphasis
is more on his guilt than upon the guilt of
the accuser.68

   If, however, the opponent were hammering away at certain weaknesses, and if those weaknesses were real and were
widely known to listeners, it would have been very difficult
to avoid dealing with the opponent's attacks in specific
terms. It still was possible, however, to mix acknowledgement and refutation of those attacks with attacks of one's
own, and this was a common enough practice, although there
was always the danger that listeners might interpret it as
a "slanging match" between enemies, neither of which was any
better than the other.
   Another variant on this strategy was "two-sided" propaganda, wherein one admitted one's own imperfections,
whether the enemy had called attention to them or not, but
on balance gave greater prominence to the positive side of
things. The British and Americans made some use of this
strategy, while the Axis powers and the Soviet Union rarely
did so. The strategy rested on the assumption that, since
few people expected perfection, and since a number of
stations never presented the imperfections of their own
countries or causes, there would be considerably greater
credibility for stations utilizing a two-sided approach.
On the other hand, there was the danger that listeners
already committed to a given cause might find that commitment weakening if they were presented with a steady diet
of partially negative information about it.
   Finally, there was the strategy of diversity, in which
a given nation might set up several different international
broadcast stations, some "white" (officially acknowledged),
some "grey" (unattributed), some "black" (false identity),
often broadcasting contradictory information. BBC, for
example, was very positive about Winston Churchill, while
the British-run Gustave Siegfried Eins berated him. In
theory, this made it possible for a broadcasting nation to
deny that it had made a certain broadcast, if that broadcast
had been made over a "grey" or "black" station. It also
made it possible to appeal to a wider variety of listeners
and, presuming each station had its own set of frequencies,
to combat jamming more effectively. All of the major powers
in the war worked through more than one international radio

service at one time or another, although the Americans,
British and Germans appear to have used a wider variety of
stations than did the Italians, Japanese and Russians.

Whether the strategy of diversity works in practice is
another matter. Such little survey and anecdotal data as
exists indicates that most listeners spent little time
listening to anything other than the "main" station of a
country, however many other choices there may have been.
A few specialized services--broadcasts to submarines,
broadcasts to enemy troops along the front lines-- appeared to
have some limited success,[69] but their impact seems to have
been minimal. Many of them were on the air so briefly,
whether measured in hours broadcast per day (some came on
for 10 or 15 minutes per day) or number of days, weeks or
months in operation, that few would-be listeners were able
to tune to them with any regularity. Toward the end of the
war, for example, German stations came into and went out of
existence almost every week. There was also the widespread
feeling on the part of the "legitimate" broadcasters that
the grey or black stations operated by their countries would
not fool any reasonably intelligent listener, who could
soon guess their real nature and identity and who might
therefore wonder whether the legitimate stations from the
same countries were all that trustworthy.[70]

Nevertheless, several nations have continued to operate
under a strategy of diversity. The Soviet Union and the
United States have been able to avoid taking responsibility
for things said by Radio Peace and Progress or by Radio Free
Europe on the grounds that they are not official stations,
even though in fact both are financed and managed by their
respective governments or bodies appointed by and reporting
to governments. The Soviet Union has been able to broadcast in Kuoyu (Mandarin) for more than 24 hours per day
because it can use both Radio Moscow and Radio Peace and
Progress for this purpose. Diversity, for all the cost and
extra effort associated with it, continues to be regarded as
a viable strategy by some stations.

The other strategic approaches also continue to exist,
although they are more apparent in some cases than in others.
Radio Moscow, for example, seemed to follow a clear-cut
"offensive" strategy in its broadcasts of the 1950s and
1960s, when it lost few opportunities to call attention to
the evils and the inevitable decline of capitalism and
colonialism, or to its own stellar record as a progressive
nation; furthermore, the station took little notice of
Western criticisms of the Soviet Union or communism. That
strategy was less clear-cut in the 1970s, when capitalism
was still being attacked, but when there were more frequent
admissions that life in the Soviet Union was not problem-
free. There also were specific responses to Western

criticisms, particularly on such events as the various
trials of Soviet dissidents and the "invasion" of Afghanistan.
And VOA has faced frequent criticism from various members of
Congress for following a two-sided approach and "telling too
much of what's bad about America."

CONCLUSION

I have contended that many of the practices of present-
day international broadcasting can be traced to World War II.
Few of those practices, to be sure, originated at that time,
but most rose to prominence then. I have also contended
that most of these practices were untested in any scientific
manner, and were of unknown value in convincing, coercing,
or even securing the attention of listeners. If the
practices live on, it is not so much because they are known
to be effective as it is that they are simply known--that
they have become familiar over time.

The perpetuation of World War II practices was also
aided by the fact that some of the same station staff
members who were active during World War II continued to
work for the stations after the war. Those nations which
became most directly involved in the Cold War--the United
States, Great Britain and the Soviet Union in particular--
had all the more reason for continuing or reviving certain
wartime practices, since this was, after all, a war as well.
It was probably even more heavily ideological than the
Second World War had been, and as such would be likely to
see greater emphasis placed on psychological warfare.

Finally, inertia must have played some role in the
perpetuation of World War II practices. Once a broadcast
staff had learned a certain manner of preparing programs,
it was easier to continue along those lines than to seek out
new broadcast content, formats and strategies. The chapters
to come will show that, while many international stations
have developed new formats, content, etc., there is a fair
amount of any station's program schedule and broadcast
style that would be recognizable to a World War II listener.

NOTES

1. See Chapter 2, footnote 13.

2. See Willi A. Boelcke, Die Macht des Radios (Frankfurt:
Verlag Ullstein, 1977), mainly Chapters 2 and 3, and Reimund
Schnabel, Missbrauchte Mikrofone (Vienna: Europa Verlag
1967), passim, for the most complete references to these

broadcasts. Also useful is Werner Schwipps, Wortschlacht
im Äther (Berlin: Haude und Spenersche, 1971). Briefer
references appear in previously cited works by Graves, Rolo,
Ettlinger, and Briggs III.

3. Boelcke, Radio, Sefton Delmer, Black Boomerang (New
York: Viking Press, 1962), and J.A.C. Cole, Lord Haw-Haw--
and William Joyce (London: Faber and Faber, 1964), are quite
revealing as to how German and British clandestine stations
came into being.

4. Gustave Siegfried Eins, Delmer's first clandestine
station, succeeded in attracting the attention of the U.S.
Foreign Broadcast Information Service, which stated in one
monitoring report that it had picked up "a new station of
unknown origin, purporting to come from within Germany and
to be operated by and for German officers." The report
went on to say that the station might well be authentic!

5. Delmer, Boomerang. The translation is Delmer's.

6. However, Ladislas Farago, in The Game of the Foxes
(New York: David McKay, 1971), p. 548, mentions that German
secret agents stationed abroad warned the home office against
using certain intelligence information in propaganda activities because it might "blow their cover".

7. Activities of clandestine stations during this
period are briefly described in the Foreign Broadcast
Information Service's "Station and Program Notes," particularly in issue no. 323 (February 12, 1945) and in
"Phony", Time, January 22, 1945, p. 88.

8. Delmer, Boomerang, especially pp. 128-130 and 272-
274, offers some anecdotal evidence of successes, as do
Asa Briggs, The History of Broadcasting in the United
Kingdom, Volume III: The War of Words (New York: Oxford
University Press, 1970), pp. 694-695, and Charles Cruikshank,
The Fourth Arm (London: Davis-Poynter, 1977), pp. 155-158.
Cruikshank discusses the use of a clandestine radio program,
"The Intruder", to cause panic among the German civilian
population in March 1945--an operation that involved the
substitution of a false "German" station for a real one
when the latter was forced to leave the air briefly. Michael
Balfour, Propaganda in War, 1939-1945 (London and Boston:
Routledge and Kegan Paul, 1979), pp. 97-99, speculates that
British clandestine radio may have "made prisoners more
inclined to talk because they thought we [the British]
knew so much already," but he also notes speculation by some
authorities that the stations may have improved German
morale because they "created a great deal of amusement."
Both Balfour, p. 413, and Briggs III, pp. 353 and 426-427,
note Churchill's interest in "Aspidistra".

9. Henry Delfiner, Vienna Broadcasts to Slovakia
(Boulder: East European Quarterly, 1974), East European
Monographs 7, notes the enormous amount of anti-semitic

material broadcast over the German-operated Slovak language
radio station in Vienna. The anti-semitic campaign was
waged by Nazi Germany throughout the war and throughout the
world, and included areas where anti-semitism wasn't much of
an issue, e.g. South Asia. It was also waged by Italy and
Japan, probably because of German influence in the latter
case (see Lucy Meo, Japan's Radio War on Australia, 1941-
1945 (Melbourne: Melbourne University Press, 1968), p. 273,
footnote 66) and possibly in the former case as well.

    10. Although the religious stations were not a part of
the Allied or Axis wartime broadcast effort, Vatican Radio
did broadcast messages to and from refugees, prisoners, etc.
and sometimes criticized the Nazis and Mussolini. Josef
Goebbels attacked Vatican Radio for its "unfriendly and at
times positively aggressive attitude towards us [Germany] "
and in April 1941 stated that he wanted to "silence" the
station, perhaps with Mussolini's help. See Willi A.
Boelcke, The Secret Conferences of Dr. Goebbels (London:
Weidenfeld and Nicolson, 1967), p. 130, p. 145.

    11. See Chapter Two, footnote 14, for references to
books containing these analyses. In addition, Z.A.B.
Zeman, Nazi Propaganda (London: Oxford University Press,
1964), contains some brief but interesting analyses, and
Robert Sherrod, "Two Weeks of Radio Tokyo", Life 18
(February 19, 1945), pp. 6+, provides a general account of
Radio Tokyo broadcasts

    12. This material was obtained primarily through the
aural and written documents available at the Sound and
Motion Picture Division of the National Archives and from
the Foreign Broadcast Information Service reports, the
"Station and Program Notes" in particular. The FBIS material
is available at the Center for Research Libraries, University
of Chicago, Chicago, Illinois, which also has a relatively
complete collection of CBS monitoring reports of foreign
broadcasts for the early years of World War II.

    13. Harold Ettlinger, The Axis on the Air (Indian-
apolis: Bobbs-Merrill, 1943), p. 185.

    14. Childs and Whitton, Propaganda, p. 134.

    15. "Sign Off", Time, May 14, 1945, p. 90.

    16. Briggs III, p. 657.

    17. Tangye Lean, Voices in the Darkness (London:
Secker and Warburg, 1943), p. 112.

    18. Ibid, p. 113.

    19. Charles Rolo, Radio Goes to War (New York: G.
Putnam, 1942), p. 207.

    20. Carl Brinitzer Hier Spricht London (Hamburg:
Hoffman und Campe, 1969), p. 155.

    21. Ernest Bramsted, Goebbels and National Socialist
Propaganda, 1925-1945 (East Lansing: Michigan State University Press, 1965), pp. 317-320.

22. Bramsted, Goebbels, p. 321.

23. Transcribed by me from tape recording of this broadcast in the collection of the Sound and Motion Picture Division, National Archives, Washington, D.C. (hereafter referred to as "National Archives Collection"), #262-25.

24. J.A.C. Cole, Lord Haw-Haw (London: Faber and Faber, 1964), p. 167.

25. Ettlinger, Axis, p. 277.

26. Rolo, Radio, p. 162.

27. Briggs III, p. 233.

28. Meo, Japan, pp. 109-110.

29. Brinitzer, London, p. 255.

30. Childs and Whitton, Propaganda, p. 286.

31. Leonard Doob, ed., Ezra Pound Speaking (Westport: Greenwood Press, 1978), p. 305.

32. Meo, Japan, p. 191.

33. Ibid, pp. 116-117.

34. However, the Allied policy of unconditional surrender for Germany and Japan prevented Allied propagandists from employing appeals to any kind of conditional surrender, even though some propagandists saw great value in such an approach. British propagandists R.H.S. Crossman, however, supported the "unconditional surrender" approach, because he thought that it projected an image of unanimous, unwavering Allied determination. Daniel Lerner, Psychological Warfare Against Nazi Germany (Cambridge: MIT Press, 1971), pp. 332-333. Delmer felt that it spoiled some excellent opportunities; see Delmer, Boomerang, pp. 204-205.

35. Meo, Japan, passim.

36. Lerner, Warfare, Chapter 6, speaks of problems faced by those Allied propagandists who tried to create division within Germany.

37. Bramsted, Goebbels, Schnabel, Mikrofone, Boelcke, Conferences and Louis Lochner, ed., The Goebbels Diaries (New York: Doubleday, 1 48) are the most readily accessible sources on the nature of Goebbels' shaping and deployment of propaganda themes. American and British efforts along these lines are covered quite well in Delmer, Boomerang, Cruikshank, Fourth Arm, Briggs II and III, Lerner, Warfare, and Wallace Carroll, Persuade or Perish (Boston: Houghton-Mifflin, 1948), while Meo, Japan, offers a fairly thorough treatment of Japan.

38. As the American invasion forces began to recapture the Pacific islands and landed on the Philippines, Radio Tokyo also deployed the "trap" angle, as in the following excerpt: "The coming of Americans to Manila is exactly what our side waited for, and our bleeding tactics, which are our aim, will now enter the positive stage." Sherrod, "Radio Tokyo", p. 8.

39. Lerner, Warfare, p. 332 and Carroll, Persuade, pp. 366-367.

40. Alan M. Winkler, The Politics of Propaganda: The Office of War Information, 1942-1945 (New Haven: Yale University Press, 1978), pp. 142-146 and Ellis Zacharias, Secret Missions (New York: G.P. Putnam's Sons, 1946). The scripts of the fourteen broadcasts are included in pp. 399-424 of Zacharias.

41. Cole, Lord Haw-Haw, pp. 65-66.

42. Doob, Pound, pp. 63-65.

43. Cole, Lord Haw-Haw, pp. 110-126.

44. Many magazine articles dealing with these personalities appeared during World War II, e.g. William Shirer, "American Radio Traitors," Harpers 187 (October 1943):397+, but previously cited books by Rolo, Ettlinger, Cruikshank, Boelcke, Radios, Lerner, Cole and Doob, plus Ronald Seth, The Truth Benders (London: Leslie Frewin, 1969), and NHK, 50 Years of Japanese Broadcasting (NHK: Tokyo, 1977), pp. 100-102, supply most of the essential detail. A good summary of the backgrounds, activities and ultimate fates of the various U.S. "radio traitors" is available in William G. Schofield, Treason Trial (Chicago: Rand-McNally, 1964).

45. Briggs III, p. 371. The fullest account of the V-for-Victory campaign is contained in Briggs, Ibid, pp. 365-384. Cruikshank, Fourth Arm, pp. 121-128, Lean, Voices, pp. 189-193, and Brinitzer, London, pp. 129-134, all add various details, but in the main collaborate Briggs' account. The campaign was very famous in its day, but Briggs, Ibid, pp. 13-14, questions its actual success.

46. Briggs III, pp. 436-437, and Lean, Voices, pp. 198-199. The "colonel" identifications for these two individuals were probably designed to invest them with a certain level of authority. "General" would not have been as suitable because there were far fewer of these, and the fiction would have been more easily discovered. Also, listeners might doubt that an authentic general would have the necessary time to make such broadcasts.

47. Brinitzer, London, p. 141. Brinitzer provides a fairly detailed picture of Fraser's style and character in Chapter 12. Briggs III, p. 429, offers a brief appraisal of him.

48. See Ellis Zacharias, Secret Missions (New York: G. Putnam's Sons, 1946), pp. 306-311, on Commander Norden, and Carroll, Persuade, pp. 366-367, on Peter Arnold.

49. National Archives Collection, #262-20.

50. Ibid., #262-100.

51. Ibid., #262-24390.

52. Ibid., #200-679.

53. Ibid., #262-25.

54. Briggs III, pp. 140-159, which also contain anecdotal references to Haw-Haw's effectiveness. See also Balfour, Propaganda, pp. 140-143.

55. Doob, Pound, p. xii.

56. However, the Vietnam War saw the creation of a
"Hanoi Hannah", and there was a "Mendocino Rose" broadcasting from the northern California coast in the mid-
1970s. In the latter case, the station broadcast to Soviet
whaling vessels in the Pacific, and balalaika and other
Russian music was introduced by a Russian-speaking woman
calling herself "Oktobriana", but known locally as "Mendocino
Rose". The station attempted through these broadcasts to
stop the slaughter of the grey whale. Tom Hennessy, "A
'Tokyo Rose' for Soviet Seamen," Philadelphia Inquirer,
January 29, 1976, p. 8C.

57. Certain international stations, e.g. the BBC's
Empire Service and the prewar international stations
operated by the U.S. commercial radio networks, did have a
number of comedy and quiz shows which were less formal,
although one might well have wondered whether a Latin
American listener could make much sense out of the likes of
Edgar Bergen and Charlie McCarthy, with their "wisecracking"
and heavy use of American slang.

58. The recorded music on these programs was quite
often from the nation to whose listeners the station was
broadcasting, particularly when those listeners were
military personnel far from home. Glenn Miller, Tommy
Dorsey, Victor Herbert and other popular and semi-classical
bands and composers were often featured by Tokyo Rose, Axis
Sally, etc. As the war went on, however, it became more and
more difficult for the Axis stations to obtain recent recordings, and much of the music they played late in World
War II was quite dated! NHK, 50 Years of Japanese Broadcasting (Tokyo: NHK, 1976), mentions a wartime incident in
which "Tokyo Rose" (an umbrella title for the women disc
jockeys on Radio Tokyo's service to U.S. forces in the
Pacific) stated in one of her broadcasts that she was sorry
not to have the latest jazz records, whereupon a U.S.
airplane dropped a package of the latest releases during a
subsequent air raid on Tokyo! The records did not survive
the drop. NHK, p. 101. Schofield, Treason Trial, pp. 193-
194 notes that Iva Toguri, the most famous Tokyo Rose,
actually claimed to be the only one. He also indicated
that one of the few defense witnesses to testify on her
behalf in her trial after the war claimed that she had
performed a positive service for the United States: she
"knew" that her programs would be seen as preposterous by
the American troops, and thus cheer them up, while her
Japanese supervisors would think that she was demoralizing
her listeners!

59. The "disk jockey" had been around in domestic
broadcasting for some time in certain countries, notably
the United States, Great Britain and Luxembourg. However,

few of them spoke about non-musical subjects, aside from
references to the weather, etc.; there was a very strict
separation between anything faintly resembling news and
anything classifiable as entertainment.

        60.   National Archives Collection, #262-19.
        61.   Brinitzer, London, p. 154, translation mine.
The original was in a broad Berliner dialect.
        62.   Deutschlandsender broadcast, reported in Rolo,
Radio, p. 99.
        63.   Tokyo to U.S. Military in the Pacific, August 12,
1945, from National Archives Collection, #262-197.
        64.   Rolo, Radio, p. 99. Sefton Delmer was employed
by the BBC to "answer" (in German) the political commentaries of Hans Fritsche, chief Nazi radio commentator. See
Brinitzer, London, pp. 189-194, Briggs III, p. 230; Delmer,
Boomerang, pp. 10-11, discusses his "reply" to Hitler.
        65.   Brinitzer, London, pp. 189-190.
        66.   Memo, Newsome to Greene, August 8, 1944, cited in
Briggs III, p. 693.
        67.   Perhaps the most peculiar example of such a
broadcast that I have ever heard was a program transmitted
by the Radio Cairo English to Israel service during the
period following the Fourth Mideast War ("Yom Kippur" War)
of 1973. The program could be heard throughout the Middle
East, and I monitored it often while living in Beirut
between 1973 and 1974. It consisted of popular music (with
no identification of specific titles, artists, etc.) and
one-line slogans, e.g. "The Arab cause is just and is bound
to triumph." It bore something of a resemblance to the
Nazi clandestine station mentioned on page 65 (this
chapter) above.
        68.   Katz, in Childs and Whitton, Propaganda, p. 129.
Much the same strategy was to be advocated for Voice of
America broadcasts to the Soviet Union in the early stages
of the Cold War; see Chapter Four below, p.99.
        69.   Lerner, Warfare, especially Chapter 11.
        70.   Briggs III, p. 434, Lerner, Ibid., pp. 271-272,
and Winkler, Politics, pp. 128-129.

4

THE VOICE OF AMERICA

Unlike BBC's External Services or most other major international radio stations, the Voice of America did not originate as part of a domestic broadcasting service. The broadcast industry in the United States was in private hands from the beginning, and private firms had little interest in communicating outside the United States. General Electric and Westinghouse experimented with international broadcasting as early as 1923, but chiefly to test and perfect their transmitting equipment; programing consisted of relays of their U.S. stations. NBC became involved in point-to-point exchanges of programs with foreign stations by 1927.[1] In that same year, GE offered the first regularly scheduled program from the U.S. designed expressly for foreign listeners: a once-per-week broadcast in Spanish to Latin America of approximately an hour of music and news.[2] The first U.S. station to devote itself exclusively to broadcasts for foreign listeners was W1XAL, which began its transmissions from just outside Boston in 1933. Its owner, Walter Lemmon, saw it as an international radio correspondence school and promoter of world peace; as you'll read in Chapter 5, it played very interesting roles in World War II and in the "Cold War".

Other U.S.-based international stations came on the air or increased their broadcast activities in the mid- to late 1930s. By the end of the decade, CBS, NBC, Westinghouse, Crosley and General Electric all had international services, but little of the programing was specifically created for foreign listeners; NBC and CBS leaned heavily on retransmissions of such fare as "Amos n' Andy" and "Charlie McCarthy", however difficult they may have been for a Chilean or a German to understand![3] The CBS and NBC stations broadcast some newscasts and occasional documentaries in Spanish to Latin America, but there was a general assumption among network executives that English was "universally a secondary [sic] language," and as such would be understood by most reasonably intelligent listeners.4 Furthermore, most stations were short on staff with a first-hand knowledge of other countries, and transmitters were often "so defective in power that reception was inferior to that of most European services."5

The U.S. Congress displayed some interest in the establishment of a governmentally-run international radio service in the late 1930s. Representative Emmanuel Celler of New York was sufficiently concerned over Fascist radio propaganda directed at Latin America to propose, in November 1937, a bill calling for the Navy to establish a short-wave station to "promote better understanding among the republics of the American continents." When hearings were held in May 1938, Celler stated: "Subtle, damnable, designing programs destroy liberty and undermine democracy. . . . The world is poisoned by propaganda." But opposition from the National Association of Broadcasters, General Electric, Westinghouse and CBS quickly appeared. NAB President Mark Ethridge told the House Naval Affairs Committee that the Celler bill "suggested the Nazi philosophy," and indicated that "the Administration would always have access to the privately-owned facilities."6 The proposal died, as did two similar bills, largely as a result of distaste on the part of Congress and industry alike for having the government undertake anything already being done by private enterprise.7

With the situation in Europe worsening, various American international stations began to put more effort into broadcasts to South America and Europe.8 However, the private stations still made little attempt to adapt their broadcasts to particular audiences, to discover the best times of day for transmission, or to follow a consistent political line. The stations were receiving increasing amounts of programming from the State Department, and later from the Office of the Coordinator for Inter-American Affairs, but the programing was not always up to their own broadcast standards.9

Even as the United States declared war on the Axis powers in December 1941, there was still no comprehensive plan for international broadcasting.10 It was not until June 1942 that President Roosevelt established a government department--the Office of War Information (OWI)--to carry out the task.11 Once it had been created, OWI moved to place all private international stations under governmental supervision. That was not completely achieved until November 1942, some broadcasters--WRUL's Walter Lemmon in particular--being reluctant to hand over their facilities without ironclad guarantees that the government would give them up when the war was over.12

OWI soon added transmitter power and language service

to what it had acquired from the private stations as it set
about the task of telling the rest of the world of America's
determination and ability to bring the war to a successful
conclusion. The collective broadcast service had been
called the Voice of America from the time it came on the
air in February 1942, and a great deal of its programing
was designed to reflect life in the United States, particularly in more personal terms, e.g. through a feature on
the day of a typical American laborer. Some broadcasts were
criticized for emphasizing America's prosperity in a largely
hungry, luxury-deprived world. Other broadcasts praised the
joint efforts of the Allies, and still others stressed enemy
military setbacks, civilian hardships and disunity among the
Axis powers.13
        Strategy sometimes dictated that misleading information
be broadcast, but that was left to the Office of Strategic
Services (OSS), lest VOA broadcasts lose credibility.14
Coordination of propaganda efforts proved difficult throughout the war, not only among the various departments and
offices engaged in it, but also within OWI. Foreign operations were based in New York City, while the domestic
branch, as well as OWI chief Elmer Davis and his immediate
staff, were in Washington, D.C. Robert Sherwood, the
distinguished playwright, had been asked by President
Roosevelt to head the organization that handled foreign
information operations before OWI was created, and that
organization was simply merged with OWI. Sherwood had been
given a relatively free hand in selecting his staff; Davis
and certain members of Congress later charged that some of
those staff members were too individualistic or not in
sympathy with Allied policy.15
        Two incidents serve to illustrate the charges made:
first, Mussolini's resignation in July 1943 was treated
skeptically by VOA, which doubted that his replacement by
King Victor Immanuel and Marshall Badoglio would herald any
real change in Fascist philosophy. VOA went so far as to
label Victor Immanuel a "moronic little king" even as the
American government was involved in delicate negotiations
with him.16 Second, in November 1943 the U.S. House of
Representatives took up the question of the presence and
influence of aliens in OWI, which was specifically criticized for allowing broadcasts by some German Social Democrats belonging to the Neu Beginnen group.17 Davis moved
in 1944 to discharge certain top OWI foreign Operations
staff, Sherwood disputed his right to do so, and President
Roosevelt himself had to intervene, all of which caused
Congress and certain journalists to wonder about the
administration of OWI and to question the need for its
continued existence after the war.18
        Well before the war was over, President Roosevelt

asked the FCC to look ahead to the postwar period and to
make recommendations on government policy regarding international broadcasting. In 1944, a special committee of
government radio engineers drew up plans for postwar international broadcasting. The State Department's Committee on
Communications asked Columbia University political science
professor Arthur McMahon to make recommendations on postwar
U.S. international broadcasting. His report, submitted in
July 1945, opened with the premise that "The United States
Government and specifically the State Department cannot be
indifferent to the ways in which our society is portrayed in
other countries."[19] The report recommended that international broadcasting be continued after the war, and
favored centralized administration, either under a private,
limited dividend corporation or under the federal government.[20]

As the war ended, President Truman announced the creation of an "Interim International Information Service,"
including the Voice of America, to be operated by the State
Department until the end of 1945. Thereafter, the Secretary
of State was authorized to terminate any or all of its
functions, or continue them within the Department. Truman
simultaneously released a statement reaffirming that private
industry should be left to do the job of international communication insofar as possible[21]--a sentiment with which the
U.S. congress certainly agreed!

THE POSTWAR "SYSTEM"

On December 31, 1945, the State Department created an
International Broadcasting Division (IBD) to assume control
of what was by then a much smaller Voice of America. VOA
was still the only U.S. international broadcasting service
in operation, since the contracts OWI had held with the
private licensees did not expire until June 30, 1946. IBD
therefore had a grace period within which to formulate a
postwar international broadcasting policy.

President Truman's original order had allowed the State
Department to assume functions in the field of international
information, but the Department had to go to the U.S. House
of Representatives in order to obtain authorization to do so.
The initial House bill, H.R. 4982, never passed, due in
part to a controversy surrounding the supplying of news to
VOA by Associated Press and United Press. The two agencies
withdrew their services from VOA in early 1946, declining
to be associated with a government-sponsored service which,
in their view, would always be suspected of spreading
propaganda.[22]

Appropriations bills passed in 1946 and 1947 assured the
continuation of the Voice of America, although many members
of Congress, Republicans in particular, attempted to cut
back on support or even eliminate it altogether.[23] Still
other bills, designed to place VOA on a permanent status,
were introduced during 1946 and 1947, and ran into opposition
along three major lines: 1) the government should not disseminate news abroad; 2) the State Department should not
have a monopoly of shortwave broadcasting; and 3) the State
Department, including VOA, employed many untrustworthy
persons who could not be relied upon to project a "fair"
image of the United States to foreign countries.

To answer the anti-monopoly argument, Assistant Secretary of State Benton produced letters solicited from five
of the seven private firms which had been active in international broadcasting before the war. At least four and
possibly five of them appeared quite ready to drop that
activity. Only CBS and WRUL seemed anxious to continue,
CBS because it saw some possibility of advertiser interest
in broadcasts to Latin America, WRUL because it felt that
its educational broadcasts were unlikely to be done by
anyone else.[24] The apparent unprofitability of international
broadcasting and a preoccupation with television, FM and
other electronic devices of greater financial promise
dampened the enthusiasm of the others for international
radio. Still, private broadcasters, principally NBC and CBS,
continued to provide substantial shares of VOA programing,
under Congressional mandate.[25]

VOA continued to receive Congressional criticism.
Representative John Taber (R., New York) told a 1947 House
hearing, "These broadcasts are doing more harm than good.
They are not checking the spread of Communism. Propaganda
that ostensibly is intended to build new respect for the
United States is being used to criticize private enterprise, to express partisan opinions, and to distort the
picture of life in the United States."[26] Those sentiments
have been expressed by countless members of Congress before
and since; in this case, however, Taber's remarks could
have pertained to broadcasts prepared by VOA itself or by
the private stations for VOA. In 1948, Congressional
investigation of an NBC-produced VOA series entitled
"Know North America" brought an end to attempts by Congress
to compel VOA to use the services of private broadcasters;
the series was held to give a distorted and overly critical
view of life in the United States.[27]

Finally, in January 1948, the U.S. Congress passed the
Smith-Mundt bill, which gave permanency to State Department
international informational and educational activities. The
ease with which it passed was undoubtedly due to the growing
intensity of the Cold War. More than 200 members of Congress

had travelled to Europe in the previous six months, and had
noted the intense criticism of the United States delivered
through various media by the Soviet Union and the nations of
Eastern and Central Europe. They also had noted the weakness
of the American response, and had been told by private firms,
broadcasters among them, that private enterprise alone could
not mount a sufficient counter-effort. The Smith-Mundt act
did not give the State Department a monopoly of international broadcasting, and in fact encouraged cooperation
with the private sector, but WRUL was the only private
station left by the end of the year.

VOA AND THE "COLD WAR"

With the Soviet blockade of West Berlin in June 1948,
the "Cold War" became tangible. The U.S. government challenged the claim made by the Soviet Union and its allies
that the Western powers were responsible for the blockade
because of their own hostile actions. VOA was not yet
blatantly anti-Soviet--its broadcasts about the blockade
emphasized positive, i.e. pro-American aspects--but Congress
tended to view it increasingly as a weapon in the growing
U.S.-Soviet confrontation and an important instrument of
foreign policy.[28] Not all of those in high governmental
positions agreed. Many of the more traditional State
Department foreign service officers found it hard to accept
broadcasting as an important element in the conduct of
diplomacy. Secretary of State Dean Acheson reportedly said
that ". . . world opinion simply does not exist on matters
that concern us."[29] Still, the views of Congress were what
carried weight in appropriations hearings, and VOA grew as
a result.

When the Korean war broke out in 1950, attempts to
limit criticism of the Soviet Union and Communism stopped.
President Truman launched a "Campaign of Truth" in April
1950, in which he called upon the media to "promote the
truth about America in order to combat Communist distor-
tions." This gave formal sanction to something that VOA
had been doing since 1947.[30] In September 1950, Truman
went a step further: he issued a classified message to the
State Department instructing it to combat Communism and
Communist media output ". . . by exposing its lies . . .
and subjecting it to ridicule."[31] Thus began the "hard
line" era, in which "tough" and even highly dramatic VOA
prose called attention to perceived Communist deficiencies:

Marching in the columns were soldiers
and sailors whose bodies supplied the bridge

over which enemies of the people, hiding
behind the red cloak of Communism, climbed
to power. Following them walked countless
victims of famine in the Volga region and the
Ukraine. Then came columns of peasants who died
facing firing squads when they dared to bring
up the promise of "Land to the People". There
were marching columns of workers turned into
state slaves; of idealists thrown into the
dungeon of the Secret Police, who lost their
lives in inexpert struggle with the careerists
surrounding the throne of Stalin; columns of
city dwellers whom the Communist local satraps
left to the tender mercies of the invading
Nazis.[32]

Oh, tender Communists in all lands: If
the milk of human kindness has not suddenly
soured in your veins, if you would save Lavrenti
Beria, you had better move fast, otherwise he
is going to be a dead duck.
Just a word of caution: If you stage any
"Save Beria" rallies in the Iron Curtain
countries, you are also going to be dead ducks.[33]

Broadcasts of this nature were inevitable, given the
climate of the times and the close scrutiny to which VOA
was subjected by Congress. The Voice itself declared in
its 1950 statement of program policies that broadcasts
should help roll back Soviet influence by all means short
of war, including

. . . making the captive peoples realize they
still belong with us. This means weakening
the will of the Red Army officers and Red
officials at home and abroad. It means
keeping the Soviet Bear so busy scratching
his own fleas, that he has little time for
molesting others.[34]

VOA's program schedule at this time was not in most
respects very different from what it had been before passage of the Smith-Mundt bill. News and commentary predominated, and Europe was the major target area. There
was considerable emphasis on developments in the United
States: culture, politics, the economy, as well as other
facets of American life. When anti-Communist material
appeared, it did so chiefly in newscasts and commentaries,
although documentaries were sometimes used for that purpose, such as a series entitled "Where Are They Now?",

which sought to portray the fates of those "who thought they could collaborate with Communists".[35]

As the intensity of the "Cold War" increased, VOA's budget increased, too, in large part for expansion of transmitter capacity to create a transmission "ring" around the Soviet Union.[36] But intensification of the conflict also brought even closer congressional scrutiny of VOA operations. Senator Joseph McCarthy made the Voice a special object of his attention in early 1953. The information branch of the State Department reacted immediately by issuing a directive which stated that ". . . no material by any controversial persons, Communists, fellow travellers, etc., will be used under any circumstances."[37] VOA director Alfred H. Morton told his staff not to take the policy literally until it had been clarified. The State Department suspended him immediately, reinstated him one day later, and shortly thereafter accepted his resignation.

McCarthy's investigations into the possible presence of Communists in the U.S. government had a particularly damaging effect on VOA. His allegations that the Voice harbored many Communists and "fellow travellers" were not new: Rep. Fred Busbey (R., Illinois) had made similar charges nearly ten years earlier.[38] However, Busbey was unable to generate a formal inquiry, whereas McCarthy held one in the full glare of publicity. A number of VOA staff resigned as a result of his accusations, whether because of pressure from superiors, fear or disgust. Innuendo frequently replaced direct accusation or hard evidence: McCarthy accused VOA of negligence favoring Communism when he discovered that the Voice had dropped its Hebrew language service in part because its officials believed that "the Jerusalem Jews were safely anti-Communist."[39]

Many senior officials remaining with the Voice in those difficult times did so, according to one U.S. Information Agency officer, because they believed in or were willing to accept a "hard line" on Communism; consequently, he feels, VOA clung to the "hard line" approach for several more years, and thus lost many neutral and pro-West listeners.[40] VOA also suffered a major budget cut in FY 1954, from $22 million to $16 million, probably because of McCarthy's attacks but also because of the end of the Korean war. There were notable decreases in numbers of language services, program hours and programs emphasizing American culture; programing in English was cut to about ten per cent of the broadcast day, whereas it had accounted for about a third of the broadcast day in 1950.

FROM STATE DEPARTMENT TO USIA

Shortly after he took office, President Dwight D. Eisenhower appointed a special committee, the Jackson Committee, to study the role and organization of international information activities. In its June 30, 1953 report, the committee argued for a separation of information services from the State Department, and recommended that a new government agency--the U.S. Information Agency--be created to administer them. Secretary of State John Foster Dulles apparently was indifferent to the presence of overseas informational activities in the State Department (although he took considerable interest in CIA-operated Radio Free Europe and Radio Liberation),[41] and he gave his blessing to the separation.

Since the new agency was to absorb all of the old information services within State, VOA was little affected by the shift, although it did move from New York City to Washington. Congress, for its part, continued to evaluate the overall effectiveness of VOA chiefly in terms of its successes in the "struggle against Communism". However, as State Department staff member Edward Barrett put it, "No one could prove last year's funds had been well-spent by producing a cage filled with 7,000 Russians who had deserted Communism."[42]

During the next four years (1954-57), VOA experienced a slight growth in numbers of languages and broadcast hours, and, toward the end of that period, became considerably less strident in its attacks on Communism. This may have come about in part because of U.S. failure to intervene militarily in the 1956 Hungarian uprising, but it also was influenced by a slight lessening of tension between the USSR and the United States. Soviet jamming of VOA nevertheless continued full-scale, although Poland had ceased jamming both VOA and BBC after its own 1956 "revolution".

When George V. Allen was selected to head USIA in 1958, he quickly decided to institute a major change in VOA programming practices, by having VOA develop a worldwide English service. Allen felt that broadcasts in specific languages to specific regions might sometimes be regarded by listeners as propagandistic, whereas, if the U.S. delivered a uniform program service to all parts of the world in the U.S. national language, it would be more believable. Allen also felt that English speaking listeners in other countries would often enjoy high prestige and greater credibility among their fellow citizens.[43]

Allen also supported the policy of "telling the truth even when it hurts". During his tenure as Agency director, VOA provided detailed coverage of several "difficult" events:

Soviet Premier Khrushchev's demands for a reunited Berlin,
Soviet space launches, the Little Rock school desegregation
problem, the U-2 "spy plane" incident. The Voice's approach
was to place the unfavorable or unpleasant (from the U.S.
standpoint) incident in a wider perspective, covering it in
terms of its past, present and likely future. Congress sometimes complained about VOA's habit of "airing America's
dirty linen in public," but Allen's testimonial skill in
Congressional hearings, plus VOA's handling of various
success stories, such as the American space program, the 1960
presidential campaign, and Khrushchev's 1959 visit to the
United States helped win VOA and USIA some small increases
in budget.

THE "MURROW ERA"

On January 29, 1961, President John F. Kennedy named
former CBS News Director Edward R. Murrow to the position
of Director of the U.S. Information Agency. His professional background, which included several years as foreign
correspondent for CBS, led to speculation that VOA might
enjoy increased prestige and budgetary support, but also
increased scrutiny from the Director's office. There were
budget increases, and there seemed to be an increase in
prestige, but, aside from an attempt to conduct a short
course at VOA in preparing and delivering copy,[44] Murrow
did not single out VOA for special attention, as some feared
or hoped he would.
During Murrow's tenure, the Voice enjoyed a significant
improvement in transmitter strength when the 4,800 kW
Greenville, North Carolina transmitter base was dedicated in
February 1963. Coupled with the development of a temporary,
and later permanent, transmitter base in Liberia, this had
the net effect of increasing the strength and clarity of the
VOA signal to Africa and Latin America, both areas major
targets of influence for the Kennedy administration. VOA
engineers had long pressed for such improvements, and had
often argued the futility of spending time and money on
broadcasts that were sometimes virtually inaudible. Congress, alarmed at Soviet and Chinese efforts to expand their
influence in developing areas, was quite willing to appropriate funds that would help the United States check that
influence.
In 1962, VOA initiated a program format that was considered revolutionary at the time: the worldwide English
service began "The Breakfast Show", a two-hour program
featuring popular and semi-classical music (mainly
American), but also containing news reports, features,

interviews, etc. The new show closely resembled NBC's
weekend "Monitor" radio program in its informality, and it
was hoped that this unstructured approach (compared to the
formality of most international broadcasting at the time),
plus the popular music, would attract listeners who could
take news and information in small doses only. VOA officials
were not at all sure that the new show would prove successful, but surveys and letters soon revealed that it rapidly
acquired a sizeable and devoted audience.[45]

Otherwise, VOA programing during the early 1960s was
little changed from what it had been in the late 1950s.
"Hard line" attacks on Communism had diminished; special
English news broadcasts, using a reduced rate of speaking
(c. 90 wpm) and modest vocabulary (c. 1200 words) had been
introduced in 1959, but were proving so popular with listeners that they were expanded to include features and short
stories; the various regional news reports to Africa, Asia,
etc. gave greater prominence to news about events taking
place within those areas, in line with President Kennedy's
desire to display greater U.S. interest in the Third World
nations; and the numbers of languages and amounts of
broadcast time for those nations increased, especially for
Africa.

Murrow was largely unable to overcome the one problem
that most Agency directors have faced: providing meaningful
influence on the government's top level policy decisions.
As one example, he was not given the opportunity to convince
other members of the National Security Council, of which he
was a full member, to consider the psychological aspects of
the imminent invasion of Cuba (the "Bay of Pigs") in 1961.
Political scientist Robert Holt examined the invasion in
light of the psychological factor:

> It also appears likely that the kind of
> preparation for the landing [at the Bay of
> Pigs] that could have been provided by Voice
> of America broadcasts was absent. It would
> not be at all surprising if the people
> responsible for broadcasts to Cuba in the
> months preceding the landings did not even
> know of the proposed invasion. . . . It
> seems clear that those responsible did not
> view the psychological instrument as a major
> instrument of statecraft.[46]

Murrow's influence in policy-making at the highest
levels of government, like that of his predecessors and
successors, seems to have been slight.[47] The effect of this
on VOA was perhaps particularly acute, because some VOA
staff members felt that there was increased interference

from high-level Agency and other government officials with
the objectivity of VOA broadcasts. One VOA official, trac-
ing this interference back to the "Bay of Pigs" invasion,
told a New York Times reporter, "Policy took over and
objectivity and credibility were pushed aside. And we just
never have gotten back in balance."48

THE STRUGGLE FOR OBJECTIVITY

Following Murrow's resignation in February 1964, unrest
on the part of the VOA staff continued to mount. The press
cited several specific instances of USIA "censorship",
including alleged Agency displeasure because VOA had carried
a mildly favorable report on Black separtist Malcolm X at
the time of his death. There was also the outright deletion
of a New York Times editorial in a VOA editorial roundup on
the grounds that it "gave too much weight to the opposition
side."49 Henry Loomis, who had been director of VOA since
1958, resigned in March 1965, and in his farewell address
referred to the pressures faced by the Voice in its attempts
to maintain objectivity, especially when others in government
wanted it to serve short term tactical policy interests:

> To sweep under the rug what we don't
> like, what does not serve our tactical purpose,
> is a sign of weakness. To acknowledge the
> existence of forces and views in disagreement
> with those of the policy makers, to take these
> specially into account in the formulation of
> our output, is a sign of strength and further-
> more is good, persuasive progaganda.50

Although Agency director Carl Rowan was mentioned and
quoted favorably in Loomis' speech, the impression arose
among some VOA staff members that he was the chief cause of
their frustration regarding objectivity. Rowan freely
admitted that he saw limits to objectivity, particularly
with respect to VOA commentaries on news: "They express
opinion, and it is the official opinion of the United States
government. . . . When there is a crisis, or when we are
militarily engaged as we are now in Viet Nam and the
Dominican Republic, we simple cannot afford to have the intentions and objectives of the United States misunderstood
by other governments."51

Perhaps as a result of the controversy over objectivity,
President Lyndon Johnson took particular interest in the
selection of a new director for VOA. When he discussed the
matter with John Chancellor of NBC, Chancellor is said to

have sought and received assurances of "freedom to report
both the good and the bad."[52] Chancellor took office in
September 1965. He resigned less than two years later to
return to NBC, and shortly thereafter pronounced himself
satisfied with the Voice's objectivity, although he did
indicate that there had been some policy battles over the
coverage of news.[53] Richard Walton, who had been a staff
member under Chancellor, intimated that Chancellor probably
didn't realize that most of the day-to-day disputes in which
objectivity was at issue never reached his desk; what he
didn't see, claimed Walton, was a determined effort by a
supersensitive administration to minimize controversy regarding its policies.[54]

Chancellor's successor, John Daly (for several years a
newsman with the American Broadcasting Company) took office
in September 1967. It was quickly apparent that Congress
was still ready to question VOA's definition of objectivity,
whatever Chancellor felt he had accomplished. Representative
Charles Joelson (D., New Jersey) read his colleagues a magazine article in which Daly said that he intended to have
VOA report ". . . fully and fairly the division in the
country [over Vietnam]." Joelson then said, "The Voice of
America is to promulgate our Government policy. If that
policy is wrong, we ought to change it here, not broadcast
statements opposing that policy." Representative John
Rooney (D., New York) added, ". . . he [Daly] should realize
that his job is to promote our way of thinking."[55]

Several months after assuming his new duties, Daly took
a six-week overseas inspection tour to learn how VOA was
regarded by its audiences.[56] When he returned to Washington,
he learned that, in his absence, a member of USIA Director
Leonard Marks' staff had tried to shift the head of VOA's
Worldwide English division to USIA's Press and Publications
division. Daly saw this as an attempt on Marks' part to
bring the Voice more directly under the control of the
Agency's head office: Marks was regarded as an unabashed
supporter of President Johnson, whose communications
interests he had once handled as a lawyer. Daly resigned in
June 1968, in part ". . . because he felt he could no longer
serve as an effective shield for the career news employees
against pressures from self-interested policymakers."[57]

BACK TO THE COLD WAR?

The Nixon administration filled the long-vacant position of VOA director in August 1969 naming Kenneth Giddens,
who owned a broadcast station in Mobile, Alabama, but who
had no experience in international communications.[58] His

appointment had been preceded by that of Frank Shakespeare
as director of USIA. Both men were thought to be politically conservative and strongly anti-Communist. Within a
year there were indications of major differences of opinion
between the State Department and USIA/VOA over "anti-Soviet"
broadcasts. VOA's John Albert, delivering a commentary on
the introduction of Soviet anti-aircraft missiles into
Egypt in September 1970, said, "It is clear that once again,
just as they did during the Cuban missile crisis, the
Soviets are attempting duplicity." A VOA news analysis of
September 12 also contained a reference to Soviet
"duplicity". The State Department was engaged in delicate
negotiations with the Russians over the missiles, and did
not find the VOA broadcasts particularly helpful! On
September 21, Secretary of State William Rogers sent
Shakespeare a memo emphasizing that, under law, USIA must
receive formal policy guidance from State. Shakespeare
responded that he considered general policy guidance sufficient, adding that he had dropped the practice of clearing
any specific news items with State shortly after he had
taken office. He told Rogers that he reported directly to
the President.[59]

When USIA submitted its FY 1972 budget request, the
Senate Appropriations Committee raised a number of questions
regarding VOA broadcasts to the Soviet Union, particularly
broadcasts to the various nationality groups.[60] The
questioning was at times slightly hostile, but became far
more so the following year, when Senator J. William Fulbright (D., Arkansas) professed to have great difficulty
understanding just how the various U.S. broadcasts (VOA,
RFE and RL) to the Soviet Union, Peoples' Republic of China
and Eastern and Central Europe could be justified at their
present magnitude and with such "aggressive" content.
After all, President Nixon himself had visited many of these
countries, had declared his respect for their sovereignty,
and had seemed to indicate that the United States would
avoid "meddling" in their internal affairs.

A crisis in Poland in December 1970, when demonstrating
workers were fired upon by the Polish militia, had drawn
strong reactions from the United States. VOA news coverage
of the event was extensive, and there was also a special
report on it, entitled "A Few Days in December":

> (MUSIC: CHURCH CHOIR, IN FULL, THEN IN
> BACKGROUND) This was the sound of Christmas
> seasons past in Poland--the sound of happy
> voices, singing of a joyous event for all
> Christendom, the birth of Jesus Christ.
> (SOUND: MACHINE GUNS AND SCREAMING) And
> this was the sound of Christmas season
> present in Poland--the sound of Gdansk,

Gdynia and Sczecsin during a few days in
December 1970. (SECOND VOICE, SOMEWHAT
ACCENTED) "According to a doctor of the
Central Hospital in Sczecsin, about 40-50
persons were killed and among them about
10 women and children." (MUSIC, SAD AND
SWEEPING, IN FULL).

Whether such broadcasts constituted "meddling" in
another country's internal affairs is a matter of personal
judgement, but Fulbright and the majority of his committee
seemed to have little doubt about the underlying intent of a
more recent action. In March 1972, Frank Shakespeare, Henry
Loomis and other Agency staff members visited Harvard
University professor Richard Pipes. Pipes had been commissioned to listen to some VOA broadcasts in Russian,
Ukrainian, Czech, Polish and English, in order to evaluate
their likely effectiveness. Pipes apparently recommended
that the broadcast might do more to stress the differences
among the various nationality groups in the USSR, because
Shakespeare soon sent a memo to Agency division heads in
which he stressed that the term "the Soviets" should not
be used, but that people living in the USSR should be
referred to by their nationality, e.g. Ukrainian. The
memo continued, "There is no 'Soviet Union' and never will
be. . . . To call it so, apart from being grammatically
incorrect, is to foster the illusion of one happy family
rather than an imperialist state increasingly beset with
national problems, which is what it is."[61] Giddens told the
Senate Foreign Relations Committee that VOA would seek to
implement the memo.[62]

The Committee, influenced heavily by Fulbright, recommended a cut in USIA's FY 1973 appropriation of just under
25 per cent, but asked for a cut of 30 per cent in VOA's
budget. Shakespeare went before the Senate Appropriations
Committee to argue for restoration of the cut, and put its
effects in "worst case" terms for VOA: a reduction in
weekly broadcast hours from 790 to 454, and in language
services from 35 to 11. (Ironically, given the source of
Fulbright's anger, the Russian and Mandarin services were to
be retained!) The Appropriations Committee, and then the
full Senate, restored the cuts.

Despite the controversy over VOA's role in a possible
new "cold war", and despite continued problems with objectivity (raised most vividly, perhaps, in the "internal
censorship" of two sets of VOA roundups of U.S. editorial
opinion on the question of military aid for Greece),[63] VOA's
basic program schedule did not change radically under the
Shakespeare-Giddens administration. In the late 1960s, VOA
developed more informal program blocks for African listeners,

and the Breakfast Show became a part of the Russian and
Ukrainian service schedules. Many of those changes represented attempts to reach specific segments of the audience,
particularly younger listeners. Yet VOA continued to place
a good deal of emphasis on programing which highlighted
specific aspects of American life, religious, scientific,
and cultural. Such programs rarely attracted large audiences, but they did serve to carry out the mandate of the
1948 Smith-Mundt Act: to present a comprehensive picture of
life in the United States.

As the Nixon administration made clear its determination to withdraw U.S. military forces from South Vietnam,
some of the pressures on VOA to soft-pedal criticism of
U.S. actions in Vietnam subsided. But they did not disappear entirely, and, when the final evacuation of Saigon
took place in 1975, U.S. Ambassador to South Vietnam Graham
Martin prevailed upon the State Department, and ultimately
the Voice, to refrain from broadcasting reports of the
evacuation. Ambassador Martin's fear was that, if an
"official" U.S. radio station presented information about the
event, there would be even greater panic among the civilian
population. VOA staff members pointed out that virtually all
major international broadcasters would be covering the
evacuation, and VOA would be conspicuous by its absence.
The protests went unheeded, and morale at the Voice fell
once again.[64] However, VOA coverage of Watergate, which
most reporters had described as comprehensive, balanced and
carefully analytical, reminded critics and VOA staff alike
that the Voice did win some credibility battles.[65]

                    AFTER VIETNAM AND WATERGATE

Watergate and Vietnam seemed to prove what certain VOA
staff members had realized long since: that VOA was far
freer to report objectively on U.S. domestic developments
than on U.S. foreign policy. And the State Department
continued to bring pressure on VOA: in 1976, the U.S.
Ambassador to Israel strongly criticized a VOA correspondent
for interviewing a member of the Palestine Liberation
Organization. According to the Ambassador, VOA correspondents were a part of the U.S. embassy "team", and,
since the U.S. had no official dealings with the PLO, it was
improper for the correspondent to have conducted the interview.[66] This further accented a problem of long standing:
to what extent were VOA correspondents professional broadcast journalists, and to what extent were they spokespersons for the U.S. government? The VOA Charter[67] refers
to VOA's obligation to mirror life in the United States as

fully and accurately as possible, but also to serve as a
channel for the statements and views of the U.S. government.
This dual mission contains all sorts of potential problems,
and journalists, who constitute only a small fraction of VOA
staff, are involved in the lion's share of them.

In order to deal with the issue, VOA director (1977-
1979) R. Peter Straus convoked a panel chaired by journalist
Chalmers Roberts. The panel examined the responsibilities
of VOA's foreign correspondents, and in its 1978 report
recommended that they be divorced as completely as possible
from U.S. government offices overseas, so that they could
pursue their work much as did other foreign correspondents,
but under the same limitations, too: no PX or commissary
privileges , no special housing, no diplomatic passports.[68]
VOA implemented the report in 1979, and it appears to have
had the desired effect: for example, the VOA correspondent
covering the Nicaraguan conflict in 1979-1980 was able to
interview freely both official government sources and unofficial Sandinista sources, despite the lack of formal U.S.
government recognition of the latter group.

But years of what they perceived as violations of their
journalistic integrity had already caused a number of VOA
staff members to speak out on the need for VOA independence
from USIA. When the opportunity presented itself to consider the matter in the context of a possible restructuring
of the U.S. Information Agency, VOA staff were more than
ready. In May 1973, the Senate Foreign Relations Committee
recommended a reorganization of U.S. international informational and cultural activities. Later that year, a
privately-sponsored Commission on the Organization of the
Government for the Conduct of Foreign Policy (the Murphy
Commission) began deliberations. They concluded in June
1975 with a recommendation that VOA should become an independent federal agency.[69] Yet another privately-sponsored
group, the Panel on International Information, Education
and Cultural Relations (the Stanton Panel), began to meet
in April 1974 and reported in March 1975; it also recommended that VOA be made an independent federal agency,
although it urged close cooperation between VOA and the
State Department.[70]

VOA staff gave testimony to both the Murphy Commission
and the Stanton Panel. The majority of those testifying
favored separation, but a few were afraid that separation
would be followed by merger with RFE and RL under the Board
for International Broadcasting, and thus saddle VOA with the
supposed reputation of RFE and RL as "cold war propaganda
instruments." In Congressional testimony over the next
three years, a number of VOA staff continued to argue the
case for separation,[71] but to no avail: when USIA was
restructured and relabelled as the U.S. International

Communication Agency (USICA) on April 1, 1978, VOA remained
a part of it. Congress seemed to have a difficult time
envisaging an "independent" VOA.

The mid- to late-1970s also featured a great deal of
internal tension over VOA broadcasts to the Soviet Union.
Depending on the precise time and circumstance, VOA was
accused of being too "soft" or too "hard". The Soviet Union
ceased jamming VOA Russian language broadcasts in September
1973 (and resumed it in August 1980, during the disturbances
in Poland), but frequently criticized VOA thereafter for
paying too much attention to issues concerning dissidents.[72]
On the other hand, dissidents and Soviet Jews frequently
criticized VOA for soft-pedalling criticism of the USSR in
matters of interest to them.[73] There were several specific
accusations of internal censorship.[74] The Carter administration's interest in human rights led to more emphasis
on that issue by the Voice, but some critics, including
Aleksandyr Solzhenitsyn, were still not satisfied that VOA
was doing what it should:

>   It is clear that the directors of the Voice
> of America are constantly trying not to arouse
> the anger of the Soviet leadership. In their
> zeal to serve détente, they remove from their
> programs everything that might irritate the
> communists in power.[75]

As it had been for the past 30 years, VOA was again
being judged chiefly in terms of its programing for or
about the Soviet Union. However, the vast majority of
VOA programing time was directed to other parts of the
world and concerned other issues and subjects. American
culture remained prominent in that schedule, but the
cultures of other countries appeared as well, particularly
in African Service shows such as "Request Time in
Africa", "African Panorama" and "Bonjour l'Afrique".
Certain programs from the 1950s were still around: "Studio
One", with documentaries about American and foreign
individuals and events (e.g. the American motion picture
industry, Galileo), "Music USA", still hosted (since 1954)
by Willis Conover and featuring American jazz and popular
music, and "Forum", with detailed and sometimes verbally
complex presentations of such subjects as heart transplants
by experts such as Dr. Michael deBakkey:

>   The arteries that supply blood to the
> heart are the coronary arteries. And it is
> a disease of the coronary arteries, a disease
> which we call arteriosclerosis or athrosclerosis,

which tends to thicken the wall of the artery
and block the lumen of the artery so that it
blocks the blood flow to the heart muscle, and
thus cuts off the nourishment to that muscle,
and that results in a heart attack.[76]

As was true for most major international stations, the
1970s were a decade of relative stability for VOA in terms
of hours of transmission and numbers of languages. In 1970,
VOA broadcast an average of over 860 hours per week, in some
35 languages; by October 1981 the figures were 904 and 39.
There was fluctuation over time, of course: hours of transmission for language services to Southeast Asia were cut
back as the U.S. withdrew from South Vietnam, Japanese was
dropped in 1970, Uzbek was added in 1975. Some new and more
powerful transmitters replaced old ones. Satellites began
to be used for relay purposes in the late 1970s. But there
were no new overseas transmission bases and no remarkable
changes in services or program strategies, although broadcasting to central Asia increased markedly as U.S.-Iranian
tensions grew and as the Soviet incursion into Afghanistan
showed signs of permanency: Farsi (Persian) was restored
to the VOA schedule, and Dari and Azeri*added, in an effort
to reach central Asian listeners. This expansion appeared
to be the result of strong pressures from Zbigniew Brzezinski and the National Security Council, rather than initiative on VOA's part.[77] The Reagan administration has continued a strong anti-Communist emphasis in certain respects:
broadcast hours in Russian and six other languages of the
USSR increased four hours per day in 1981, and there was
serious consideration of a special broadcast service for
Cuba as of late 1981, although it was not altogether clear
who would operate the station.[78]

PROGRAMING

English is easily the largest of the VOA language
services--24 hours a day for Worldwide English, plus daily
special services to Africa (5½ hours), Latin America (one
hour) and the Caribbean (30 minutes). Other language
services include almost all of the world's major languages
(Japanese is the chief exception) and many smaller ones,
especially for Eastern Europe and the Soviet Union.
    News and information form the mainstay of VOA's schedule
both in terms of quantity (roughly two-thirds of all program
time) and assumed importance. Most of the information
included in the newscasts, which are broadcast by all of the
language services, comes from VOA's central news room. The

*As of November 1981, the Azeri service had not yet come on
 the air because of difficulties in recruiting qualified staff.

news room in turn receives its raw material from a combination of several wire services, its own domestic and foreign
reporters and various "stringers", the American commercial
and public broadcasting services, and domestic and foreign
newspapers and magazines. The language services are supposed to translate the newscasts as accurately and completely
as possible. Because of the sheer number of languages
involved, and because of the need for rapid translation if
the news is to be up to the minute, mistakes and unauthorized additions can and sometimes do occur.

VOA prides itself on the completeness and immediacy of
its newscasts, and, when compared with most U.S. domestic
news broadcasts, they certainly are more complete. At
certain times of day, Worldwide English broadcasts a full
hour of news, with liberal use of reports from its 15
overseas correspondents. One study showed that the VOA's
Russian language service was not as timely with its newscasts as were some of its Western competitors (BBC, RL,
Deutsche Welle),[79] and another study showed that certain
language services made some very arbitrary decisions as to
whether and how to broadcast certain newscast items
furnished by the central news room,[80] but a reexamination of
news policy and practice in 1979 appears to have led to the
correction of most of those problems. There remains some
internal criticism that the central news room places too
much emphasis on U.S. domestic events that are of little
interest to overseas listeners. Since most VOA news room
personnel worked for U.S. newspapers and broadcast stations
before coming to the Voice, and since many staff members in
the language divisions were born and brought up in the
countries to which they now broadcast, there is bound to be
some disagreement over which stories are important and for
what reasons.

There are many other news and information broadcasts,
including summaries of U.S. newspaper editorial opinion,
interview shows (Press Conference USA) and various feature
reports, but one of the most distinctive and controversial
formats is the VOA commentary. Very few international
stations broadcast editorials or commentaries written by
their own staff members, although several broadcast commentaries written by "outsiders". VOA editorials and commentaries have come and gone several times over the history
of the station; they came most recently in 1978. They
are expressions of official U.S. government opinion, and
must be cleared by USICA policy officers (housed within
VOA) before they can be broadcast. They are heartily disliked by most VOA staff and it is questionable whether they
are particularly useful, since they are not a daily feature
of the schedule, and thus listeners have no regular expectation of receiving them. Their "advocacy" position also

may serve to remind listeners that VOA is a U.S. government
operation, with whatever limits on objectivity that might
imply.

>ANNOUNCER: Here is a commentary--reflecting
>the views of the U.S. Government--on Libya's
>disruptive international behavior and the
>necessity for increased African and inter-
>national attention to this question.
>VOICE: The facts are painfully clear. Under
>its ruler, Colonel Qadhafi, Libya has embarked
>on what can accurately be called a peace-
>threatening course of diplomacy-by-subversion.
>The expressions that brand of diplomacy takes
>are varied and ugly. They range from military
>intervention in Chad, Libya's next-door
>neighbor, to the sponsorship and implementation
>of international terrorism--including the
>murder of Libyan nationals overseas who dis-
>agree with Colonel Qadhafi's policies and
>ambitions. . . .
> In the general context of supporting
>African countries threatened by Libya, the
>Reagan administration is asking the U.S.
>Congress for additional military assistance
>funds for Tunisia and Sudan, two countries
>particularly threatened by Libya. Beyond
>that, the administration is also seeking ways
>to provide economic and military support to
>other countries similarly threatened.
>VOA Commentary, July 11, 1981

VOA also broadcasts a great deal of "soft" information
(on less timely and/or "vital" events), although there is a
higher proportion of it on the major language services such
as English, Russian and Mandarin than on the minor services
such as Hausa and Azeri, simply because the major services
have longer broadcast hours and more staff. There are
Breakfast Show-like programs in Ukrainian, Russian, Spanish,
French to Africa, and Spanish to Latin America, and many of
the larger services have music request shows and listener
mailbox programs. The Mandarin, Polish, Czech, Arabic and
Portuguese (to Europe) services offer lessons in English.
VOA's Worldwide English Servide provides a wide variety of
popular and classical music, reviews of books and cultural
events, features about religion in the United States,
American history, scientific developments, and even new
industrial products:

>ANNOUNCER: Our next product is a trencher/
>plow combination, a large piece of heavy

equipment designed to be used by utility
companies to bury cables and pipes. Its
manufacturers advertise that buyers will
be attracted to it not so much because of
what it <u>does</u> have, but because of what it
<u>doesn't</u> have. The Parson hydrostatic
trencher/plow combo has been designed with
a special four-speed forward drivetrain--
and what it lacks are all superfluous belts,
splines and clutches. . . .
New Products, USA, June 7, 1981

   Most feature programs are scheduled once a week, last
either 15 or 30 minutes (except for the three or four
minute feature reports included with the Breakfast Show),
and are repeated several times. The Special English service
includes considerable feature material: American short
stories, space exploration, American history, etc., each
feature running 15 minutes and repeated twice a day. The
African service in English provides at least an hour a day
of African, U.S. and Caribbean popular music, plus numerous
short feature reports about developments in African, Caribbean and Afro-American culture, sports, political life, etc.
Some of the "soft" information on VOA seems to be there
because VOA staff feel it will help attract listeners to
the "harder stuff", although they also see it as a valuable
element in its own right: a way of conveying an image of
an America made up of individual human beings with individual emotions and individual ways of expressing them, a way
of telling listeners that America is more than a political
entity. To help convey that image, much of the "soft"
programing is written and delivered in an informal manner,
with a good deal of ad-libbing in the various Breakfast
Shows and in the music request shows, as in the following
excerpt from a Yvonne Barclay-hosted broadcast of "Request
Time", September 29, 1977, where she picked up on the final
line of the song "Mexican Divorce":

      "One day married, the next day free." Ya
   know, it's really kinda strange that a lot of
   people look at marriage as sort of imprisonment,
   right? I should imagine that, if people get
   married, that they should still be free, right?
   You don't change. I mean, you're still the
   same individual, you're a human being, you're
   a person, right? And because you get married
   doesn't mean that you're a prisoner. . . .

   Program staff members in the central news room and
Worldwide English service are almost 100 per cent U.S. citizens

and many have had previous experience in domestic radio,
television and newspapers. A few of the foreign language
services employ Americans who have exceptional written and/or
oral command of that language, but most announcers and
writers are either naturalized American citizens or are
citizens of other countries under contract with VOA for two
or three year periods. Contract staff often help to bring a
fresh perspective to a language service: most are well
acquainted with recent developments in their countries, and
most are up to date on idioms, slang, proverbs, etc.

The foreign language desks frequently are headed by
USICA foreign service officers who have served in the
country or area in question, and who usually, but not always,
speak its language. However, many do not speak it well
enough to be able to catch its subtleties, especially the
more emotional ones, and post-examination of broadcast
scripts and recordings has revealed occasional insertion of
an individual writer's or announcer's personal opinion in
newscasts and news analyses. For example, during the Anglo-
French-Israeli attack on the Suez Canal in 1956, certain of
the Arabic language service staff, themselves citizens of
Arab countries, added their own editorial condemnations to
the official condemnations of the attack contained in the
scripted news items. Post-examination revealed the additions, but also exposed one of the pitfalls of translation:
a literal translation of the editorial additions from
Arabic to English made them sound far more emotional than
they really were.

                          THE AUDIENCE

VOA has no research division of its own, although it
has had at times a research officer who was responsible for
conducting research on VOA's internal practices and for maintaining liaison with USICA's Office of Research. The Office
of Research is responsible for a wide variety of research
projects, so VOA has not necessarily gotten the sorts and
amounts of research that it would like. Furthermore, the
flow of USICA radio research almost totally ceased between
1978 and mid-1981, apparently because the then Director of
USICA, John Reinhardt, did not regard it as particularly
useful.[81] Radio research picked up again in late 1981
following Reinhardt's departure.

Various studies (see Chapter 11) have revealed that
VOA's audience profile is much the same as that for most of
the other major international broadcasters: a young to
middle-aged, relatively prosperous, well-educated, urban
audience, many of them the so-called "opinion leaders"

(government officials, business executives, teachers, sometimes military and religious leaders). The size of that
audience seems to vary a great deal from country to country,
being smallest in countries already well served by a wide
variety of uncensored domestic media (e.g. Western Europe,
to which little but VOA Worldwide English is directed, and
where no more than two or three per cent of the population
listens to VOA once a week or more) and largest in countries
with a scarcity of media, especially reliable media (e.g.
parts of Africa, where VOA sometimes attains "regular"
(once a week or more) listenership levels of 30 or 40 per
cent). In the few surveys where listeners have been asked
about the credibility of VOA broadcasts, the Voice has
received relatively high marks, usually coming second to, and
occasionally surpassing, the BBC. When listeners have been
asked about the relative popularity of specific VOA programs,
news usually has topped the list by a considerable margin,
with music request shows often coming in second. Programs
for highly specific audiences, such as "Forum", usually
finish at or near the bottom of the list, as one might
predict.

VOA conducted several listener panel studies in the
mid- to late-1970s. They are covered in Chapter 11, but it
is worth noting here that the studies reveal a keen interest
on the part of those listeners who took part in them in the
"personality" side of broadcasting: programs were deemed
more listenable, more credible, etc., if they were connected with names and voices of specific individuals. On
the other hand, the panels also elicited some criticism of
VOA programing--a rare commodity, since surveys are rarely
structured to bring out criticism, and listener letters
(almost 200,000 in 1980) seldom contain it[82]--mainly along
the lines that VOA was too preoccupied with life and events
in the United States.

It is difficult to estimate the size of VOA's worldwide audience (VOA put it at 80 million listeners per day as
of 1981, and excluding China) but the various research
studies already mentioned have shown that it compares quite
favorably with the size of the audience for the BBC's
External Services. It comes out ahead of BBC in some
countries (notably in Latin America and in Francophone
Africa), does about as well in others (Central and Eastern
Europe and the USSR), and is behind in still others
(Anglophone Africa, the Middle East, South Asia). The two
stations finish ahead of most of the competition in most
countries, although Radio Havana does well in some parts of
Latin America, Radio Cairo and Radio Monte Carlo-Cyprus in
the Middle East and North Africa, and Deutsche Welle in parts
of East Africa.

TECHNICAL SERVICES

Prior to and during World War II, the United States could manage to reach most of its target audiences from transmitters located in the United States. Since that time, the worldwide increase in international broadcast activity, coupled with the U.S. desire to reach audiences all over the world, has led to the establishment of transmitters all across the globe.

Thanks to its position as one of the major victorious powers in World War II, the United States was able to establish transmitters in occupied territory: West Germany and Okinawa. Its special relationships with the Philippines and Liberia allowed it to develop transmitter sites there, and the French government permitted it to erect transmitters in French-governed Morocco. It had had wartime arrangements with Great Britain allowing transmitter bases there, and those arrangements have continued. Negotiations with the governments of Greece, Sri Lanka and Thailand produced agreements for the establishment of transmitter bases in those countries, and the government of Morocco agreed to allow the continued presence of that transmitter base. The Okinawa site was "lost" in 1978, following the reincorporation of Okinawa with Japan, but all of the others remain in service as of 1981, and have been joined by a 50 kW medium wave transmitter on the Caribbean island of Antigua, where BBC and DW already share a transmitter site.

There are prices to be paid for overseas bases, of course, and not all of them are monetary, although dollar costs may come to the fore when a site-leasing agreement calls for lease costs of several million dollars a year or when the decline of the American dollar against the Japanese yen or German mark causes annual operating costs to shoot up. More important in terms of U.S. foreign policy and the broadcast policy of VOA are lease arrangements which link the U.S. with dictatorial governments or which allow other countries the use of time on the VOA transmitter to disseminate broadcasts which themselves may serve to counteract U.S. foreign policy, as Greece did in the early 1970s.[83] It is also possible that, even without a specifically prohibitive agreement, VOA will engage in self-censorship in order to avoid the risk of endangering the overall agreement, as appeared to have happened with respect to Greece in 1971 (above, p. 107).

The overseas transmitter bases give VOA a tremendous advantage in reaching audiences with more powerful, and hence clearer, easier to tune, signals. Several of the bases have medium wave transmitters, which usually means that an even larger public can be reached, since medium wave receivers are far more common than short wave receivers, and since medium wave is ordinarily less subject to inter- ference and fading. Local placement of VOA relayed broad- casts and pre-recorded tapes also helps to reach more listeners, although VOA is not as active in that respect as are BBC and DW.

If VOA were suddenly deprived of access to its overseas bases, it could still manage fairly well from the United States. It has bases on the east and west coasts (the east coast base, in North Carolina, has a total power of nearly five million watts), in Ohio, and near Key West. However, signal quality for much of the Soviet Union, the Middle East, South Asia and Africa would suffer greatly; as it is, much of East and South Africa receives poor coverage even now.* Medium wave broadcasting would be out of the question for all but a few areas. Satellites, which VOA has used to relay broadcasts to its overseas transmitters since 1979, cannot yet be used to reach home radio receivers directly. For better or for worse, VOA appears to have become heavily dependent upon its overseas transmitter bases.

FUTURE PROSPECTS

VOA faces a number of potential problems and oppor- tunities as it enters the 1980s, although some of them may be more apparent to VOA staff than they are to its listeners. As I have just noted, there are weak spots in transmission coverage, and more could develop, particularly if other broadcasters manage to install more and bigger transmitters and VOA does not. Requests to Congress for funds to update and expand transmitter bases have met with mixed success, and countries where transmitters are located do not always appear anxious to allow expansion. In Sri Lanka, it took the U.S. several years to negotiate an agreement--finally signed in 1981--allowing it to replace VOA's antiquated 35 kW transmitters with six 250 kW transmitters.

Insofar as the United States is destined to remain a chief actor in a turbulent world, VOA should be able to count on widespread world interest in what the United States does and says. However, that world may be changing in certain respects, most notably in the increasing desire on the part of developing nations to make their voices heard. Debates over the "new world information order" in the late 1970s and early 1980s have made it clear that many countries are dissatisfied with the imbalance, as they see it, in world news coverage. To the extent that VOA fails to take this dissatisfaction into account, it may find itself increas- ingly criticized for its apparent preoccupation with the

_____
*However, service to southern Africa should be improved by the addition of a 50 kW transmitter in Botswana, placed in service by VOA in mid-September 1981.

United States and with U.S.-Soviet relations.

VOA will probably face continued credibility problems in the coming years. After all, they never have been altogether absent, even during the halcyon days of Kennedy and Murrow, and recent organizational changes (implementation of the Roberts report, passage into law of the VOA charter) certainly have not eliminated the pressures VOA faces from Congress and the State Department to emphasize, moderate or suppress coverage of certain events. The fact of the matter is that USICA, and therefore VOA, is low in the pecking order of government agencies, and most USICA and VOA directors have not felt themselves in a position to protest outside pressures, at least where foreign policy matters were concerned. (The record is considerably better for VOA coverage of domestic issues).

Although there are many parts of the world where listeners cannot receive VOA broadcasts in their own languages (notably within India and Africa), there seems little prospect for an increase in VOA language services. And if languages were to be added, would they be chosen for their short-term, strategic value, or for their long-term value? The most recent language to be added--Azeri, in 1980--seemed at the time to be a short-term strategic choice, although it may turn out to be long-term. Short-term choices may be poor choices for two reasons: the crises that give rise to them may pass by the time properly staffed and supervised teams are ready to broadcast; and if a short-term service disappears from the airwaves when the crisis is over, its listeners may get the impression that VOA considers them worthy of its attention only when U.S. foreign policy interests are at stake.

As VOA moves into its fifth decade, it appears to have attained a certain sanctity of age, and there are few members of Congress or other government officials who question the need for it. Some of those members and officials still evaluate the station in terms of how effectively it reaches "the Communist world"; yet its weekly broadcast hours in the languages of non-Communist nations EXCLUDING English (which itself makes up about a fourth of the weekly total) nearly equal its weekly hours in the languages of the Communist nations. Furthermore, many of its broadcasts have little to do with the Soviet-American (or East-West) "confrontation", but much to do with music, science, sports and other fields in the United States and abroad. The informal, personal style of many of its programs appear, if listener letters are any indication, to succeed in "humanizing" the United States.

If VOA can continue to make itself heard in the face of the transmitter superpower race, if it can manage to avoid credibility problems of the sort exemplified by the

evacuation of Saigon, and if it can keep the amount and
style of coverage of U.S.-Soviet relations in reasonable
balance with its other broadcasts,* it should be in a good
position to retain its apparent popularity with international broadcast listeners for some time to come. But
perhaps most important for VOA's future success, as former
VOA staff member Fred Collins put it:

> . . . Radio's strong suit is disseminating
> information, not changing minds. A key
> point so often neglected by those who demand
> that VOA pound out the policy line in war or
> peace is simple: the listener has the final
> say. He--or she--can always turn off the set.[84]

NOTES

1. E. Roderick Diehl, "South of the Border: the NBC
and CBS Radio Networks and the Latin American Venture,
1930-1942," Communication Quarterly 25 (Fall, 1977):4-5.
See also Douglas Boyd, "The Pre-history of the Voice of
America," Public Telecommunications Review 2 (December 1974).
2. Jerry Ray Redding, "American Private International
Broadcasting: What Went Wrong and Why," unpublished Ph.D.
dissertation, The Ohio State University, 1977, pp. 98, 108,
121-122.
3. As of early 1939, the NBC and CBS international
stations were carrying 10 to 25 per cent specially prepared
material, not all of it in Spanish and Portuguese; the
remainder of the time was devoted to regular network shows
in English. Thomas Grandin, The Political Use of Radio
(Geneva: Geneva Studies, 1939), p. 63.
4. U.S. House of Representatives Naval Affairs Committee, Hearings on H.R. 4281, "Promotion of friendly
relations among the nations of the Western hemisphere,"
(75th Congress), May 16, 1938, p. 3532.
5. John B. Whitton and John H. Herz, "Radio in International Politics," in Propaganda by Short Wave, Harwood
Childs and John B. Whitton, eds. (Princeton: Princeton
University Press, 1942), p. 45.
6. Grandin, pp. 64-65, provides a brief account of the
Celler bill and the debates surrounding it, including the
passages quoted here.
7. The U.S. Navy attempted frequently during the 1930s
to establish a shortwave broadcasting service for Latin
America, but without success. See Redding, "American
Private International Broadcasting", pp. 123-129.

---

*However, the Reagan administration's "Project Truth",
launched in late fall 1981, seems to herald a renewal of
strongly anti-Communist broadcasts by VOA. See "A Hot
New Cold War at ICA," Newsweek 98 (November 16, 1981):36-37.

8. They were aided in their Latin American efforts by
a special division of the State Department, established in
August 1940. This division eventually became the Office of
the Coordinator of Inter-American Affairs. CIAA remained
in existence throughout World War II, and had jurisdiction
over VOA broadcasts to Latin America. The Foreign Information Service was organized in August 1941, and, like CIAA,
attempted to enlist the cooperation of the private broadcasters in "telling the (official) story of America to the
rest of the world." Robert Pirsein, The Voice of America:
A History of the International Broadcasting Activities of
the United States Government, 1940-1962 (New York: Arno
Press, 1979), Chapters 1 and 2.
    9. Whitton and Herz, Radio , p. 48. CIAA officials
were so disturbed about lack of cooperation that they
developed a plan for leasing air time, rather than depending
upon the stations' charity. The plan failed, chiefly
because other government officials could not accept the
principle of paying for air time. Pirsein, VOA, Chapter 1.
Therefore, the private stations were under no obligation
to accept any CIAA or FIS newsfiles or other programs, and
frequently did not, on the grounds that they were too clum-
sily or unprofessionally prepared. See "U.S. Takes Over
Short Waves," Newsweek 20 (October 19, 1942):31; also John
Hutchins, "This is America Speaking," New York Times
Magazine (May 10, 1942):10+. Even as of September 1942,
there were problems of coordination between the various
U.S. stations which allowed the Germans to point out dis-
crepancies in their accounts of the news; see Stefan U.
Rundt, "Short Wave Artillery," The Nation (September 12,
1942):212.
    10. Charles A.H. Thomson, The Overseas Information
Service of the United States Government (Washington: The
Brookings Institution, 1948), pp. 3, 120-123, 129-130.
    11. One OWI official attributes this delay to Roose-
velt's distaste for propaganda. Wallace Carroll, Persuade
or Perish (Boston: Houghton Mifflin, 1948), p. 7. Carroll
also contended that Roosevelt ". . . never knew what (the
OWI) was doing and sometimes, apparently, confused it with
the Office of Censorship." James Warburg, Unwritten Treaty
(New York: Harcourt Brace, 1946) provides many details on
OWI, and is often highly critical of its chief, Elmer Davis.
A more thorough and more dispassionate account can be found
in Alan Winkler, The Politics of Propaganda (New Haven:
Yale University Press, 1978), pp. 104ff.
    12. Lemmon encountered several problems and delays in
recovering his station after World War II; see "W.S. Lemmon
Seeks Release of WRUL from War Communications Board," New
York Times, April 24, 1946, p. 12, and Thomson, Overseas
Information Service, p. 235.

13. For further information on programming during this period, see "U.S. Arsenal of Words," Fortune (March 1943) pp. 82-85+; "The Voice of America Speaks," Popular Mechanics (June 1944) pp. 1-5+; Harold Callender, "The Voice of America Echoes Widely," New York Times Magazine (November 15, 1942) p. 10+; Harold Callender, "U.S. Broadcasters Recall Nazi Boast," New York Times, November 7, 1942, p. 4; and Pirsein, VOA, Chapters 3 and 4.

14. Daniel Lerner, who worked with OWI, has asserted that OSS and other "disguised" broadcast operations harmed the OWI effort, since most reasonably intelligent listeners could guess the origins of the OSS stations, which may have led them to mistrust the OWI stations, as they came from the same government. Daniel Lerner, Sykewar (New York: George W. Stewart, 1949), passim.

15. Davis moved to discharge several OWI staff members in 1944, James Warburg among them. Warburg in turn criticized Davis for failing to impress the makers of foreign policy with the need to consider the psychological dimensions of policymaking. Warburg, Treaty, pp. 112-113.

16. Warburg, Ibid., pp. 109-111, contains a description of this incident.

17. Robert Spivack, "The New Anti-alien Drive," New Republic (November 29, 1943):740-741.

18. In 1944, Representative Clarence Brown (R., Ohio) claimed that OWI broadcasts failed to report opposition to President Roosevelt, or did so with insufficient detail; see "Says High Officials Block OWI Inquiry," New York Times, March 15, 1944, p. 21. Warburg, Treaty, passim., p. 89.

19. Arthur McMahon, Memorandum on the Post-war International Information Program of the United States (Washington, D.C.: Department of State, Publication 2438, 1945), p. 2.

20. A concise summary of the McMahon plan appears in Burton Paulu, "The Voice of America from 1945 to 1949," unpublished Ph.D. dissertation, Columbia University, 1949, pp. 23-28.

21. The full statement is contained in State Department Bulletin 13 (September 2, 1945), pp. 306-307.

22. Paulu, VOA, pp. 40-49.

23. Donald R. Browne, "The Voice of America: Policies and Problems," Journalism Monographs 43 (February 1976): 7-11; also Paulu, VOA, p. 111.

24. U.S. Senate, Committee on Appropriations, Department of State etc. Appropriation Bill for 1947, Hearings... (79th Congress, 2nd Session), (Washington, D.C.: Government Printing Office, 1946), pp. 91-94.

25. Paulu, VOA, p. 190.

26. Cited in Marjorie Foulkrod, "Short Wave of the Future," Current History 13 (July 1947):13.

27. Browne, "VOA", pp. 13-14; also Paulu, "VOA",
pp. 184-200.

28. However, Newsweek reported that VOA was told by
the State Department to "lay off" broadcasts on the Berlin
Blockade when it was first imposed, until "Washington could
make up its mind." See "U.S. to the World," Newsweek,
(August 16, 1948):p. 51.

29. Cited in Thomas Sorensen, The Word War (New York:
Harper and Row, 1968), pp. 29-30.

30. VOA broadcasts in Russian to the Soviet Union
began in February 1947; when the State Department, in
December 1946, publicly announced its intention of initiating these broadcasts, it stated that they would probably
be used ". . . to answer charges sometimes contained in the
Russian press and radio." New York Times, December 17,
1946, p. 11.

31. Wilson Dizard, The Strategy of Truth (Washington,
D.C.: Public Affairs Press, 1965).

32. From Overseas Information Programs of the United
States, Hearings before a subcommittee of the Committee on
Foreign Relations, U.S. Senate, Part 2, pp. 1458-1459
(1953), cited in Urban G. Whitaker (ed), Propaganda and
International Relations (San Francisco: Chandler Publishing
Company, 1962), p. 113.

33. Cited in Oren Stephens, Facts to a Candid World
(Stanford: Stanford University Press, 1955), p. 85.

34. Cited in Edward Barrett, Truth is Our Weapon (New
York: Funk and Wagnalls, 1953), pp. 78-79.

35. See "The Voice of America: What It Tells the
World," Time (May 1, 1950):22-23.

36. VOA had begun its quest for more medium wave
transmitters in World War II. Elmer Davis realized the
difficulties inherent in reaching listeners with shortwave
broadcasts only, and had developed plans for a fairly
comprehensive network of medium wave transmitters by 1943;
many of these transmitters were never built, but the intent
was clear. See Elmer Davis, War Information and Censorship
(Washington: American Council on Public Affairs, 1943),
p. 20. For details on increases in transmitting power, see
"State Department is Due for a Louder Voice," Business Week
(August 5, 1950):89-90. However, Senator McCarthy, in his
investigation of VOA in 1953, turned up "evidence" that the
design and/or location of certain transmitters was faulty,
blamed Communist influence in part and the expansion program
came to a halt. This program, the "ring" plan, had already
been set in motion, and some transmitters were under construction.

37. Thomas Sorensen, The Word War (New York: Harper
and Row, 1968), p. 33.

38. Busbey was particularly concerned about VOA broadcasts discussing the possibility of a "second front" in Europe. This, he argued, was not U.S. military policy, but was that of the Russians. See "Asks House Inquiry on Aliens in OWI," New York Times, December 11, 1943, p. 8. Senator Pat McCarran held hearings on possible Communist and fellow traveler infiltration of the Voice in July 1951; see "McCarran Charges 'Slanting' of Voice," New York Times, July 10, 1951, p. 7. McCarthy himself had challenged the loyalty of certain VOA staff members earlier that year; see New York Times, April 29, 1951, p. 29. Consult Pirsein, "VOA", Chapters 7-10, for a thorough review of VOA's problems during the McCarthy era.

39. Sorensen, Word War, p. 34. Elmer Davis observed that "In the spring of 1953 the Veterans of Foreign Wars extracted a promise from VOA that it would not put on its programs any of the music of Roy Harris, who in 1943 had composed a symphony which he dedicated to the Soviet Union," Elmer Davis, But We Were Born Free (London: Andre Deutsch, 1955), p. 41.

40. Dizard, Strategy, pp. 74, 87. As of mid-1953, VOA Director Erikson was still arguing for hard-hitting, forceful, emotional presentations for audiences behind the Iron Curtain, although he favored more dispassionate broadcasts elsewhere. Sorensen, Word War, p. 43. But one of his predecessors, Foy Kohler, mistrusted the negativism of such a policy, feeling that, if the Communists began to "open some of the doors" that both we and they had so resolutely blocked, we would "fall flat on our faces." Edwin Kretzmann, "McCarthy and the Voice of America," Foreign Service Journal, February 1967, pp. 26ff.

41. Erik Barnouw, The Image Empire (New York: Oxford University Press, 1970), pp. 93-94.

42. Barrett, Truth, p. 85.

43. George Allen, "U.S. Propaganda a Big Mistake," Boston Globe, August 11, 1963, Section 1, p. 2.

44. Interview with Louis T. Olum, staff director of the U.S. Advisory Commission on Information, conducted by Robert Joy, July 22, 1968. Cited in Joy's "The Influence of Edward R. Murrow on the USIA," unpublished M.A. thesis, (Ohio University, Athens, Ohio, 1968), p. 98.

45. See VOA Memorandum "Analysis of Breakfast Show Contest Mail," August 16, 1967.

46. Robert T. Holt, "A New Approach to Political Communication," in Propaganda and the Cold War, John Whitton (ed.) (Washington: Public Affairs Press, 1963). Schlesinger believes Murrow in fact knew nothing of the proposed Bay of Pigs invasion. See Arthur Schlesinger, A Thousand Days (Boston: Houghton Mifflin, 1965), pp. 259, 272. Kendrick states that Murrow was qualified to attend

the crucial National Security Council meeting at which the
final decision to launch the invasion was taken, but that he
was not invited. Alexander Kendrick, Prime Time (Boston:
Little-Brown, 1969), p. 462.

47. Sorensen disagrees, claiming that Murrow had considerable influence at the highest levels: "Other directors
of USIA sat in high councils of Government; but none had the
influence Mr. Murrow had. He spoke little, but when he
spoke he had something to say and the President and his
colleagues in the Executive Branch listened." Sorensen,
letter to the editor, Washington Post, May 5, 1965, p. 14.

48. "Voice Policies Disturb Aides," New York Times,
June 6, 1965, p. 21.

49. "Voice Policies Disturb Aides," Ibid. There was
also a very confused situation regarding the possible role
of the Kennedy Administration in "using" the VOA to weaken
the authority of Vietnamese President Ngo Dien Diem in 1963.
Roger Hilsman, a member of the Kennedy administration, gives
an account of this complex episode in To Move a Nation
(Garden City: Doubleday, 1967), Chapter 31, passim, but
especially p. 289. At about the same time, a Soviet writer,
Artem Panfilov, criticized seemingly "objective" VOA broadcasts on civil rights, saying they ignored consideration of
the basic faults of capitalism. See U.S. Radio in Psychological Warfare (Moscow: International Relations Publishing
House, 1967), Chapter 4, Section 3.

50. Henry Loomis, "Remarks made by Henry Loomis on the
Occasion of his Departure as Director, Voice of America,
USIA," HEW Auditorium, Washington, D.C., March 4, 1965,
pp. 16-17.

51. "Voice Policies Disturb Aides". Rowan, like
Murrow, sat on the National Security Council. President
Johnson's memoirs take account of his presence, but give no
indication of the nature of Rowan's contributions, if any.
Lyndon B. Johnson, The Vantage Point: Perspectives on the
Presidency (New York: Holt, Rinehart & Winston, 1971).

52. Lloyd Garrison, "John Chancellor of NBC Named
Director of the Voice of America," New York Times, July 29,
1965, p. 1f.

53. "And Fie on You," Letter to the editor, The Nation,
205 (September 25, 1967), p. 258.

54. Richard Walton, "Memorandum to John Daly," The
Nation, 205 (August 28, 1967), pp. 135-138; also letter to
the editor of The Nation, 205 (September 25, 1967), pp. 258f.

55. "Daly View of 'Voice' Criticized in House," New
York Times, June 1, 1967, p. 15. John Rooney was one of the
severest Congressional critics of the United States Information Agency and of VOA.

56. "Voice of Truth?", New York Times, April 10, 1969,
p. 46. See Benjamin Wells, "Daly Quits the Voice of America
. . .", New York Times, June 7 1968 p. 1.

57.   "Voice of Truth?", Ibid.

58.   Giddens himself told the Senate in 1972 that he ". . . didn't know anything about it (VOA)" when appointed other than being aware of its existence. "USIA Appropriations Authorization, FY 1973," Hearing before the Committee on Foreign Relations, U.S. Senate, 92nd Congress, 2nd session, p. 274. Giddens was the subject of an attack by Pravda in August 1972, which accused VOA of attempting to "inject bourgeois propaganda into the minds of young people under the narcotic effect of music and entertainment," and called Giddens an Alabama millionaire who "maintains the closest relations with the chieftains of the Fascist-acting John Birch Society." Hedrick Smith, "The Soviet Press Steps Up Attack on U.S. After Lull," New York Times, September 3, 1972, p. 11.

59.   Tad Szulc, "Tough USIA Line Drew a Complaint From Rogers," New York Times, October 25, 1970, p. 3. Shakespeare reiterated these points in a November 13, 1970 breakfast meeting with reporters; see Robert M. Smith, "USIA Chief Sees a Soviet Ferment," New York Times, November 14, 1970. The VOA's more "aggressive" position in terms of its broadcasts on Soviet actions in Egypt may have been prompted by testimony given by columnist William Buckley to a House of Representatives Foreign Affairs Subcommittee on July 22, 1970. Buckley, returning from a trip to Eastern Europe, conveyed the desire of U.S. Ambassador to Moscow Jacob Beam for a "crisper" anti-Communist line from VOA. Buckley also wished to see the Voice become more "realistic and aggressive" in commentaries on the Soviet Union. See "Buckley Bids 'Voice' Be Tough on Soviet," New York Times, July 23, 1970, p. 7.

60.   U.S. Senate, Committee on Appropriations, Hearings on H.R. 9272, 92nd Congress, 1st Session, FY 1972, p. 832.

61.   "USIA Appropriations Authorization, FY 1973," Committee on Foreign Relations, U.S. Senate, p. 282.

62.   Ibid., p. 285. Several VOA staff members have told me that they virtually disregarded the memo, in part because its implementation would have led to very clumsy phraseology in many cases, in part because VOA, like many bureaucratic organizations, resists such changes, realizing that in most cases there will be no effort to see whether the directive has been implemented.

63.   Browne, "VOA", p. 34.

64.   "Should Voice of America Speak for U.S. Policymakers or Truth?", UPI release, July 16, 1975; "Voice of America Suppressed News on Cambodia, South Vietnam Fall," St. Louis Post Dispatch (UPI release), May 21, 1975, Section 1, p. 8B. On May 20, 1975, the House Subcommittee on Government Operations discussed VOA coverage (or non-coverage) of the Saigon evacuation and a Cambodian demonstration in opposition to Lon Nol.

65. There were many newspaper stories on VOA coverage
of Watergate; one of the most thorough was Arlen Large,
"At Voice of America, There's No Cover-Up on Watergate
News," Wall Street Journal, May 16, 1974.

66. "The Voice is Shaky," editorial, Los Angeles
Times, October 17, 1976, Section 6, p. 4.

67. The full text of the VOA charter is as follows:
1. VOA will establish itself as a
consistently reliable and authoritative
source of news. VOA news will be
accurate, objective, and comprehensive.
2. VOA will represent America, not any
single segment of American society. It
will therefore present a balanced and
comprehensive projection of significant
American thought and institutions.
3. VOA will present the policies of the
United States clearly and effectively.
VOA will also present responsible discussion and opinion on these policies.
The charter became public law in 1976.

68. Richard Weintraub, "Sweeping Changes Urged for
VOA Correspondents," Washington Post, March 12, 1978,
p. A32; Linda Charlton, "Shift Urged for Voice of America,"
New York Times, March 13, 1978, p. 4. Roberts himself
wrote an article about some of the problems that his
committee's report was designed to address, and some of the
changes it led to; see "New Image for the Voice of America,"
New York Times Magazine, April 13, 1980, pp. 107-114.

69. Commission on the Organization of the Government
for the Conduct of Foreign Policy, Report, June 1975.
(Washington: Superintendent of Documents, 1975).

70. Panel on International Information, Educational
and Cultural Relations, "Recommendations for the Future,"
Georgetown: Georgetown University Center for Strategic
and International Studies, March 1975.

71. See particularly "Public Diplomacy and the Future,"
Hearings before the Subcommittee on International Operations,
House of Representatives, 95th Congress, 1st Session, June
1977, pp. 100-135.

72. Christopher Wren, "Soviet Lampoons Dissident
Debates," New York Times, May 2, 1974, p. 13.

73. "Russians Listening Avidly to Western Radio," Los
Angeles Times (AP release), November 28, 1976, Section 4,
p. 6; Christopher Wren, "Soviet Reneges on Visas for the
Leviches," New York Times, December 25, 1974, p. 2.

74. "Muted Voice of America," Time, December 16, 1974,
pp. 84-85; "Voice of America: News, Diplomacy Hard to Mix,"
Christian Science Monitor (AP release), March 26, 1976.

75. Aleksandr Solzhenitsyn, The Mortal Danger (New
York: Harper and Row, 1980), p. 51.

76. From the VOA series "Forum at Twenty"; transcribed by me from tape recording.

77. David Binder, "U.S. Concedes it is Behind Anti-Khomeni Broadcasts," New York *Times*, June 29, 1980, Section 1, p. 3; Stephen S. Rosenfeld, "On the Beam," Washington *Post*, December 28, 1979. Brzezinski's deep interest in broadcasting to Iran and Soviet Central Asia was confirmed by several VOA staff members with whom I spoke in late March 1980.

78. See "Radio Free Cuba," *Broadcasting*, September 28, 1981, p. 23 and "Florida Broadcasters Offer Help . . .," *Broadcasting*, October 5, 1981, p. 30.

79. James Oliver, "Comparison of the Russian Services of the Four Major Broadcasters (VOA, BBC, DW, RL)", Washington: U.S. Information Agency, Office of Research, Report R-8-75, July 28, 1975.

80. A VOA internal study of the manner in which the coverage of the "Jonestown (Guyana) Massacre" was handled by VOA's language divisions circulated throughout VOA in spring 1979, and caused something of a sensation, since the study revealed that certain language divisions had spent little or no air time on the story, or had delayed trans-mission of it, even though an abundance of material was available from the central news room; reasons for omis-sions and delays ranged from "horror stories shouldn't be carried" to "the reputation of the United States would only be damaged if we had carried this story." I have seen a copy of the study, but it is not available for public in-spection.

81. Mr. Reinhardt's feelings, according to several USICA Office of Research staff members with whom I spoke in March 1980, were influenced heavily by a report on USICA research practices written for him by pollster Daniel Yankelowitz.

82. "A Content Analysis of VOA Mail," Washington: U.S. Information Service, Office of Research, Report E-25-76, December 28, 1976.

83. When I visited Nicosia, Cyprus in April 1974, several officials of the Cyprus Broadcasting Corporation told me that a major problem in keeping some measure of peace between the Greek Cypriot and Turkish Cypriot com-munities was the "inflammatory" broadcasting directed to the island by the Greek Government over the powerful VOA medium wave transmitter on Rhodes; in return for being allowed to set up that transmitter, VOA had had to agree to let the Greek Government broadcast over it during one period of the day, and its power and location made it ideal for reaching listeners in Cyprus with broadcasts emphasizing the es-sentially Greek identity of the island.

84. Collins, letter to *Foreign Affairs*, 60, Fall 1981, p. 192.

Forces Radio Service was in business; by the end of the war, it was coordinating the activities of some 300 stations overseas, and broadcasting a shortwave service for U.S. military personnel around the world.

Peacetime brought a considerable decrease in number of stations, to a low of 60 in 1949, but Cold War tensions and the Korean War, followed by the war in Vietnam, saw the number rise again. By the late 1960s there were over 300 stations in 30 foreign countries and nine U.S. territories. That number has again declined in the 1970s, and there are roughly 100 stations in 15 foreign countries as of 1981. The shortwave service has remained throughout AFRTS' 40-year history.

Armed forces radio services have received little attention from the U.S. media, with one exception. During the late 1960s and early 1970s, stations in Vietnam and Europe came under attack, sometimes from military staff themselves, for censoring the news.[2] The AFRTS central news bureau in Washington, D.C. (the Armed Forces News Bureau, which, along with AFRTS, moved to Los Angeles in 1981) escaped such criticism, by and large. However, a combination of shrinking budgets and an "anti-censorship" climate led to the virtual disappearance of the AFNB practice of assembling its own newscasts from edited and unedited U.S. network newscast and items filed by its own reporters. Since the early 1970s, AFNB has simply retransmitted unedited U.S. commercial and public radio network newscasts.

There is no doubt that AFRTS and U.S. overseas military station broadcasts are clearly intended for U.S. citizens-- military personnel, dependents and civilian support staff-- who happen to be working outside the country. Many of the overseas stations have transmitters of one kilowatt or less (only Frankfurt and Tokyo use 50 kW or more), making it difficult for host-country listeners to pick them up. Almost all of the broadcasts come from U.S. sources, with none of the background material that VOA supplies to help foreign listeners understand U.S. life and institutions. And, with very few exceptions (the Far East Network station in Tokyo tries to teach its American listeners a new Japanese word each day), all of the programs are in English. What's more, the disk jockeys, who are the mainstay of the overseas stations' broadcast schedule, sometimes speak a brand of English that would be well-nigh unintelligible to a classroom-educated Japanese or German student of the language!

Yet it's clear that these broadcast services do reach foreign listeners. Requests for QSL cards (verification of reception of station) come to AFRTS from thousands of citizens in other countries each year. Various polls and surveys done by domestic stations in countries where there are also U.S. military stations indicate listenership for

the latter on the order of two to four per cent of the adult
population once a week or more; if teenagers were surveyed,
the percentages probably would be higher. The overseas
stations also receive many telephone calls and letters from
the "locals" to play and dedicate various records. Station
personnel are well aware of this so-called "shadow" audience,
and the Department of Defense training program for military
information specialists who are to be assigned to overseas
stations includes a unit on being sensitive to that audience.[3]
     What a foreign listener might think of U.S. armed forces
radio would depend on which service she or he listened to.
The AFRTS shortwave service has a 24-hour-a-day transmission
schedule (it uses VOA transmitters in the U.S. and the
Philippines), and provides little but unedited U.S. network
newscasts and coverage of U.S. college and professional
sports events. Commercial breaks in the U.S. broadcasts are
filled with public service announcements suitable for the
military:

> It's not like the old days. The air force
> used to have a much larger force of personnel
> and a bigger budget. But the cutbacks haven't
> affected their performance. The only difference
> in the air force is the attitude: it has un-
> officially been dubbed "leaner and meaner".
> The muscles that prepare it as a modernized force
> which enables our air force to maintain aero-
> space superiority have simply become more
> efficient. Air force personnel are better
> trained than ever before, and the readiness and
> determination of the entire air force is re-
> flected in each and every one of them. It's
> been a long haul, these two hundred years of
> freedom enforcement, and the military services
> have performed admirably. Our liberties are
> directly related to the constant vigilance of
> the air force experts and all of our military
> personnel. The air force operations today
> involve both air and space. When man makes
> the big step across the stratofrontier, you
> can be sure the air force will be there. Yes,
> it's not like the old days. With today's all
> volunteer air force, it's better.
> AFRTS, August 1979

AFRTS also prepares and broadcasts news of particular interest to military personnel, such as "Armed Forces Digest"
and "Marine Diary". Such music as it transmits is used only
to fill time, and goes unidentified.
     The armed forces stations overseas are considerably
better-rounded than AFRTS, although AFRTS material does

account for about 10 per cent of their schedules. The remainder includes locally-produced newscasts, music (largely
popular), local U.S. military sports, religious services,
community calendar programs (sometimes containing bits of
information about the host country), and, for some stations,
old radio shows such as "Gunsmoke" and "The Lone Ranger".
The smaller stations, such as those in the Benelux countries,
often simply relay the broadcasts of the larger stations,
such as AFN Frankfurt.

Some anecdotal evidence indicates that foreign listeners are more willing to believe U.S. armed forces broadcasts, on the assumption that the U.S. wouldn't lie to its
own citizens and that most of the programs are identical to
what U.S. listeners receive.[4] For a brief period in the
mid-1960s, VOA placed a specially-prepared commentary on the
AFRTS program schedule, thinking it might be a way to penetrate the psychological defenses of listeners who didn't
trust VOA.[5] No one attempted to scientifically test the
effectiveness of this ploy, and armed forces broadcast
staff, resentful at being "used" by VOA, helped get the
program cancelled.[6]

There is no doubt that a foreign listener would hear an
authentic voice of America when listening to a U.S. military
station or to AFRTS, but it would be a very domestic voice.
U.S. foreign policy would appear as one of many concerns and
interests of the United States--and perhaps a less important
concern than popular music and sports. It would not be a
perfect mirror of the United States, but then neither is the
Voice of America. A listener who combined the two voices
would end up with a fairly well-rounded picture of life in
the U.S.

RADIO IN THE AMERICAN SECTOR OF BERLIN (RIAS)

The same Cold War tensions that gave rise to an expansion of American military activity were also responsible for
the "internationalization" of a radio station which had
begun life in the most modest, uninternational fashion
possible. RIAS Berlin came on the air in February 1946 as a
wired radio service for Germans living in the American
sector of Berlin. With the Berlin Blockade of 1948, RIAS
found itself playing an international role, as it carried
the message of Allied determination to resist the Blockade
to listeners in West Berlin, East Berlin and East Germany.
During the next ten years, the station grew to become one
of the larger radio operations in Western Europe, with three
separate broadcast services over longwave, medium wave,
short wave and FM.[7]

    While certain programs remained on the schedule to serve
listeners in West Berlin, they were far outnumbered by those
intended for listeners in East Berlin and East Germany.
There were specific programs for farmers, factory workers,
SED (Communist party) officials, religious groups and others.
Popular, jazz and classical music, especially of the sort
generally unavailable over East German radio, was plentiful.
News, commentary, press reviews and other informational
programs abounded. A number of satirical programs and series
lampooned SED officials and Soviet policies in East Germany.
The station attempted to serve as "the sort of radio service
East Germans would want if they had a choice in the matter,"
according to its own staff; it thus became something of a
prototype for Radio Free Europe and Radio Liberty.
    That statement of purpose might be considered pre-
sumptuous, but it did rest on a considerable body of audience
research and anecdotal evidence: prior to the erection of
the Berlin Wall in August 1961, it was comparatively easy
for East Germans in general, and East Berliners in particular,
to visit West Berlin for the day, where many of them called
the station, mailed post cards and letters to it, and were
interviewed by survey research organizations. From this
evidence, RIAS was able to conclude that between one-third
and two-thirds of the adult population of East Germany
listened to it each day, and that many of those listeners
claimed to depend on the station for spiritual sustenance,
cultural sustenance and information on developments outside
and inside the Communist world.
    In order to provide "inside information", RIAS invested
a great deal of time, effort and money in finding out what
was going on in East Germany. Most of the information came
from monitoring East German radio stations and reading East
German magazines and newspapers. All of this material was
carefully indexed and filed, and more than once enabled the
station to compare past promises made by East German
officials with their present performances. RIAS also collected a large amount of information on the socialist
nations of Eastern and Central Europe in order to lead its
listeners to compare their own situations with those of
Hungarians, Russians, etc. The hope was that if, for
example, a youth group in Hungary were allowed greater
freedom to do certain things than were East German youth
groups, the East Germans might demand the same freedom, on
the grounds that what is permissible for one socialist
(Communist) state should be permissible for others. This
technique, known as "cross-reporting", has been widely
practiced by Radio Free Europe and Radio Liberty, as well.
    The construction of the Berlin Wall in 1961 deprived
RIAS of ready access to many of its sources of information
about daily life in East Germany. That event also

symbolized one more limit to U.S. willingness to intervene
in a potential military conflict between East and West, much
as had been the case with demonstrations in East Berlin and
East Germany in 1953, when the Western powers also chose not
to become involved militarily. RIAS had never promoted
armed action against the East German government, although
some of its programs did encourage workers, peasants, youth
groups and others to bargain with and even challenge the
government. For example, when the Zeiss factory contract
came up for renewal in 1950, RIAS compared the old contract
with the new one, clause by clause, showing workers where
the advantages and disadvantages were, and urging them to
strike the best bargain they could.[8] However, following the
erection of the Wall, the station had to alter its tactics
to some degree.
       In fact, one shift had begun around the mid-1950s. At
that time, RIAS adopted a policy of serving as a "bridge to
the West", keeping East Germans well informed as to what
was going on in Western Europe, especially in such socialist
nations as Sweden. This was a recognition that socialism
was probably more appealing for many East Germans than was
capitalism. Rarely did the station deal with U.S. domestic
affairs, unless they were major events, and U.S. culture,
outside of a certain amount of popular music, was presented
infrequently--this despite the fact that RIAS was financed
by the U.S. Government and supervised by U.S. Information
Agency staff.[9] News items and programs stressing the
"bridge" theme increased in the 1960s, particularly where
economic development was concerned, since that subject was
of particular concern to most East Germans. RIAS largely
discarded its satirical programs lampooning the East German
government.
       When East and West Germany officially recognized each
other's independent existence in a 1973 accord, it again
became possible for RIAS to gain access to a fairly wide
range of information, and even to send reporters into East
Germany, particularly to cover meetings, athletic contests,
etc., involving the two Germanies. Over the years, RIAS has
paid close attention to coverage of West Germany, partly
because a number of its listeners were West Berliners,
partly because reunification of Germany has been part of
Western policy, partly because East Germans are connected
with West Germany by ties of language, cultural tradition
and blood: few East Germans do not have a relative across
the border. The station always has been operated as a
German station above all else, and, if the supervision and
financial support came from the United States (through USIA),
the day-to-day programing decisions were made by the German
staff. In the 1970s, the U.S. supervisory staff shrank to
two individuals, compared with a German staff of roughly 600,

and as of 1980 the West German government was making annual
financial contributions roughly ten times greater than U.S.
portion of the RIAS budget. Thus, by the end of the 1970s,
RIAS was more German than ever.

Today RIAS appears to be less important than it once
was in reaching East German listeners with a "Western"
message. There are fewer pressures on East Germans not to
listen to Western broadcasts now, and there is a wide range
to choose from: various West German stations, including
television in certain parts of East Germany; Swiss and
Austrian radio; and international stations broadcasting in
German from England, Sweden and a host of other countries.
Like RIAS, most of the stations offer a wide variety of
informational and entertainment programing, although only
one (West Germany's Deutschlandfunk) even begins to approach
RIAS' degree of concentration on covering life in East
Germany. East German broadcasting also has become more
interesting and diversified. But RIAS also stands as a
symbolic guarantee of U.S. presence in West Berlin and U.S.
interest in East Germany,[10] and its reduction or abolition
would doubtless touch off speculation as to U.S. motives.
The station is likely to remain on the air for some time to
come, even in the face of what is almost certainly a dwindling audience.

RADIO FREE EUROPE AND RADIO LIBERTY

Radio Free Europe and Radio Liberty are, after a
fashion, larger versions of RIAS. Both were founded in the
early 1950s as part of the U.S. "Cold War arsenal", whereas
RIAS more or less grew into that role, and both were charged
with the task of encouraging and exploiting discontent in
Communist nations. Also, much like RIAS, both stations
developed elaborate information-gathering systems. And
finally, as RIAS also had done, RFE and RL employed a number
of individuals who had left the countries to which they were
now broadcasting. Coincidentally, RFE and RL also were
located in Germany, albeit in Munich rather than Berlin,
although some administrative functions and recording facilities were in New York City.

The stations began their respective lives with a good
deal of publicity. They were to serve as outlets for
exiles broadcasting back to their "captive homelands".
They were to function independently of the United States
government, as "a non-official instrument of American
foreign policy". In order to preserve that independence,
U.S. citizens were urged through announcements appearing in
and on radio, television, magazines, newspapers, mass tran-
sit placards, billboards, etc. to contribute their dollars

so that Eastern Europe and the USSR might someday be "freed
from Communist rule." Private boards of directors, composed
of distinguished U.S. citizens such as retired General
Lucius Clay were to oversee the stations and assist in fund-
raising activities.[11]

All of that was an elaborate fiction. In fact, the
stations were financed through and supervised by the U.S.
Central Intelligence Agency, and the fund-raising campaigns
never collected more than a small fraction of annual operating budgets.[12] The fiction was maintained until 1967 when
a series of events forced the revelation of the extent and
nature of many CIA activities, including operation of RFE
and RL.[13] However, the CIA itself did not admit to that
role, and it was not until 1971 that the U.S. Congress (and
chiefly Senator Clifford Case of New Jersey) held a full
investigation of CIA involvement with the stations, and
called for an end to that involvement. Finally in 1973,
Congress authorized an annual expenditure of public funds
for support of the stations, and also approved a public
supervisors (oversight) board: the Board for International
Broadcasting. The Board makes an annual report to Congress
and makes the annual budget request for the stations. The
estimated FY 1982 budget was to be between $90 and 100
million, or not much less than VOA's FY 1982 appropriation.
Also like VOA, the stations have been the subject of controversy throughout much of their history, but often for very
different reasons.

The Years of "Liberation" (1950-1956)

Initially, RFE and RL were to carry the message of
"liberation" to the "captive" nations of Eastern Europe and
to the Soviet Union. RL's full title at first was "Radio
Liberation from Bolshevism," which was shortened to "Radio
Liberation" in October 1956 (ironically, just before the
Hungarian Revolution) and not changed to Radio Liberty until
1959. What "liberation" meant never was clearly defined,
but the U.S. government appeared to think in terms of
"freeing nations from Communist rule", while at least a few
of the exiles who wrote, produced and delivered most of the
broadcasts thought in terms of taking or retaking political
power. Yet other exiles, as we shall see, doubted the
efficacy of a policy of liberation.

As Cold War tensions continued, the stations quickly
grew to something close to their present size and scope.
RFE began life in 1950 with one 7,500 watt transmitter; by
1955 it had 29 transmitters with a total power of more than
a million watts, beaming several hours per day in each of

seven languages (Polish, Hungarian, Czech, Slovak, Romanian, Bulgarian, and, from 1953 to 1955, Albanian).[14] RL enjoyed something of an advantage in initial (1953) transmitter power--two 10,000 watt transmitters. That power was increased to 300 kW within five years, and during the same period, RL's language broadcasts increased from one (Russian) to ten (ranging from Ukrainian to Tatar and Azerbaijani). If negative reactions from the press in the target countries could be taken as a valid measure of effectiveness, the stations were proving most effective: it was a rare week that went by without an attack of some sort on the stations' motives, credibility or accuracy. The stations themselves were not inclined to mince words when attacking the governments of those countries:

>The rulers of the Kremlin are trembling. In the sleepless nights of their bad conscience the slightest whisper of the suppressed millions sounds like a threatening roar to them.
>RFE to Hungary, 1953[15]

Some of the broadcasts strongly resembled those of World War II, as for example in work slowdown campaigns:

>Work slowly, do only what has to be done daily. Low speed, unfinished business, call it passive resistance. As slow as possible, strike unnoticed, and be circumspect. Speed has no value. Freedom . . . is near. And it gets nearer, the slower you work.
>RFE to Czechoslovakia, 1954[16]

The resemblance between RFE/RL broadcasts and World War II broadcasts, especially those carried over the BBC and various American and British psychological warfare stations, may have been due partly to the fact that a number of the American managerial staff and exiles had worked for, or were well acquainted with, those stations.[17] However, there were apparently some differences of opinion between exiles and Americans over the policy of liberation, the exiles claiming that the Americans wanted to "push us too far" in the direction of encouraging revolution in their homelands.[18]

When the Hungarian Revolution occurred in late October 1956, the situation seemed tailor-made for Western intervention within the framework of liberation. While there is very little evidence to suggest that RFE broadcasts specifically encouraged liberation through revolution at that or any other time,[19] the general tone of its programs for the previous six years had been one of encouraging the expectation of liberation:

> Our aim is liberty. Our aim is your
> liberty. We shall reach our goal.
> RFE to Czechoslovakia, 1952[20]

> But continued passive resistance will
> bear fruit. It will not only weaken the
> regime's desparate efforts toward consoli-
> dation, but will pave the way for a better
> and more democratic future.
> RFE to Hungary, 1953[21]

The first fruits to be borne had appeared in Poland
some four months earlier, and the resistance was far from
passive. Workers in Poznan, discontented with poor managerial practices in a locomotive works and upset over an
increase in work norms, staged a demonstration march that
turned into a riot. RFE urged caution:

> Let us have no illusions. Incidents like
> that play into the hands of Ochab and his
> Stalinist clique, who want the return of terror
> and oppression. The struggle for freedom must
> end in victory, for no regime based on repres-
> sion can last. But in that struggle prudence
> is necessary. And therefore in the name of that
> ardent desire, common to us all, Poland's
> freedom, we must call on the people to preserve
> calm and refrain from acts of despair.
> RFE to Poland, June 1956[22]

Over the next few months, the situation was often
tense, and Soviet intervention appeared likely, but it was
averted. RFE broadcasts encouraged Poles to be firm in
their demands for relaxation or removal of some of the
Polish government's more oppressive measures, but to be
realistic enough to recognize the ability of the Soviets to
intervene.[23]

The success of the Poles in achieving reforms was
widely reported by RFE in its other language services, and
may well have had a stimulating effect in Hungary.[24]
Demonstrations there began far more peaceably, but soon
grew into outright confrontation with Soviet forces. Radio
played an important role in that process, with small
"freedom stations" springing up in cities all across
Hungary. The stations at first gave voice to demands for
reform and reports of victories, but as Soviet armed forces
entered the conflict, the stations began to call upon
Western nations, individually or collectively, to send
supplies and even military support.

RFE rebroadcast many programs from the "freedom

stations," and added some encouragement of its own. Its
specific role in "fanning the flames of revolution" is not
altogether. clear although one broadcaster "instructed"
listeners in how to make incendiary bombs for use against
Soviet tanks,[25] while another reported on a British newspaper article concerning "Western" support for the Hungarian
"freedom fighters", then himself added this comment:

> The reports from London, Paris, the United
> States and other Western reports show that the
> world's reaction to Hungarian events surpasses
> every imagination. In the Western capitals a
> practical manifestation of Western sympathy is
> expected at any hour.[26]

RFE came in for heavy U.S. and European press criticism following the revolution, on the grounds that, through
its encouraging tone, it had prolonged what was bound to be
a futile attempt at revolutionary change, thus placing the
lives of many Hungarians in needless jeopardy. Investigations of RFE's broadcast activities during the revolution
were conducted by the West German government, a United
Nations special committee, and a special committee of the
Council of Europe.[27] Those investigations indicated that,
if RFE had acted irresponsibly, it had done so largely by
generating over time a climate within which a Hungarian
listener might well have been led to expect "Western"
support in the event of a revolution. A survey conducted
among over 1,000 Hungarian refugees in December 1956 showed
that of the 96 per cent who expected U.S. and/or "Western"
aid, over one-third claimed that the expectation was based
on RFE broadcasts, "Western" broadcasts, or "Western"
propaganda.[28]
While this was not an outright condemnation of RFE's
existing practices, it certainly called into question the
RFE and RL policy of stressing liberation. Within a short
time, RFE had tightened up its supervisory practices and had
begun to place more and more emphasis on a programing concept that some, including RFE itself, have labelled "a
bridge to the West". Talk of liberation virtually disappeared.

The "Bridge to the West" (1957-1968)

The "bridge to the West" policy certainly did not mean
that RFE and RL had given up hopes of promoting change
within the target countries--change in directions more
favorable to U.S. policies and interests. As agencies of

the United States government, whether officially acknowledged or not, the stations simply were reflecting a change
in the overall policy of that government--or non-policy, as
some have labelled the original concept of "liberation."[29]
Under the "bridge" policy, the stations were to encourage
gradual, evolutionary change, not by hard-hitting and often
personalized attacks on the governments of the target
countries (although some attacks have never disappeared
altogether), but by reminding listeners of the relative
prosperity and freedom of thought enjoyed by Western
Europeans. RFE and RL policy makers hoped that such broadcasts would increase pressures for economic reforms and
further contact with the Western European nations.

The passing of RFE/RL's "liberation" phase may have
seen changes in program content, but the overall shape of
the broadcast schedule, over 70 per cent of it devoted to
news and current affairs, remained unchanged. The stations
also continued their attempts to reach specific groups
within the population, such as farmers, young people,
scientists and Communist party officials, although the
larger services, such as Russian, Polish and Hungarian, did
far more of this than did smaller ones such as Kirghiz.

In some cases, the stations had insufficient knowledge
of the particular area or country to permit much specialized
broadcasting. RFE and RL, like RIAS, have extensive monitoring services and research divisions to comb the airwaves
and various publications originating within the target
countries in order to obtain news of developments and trends
there, especially news that is not widely circulated within
and among the countries. However, it's far more difficult
to obtain information on internal matters for the Kirghiz
Republic than for Poland. Thus, while the two stations
attempted to provide their listeners with "the sort of
broadcast service they would wish if they had a choice in
the matter" (much as RIAS claimed to do), there were severe
limits to the thoroughness and completeness of many of the
individual language services.

The program concept of "cross-reporting," which I have
already mentioned in connection with RIAS, had always been
employed by RFE and RL, but it proved particularly suitable
in the context of the "bridge to the West" policy. "Cross-
reporting" enabled the stations to suggest internal reforms
that should be practicable on the assumption that what was
proper for one Communist country should be proper for all.
If one Communist country were to "borrow" something from the
West, it might be possible to build that one adoption into
several. Approximately two-thirds of the news and information (features, press reviews, etc.) program time was
devoted to items about the Communist world (not all of them
within the category of "cross-reporting", to be sure).

Audience research also increased markedly in the 1960s,
particularly for RFE. More and more "average" Central and
Eastern Europeans, as well as some groups from the USSR,
were being allowed to visit Western Europe for scientific
and cultural conferences, and even tourism. Working through
interviewers in Vienna, Stockholm, Paris, etc. which it had
trained and supervised, RFE conducted interviews on media
habits and on attitudes toward such issues as the relationship between church and state, prospects for their country's
economy, etc. Such information helped RFE to shape its
programing more specifically to the tastes, habits and
opinions of its potential audiences.

However, a number of Eastern and Western Europeans,
including some specialists in audience research, have
questioned whether people interviewed under such conditions
will provide "true" answers, given their possible concern
with surveillance on the part of their fellow citizens or
anyone else.[30] Others have wondered whether the interviews
themselves were properly supervised by RFE, or even whether
the interviews were actually conducted in all cases.[31]
It is obvious that such surveys cannot represent a truly
random sample of the population, nor does RFE claim that
they do. Most of RL's audience research has been even less
random, since the major share of studies has been conducted
in refugee centers, although it too has conducted surveys
among Soviet visitors to Western European cities.[32]

Data from the surveys were quite consistent throughout
the 1960s. They showed that audience for both stations
were predominantly urban, better-educated and in an age
range from 30 to 60, with considerable numbers of younger
listeners for the jazz and popular music shows. It also
indicated that listeners were generally inclined to believe
the stations. (It would be surprising to learn otherwise,
since few would continue to listen to a station that they
couldn't believe, unless they wished to be better able to
expose its "lies" to those who were more naive!) and that
they listened primarily to news and information programs
(again, quite predictable, given the preponderance of this
program category in the overall schedule).[33]

The "New Cold War?" (1968-1980)

By 1968, RFE and RL had a more precise idea of the size
and composition of their audience, and various bits and
pieces of anecdotal information, as well as reactions to
their broadcasts by the mass media in the target countries,
led them to feel that their increased emphasis on evolutionary development in the post-1956 period was bearing

fruit. The nations of Central and Eastern Europe, and, to
some extent, the Soviet Union, did appear to be evolving in
directions more congenial to the West.

However, in 1968 the evolution in one country--
Czechoslovakia--came to an abrupt halt. As with Hungary in
1956, the Soviet Union played the major role in arresting
the liberalization movement (widely known as the "Prague
spring"). This time, however, there were few accusations
of RFE misconduct by the Western media, and no post hoc
examinations of its broadcast policies before and during the
crisis. "Liberation" messages had virtually disappeared
from RFE and RL broadcasts following the Hungarian uprising
in 1956, and policy making and implementation were under
tighter control than they had been 12 years earlier, thanks
in part to a formal statement of editorial policy.34 RFE's
coverage of the Polish workers' demonstrations in December
1970 likewise drew very little criticism from the Western
media.

RFE and RL faced a crisis of their own early in 1971.
Senator Clifford Case (R., New Jersey) introduced a bill
(S. 18) calling for the stations to be removed from CIA
and brought within the Congressional appropriation process;
their budgets ($30 million for FY 1972) would be appropri-
ated to the Department of State, which would then disburse
the funds. The Nixon administration supported another bill
(S. 1936) which proposed a non-profit corporation to supervise the stations and an annual Congressional appropriation
for them. Over the next two years, the State Department did
disburse funds for the stations, but in 1973 a special
Presidential Study Commission reported favorably on them and
recommended their continuation.35

The debates during 1971-1973 period were often acri-
monious, particularly on the issue of the administration's
desire to maintain the stations' "private" identity. Senator
J. William Fulbright (D., Arkansas) was especially suspicious
of the administration on that point, stating "Neither the
CIA nor any other agency is going to put out the money like
this and allow some unknown or private individual to determine a policy."36

By early 1972, Senator Fulbright was calling for the
dissolution of the stations, labelling them "relics of the
Cold War." Most of his colleagues in the U.S. Senate and
House disagreed with him. The Nixon administration, which
appeared to follow a two-pronged policy of promoting détente
with the Communist world while simultaneously criticizing
it, particularly through international broadcasting, worked
hard to gain passage of its bill. Finally, in 1973, Congress
authorized the establishment of a nonprofit corporation, the
Board for International Broadcasting, whose members would
be chosen by the President with the advice and consent of
the Senate.

Criticism of the governments of the Soviet Union and
Eastern and Central Europe continued throughout the Nixon
administration. Even Watergate was enlisted as a basis for
comparison of political practices:

> This matter could be approached with the
> cynicism that is sometimes present in some
> European commentaries: there always have been
> scandals, and always will be, but the world will
> go on. Or it could be seen through the eyes of
> a Communist politician, for whom such things as
> bugging and wiretapping belong among the normal
> means of governing, and who will never understand
> how they could become a public scandal.
> RFE in Czech, June 1973[37]

RL became particularly active in broadcasting an unusual form of programing during this same period. Samizdat
(Russian term for "self-publishing") are materials written
(or allegedly written) by individuals who disagree with some
aspect or other of Soviet government policy, conditions of
life in the USSR, etc. Their authors may express themselves
in prose, poetry or other literary forms, and they may be
short or long. Samizdat circulate as handwritten or type-
script copies, and many find their way to Western Europe.
Determining their authenticity is often next to impossible.
RL was broadcasting them for an average of four hours per
month in 1969, and that figure climbed to 80 hours a month
(including repeats) in 1971.[38]   (The 1981 figure is about
16 hours per month, not including repeats). Often read at
dictation speed so that listeners could transcribe them--
something RL had done from the late 1950s with "banned"
novels and plays by Soviet authors--they were further evidence that, détente notwithstanding, RL continued to serve
as a vehicle for criticizing the Soviet government.[39]

Once the Board for International Broadcasting had been
established, it was not long before Congress began to examine
ways in which to get the stations to economize. The General
Accounting Office had issued a report in 1972 in which the
physical consolidation of the two stations was recommended,
both because it would result in budgetary savings and because it would help to increase policy coordination. RFE's
Munich building was remodelled and enlarged, and in 1975,
RL moved in. Likewise, RFE/RL offices in New York City
were consolidated and moved to Washington, D.C., also in
1975.

The decline of the U.S. dollar vis-a-vis the West
German Deutschmark more than wiped out the savings realized
through consolidation. The General Accounting Office examined the administrative practices of RFE and RL in 1976,

and concluded that the stations could realize still further
savings by revising the salary schedules for many of the
staff, since those schedules seemed out of line compared
with what other U.S. governmental organizations in West
Germany were paying. The GAO report also suggested that the
stations consider moving most of their operations to the
United States, as a further cost-cutting measure, and it
expressed serious reservations as to whether station management on the one hand and the Board on the other agreed on
the amount and nature of each other's authority.[40] Following release of the report, the stations did revise their
salary schedules, and the Board asserted its oversight
functions in clearer terms. But Board and stations alike
rejected the idea of a move to the United States, both on
the grounds that economies would not be that great and that
Munich had particular advantages in the recruitment of staff
and as a center for the gathering of anecdotal information
on developments in the target areas.

The early 1970s were difficult years for the stations
in yet another way. Both had major transmitter bases in
West Germany, but both also operated transmitters in other
countries: Spain for RL, Portugal for RFE, and until 1972,
Taiwan for RL.[41] The leases for the Spanish and Portuguese
bases expired in 1976 and 1974, respectively, and the new
governments in each country were considerably more reluctant
to renew them than their predecessors had been. Both
governments finally agreed to renew the leases, but under
terms which gave them greater scope to examine broadcast
content and to refuse to allow the retransmission of material
harmful to their own interests.[42]

In the 1976 presidential campaign, candidate Jimmy
Carter made the stations a campaign issue when he criticized
the Ford administration for its failure to request funding
for additional transmitters, saying:

> I believe that this failure to act stems
> from the inability of the present Administration
> to appreciate the importance of an open foreign
> policy and a free flow of information and ideas
> through mass communication. There are also
> signs of a more insidious problem--a preference
> by our Secretary of State to deal privately with
> the Soviets, while they have launched a massive
> diplomatic attack on the radios demanding that
> they be shut down and attempting to prevent RFE
> and RL commentators from covering the Olympic
> Games.[43]

Carter clearly saw the stations as a major element in
bringing his message on human rights to listeners in

Central and Eastern Europe and the Soviet Union. Once
elected, he pushed for the necessary budgetary appropriations,[44] and was largely successful: Congress authorized
an expenditure of roughly $5.2 million on purchase and
installation of four new transmitters in FY 1978 and another
$9.7 million on seven new transmitters in FY 1979.

    Carter frequently invoked the "free flow of informa-
tion" provision of the Final Act of the Conference on
Security and Cooperation in Europe (1975) when speaking in
support of RFE and RL. Under his administration, there were
renewed efforts to obtain elimination of jamming of RFE and
RL broadcasts. RL had been jammed continuously from its
first day of broadcast; while RFE's Hungarian and Romanian
services had been free of jamming since the mid-1960s, the
Polish, Bulgarian, Czech and Slovak services were still
jammed as the Final Act of the CSCE was signed. The Central
and Eastern European and Soviet delegations to the Conference justified exclusion of RFE and RL broadcasts on the
grounds that they were a form of meddling in the internal
affairs of the target countries.

    In one respect, at least, Soviet suspicions of RL in-
tentions received some reinforcement even as the Conference
was being held. Acting under a "mandate" from Congress,
RL initiated weekly broadcasts in Lithuanian in January
1975, then increased them to a daily schedule in March;
Latvian and Estonian were first offered in July 1975, again
on a weekly basis, and became daily in September. Since the
three Baltic republics had been incorporated with the Soviet
Union only 35 years earlier, and since there were large
numbers of emigrés from them, often well organized, in
certain Western European countries and the United States,
the Soviet Union was extremely sensitive about any action
that might appear to challenge the legitimacy of their in-
corporation.[45]

    In February 1980, RFE ran afoul of some Congressional
criticism for its 1979 broadcast of an RFE Romanian service
interview with Archbishop Valerian Trifa who, as it turned
out, was facing deportation proceedings in the United
States because of his alleged role as member of Romania's
fascist Iron Guard in Bucharest during World War II. The
House Foreign Affairs Committee was not fully satisfied
with RFE's explanation, particularly in terms of what it
seemed to reveal about the station's mechanisms for internal
control of broadcast content.[46] Shortly after the committee
hearing, the General Accounting Office conducted an investi-
gation--its third in less than ten years--of RFE/RL. That
investigation led GAO to state that, although the stations
had shown much improvement since its 1976 investigation, the
relationship between them and the Board for International
Broadcasting remained somewhat strained and unclear.

More to the point of the specific problem of program supervision, the GAO investigators discovered that RFE/RL's Broadcast Analysis Department (BAD seems an unfortunate acronym for script "censors"!) was understaffed and perhaps ineffectual. For example, there were no BAD analysts available to examine scripts for four of RL's services, another BAD analyst covered two RL languages, and yet another had to manage six! There also appeared to be a lack of clarity in the guidelines for BAD to use in its evaluation of scripts. The BAD files also contained copies of scripts on which BAD notations raised serious questions, e.g. "There is a pervasive overtone of incitement about this program. It should never have been allowed to go on the air." But the broadcast had gone on the air, because, while BAD may make both pre- and post-broadcast assessments, the former rarely occur.[47]

In April 1981, columnist Jack Anderson uncovered further evidence of problems with supervision of programing. He quoted from an internal report prepared by a B.I.B. staff member who had monitored RL in January 1981. That exercise produced examples (isolated ones, I was told by the staff member, James Critchlow) of programs featuring Russian Orthodox church spokespersons making "anti-Catholic" statements, and other programs containing "anti-Polish" statements. That the incidents took place at all, but especially in such tension-ridden circumstances in Poland, only seemed to point up the need for more careful program supervision, however difficult it might be to achieve.[48]

Conclusion

Despite various Congressional, GAO and press criticisms, RFE and RL appear to be firmly fixed in the galaxy of international radio, however temporary they were supposed to be as they began their respective lives. Their combined forces --some 21 languages[49] for just over 1,000 hours per week-- make them one of the world's largest international broadcasters. Their program schedules, dominated as they are by informational broadcasting about life within the Communist world, clearly show the more tactical nature of the RFE/RL broadcasting mission. Yet there is entertainment (mostly popular music), and coverage of events in the West certainly has increased over the past two decades. With tens of millions of dollars invested in equipment and with a staff of over 1,700, the stations show every sign of permanency.

Even if a radical change in political conditions should come about in one or more of the target areas, the stations and their supporters very likely would claim that it would

be wise to wait and see whether the changes were lasting
ones before dismantling any of the broadcast services. Such
a wait could be almost indefinite, although it's quite
possible that a given service might be reduced in air time,
if that would seem useful as a diplomatic gesture of U.S.
recognition of political change.

Policy guidance for the stations clearly remains a
problem. The B.I.B. administrative staff of 40 is miniscule
in comparison with the total enterprise. The Board's five
members are not full time, and there are accusations that
some administrations have "played politics" with Board
appointments.[50] Congress might like to have a Board which
could act as final arbiter in program decision-making, but
that simply isn't practical: radio must rely on its timeliness for maximum impact, and the stations in Munich must
be in a position to react quickly when critical events
occur. Yet this raises the question of who decides whether
RFE/RL broadcast policies (see footnote 34) would be or have
been violated and, as we have seen, the answer is not altogether clear.

But because the stations are organizationally independent of both the State Department and USICA, they are
also independent of official policy guidance and of any
requirement to coordinate broadcast policies. While it is
unlikely that there would be a reoccurrence of the ir-
responsible broadcasts that were beamed to Hungary in 1956,
it is perfectly possible for RFE and RL broadcasts to be at
variance with VOA broadcasts and/or with official policy.
Before 1971, the U.S. government could claim that it had no
real control over the stations, although the domestic
media in the target areas pointed out the stations' CIA
connections year after year. The Western media, including
some international broadcasters, publicized the 1971-1973
Congressional debates over the future of RFE and RL. Since
1977, the stations have broadcast a uniform identification
statement that mentions U.S. governmental financial support.
It is most unlikely that listeners do not associate the
stations with U.S. governmental policy, whatever their
claims of independence from the government. What RFE and
RL say is almost certain to be taken as a reflection of
that policy.

There seems little doubt that the stations do continue
to attract many listeners. Radio stations within the target
areas have improved considerably over the past 30 years, and
are much livelier, more entertaining and even more timely
than they used to be. Still, newscasts and other information programs remain their Achilles' heel, because there
are still many news items which they broadcast late, incompletely or not at all, ranging from airplane crashes to
labor unrest to changes in political leadership. RFE and

RL, thanks to their elaborate information-gathering system, can provide listeners with quicker, more detailed accounts of events taking place within and among the target countries, and with informed analysis of those events. Some of that information is available through BBC, VOA, Deutsche Welle and other stations, but the combined total of their broadcast hours in a given Eastern European or Soviet language rarely equals what RFE and RL provide.

However, the stations are concerned about the composition of their audiences. A major persuasive element in RFE fund raising campaigns in the 1950s and 1960s was that young people were the best hope for eventual change in Eastern and Central Europe; therefore, it was especially important that they have access to a "voice of truth". By the 1970s, RFE/RL audience research was revealing that numbers of younger listeners were declining for several of the services. RFE and RL staff feel that this is probably due to two factors: the superannuation of writers and announcers for some of the services (many people have been with the stations since the early to mid-1950s, and may well sound as if they come from and are speaking to an older generation),[51] and a climate of apathy among younger people, described in one BIB Annual Report as an "apolitical" or "non-political" trend.[52]

As the stations enter their fourth decade, they appear to face much the same situation as does RIAS: citizens of the target countries have, to varying degrees, reached a modus vivendi with their respective governments, and they have seen their own standards of living rise. If they are aware of higher standards of living elsewhere, or of the shortcomings of their governments, it won't necessarily follow that they wish to be reminded continually of those things. RFE and RL have done a great deal to "objectify" the tone and content of their broadcasts during the 1970s, but when all is said and done, those broadcasts still are critical in tone. The establishment and maintenance of credibility do not rest on an abstract definition of truth; they have far more to do with what listeners are willing to accept as credible. While that is true for all international stations, it seems especially so for stations which have as their most basic purpose the transmission of information about life in someone else's country.

OTHER CIA RADIO OPERATIONS

During the time they were financed and administered by CIA, RFE and RL were far and away the Agency's largest radio operations. However, CIA has been and continues to be involved in a wide variety of other radio activities; the following should give some idea of their range.

Radio Free Asia (1951-1955)

Developed as part of the "arsenal" of radio stations
that was supposed to help bring about the liberation of
Communist nations, RFA soon proved to be less useful than
RFE or RL. Its administrative and programing headquarters
was in San Francisco, where it prepared taped material for
placement over stations in Asia and the Pacific (e.g.
station DZBB in Quezon City, the Philippines). It also
broadcast from transmitters in San Francisco and on Guam.
The Peoples' Republic of China was the chief target of RFA
broadcasts; however, few Chinese listeners had private broadcast receivers, and fewer still had receivers capable of
picking up shortwave broadcasts. Furthermore, RFA never
managed to develop the elaborate information-gathering
system that characterized RIAS, RFE and RL, so it was unable
to serve very effectively as an alternate source of information on daily events. Also, several countries and
religious organizations, such as The Republic of China-
Taiwan, the Far East Broadcasting Company in the Philippines, became involved in broadcasting anti-Communist
material to listeners in the Peoples' Republic during the
early 1950s, thus reducing the need for RFA broadcasts.[53]

Radio Swan-Radio Americas (1960-1967?)

Radio Swan closely resembled the tactically-oriented
"black" propaganda stations so common in World War II. Like
them, it operated under a false identity and for a limited
purpose. It supposedly was operated by the "Gibralter
Steamship Line" as a commercial venture earning profits
through the sale of advertising time. (There is no evidence
that it sold as much as one minute of time). It supposedly
was directed at Spanish-speaking listeners throughout
Central America and the Caribbean. In fact, it was aimed at
Spanish-speaking listeners in Cuba, and its intent from the
time of its first broadcasts in May 1960 was to discredit
the Castro Government and help to prepare the way for the
"liberation" of Cuba by Cuban exile forces. Presumably,
once the Castro government had been deposed, the station
would go out of existence.
    Radio Swan was located on Great Swan Island, which at
that time was claimed by both the U.S. and Honduran governments, and from which the station's 50,000 watt medium wave

transmitter could beam an unobstructed signal north to Cuba.
The Cuban media reacted quickly to it, calling it "a new
aggression of imperialistic North America."[54]

The station's usual fare of attacks on the Castro government, interviews with Cuban exiles in the United States, and
music, began to include coded messages, supposedly to anti-
Castro forces within Cuba, as preparations for the "Bay of
Pigs" invasion increased. Finally, when the invasion was
launched on April 17, 1961, Radio Swan urged its support:

> Forces loyal to the Revolutionary Council
> have carried out a general uprising on a large
> scale on the island of Cuba. . . . the militia
> in which Castro placed his confidence appears
> to be possessed by a state of panic. . . . An
> army of liberation is in the island of Cuba to
> fight with you against the Communist tyranny of
> the unbalanced Fidel Castro . . . attack the
> Fidelista wherever he may be found. Listen for
> instructions on the radio, comply with them and
> communicate your actions by radio. To victory,
> Cubans![55]

Victory did not come, but Radio Swan continued to broadcast, albeit in a less specifically revolutionary vein. The
station's name was changed to Radio Americas within a year,
and it remained in service for several more years. It may
have resurfaced in the late 1970s: a Czechoslovak book on
CIA activities cites a Honduran newspaper as claiming that
the station had reappeared in the Honduran city of San
Pedro Sula around 1975, that it was run by a group of Cuban
exiles working under CIA direction, and that it "spews
forth anti-communist poison against the country's most
honest citizens," attacks the Castro government, supports
the Pinochet government of Chile, etc.[56] There is a Radio
Swan de Honduras in San Pedro Sula, it does broadcast over a
very powerful transmitter by Honduran standards (25 kW--just
half the power of the "old" Radio Swan), and it utilizes the
same medium and short wave frequencies as did its alleged
predecessor. In response to my queries about the "new"
Swan, CIA labelled it a "sensitive" matter and provided no
details on it.[57]

Stations on Foreign Soil

From time to time, CIA has set up field (portable)
transmitters in other countries, in order to broadcast to
their immediate neighbors. There may have been such an

operation from Honduras in 1954, when a clandestine station
began to broadcast anti-communist material into Guatemala,
although specific evidence of CIA involvement is lacking.[58]
Marchetti and Marks mention the Agency's establishment of
clandestine stations on Taiwan in the mid-1960s for the
purpose of exploiting popular discontent with "Red Guard"
activities in the PRC.[59] A CIA clandestine station set up
in Laos in 1971 attempted to insure that exiled Cambodian
Prince Sihanouk would find little popular support for his
return by imitating his voice and having him appear to
"exort young women in 'liberated areas' [of Cambodia] to aid
the cause by sleeping with the valiant Viet Cong."[60]

The Agency has also "borrowed" facilities in friendly
countries for use in transmitting clandestine broadcasts.
In May 1980, a station calling itself "The(Free?) Voice of
Iran" began to broadcast from Egypt to Iran. Its programs
contained Iranian popular music and news and information.
The Ayatollah Khomeini was called "racist and fascist" and
there were calls for the "liberation of Iran" and appeals to
Iranians to "take guns into your hands" to accomplish it.
CIA would not confirm or deny its involvement, but other
U.S. government officials did confirm it.[61]

Agency Support for "Legitimate" Stations

Perhaps the hardest form of CIA support for radio
operations to prove is Agency involvement with "legitimate"
stations. As the 1967 Ramparts magazine article (footnote
13) and numerous books (e.g. Agee, Inside the Company) have
shown, money furnished by the Agency for various activities
can be "laundered" to the point where its origins are
almost impossible to trace. Inferentially, CIA would appear
to have been involved in the broadcast activities of several
"legitimate" stations. For example, in February 1963, Radio
Liberty reached an agreement with Charlotte, North Carolina
radio station WBT (50 kW, medium wave) for the transmission
of RL Russian language broadcasts to Soviet personnel
stationed in Cuba.[62] It is quite possible that WBT management did not know of CIA connections with RL.

Just as inferential is CIA involvement with station
WRUL. As I pointed out in the previous chapter, WRUL
probably has the best claim to the title of "first international radio station in America". During the 1930s, it
was also a highly unusual international station, in that it
broadcast educational programs, partly with the support of
the Rockerfeller Foundation. When war broke out in Europe
in 1939, British intelligence "infiltrated" the station and
began using portions of broadcast time to carry the views of

exiles from various European countries then under Nazi
rule.[63] Some 20 years later, WRUL assisted in another intelligence organization effort, as it made available for
retransmission over Radio Swan an interview series that it
had developed in April 1960. A Cuban exile conducted interviews with other Cuban exiles, and their frequent criticisms
of Castro accorded well with Radio Swan's broadcast policy.
It's unlikely that WRUL owner Walter Lemmon would have been
unaware of Swan's CIA connections, but it is uncertain
whether Lemmon offered the series upon specific request from
the CIA.[64]

CONCLUSION

When Marchetti and Marks wrote about the Central Intelligence Agency, they noted that it was only one of
several U.S. governmental organizations involved in intelligence activities; furthermore, it was neither the largest
nor, seemingly, most powerful of those organizations. The
Voice of America appears to be in much the same position
where U.S. international radio is concerned: RFE and RL
feature a larger combined total of broadcast hours than does
VOA, and a combined budget of approximately the same size.
Then there are RIAS, AFRTS, the various overseas armed
forces stations, and a scattering of CIA operations. There
is no mechanism for coordinating the stations, just as
there appears to be no mechanism for coordinating the
"intelligence establishment". Even within CIA, it seems
possible for the left hand to be unaware of what the right
hand is doing: some radio operations come under the jurisdiction of the Covert Action branch of CIA's Clandestine
Services, while others may be assigned elsewhere.[65]
    Why does the U.S. government need so many broadcast
outlets? There is no simple answer, but the State Department, the National Security Council and the CIA have at one
time or another seen VOA as inappropriate or underbudgeted
for the particular tasks they had in mind. But particular
missions have a way of becoming general ones, and RFE, RL,
RIAS, the U.S. military stations and even perhaps Radio
Swan have acquired a life of their own, with their staff
members and supporters lobbying vigorously on their behalf.[66]
The U.S. government also can excuse itself from responsibility for "objectionable" broadcasts made over the clandestine or the "publicly funded, privately operated" stations, all the while profiting from the diversity of
messages they are able to transmit. Yet that very diversity
adds to the potential for listener confusion regarding U.S.
policies, and increases the possibility that stations that

come to be disbelieved will have a "guilt by association"
effect on other stations.

There is also some question as to how much right one
nation has to so much space in the frequency spectrum,
especially when that spectrum is so overcrowded. Erik
Barnouw once referred to "An air already crowded with
American transmissions . . ." and he invoked this phrase
in connection with the initial broadcasts of Radio Liberation from Bolshevism (Radio Liberty) in 1953.[67] Expansion
of U.S. government international broadcasting activity since
that time, with no commensurate expansion of the frequency
spectrum for radio, has added to that crowding. Virtually
every nation that engaged in international broadcasting in
1953 has expanded its services, too, but only the USSR
comes close to matching the U.S. record for number and
variety of services--and it certainly does not have international religious stations!

NOTES

    1. My article, "The World in the Pentagon's Shadow,"
Educational Broadcasting Review 2 (April 1971):31-48,
provides a more detailed account of the early years of armed
forces radio.

    2. See "Under Military Control," Time 91 (January 5,
1968):57; Randall Moody, "The Armed Forces Broadcast News
System: Vietnam Version," Journalism Quarterly 47 (Spring
1970):27-30; Charles Moore, "Censorship of AFVN News in
Vietnam," Journal of Broadcasting 15 (Fall 1971):387-395.

    3. The unit includes a number of "horror stories"
which illustrate lack of sensitivity, e.g., a U.S. armed
forces station in Turkey playing American popular music at
a time when the Turkish national radio service was "in
mourning" for a deceased national leader and was playing
suitably sombre music.

    4. Those and other assumptions were reflected in
various newspaper articles written in the 1960s, e.g. Jack
Gould, "A Voice That Europe Trusts," New York Times,
April 17, 1966.

    5. Browne, "The World," p. 46, footnote 24.

    6. Interview with Robert Harlan, Program Manager, AFN
Frankfurt, August 1967.

    7. More complete details on RIAS' activities from 1946
to 1960 are available in my Ph.D. dissertation, "History and
Programing Policies of RIAS: Radio in the American Sector
of Berlin," University of Michigan, February 1961. My
article "RIAS Berlin: A Case Study of a Cold War Broadcast
Operation," Journal of Broadcasting 10 (Spring 1966):119-

135, provides a summary of the dissertation and information on the period 1961-1964.

8. Browne, "History," pp. 296-297. See also Roy Rowan, "Pinsel Propaganda," <u>Life</u> 31 (December 3, 1950):27-28.

9. The station has long since dropped the use of its full title for purposes of station identification. "Radio in the American Sector of Berlin" was lengthy, formal and specifically identified the station with the United States. It was succeeded by "RIAS: A Free Voice of the Free World," and then by the present station identification "RIAS Berlin."

10. RIAS broadcasts do not contain any acknowledgement of U.S. support, but East German media frequently refer to it, and it is unlikely that most East Germans are not aware of it.

11. Radio Liberty generally avoided making any public appeals, preferring instead to claim that it received most of its support through corporate donors, which was true enough, inasmuch as the CIA funneled most of its support through corporate structures of one sort or another.

12. U.S. governmental support for the stations was an ill-kept secret from the beginning: an International News Service dispatch of March 11, 1953 notes a statement by George Creel (who had headed U.S. government informational activities in World War I) that VOA had proven so ineffective that RFE and Radio Free Asia had to be developed, "both supposedly supported by public subscription but secretly aided by federal funds." Cited in Eugene V. Castle, <u>Billions, Blunders and Baloney</u> (New York: Devin-Adair Company, 1955), pp. 168-169.

13. Sol Stern, "A Short Account of International Politics and the Cold War with Particular Reference to the NSA, CIA, etc." <u>Ramparts</u> 5 (March 1967):29-38, noted some CIA-supported activities and the foundations which were used to channel support. A February 21, 1967 article in the New York <u>Times</u> (E.W. Kenworthy, "Hobby Foundation of Houston Affirms CIA Tie," p. 32) linked CIA, the Hobby Foundation and RFE. Several articles then appeared in which called for a dissolution of the connection, e.g., Jack Gould, "A New Twist for Espionage," New York <u>Times</u>, March 14, 1967, p. 12. When I visited RFE and RL offices in New York and Munich in August 1967, several staff members told me that they wondered how long the stations would be able to continue. They were convinced that U.S. public opinion in general, and congressional opinion in particular, would soon force the stations off the air.

14. Albanian was dropped because RFE officials felt that too few Albanians had unfettered access to radio receivers to make the broadcasts worthwhile.

15. Allan Michie, <u>Voices Through the Iron Curtain</u> (New York: Dodd-Mead, 1963), p. 71.

16. "News From Behind the Iron Curtain," October 1954, cited in Donald Shanor, "The New Voice of Radio Free Europe," (New York: Columbia University) Journalism Research Memorandum GSJ-68-1, 1968, p. 27.

17. Robert Holt, Radio Free Europe (Minneapolis: University of Minnesota Press, 1958), Shanor and Michie all contain numerous references to staff backgrounds, e.g. Jan Nowak, Head of RFE's Polish Service for nearly three decades until his retirement in the late 1970s, had worked for the BBC Polish Service, albeit after World War II.

18. Shanor, "New Voice," pp. 26-27. Shanor's interviews with "exile" staff took place long after that period, so there could be a certain amount of self-justification in some of the responses he received.

19. In fact, a number of RFE broadcasts specifically asked listeners not to think in terms of armed uprisings; see Shanor, Ibid., p. 28, and Holt, RFE, p. 175.

20. Shanor, Ibid.

21. Shanor, Ibid.

22. Holt, RFE, p. 175.

23. Holt, Ibid., Chapter 10, passim.

24. Holt, Ibid., pp. 186-187.

25. Michie, Voices, p. 258. Michie also indicates that two other specifically encouraging broadcasts were done by a fictional "Colonel Bell." The device of a fictitious military expert was used quite widely by VOA and BBC in World War II; see Chapter 3, pp. 76-77.

26. Michie, Ibid., p. 260.

27. Michie, Ibid., pp. 261-263. Shanor, "New Voice", discusses the West German investigation only, and Holt simply notes that particular investigation.

28. Michie, Ibid., pp. 265-266. RFE's role in the Hungarian revolution was the subject of literally dozens of newspaper and magazine articles, many of them condemnatory, e.g., Leslie Bain, "Have We Failed in Hungary?", The Reporter, January 24, 1957. A summation of the anti-RFE arguments appears in D.F. Fleming, The Cold War and Its Origins (New York: Doubleday, 1961), pp. 806-814.

29. Holt, RFE, pp. 208-212, provides an excellent analysis of this issue. Shanor, "New Voice", pp. 25-26, cites the statement of one RFE exile editor: "The policy [of liberation] was so ambiguous and vague . . ."

30. My own discussion with heads of audience research units in the BBC, DW and VOA-USIA from 1967 to the present have elicited a consistent response: those individuals acknowledge the extreme difficulty of conducting such research, but all are doubtful of its accuracy.

31. Certain Eastern Europeans claim to have worked for RFE in order to gather information for their intelligence services. Radio Prague's North American Services broadcast

an interview on September 26, 1975 in which an individual
claimed to have worked for one of the research firms employed
by RFE; he stated that he, and other researchers he knew,
simply filled out the questionnaire forms in their apart-
ments, and submitted them as valid interview data. Radio
Free Europe has responded to some of this criticism by
noting that it attempts to correct for "deviant" or even
fictitious responses. See "The Method of Continuous and
Comparative Sampling," Audience Research Department, Radio
Free Europe, September 1975. In my own discussions with
audience research staff at RFE in August 1967 and September
1975, I have felt that quality control of research was
indeed a problem for that staff. James Price, "Radio Free
Europe--A Survey and Analysis" (Washington, D.C.: Library
of Congress, March 22, 1972) contains an assessment of RFE's
research practices by Lorand Szalay (pp. 1-8, Annex A); it
is generally positive.

32. Ithiel de Sola Pool and associates have applied a
computer simulation technique to data gathered by RL in the
early and mid-1970s; their findings appear in highly sum-
marized form in the Board for International Broadcasting's
Fourth Annual Report (1978), Washington, D.C.: Board for
International Broadcasting, 1978, pp. 22-24. Joseph Whelan,
"Radio Liberty--A Study of its Origins, Structure, Policy,
Programming and Effectiveness" (Washington, D.C.: Library of
Congress, March 22, 1972), pp. 310-319, contains an evalua-
tion (positive) of RL's research practices.

33. The situation remained much the same in the 1970s;
see a series of RFE research reports for the various RFE
target countries entitled "Listening to Western Radio in
_____," and released between May and July 1975. The most
recent study, "Listening to Western Radio in East Europe,
1979 to 1980," RFE-RL Audience and Opinion Research, East
Europe Area, January 1981, shows strong overall listening
figures for RFE (usually 30 to 50 per cent once a week or
more), but provides no demographic breakouts.

34. A list of editorial policy restraints appears in
the BIB Fourth Annual Report, pp. 48-49; these are two
particularly relevant provisions:

5. Avoidance of tactical advice, by which
is meant recommendations for specific action in
particular cases, except in unusual circumstances, and then only to calm moods in tense
situations. . . . Such advice is likely to be
resented and, if acted upon, could cause harm to
the people involved.

8. Avoidance of any suggestion that might
lead audiences to believe that, in the event of
international crisis or civil disorder, the West
might intervene militarily in any part of the
broadcast area.

35.   "The Right to Know," Report of the Presidential
Study Commission on International Radio Broadcasting
(Washington, D.C.: U.S. Government Printing Office, 1973).

36.   U.S. Congress, Senate Committee on Foreign Relations, Public Financing of Radio Free Europe and Radio
Liberty, 92nd Congress, 1st Session, 1971, p. 39.

37.   U.S. Congress, Senate Committee on Foreign
Relations, Hearings on the Establishment of the Board for
International Broadcasting, 93rd Congress, 1st Session, 1973,
p. 102.

38.   Whelan, Radio Liberty", p. 180.

39.   James Oliver, "Comparison of the Russian Services
of the Four Major Broadcasters (VOA, BBC, DW, RL),"
(Washington, D.C.: Office of Research, U.S. Information
Agency, Report R-8-75, July 28, 1975), includes a fairly
detailed analysis of RL programing for the week of June
9-15, 1974. The USIA-prepared overview of the findings
notes that "RL is highly critical of the Soviet system, its
government and policies, but very sympathetic towards the
Soviet people, especially anti-regime groups and individuals"
(p. ii).

40.   Comptroller General of the United States, "Suggestions to Improve Management of Radio Free Europe, Radio
Liberty," Report to the Congress, June 25, 1976. The same
arguments surfaced again in the late 1970s; see BIB Sixth
Annual Report, 1980, pp. 32-37.

41.   The transmitter base on Taiwan was closed down as
an economy measure. Interview, Robert Redlich, Office of
Public Information, RL, Munich, September 9, 1975. Redlich
added that RL also considered the Far East portion of the
Soviet Union to be strategically less important that its
other areas. A letter to me from Anatole Shub of BIB,
July 14, 1981, states that the Taiwan site was considered
too far away from the target area to be effective.

42.   Patrick Chapman, "Portuguese Say RFE Gave 'Assurances' on Broadcasts," Washington Post, June 15, 1975,
p. A20; Richard Weintraub, "No Policy Change, RFE Officials
Say," Washington Post, June 15, 1975; Miguel Acoca, "Spain
Gives U.S. Radio Six Months," Washington Post, March 18,
1976, p. A34; "Spanish May Extend Radio Liberty Setup,"
New York Times, March 18, 1976, p. 8.

43.   "Jimmy Carter on Radio Free Europe and Radio
Liberty," Jimmy Carter Presidential Campaign Statement,
P.O. Box 1976, Atlanta, Georgia, undated, probably summer
1976.

44.   Office of the President, Report on International
Broadcasting, submitted by the President of the United
States to Congress, March 22, 1977. Reprinted in BIB
Fourth Annual Report, pp. 39-42.

45.   On my first visit to RL in August 1967, several

staff members expressed the hope that the station would
develop broadcast services for the Baltic republics. While
Congress was interested in the initiation of such services,
partly because of lobbying by exile organizations, RL management also worked for their initiation. One reason for RL's
interest appeared to be their perception of the citizens of
the Baltic republics as having a greater sense of national
tradition than did many areas of the USSR and as possessing
a greater degree of resentment of the Soviet government and
a greater disdain for Russian culture than did many of the
Soviet republics. While RL has never followed a policy of
encouraging the breakup of the Soviet Union by playing to
the nationalist sentiments of its component republics, there
is no doubt in my mind that some of its broadcasts are designed to appeal to those sentiments, for whatever ultimate
purpose.

46. U.S. Congress, House of Representatives, Committee
on Foreign Affairs, Subcommittee on International Operations,
"Allegations Concerning the Romanian Service of RFE,"
February 21, 1980.

47. Office of the Comptroller General, "Improvements
Made, Some Still Needed in Management of Radio Free Europe/
Radio Liberty," Report to the Congress, ID-81-16, March 2,
1981, pp. 9-12.

48. Jack Anderson, "Radio Liberty Making Static on the
Air," Washington Post, April 14, 1981, p. B15. Telephone
interview with Critchlow on October 15, 1981. Anderson also
wrote an article about transmitter problems at RFE/RL; see
"The Ante Rises Over Radio Free Europe," Washington Post,
July 25, 1981, p. B7.

49. RFE continues to broadcast in its original languages, with the exception of Albanian; RL broadcasts one
service in Russian and another in Russian, Byelorussian,
Ukrainian, Armenian, Georgian, Tatar-Bashkir, Azeri,
Estonian, Latvian, Lithuanian, Kazak, Uzbek, Kirghiz, Tajik,
and Turkmen. Uighur was dropped in 1978.

50. See A.E. Sulzberger, "U.S. Overseas Radio Stirs
Dispute Again," New York Times, May 15, 1980, p. 17. Some
members of the U.S. Senate Foreign Relations Committee felt
that "intelligence community pressure" was being applied to
influence the appointment of BIB members more compatible
with their views.

51. Certain of the services have been able to recruit
younger staff over the past decade or so: several Czecho-
slovakians joined RFE following the 1968 uprising, and the
Russian language service benefitted greatly from the
emigration of Soviet Jews in the early to mid-1970s. Interview, Jean LeCach, Personnel Division, Radio Liberty,
September 9, 1975. However, sometimes there are strong
differences of opinion between younger and older staff

members; BIB took note of those tensions in its Fourth Annual
Report, p. 31.
      52. Second Annual Report, p. 24 (footnote 6). However,
a 1978 RFE research report, "East European Youth and Various
Value Systems," December 1978, concludes that young people
in Eastern and Central Europe are for the most part "far
more idealistic than all segments of the older generation in
spite of a repressive social order. . . ." (p. 12). BIB's
Fifth Annual Report, 1979, essentially repeats the Second
Annual Report; see p. 22.
      53. David W. Conde, CIA: Core of the Cancer (New
Delhi: Entente Private Limited, 1970), claims that following
RFA's demise, "some of the [RFA] radio stations in the
Pacific became outlets for 'Christian religions' and always
identified the close relationship between 'God' and the
United States," (p. 111). Conde notes the creation of
another Radio Free Asia in 1966, but does not directly state
that it is financed by CIA (p. 115). The station he refers
to actually was called Radio of Free Asia. It had its headquarters in Washington, D.C., and was part of the Korean
Cultural and Freedom Foundation, which conducted a fund-
raising campaign much like RFE's. The station broadcast
through leased facilities, primarily in South Korea, and
attempted to reach listeners in the PRC and North Korea.
ROFA may or may not have received CIA support, but in 1971
the U.S. Department of Justice decided not to press an
investigation into whether it was an agent of the South
Korean government, and thus in violation of the Foreign
Agent's Registration Act. See Anthony Marro, "Republican
Ties to Korea Lobby Under Scrutiny," New York Times, June 8,
1977, p. A18. For further details on RFA, see Donald
Feinstein, "Free Voices in the Battle for Men's Minds,"
Journalism Quarterly 31 (Spring 1954):193-200.
      54. "American Radio in the Caribbean Counters Red
Campaign in Cuba," New York Times, September 9, 1960, p. 1+.
See also "Cuba Sees 'Aggression'," New York Times, September
15, 1960, p. 12.
      55. David Wise and Thomas Ross, The Invisible
Government (New York: Random House, 1964), pp. 54-55. Wise
and Ross devote an entire chapter to Radio Swan (Chapter 24),
and include several excerpts from the station's broadcasts.
Also useful is Peter Wyden, Bay of Pigs: The Untold Story
(New York: Simon and Schuster, 1979), especially pp. 23, 118,
208-209.
      56. From Vanguardia Revolucionaria, 21 de Junio de
1975, cited in Vitaly Petrusenko, A Dangerous Game: CIA
and the Mass Media (Prague: Interpress, no date, probably
1977), p. 28.
      57. Letter to me from U.S. Congressman William
Frenzel (R., Minnesota), December 16, 1980.

58. Paul F. Kennedy, "Guatemalans Get Appeal to
Revolt," New York Times, May 5, 1954, p. 17.

59. Victor Marchetti and John D. Marks, The CIA and the
Cult of Intelligence (New York: Alfred A. Knopf, 1974),
pp. 156-160.

60. Newsweek, November 22, 1971, p. 39.

61. David Binder, "U.S. Concedes it is Behind Anti-
Khomeini Broadcasts," New York Times, June 29, 1980, Section
1, p. 3. It is probable that the station in question is the
"Voice of Iran," as the "Free Voice of Iran" almost certainly
operates from Baghdad. Some four or five different clandestine stations were directed at Iran from various countries
in 1981!

62. "Radio Liberty to Reach Cuba," New York Times,
February 21, 1963, p. 5. RL also sent anti-Communist
Spanish language tape recordings to stations throughout Latin
America during the 1960s. The CIA furnished financial
support to the Cuban Freedom Committee for a group called
Christianform; the Committee prepared Spanish language tapes
attacking the Castro government, and arranged for them to be
broadcast over stations in Miami, Key West and New Orleans;
see Robert G. Sherill, "The Beneficient CIA," The Nation 202,
May 9, 1966, pp. 542+.

63. H. Montgomery Hyde, The Quiet Canadian (London:
Hamish Hamilton, 1962), pp. 157-162; also Corey Ford,
Donovan of the O.S.S. (Boston: Little, Brown, 1970), p. 113.

64. Wise and Ross, Government, p. 318, p. 333. See
also "American Radio in the Caribbean," New York Times,
September 9, 1960, p. 1+.

65. Marchetti and Marks, CIA, p. 162.

66. Marchetti and Marks, Ibid., p. 155, indicate that
a number of CIA officials were ready to cease financial
support of RFE and RL well before the 1967 revelations, on
the grounds that the stations were no longer that useful to
the Agency; however, station staff, certain CIA staff and
various influential supporters of the stations were able to
argue for continuation of CIA support.

67. Erik Barnouw, The Image Empire (New York: Oxford
University Press, 1970), p. 92.

6

BBC'S EXTERNAL SERVICES: PACE-SETTER FOR THE FIELD?

BBC's External Broadcasting Services have been around for so long and have achieved such fame that many listeners probably consider the station to be the originator of international radio. It wasn't, by at least five years.[1] And for the first six years of its existence, it confined itself to one form of international broadcasting: an "Empire Service" to English speaking listeners in Great Britain's many colonies, protectorates and Commonwealth partner nations throughout the world.[2] However, the rise of fascism in Europe thrust upon BBC a new mission: the re-futation of propaganda broadcasts by Italy to the Middle East (a good share of which was then under some form of British rule) and by Germany and Italy to Europe and Latin America.

This new mission was not without cost. During its initial period as Empire Service, this branch of BBC had been financed as was the rest of the BBC: through the annual license fee levied upon owners of individual radio sets in British households. Control over the broadcast content of the Empire Service remained in the hands of BBC itself. But when BBC began in 1938 to broadcast in Arabic (in order to counteract the Arabic broadcasts of Italy's Radio Bari), and soon after in various other languages, it was now serving the needs of British foreign policy. By the same token, it was not considered right that the British listener should bear the additional costs of these new and frequently expensive services. The British Foreign Office was willing to step in with some financial support, but it also wanted to exercise some measure of guidance.[3]

WORLD WAR II

BBC resisted Foreign Office controls with partial success, but wartime necessities sealed the bargain: the

161

Empire Service remained largely master of its own house where English-language broadcasts were concerned, while the new foreign language services were subject to guidance and even a measure of control on the part of the Foreign Office, the Political Warfare Executive, the Special Operations Executive, the Ministry of Information and others. Never again did BBC enjoy complete internal control of its foreign broadcasting.[4] But World War II brought BBC something else that it _has_ enjoyed ever since: its reputation for credibility. That did not develop overnight; reporting of the Battle of Norway (1940) appears to have been notably inaccurate.[5] Yet, by making greater and greater efforts to report war news as carefully and accurately as possible, even when the news was not in Britain's favor (and that was very frequent in the first few years of the war), BBC did establish a reputation for telling the truth, even when it hurt. BBC officials had to struggle with military departments to obtain accurate figures on such matters as exact numbers of losses of British aircraft.

BBC received a great deal of criticism from a number of officials for publicizing the extent of Britain's losses,[6] but the effect on listeners in Europe must have been devastating, especially if one lived in Germany. It was possible for German radio to announce that the _Luftwaffe_ had shot down, say, 20 British planes, and for BBC to announce that Britain had lost 21. This probably made some listeners wonder at BBC's sanity or loyalty, but it also helped to insure that, when BBC said that 25 German planes had been shot down and German radio said that five had been lost, the British account would be believed. There was a touch of the Machiavellian to this policy, however; it was well summarized by British World War II propaganda expert (and later leading political figure in the Labour Party) Richard H.S. Crossman:

> From what I am saying, there arises this conclusion: if the art of propaganda is to conceal that you are doing propaganda, then the central substance of propaganda is hard, correct information. . . . If you give a man the correct information for seven years, he may believe the incorrect information on the first day of the eighth year when it is necessary, from your point of view, that he should do so.[7]

The first day of the eighth year never came. Such deceptive broadcasting as had to be done was handled largely by the various clandestine stations of the sorts described in Chapters 2 and 3—for example, _Gustave Siegfried Eins_. BBC was concerned that listeners might not be able to

distinguish between itself and these other stations, although
there was a period early in the war when its German Forces
Programme may have been used to disseminate misleading
information.[8] Also, at various times during the war, some
of the BBC programs carried messages in code for Allied
agents and resistance groups operating within enemy-held
territory.[9] By and large, however, the station was able to
avoid dealing in half-truths, polemics and espionage-related
activities.

More than once during the war, BBC had difficulties with
the Foreign Office, particularly over the question of how to
deal with the broadcast activities of exiles from the occupied European nations. Ironically, John Reith, who had
been Director-General of the entire BBC from its inception
until 1938, pushed hard for direct Ministry of Information
control of the overseas broadcasting services (languages
other than English) during World War II.[10] That never
occurred, but relations between the Foreign Office, the
Ministry of Information and BBC were not always good.[11]

FROM WAR'S END TO SUEZ

When the Second World War ended, the British faced the
question, much as had the Americans, of what to do with
international radio broadcasting. It may have been easier
for BBC to answer than it was for VOA, since the only
British international broadcast station that had existed
prior to the war was BBC. But the nature of that operation
had expanded considerably. Where it had broadcast solely
in English up to 1938, drawing most of its material from BBC
domestic radio, it now employed over three dozen foreign
languages, all of which required original programs or translations of existing program material.

Also, Great Britain faced extreme financial austerity
just after World War II, which led some members of Parliament and the government to think of the BBC overseas services
as a potential contributor to budget trimming. (After all,
few in Great Britain would be inconvenienced directly by its
reduction!) Trimmers argued that the English service could
stay, inasmuch as there was still a British Commonwealth
and a British Empire. Some of the European languages still
might be useful. A few, such as Russian, might even be
added (Russian was, in December 1946), given signs of
deterioration in East-West relations. But much else should
go. Numerous "internationalists" within and outside of
Parliament, and the BBC itself, plus a changing world in
which Communism was spreading and colonial empires fading,
tipped the balance, and the overseas services survived, with
relatively small cuts.[12]

That did not mean that governmental pressures, whether from the Foreign or Colonial Offices, Parliament, or wherever, ceased. During the early 1950s, the BBC External Services (a title used to cover all of the BBC international broadcast activities since 1948) suffered occasional budget cuts and a fair measure of criticism for not being "tough enough on Communism."[13]   That did not mean that BBC took a neutral position in the Cold War. Its broadcasts could and often did sound very "tough", sometimes assuming forms reminiscent of World War II, as in this satirical poem on the German service's weekly program "The Westerly-Easterly Ivan":

Refrain: There was a big fat rat
           That ate and ate
           The fat rat had all in plenty

1.   It crept from the Kremlin to Poland
     It hauled away steel and coal
     It took whatever it found
     It took the whole country

2.   It crept in one short day
     From the Kremlin into old Prague
     It ate itself into Budapest
     And celebrated a great feast . . .

4.   It ate itself into the GDR
     The rat was a great lord
     It said: "Goatee,* bleat, bleat, bleat!"
     It ate away all the machines

5.   (partial)
     Yet as the rat was smacking its lips
     What happened was: the rat burst

6.   Then there was no big rat
     That ate and ate
     Over the dead, Red rat
     Finally grew the grass.[14]

Also, many of the broadcast transmitters were beginning to show their age, and the other major international broadcasters, Radio Moscow and VOA chief among them, were building more and more transmitters, and as a result "outgunning" BBC.[15]

---

*"Goatee" was a term of derision for East German (GDR) Prime Minister Walter Ulbricht, who wore one, hence the "bleat, bleat, bleat" of the "goat".

Perhaps the severest test for the External Services came in 1956, on the occasion of the Anglo-French-Israeli attack on the Suez Canal. Following its long-established tradition of telling the truth even when it hurt, BBC broadcast round-ups of British editorial opinion on the attack, and covered the event thoroughly in newscasts. Since much British reaction was negative, this came through in BBC broadcasts, as did expressions of support for the invasion. Prime Minister Anthony Eden was deeply displeased with the amount of BBC coverage of negative reaction, and one high-ranking BBC staff member subsequently claimed that Eden had plans to take over BBC for the duration of the conflict.[16] Whether the plans existed or not, they were never carried out, and BBC continued to broadcast what it regarded as balanced accounts of British viewpoints on the event. (BBC itself did not comment or editorialize on the situation in the Middle East; a Prescribing Memorandum requires it to "refrain from expressing its own opinion on current affairs or matters of public policy."[17] However, BBC can and does invite commentators from outside the Corporation to air their views).

A number of members of Parliament, including a few from the opposition Labour Party, felt that BBC should have co-operated with the government and at the least scaled down broadcast coverage of viewpoints opposed to official govern-mental policy. The next few years saw considerable question-ing of the External Services by Parliament in the course of appropriations hearings, and the Services did not fare well in terms of budget increases during this period. Also, the Foreign Office, which served (and which continues to serve) as the main channel through which the External Services requested and received their budget, appointed an "observer" to assist in coordinating activities between itself and the External Services.[18]

BBC also was under pressure during the 1950s to reduce its broadcast services to Western Europe, on the assumption that listeners there were already sufficiently well-informed about and friendly toward Great Britain.[19] There were cut-backs, mainly in the Scandinavian languages and Dutch, but French, Italian, German, Spanish and Portuguese remained, although few years pass without some member of Parliament, special government committee or Foreign and Colonial Office (FCO) official calling for their elimination, too. But as European services were being reduced, new language services for the emerging nations of Africa came on the air. In 1957, BBC introduced Hausa, Somali and Swahili. It also began to expand the small amount of special programing in English for Africa that had begun in 1948 with "West African Voices," until today it offers nearly 3½ hours per day of English language news and features for African listeners.

(It also provides 15-30 minutes per day of special service
for English language listeners in South Asia).

GROWTH, CHANGE AND PROBLEMS IN THE 1960S

Already in the 1950s, BBC had begun to broadcast about
British industrial products and services, with a view to
promoting orders from other parts of the world.[20] In the
1960s, this category of broadcasting developed still further,
chiefly through the program "New Ideas", which gives details
each week on three to five new British products available
for export and potentially useful to buyers overseas:

> . . . . [It derives] its lightweight properties
> from the incorporation of an expandable poly-
> styrene bead (?) into the mix. This adds con-
> siderable insulating property to the concrete,
> which should make it very attractive for use in
> countries with extremes in climate, whether
> hot or cold. The blocks can be used for housing
> projects . . . and for load-bearing piles in
> walls and ceilings. One of the potential uses
> for CEMPAL blocks is in disaster zones, where
> lightweight houses have to be built very quickly.
> . . . Behind CEMPAL lies 12 years of research
> and development. The manufacturers are sure that
> they have a product that will find an enormous
> market the world over.
> New Ideas, July 18, 1981

New Ideas hosts invited interested listeners to write
for further information, and they did, by the thousands.
For example, some 12,000 inquiries were addressed to New
Ideas in 1977 and many of the inquiries eventually resulted
in orders. It was also increasingly evident that broadcasts
to listeners elsewhere could help to promote tourism, most
easily from Western Europe, but from other parts of the
world, as well. BBC frequently has offered these two types
of broadcast programing as evidence that the organization
actually helps to bring money into Britain, and thus to some
extent pays its own way.[21]
Money remained something of a problem for BBC in the
1960s. The External Services continued in their attempts
to secure a five-year budgetary allocation, in order to
facilitate long-range planning, but governments were not
sufficiently receptive. Increases in the budget were not
adequate to allow for expansion, and the BBC fell lower in
lists of major international broadcasters, as measured by

weekly hours of transmission and by languages employed. To
some, this was regretable; to others, it was appropriate, in
view of Great Britain's decline as a major world power. The
Foreign Office seemed uncertain as to the relative importance
of international broadcasting, and used its power of pre-
scription of language services to force BBC to drop two of
its languages--Albanian and Hebrew--in the late 1960s.
Whether it did so for reasons of economy or for reasons of
foreign policy is disputed, but it showed once again that
the organization had less than total control of its own
destiny.[22]

As the decade closed, a review committee (Duncan) report
released in mid-1969 praised the BBC's External Services for
a job generally well done, but also expressed the view that
the organization could do without many of its foreign
language services. English, the report stated, was a universal language, especially for the elite, who were assumed
to be the primary target of international broadcasting.
Committee members also felt that language services to
Western Europe and to Latin America could be cut back or
even dropped, the former because listeners there were already
well served by their own media where information about Great
Britain was concerned, the latter because the area was seen
as less crucial to British foreign policy than were other
parts of the world.[23]

Various criticisms of "questionable" programing practices by the External Services added to BBC's problems over
the next several years. As one example, the Rhodesian unilateral declaration of independence had led to BBC's setting
up a transmitter in neighboring Bechuanaland in 1965. A
special Rhodesian service attacking the Smith government was
operated over this transmitter until 1969--a step taken at
the request of the British government, and not on BBC's
initiative. Few thought that it did much good; many, including some BBC staff, felt that it was far too propagandistic to fit in with the general tone of the External
Services.[24]

There also were numerous allegations, chiefly by members
of Parliament, of "Communists in the ranks of the External
Services". This accusation was an old one (see footnote 12)
but it acquired new strength, particularly where the Yugoslav service was concerned.[25] BBC External Service coverage
of the Nigerian Civil War (1967-1970) also sparked a good
deal of controversy, some members of Parliament feeling
that BBC had displayed either pro-Biafran or pro-Federal
Government sentiment (more often the latter).[26]

BBC also came under Parliamentary and press criticism
in 1975 for failing to exercise adequate supervision over
one of its language services--in this case, Portuguese. Two
members of this service were supporters of "left wing"

elements in Portugal, and showed their support by delivering
sarcastically various news items concerning Portuguese
political figures opposed to their viewpoint. BBC's
Managing Director of External Services, Gerard Mansell,
publicly admitted that this had occurred (various Portuguese
politicians had complained about it), and the two announcers
were dismissed, but a few members of Parliament expressed a
desire for a more extensive investigation of supervisory
practices.[27]

Such an investigation never took place, but the controversy over the Portuguese incident illustrated the problem
of adequately supervising translation practices, for news
broadcasts in particular, in a vast, multi-lingual service.
BBC's Controller of European Services, Alexander Lieven,
commissioned in 1975 a study of translation accuracy in newscasts. The study revealed that accuracy was generally high,
but that there were horrendous errors in translation from
time to time, caused by ignorance, sloppiness, or, occasionally, an apparent desire to develop a different interpreta-
tion in the translated item.[28] This led to an attempt on
the part of the External Services management to tighten up
supervisory practices, but the basic problem will never
disappear entirely. And if BBC regards it with particular
seriousness, that is not so much a reflection of its magnitude (which seems in any event to be small) as it is of its
importance in terms of maintaining BBC's reputation for
accuracy and objectivity, which it considers to be one of
its major stocks in trade.

THE DISAPPEARING POUND IN THE 1970S

Few years in the 1970s were without their budgetary
problems, and in 1974 the Foreign Office was rumored to be
considering a large cut in the External Services budget.
BBC resisted this strongly, and publicized the rumor, as
well as many statements from people in Britain and overseas
opposed to any cuts.[29] The cuts never materialized, but the
scenario was repeated, with greater and lesser degrees of
drama, almost every year thereafter. The External Services
budget actually rose from 17 to 55 million pounds between
1974 and 1981, but inflation in Great Britain and the
generally weak performance of the British pound against
most major Western currencies wiped out most of the apparent
gain.

A 1977 report on overseas representation of Great
Britain added to BBC's monetary worries. The report,
compiled by the Central Policy Review Staff, agreed with the
generally positive appraisal made by the Duncan Committee,

but also reached some of the same budget-cutting conclusions, and for some of the same reasons. It felt that many language services could be cut because they were not vital to Britain's overseas interests and/or because they were directed to countries already well informed about Great Britain. It proposed a cutback in all but the "most essential" languages --those spoken in "closed" and/or strategically important countries, such as the USSR, China and the Arab World. It also proposed a cutback in the English language World Service, partly on the grounds that North America and Australia "have access to British culture and information about the UK through newspapers, films, books and the many contacts that exist between them and Britain."[30]

When the Conservative Party returned to power in 1979, it quickly embarked upon a program of fiscal austerity. Prime Minister Margaret Thatcher praised the External Services, but her government proposed a 10 per cent budget cut for them.[31] Again there was a strong show of support for the Services from listeners overseas, the British public and the British press, and the cut was largely deferred, but it resurfaced in 1981. The Foreign Office proposed a cut of roughly three million pounds, and stipulated the language services that should be cut: French to France, Spanish to Spain, Italian, Somali, Portuguese to Brazil, Burmese and Maltese. Some of the supporting arguments sounded much like those raised in the 1977 Central Policy Review Staff report, as did one "tradeoff": the government would cut languages, but would seek to appropriate more money for updating the transmitter system. In the words of the Prime Minister as she addressed the House of Commons on July 6, 1981, ". . . we do think it better that some 33 language services should be properly heard than that 40 should be inadequately heard," but many, including some members of Parliament and the Association of Broadcasting Staff, were skeptical that the Conservative government could or would deliver on its "pledge".[32]

The House of Lords on July 30, 1981 voted 82 to 45 to express their concern over the proposed cut--tantamount to asking the government to reconsider it--and nine Conservatives joined with the majority. The cuts had not been ordered as of October 1981, even though the Foreign Office could do so, and might not be imposed at all,* but BBC staff have little doubt that the 1980s will prove as financially turbulent as were the 1970s.

The various budgetary crises have made it abundantly clear that the External Services need strong shows of support from more than just their listeners. BBC's Board of Governors and domestic broadcast services are one important line of support in that they speak out vigorously against most proposed cuts. The British press generally has

---

*A compromise position emerged at the end of October: the budget would be cut by 1½, rather than 3 million pounds, and Italian, Maltese, Spanish to Spain and the subsidy for the Transcription Services would be halted.

supported the External Services strongly over the years,
both through articles and editorials and through publication of readers' letters praising the Services and arguing
against cuts. Many members of Parliament have spoken in
support of the Services, although some have raised questions:
are the services sufficiently critical in broadcasts to and
about the USSR; are they subject to undue influence by the
government of the day; do broadcasts adequately support
British foreign policy; is there Communist influence at
work within the staff; are the Services cost-efficient?
Often the questions are answered by other M.P.s, and those
answers generally support the Services. But BBC has on the
whole had a far easier time of it in Parliament than has VOA
in Congress!

But it is the Foreign and Colonial Office that presents
the External Services budget to Parliament, and which pre-
scribes its language services and hours of broadcast. Yet,
while there are many contacts between FCO and BBC, including
briefings on policy and discussions of budget, BBC does not
seek FCO guidance, and the latter offers it seldom. BBC
has on two occasions delayed broadcasts upon FCO request--
in 1967 it delayed a reading of Svetlana Stalin's "Letter
to a Friend" so as not to jeopardize discussions about to
be held in Moscow by the British Foreign Secretary, and in
1975 it delayed an interview with an author who had written
a book critical of Ugandan President Idi Amin so as to not
jeopardize FCO negotiations with Amin for release of a
British prisoner--but has always emphasized that it retains
final power of editorial decision.[33]

That does not mean that FCO is disinterested in what the
External Services broadcast. Few months go by without
protests from abroad about specific BBC broadcasts, and many
of them come from British embassies abroad. In some cases,
the embassies are simply conveying protests received from
local government officials, while in others they are indicating their own disagreements with BBC broadcasts. As one
example, BBC broadcasts in Farsi to Iran in the late 1970s
(including an interview with the then-exiled Ayatollah
Khomeini) caused Iranian government officials to protest to
the British Embassy that BBC was being "far too critical" of
the Shah and his government. The Embassy relayed the complaints, but BBC officials indicated that, since the pro-
tested material was not being contested on grounds of in-
accuracy, the broadcasts would continue.[34] BBC officials
listen to Foreign Office officials and request their support
for proposed expansion of language and transmitter services,
but there has not been an FCO observer at Bush House (the
External Services headquarters) since shortly after one was
installed following the Suez Canal episode. The post
disappeared within a matter of months,[35] and BBC officials

have sought to keep an arm's length relationship with the
Foreign Office ever since.[36]

PROGRAMING

The External Services are made up of a European Service,
embracing the 17 European languages broadcast by the BBC,
the Overseas Services, which cover another 22 languages,
and the English Service, whose World Service broadcasts to
the entire world in English for 24 hours a day, with
additional special services for Africa, South Asia and the
Falkland Islands. The combined services were on the air for
over 740 hours a week as of 1981, a figure that has changed
little over the past decade; it was 723 hours in 1970.
The mainstay of the program schedule, at least in terms
of amount of praise as well as quantity of listener response
it elicits, is the news. Newscasts are prepared by the
Central News Room, which culls its material from several wire
services, BBC correspondents overseas, BBC Monitoring Services reports (which include both foreign broadcasts and
press and wire service reports), and other printed material,
including the British domestic press. All of this material
is processed and distributed in the form of regular news
bulletins and subsequently is translated by the individual
language services. Items used by the services are to be
translated as accurately as possible, but there is little
opportunity for anyone not connected with the language
services themselves to regularly monitor the translations
for accuracy.[37]
The network of BBC correspondents overseas is perhaps
the most impressive part of the array of newsroom sources,
because it is the main element that most clearly differentiates BBC from most other international radio stations.
There are some 20 BBC correspondents stationed aboard at any
one time, plus numerous freelance reporters and further BBC
correspondents out on special assignments, and they out-
number similar forces employed by any other international
station.[38] Furthermore, their reports are used not only in
the news broadcasts, but in a variety of other informational
programs: The World Today, Twenty-Four Hours, Outlook.
The average BBC correspondent report is longer and more
carefully detailed than are reports from other international
radio station correspondents and stringers, and often better
written in terms of structure and word choice. Careful
selection and training procedures help to assure generally
high quality for both correspondents and stringers.
Aside from news and other informational broadcasts,
including press and magazine editorial and opinion roundups

and the aforementioned New Ideas, there is a wide variety of entertainment, ranging from pop music (some of it by listener request) to classical music and from comedy skits to serious drama. While some of the entertainment programing, in contrast with the informational programing, is drawn directly from BBC's domestic radio services, a number of programs are not. Pop music, especially by request, has grown in importance over the past 15 years; the World Service in particular carries a number of DJ request shows. There are also dramatic programs written by individuals in other countries and produced by BBC's External Services.

Sports of various kinds also have long been a major element in the program schedule and appear in various forms: reports of scores and highlights from football, cricket, golf and other contests, interviews with figures from the world of sports, and live broadcasts of contests. Few other international broadcasters do as much with this particular category of broadcasting, which BBC considers an excellent means of attracting the attention of a wide variety of listeners--especially listeners who would be hostile to political propaganda.[39] In a similar vein, there is a widely acclaimed and widely rebroadcast "English by Radio" series, which began on the Arabic Service in 1939, and most of the language services now offer lessons in English.

Quite naturally, program choice is widest on the 24-hour-per-day World Service,[40] but a number of other language services provided by the External Services--Arabic, Russian, French, German and Spanish (for Latin America) chief among them--also provide a wide variety of programing. The Arabic Service in particular benefits from a record library of Arabic popular and classical music that would be the envy of most broadcast stations within the Arab World. Some of the other major language services, and a few of the smaller ones, also have substantial record libraries of the music of their countries or areas.

The announcing and writing staff for BBC's World Service comes largely from within Great Britain itself, but a large number of the announcers and writers for the various services other than English are brought in on short-term contracts, ranging from two to five years. A few of those individuals manage to stay on for longer periods, and eventually may become British citizens, but the majority return home and are replaced by fresh recruits (sometimes enlisted by BBC correspondents overseas, as are many overseas stringers). This has the advantage of bringing in announcers and writers who have up-to-date acquaintance with the country to which they will broadcast, including an acquaintance with stylistic changes in the language.[41] Most language desks are supervised by British citizens (many of them naturalized) to better insure adherence to overall policy guidelines.

BBC generally tends toward formality of style in written copy and oral delivery, with disk jockey shows, broadcasts of sports events, the daily "Network Africa" and rebroadcasts of certain domestic programs (e.g. quiz shows such as "Animal, Vegetable or Mineral?" and other programs featuring audience participation) as notable exceptions to the rule. VOA's Breakfast Show has no direct counterpart on BBC, in that BBC treats such elements as news, features and music as separate entities, and seems to feel that some of their impact would be lost if they were to be mixed together in the fashion of the Breakfast Show. The level of comprehension required to follow most BBC broadcasts, whatever the language, is somewhere around a "beginning secondary" standard (eighth or ninth grade in U.S. terms). Few programs demand more, but neither is anything designed for the beginner in any language, as is VOA's Special English. (There was an English-language broadcast of news at dictation speed until around 1970, but it was not simplified English).

By various measures, BBC's programs are not only understood by most of its listeners; they also appear to be widely believed. That may stem in part from the reputation for believeability earned by BBC during World War II, but I have often wondered whether BBC's credibility might also be due to Britain's diminishing role in world politics, so that listeners might regard the BBC as better able to broadcast accurate and complete information because Britain has less of a stake in major events. BBC news items about life within Great Britain may also contribute to that reputation, because some of them present unpleasant aspects of British life, including possible racism:

> A court in the city of Warwick has jailed
> three young white men who made a [word indistinct]
> attack on an Indian temple in a Commonwealth
> club there two months ago. All three had
> travelled to Warwick from the neighboring city
> of Coventry to make the attack. They were
> each sentenced to four years' imprisonment.
> They pleaded guilty, but denied that the
> attacks were racially motivated.
> BBC World Service, News About Britain, July 17, 1981

That reputation might also be enhanced by the station's non-threatening aura. Sports, music and entertainment make up about a third of the typical weekday schedule and almost half of the weekend schedule for the World Service. Plays in various English dialects, some of them almost incomprehensible to a listener who has never heard anything but the Queen's English, or roaring crowds at football matches,

topped by roaring announcers, add to that aura. Could a
station that broadcasts the day's cricket scores, including
those for towns the size of Bourton-on-the-Water, possibly
have any evil intent?

THE AUDIENCE

The External Services have long had a commitment to
discerning as clearly as possible who is in the audience
and what those listeners think about what they receive. The
Audience Research Department of the External Services had
its beginnings in 1946, and has carried out research studies
continuously since that time. Much of its effort involves
preparing, supervising and analyzing results of survey
research studies on BBC and other international broadcast
listening in individual countries or languages. Surveys
generally ask listeners to indicate times of day and
frequency of listening to the BBC and other stations. Surveys undertaken jointly with USICA may also ask listeners
how credible they find certain international stations. In
the West European, Middle Eastern and South Asian nations,
BBC generally ranks at or near the top in frequency of
listening and in credibility. It also does well in those
respects in English-speaking Africa and in Southeast Asia,
but slightly less well in Latin America, at least where
frequency of listening is concerned.
     Each year's BBC Handbook contains a brief summary of
audience research studies conducted by the External
Services during the year. Although those summaries rarely
state it, my own examination of studies done by the BBC,
VOA and other international broadcasters has revealed that
the BBC tends to attract a slightly to much larger share of
older, better-educated, more "significant" (teachers,
government officials, businessmen and women) listeners than
do most of the other international stations.
     A second form of listener research includes the BBC
Listeners' Panel, comprised of listeners who have agreed
to respond to BBC mail questionnaires about specific
External Services programs. There also are questionnaires
mailed to listeners who have recently written to BBC. Thousands of these questionnaires, dealing with listener reactions to everything from pop music programs to presentations of the news to radio drama, have been sent out each
year since 1948, currently in some 15 languages. (In 1979,
over 13,000 questionnaires were returned). In them,
listeners answer questions regarding such matters as frequency of listening, liking for specific announcers, comprehensibility of broadcasts, etc. While these data do not

constitute truly scientific evidence, they do reveal many
specific reactions to specific programs. They also act as
something of an early warning system: if loyal listeners
(as most panel members would be, since they have volunteered
their services) take exception to a program series or
announcer, or find a given broadcast difficult to comprehend, the problem is likely to be even greater for the
larger audience.

The Audience Research Department also has carried out a
laboratory study of sorts. In 1971, it conducted a research
project in Nigeria to determine what sorts of broadcast
material seemed to cause difficulties in comprehension.
Individual Nigerians were played a specially-prepared
tape recording of standard BBC material, then asked specific
questions about their understanding of the material. Words
which caused misunderstandings or temporary loss of comprehension were noted. This small-scale experiment has not
been repeated, in part because of the considerable cost
involved but also in part because of the lack of sufficiently generalizeable conclusions it produced: specific
words caused difficulties for specific listeners, but there
wasn't much of a pattern emerging from the data.[42]

The External Services also receive between 300,000 and
350,000 unsolicited letters from listeners each year, many
of them containing requests for music, some of them requests
for information, some of them simply complimenting BBC, a
few of them criticizing certain broadcasts. Most of this
mail cannot be analyzed systematically because writers
rarely indicate their ages, occupations, educational levels,
etc., but it does contain much helpful anecdotal material
which is extracted and shared with relevant units within
the External Services.

Finally, BBC learns a good deal about its audience
through anecdotal reports from BBC and British newspaper
correspondents and British Embassy officials in other
countries, as well as from foreign newspaper articles about
BBC broadcasts (often critical, and thus possibly indicating
that BBC has struck a sensitive nerve).[43] Such reports
have revealed that many of the world's leading statesmen
and -women are regular listeners to BBC. The External
Services attempt to cultivate a habit of regularly listening to BBC on the part of those individuals and their more
humble but more numerous countrymen and -women in all parts
of the world by placing BBC schedules in many local papers
and by distributing hundreds of thousands of program guides
to listeners each month, in several different languages
("Huna London", the BBC Arabic Service program guide, goes
out in some 70,000 copies monthly), as well as by providing
listeners' letterbox programs in which listener questions
are answered. To further encourage listener mail, BBC has

rented postal boxes in a number of countries, so that correspondents might send their letters at lower postal rates.

TECHNICAL SERVICES

Unlike the United States, the Soviet Union, Canada or
Australia, Great Britain is a small nation, and does not
enjoy the natural advantages possessed, if not necessarily
exploited, by those nations in terms of erecting transmitters for international broadcasting at a variety of
geographical locations. It does still enjoy the advantage
of retaining some far-flung overseas territories, and the
further advantage of enjoying friendly relations with most
of its former colonies and protectorates. Consequently, BBC
has located transmitter sites in a more or less globe-gird-
ling belt, encompassing Cyprus, Masirah Island (Persian
Gulf), Singapore, Antigua (Caribbean)and Ascension Island
(mid-Atlantic), in addition to an array of 43 transmitters
in Great Britain itself, a smaller transmitter in West
Berlin, a low-power UHF transmitter in Lesotho, and leased
or exchanged time over VOA and Radio Canada International
transmitters in North America. Few areas in the world are
outside the reach of a reasonably clear BBC signal at least
some of the time (although some of the transmitters are
beginning to show their age) and that signal is available on
medium wave as well as short wave to listeners in much of
Europe, the Middle East and South Asia.
      There are certain prices to be paid for having access
to some of those sites, while other sites have been lost
because of changes in political leadership or foreign
policy. Many of the locations were either British pos-
sessions (Ascension Island) or British protectorates or
colonies (British Somaliland) when transmitters originally
were placed there. However, as some of those colonies and
protectorates became independent nations, their new governments decided that they didn't want the BBC transmitting
from their territories. The External Services lost transmitting sites in Malta, Malaysia and Somalia, and had to
reach a new and more restrictive agreement with Cyprus.[44]
Some of the losses were temporary, as BBC found nearby sites
which served its purposes just as well, but the construction
of new facilities was costly, and the most recent (1976)
BBC transmitter site--on Antigua, in the Caribbean--had to
be jointly financed and developed with West Germany's
Deutsche Welle.
      BBC is willing to pay the price of foreign trans-
mitters, but the External Services have not placed all of
their eggs in that particular basket; local placement of

tapes and discs, as well as direct broadcast relays to local
stations around the world, are heavily practiced. No other
international broadcast servide is as active in those
respects: hundreds of stations take thousands of hours of
BBC programing each year by these means, and one broadcast
service in Hong Kong carries an entire nine-hour bloc rebroadcast of the BBC World Service daily.[45]

FUTURE PROSPECTS

     The BBC External Services of the 1980s are quite likely
to bear a close resemblance to those of the 1970s. Languages
employed and program hours broadcast have changed hardly at
all during the past decade, and budgetary and supervisory
problems, particularly where the more exotic language services are concerned, militate against expansion. BBC's
most recent addition--Pushto (to Afghanistan) in 1981--took
over six months of intensive recruiting and training before
coming on the air. There may be continued upgrading and even
expansion of transmitter facilities, but cost alone makes
new sites questionable, even though BBC would like to be
able to deliver a better signal to southern and eastern
Africa and to China, and has proposed transmitter sites in
Hong Kong and the Seychelles Islands.
     Programing could conceivably change in the future, but
where the World Service is concerned, indications are that
its audience appreciates the wide variety of programs it
receives.[46] However, since a number of these programs,
entertainment in particular, come from BBC's domestic
services, there is always the possibility that the domestic
services may drop some of them and not replace them with
similar material. Given the many budgetary problems of BBC
domestic broadcasting in the 1970s, it is entirely possible
that radio will find itself with ever-smaller shares of the
budget, and may cut back on some of the more expensive productions. This would tend to reduce the "homey" atmosphere
projected by the present World Service, unless the World
Service itself decided to continue to produce such programs,
which seems unlikely, given its own budgetary problems.
     The External Services also are likely to continue to
come under pressure from the Government to cut back as a
part of overall reduction in governmental budgets. During
the 1970s, BBC resisted those pressures quite successfully,
thanks in part to its careful attention to public relations
within and outside of Great Britain.[47] The 1981 proposal of
cuts seemed to be more strongly supported by its proponents
than were past proposals, so how long the struggle will
continue without a truly sizeable cut is difficult to say.

Great Britain's poor financial situation is not the only
factor; there are voices raised in newspapers, in Parliament
and in government which contend that the nation's less
central role in world politics should warrant a reduction in
the External Services.[48] Another oft-cited rationale is
that many nations (Western Europe, the United States,
Australia) are so information-rich and so well-disposed
toward Great Britain that broadcasting to them is unnecessary. Unless relations with the United States and/or
Western Europe deteriorate in the 1980s, that line of argument may gain strength.[49]

It also appears that the External Services will face
continued struggles with the Foreign and Colonial Office over
short-term versus long-term strategies. External Services
administrators remain committed to long-term (see footnote
31), but face considerable pressure at times from FCO for
short-term approaches. When it's a matter of increasing
broadcast hours in given languages at FCO request, as it
was for Portuguese to Portugal in the mid-1970s and for
Turkish and Russian in 1981, the expansion is usually a
short-term response to political unrest, but BBC ordinarily
will seek to retain the increases after the crisis has
passed. It strongly resists dropping language services
which, in the opinion of the FCO, have outlived their usefulness, but it has lost some of those battles in the past
(Albanian, Hebrew, Sinhala) and well may lose more in the
future.

BBC also is likely to continue to come under attack for
occasional lapses from its generally high standards of
credibility and impartiality. Those attacks often may be
motivated by publicity-seeking considerations, but most will
receive ample press, if only because of the contrast they
present with the usual performance of the External Services.
Then, too, BBC never has claimed to be totally impartial.
Its coverage of events in the Communist world traditionally
has featured a decidedly pro-Western perspective, and the
upbringings and backgrounds of its own staff mean that
minority viewpoints probably will be far outweighed by what
former BBC staff member Julian Hale has called a "centrist
bias".[50] There also are occasional criticisms of an overly
Western perspective on coverage of events taking place in
the Third World.[51] But it is difficult to detect any particular "theme" in BBC broadcasts, unlike VOA's sometimes
heavy concentration on anti-Communist or anti-Soviet material.
Perhaps Julian Hale put it best when, in Radio Power, he
said (p. 49), "As Chile exports copper, and Australia wool,
so Britain exports honest information." That information
might help promote British trade or tourism, might discomfit
dictatorial politicians, might show Britain's interest in
developing nations, etc., but little other than the promotion

of trade or tourism appears to be a calculated policy.

If the External Services are not the paragon of international broadcasting virtue that some observers hold them to be, that should come as no surprise. There are bound to be mistakes and oversights, sins of commission and omission, in such a multi-faceted organization. That there are a few sins and errors as there seem to have been is a considerable tribute to the sense of professionalism and pride its staff have in their work. That sense is strengthened, I feel, by the largely successful ongoing struggle BBC management has waged to keep the Services free of outside pressures. Staff and management alike would oppose the suggestion, much less the demand, that they not broadcast news of an important event such as the evacuation of Saigon. BBC's proud independence may have rankled domestic and foreign government officials, members of Parliament, ambassadors, the domestic and foreign press and others on various occasions, but it has also had a great deal to do with the development of an extremely high standard of excellence in international broadcasting--a standard many other international broadcasters acknowledge and seek, but have not yet attained.

NOTES

1. However, the BBC began experimental transmissions for international broadcasting in November 1927, primarily for relay purposes. See "International Station Testing on 24 Meters," The New York Times 10 (November 13, 1927):18.

2. As early as 1929, several BBC officials were suggesting a broader mission for what was to become the Empire Service--a mission that would include the influencing of world public opinion. Asa Briggs, The History of Broadcasting in the United Kingdom, Volume II, The Golden Age of Wireless (New York: Oxford University Press, 1965), pp. 374-375.

3. Briggs, II, Ibid., documents the discussions between the BBC and the Foreign Office with characteristic thoroughness; see pp. 399-401. My own inspection of letters, memos, minutes of meetings, etc. on the discussions seems to show that then Director General of the BBC, John Reith, took a public stand that "the BBC has the final say in all matters of broadcast content." However, his more privately expressed sentiments indicate a greater willingness to compromise with the Foreign Office; in a conversation with the person appointed by the Foreign Office to head the newly-created Arabic service, Reith, discussing what might happen if "irreconcilable" differences arose, said ". . . my answer officially would be that the BBC must have its way, but personally not; in other words, I did not like to contemplate

our doing anything that the Foreign Office opposed." From
memo of conversation with Calvert by Reith, January 7, 1938,
on file at the BBC Written Archives Center, Caversham Park,
Reading, England. Briggs, II, pp. 397-405 and Norbert
Tonnies, Krieg vor dem Krieg (Essen: Essner Verlagsanstalt
G.m.b.H., 1940), pp. 176-209, present considerable information on BBC broadcasts just before the war, Tonnies from
a Nazi point of view.

4. See especially Charles Cruikshank, The Fourth Arm
(London: Davis-Poynter, 1977), pp. 52-57, for a description
of some of the coordinating procedures followed by PWE and
some of the difficulties involved in implementing them where
various governments-in-exile were concerned. Asa Briggs,
The History of Broadcasting in the United Kingdom, Volume
III, The War of Words (London: Oxford University Press,
1970), passim, but especially pp. 482-483, provides further
examples, as does D.G. Bridson, Prospero and Ariel (London:
Gollancz, 1971).

5. Daniel Katz, "Britain Speaks," in Propaganda by
Short Wave, Harwood Childs and John Whitton, eds. (Princeton:
Princeton University Press, 1942), p. 120. Katz was generally
critical of BBC broadcasts to North America in the first
year or two of the war. He found that quite often they
lacked timeliness, were somewhat stuffy, and sometimes inaccurate.

6. Again, Briggs, III, and Cruikshank, Fourth Arm, as
well as Sefton Delmer, Black Boomerang (New York: Viking
Press, 1962), contain numerous references to the tensions
between the BBC, the military departments, the Political
Warfare Executive, the Special Operations Executive, and
other offices and departments. See especially Briggs, III,
pp. 35-43, 83-87, 169, 274-275, 308-310. Briggs also
questions the absolute reliability of BBC reporting of war
losses; see p. 288.

7. R.H.S. Crossman, "Psychological Warfare," Journal
of the Royal United Service Institution (August 1952):323.

8. John Baker White, The Big Lie (London: Evans
Brothers Limited, 1955), especially pp. 64-66 and 84. A
letter to me from Gerard Mansell, then Managing Director of
BBC External Services, February 13, 1980, states that (Lord)
Patrick Gordon-Walker, a senior official with the BBC German
Service during World War II, has denied that misleading
information was broadcast, and regards White's book as
"appallingly inaccurate." Michael Balfour, Propaganda in
War, 1939-1945 (London and Boston: Routledge & Kegan Paul,
1979), cites an instance in which BBC was "used" by PWE and
SOE to deceive the Germans into thinking that the Allies were
about to launch a cross-Channel invasion (p. 358), but he
later states that BBC itself had been deceived by PWE and
SOE, and that his research disclosed "no case of the BBC

putting out statements known by it to be false" (p. 428).
BBC did become involved with work slowdown campaigns for
listeners in Nazi-occupied Europe in 1941 (Cruikshank,
Fourth Arm, pp. 123-124; White, Big Lie, p. 94), and it led
to a dispute among BBC, PWE and SOE as to who should conduct
such propaganda. Enthusiasm over the success of its "V for
Victory" campaign led BBC's European News Department to
develop a memo on "broadcasting as a weapon of war" which
contained the statement "When the British government gives
the word, the BBC will cause riots and demonstrations in
every city in Europe . . ." (Cruikshank, Fourth Arm, p. 122).

   9. Specific instances are cited in Anthony Cave Brown,
ed., The Secret War Report of the OSS (New York: Berkley,
1976), p. 401, and Bickham Sweet-Escott, Baker Street Ir-
regular (London: Methuen and Company, 1965), pp. 103 and
195. Sweet-Escott also mentions the problems the BBC's
"inaccurate reporting" caused the British agents who were
dealing with various Yugoslav partisan units (p. 192).

   10. Briggs, III, p. 162.

   11. While there is no comprehensive treatment of the
BBC's overseas broadcast activities in World War II, Briggs,
III, is as thorough an account as any. Balfour, Propaganda;
Jeremy Bennett, British Broadcasting and the Danish Resist-
ance Movement (Cambridge: Cambridge University Press, 1966);
Carl Brinitzer, Hier Spricht London (Hamburg: Hoffman und
Kampe, 1969); E. Tangye Lean, Voices in the Darkness (London:
Secker and Warburg, 1943); Bernard Wittek, Der britische
Atherkrieg gegen das dritte Reich (Münster: University of
Münster, Studien zur Publizistik, Bd. 3, 1962); and Paul
Allard, Ici Londres! (Paris: Les Editions de France, 1942),
all add considerable detail to the picture of BBC's wartime
activities, Allard from a Nazi perspective and Brinitzer
from the standpoint of a German working for BBC's German
service.

   12. Asa Briggs, The History of Broadcasting in the
United Kingdom, Volume IV, Sound and Vision (London: Oxford
University Press, 1979), pp. 137-140, provides a brief
account of the transition from wartime to peacetime. Noel
Newsome, "International Radio," The Political Quarterly 17
(January-March 1946):48-60, offers a strongly-worded argument
for maintaining BBC at full strength in peacetime, and pushes
hard for a truly international radio station, run on a multinational basis and located in Luxembourg; both he and Briggs
see BBC as losing its more European character as it moves
into the immediate postwar years. See also House of Commons,
Session 1945-1946, First Report of the Select Committee on
Estimates, British Broadcasting Corporation (Reports--
Committees--Civil Aviation to Estimates, 1945-1946, Vol. 6),
especially pp. vii-viii, 4-5, 12, where several Committee
members wonder how the costs of the overseas services should

be borne, and where one individual testifying before the
Committee (Sir Eric Bamford) gives the impression that it is
the Government, and not BBC, which wants the overseas services
to continue (p. 12). As for the Russian service, it would be
more correct to state that it was restored to the schedule in
1946. BBC broadcast briefly in Russian in 1942-1943, but the
Soviet government asked that the service be suspended, and
it was.

    13. Much as was the case with VOA during and after
World War II, BBC announcers were sometimes accused of being
too favorable towards Communism. See D.G. Bridson, Prospero,
Chapters 3-5, passim.

    14. Brinitzer, London, pp. 315-316, broadcast of
November 11, 1953, translation mine. (The original verse,
which is Brinitzer's, did rhyme!) The famous folk singer and
poet Theodore Bikel wrote the music.

    15. House of Commons, Session 1951-1952, Ninth Report
from the Select Committee on Estimates, Overseas Broadcasting
(Reports--Committees, 1951-1952, Volume 6) and "Summary of
the Report (1952) of the Independent Committee of Enquery
into the Overseas Information Services" (Drogheda), Cmnd.
9138, April 1954, presented by the Secretary of State for
Foreign Affairs to Parliament, Volume 31, Accounts and Papers,
1953-1954, are the two best sources of official thinking on
the role of the BBC External Services at this time. Both
reports strongly supported BBC, but Drogheda, somewhat reluctantly, sees some justification for the Government's
"using" the External Services (pp. 4, 6) while the Select
Committee on Estimates seems puzzled as to the precise
manner in which the External Services are guided by various
prescribing authorities (e.g., Foreign Office, Colonial
Office, military) (pp. vii, 5-7). At one point, the Select
Committee Report states that "the real control exercised by
Departments, especially the Foreign Office, the Service
(military) Departments and the Colonial Office, has increased
considerably." (p. xxvi). Briggs, IV, pp. 505-541, also
provides much useful information on the External Services
during this period. My own examination of BBC internal
memos, correspondence between BBC, the Foreign Office,
British Embassies, etc. for the period 1946-1950 (on file at
the BBC Written Archives Centre, Caversham Park) reveals a
number of instances of Foreign Office and Embassy expressions of displeasure at BBC External Services reporting,
especially about the Soviet Union. In some of those instances
BBC officials clearly were in a position of having to wait
for Foreign Office permission before carrying certain news
items, including one (on political arrests in Romania in
1947) which had already appeared in the Times of London!
Letter, Ian Jacob (BBC) to Ivone Kirkpatrick (FO), April 26,
1947.

16. Harman Grisewood, One Thing at a Time (London:
Hutchinson, 1968), pp. 195-204. Charles Hill (Lord Hill of
Luton) casts doubt upon Grisewood's allegations; see Behind
the Screen (London: Sedgwick and Jackson, 1974), pp. 169-
170. However, several staff members presently or formerly
with the External Services have told me that they were convinced of the existence of such a plan. While she does not
comment on the subject of a specific plan, Grace Wyndham
Goldie, in Facing the Nation (London: The Bodley Head, 1977),
pp. 185-186, does support Grisewood's basic contention that
BBC faced enormous pressure from the Eden administration
over this issue.

17. BBC Handbook 1979 (London: BBC, 1979), p. 262.

18. Debates in the House of Commons and House of Lords
over the roles played by BBC and the Government during the
Suez conflict are quite instructive, in that BBC received a
great deal of support and commendation from Conservatives
and Labourites alike, although one House of Commons Labour
Party member saw the entire discussion as a "smokescreen" to
hide the BBC's "anti-Socialist bias". See House of Commons,
Debates, Volume 560 (1956-1957), Col. 1023-1102; Volume 565
(1956-1957), col. 1219; House of Lords, Debates, Volume 201
(1956-1957), cols. 538-561, 564-598. It took the BBC's
External Services several years to overcome one effect of
its Suez policy, however: its budget rose at a very modest
rate in the late 1950s, largely, I have been told by numerous
BBC officials, because a number of members of Parliament
felt deep down inside that the nation, and therefore the BBC,
should have presented a "united front" during the Suez
crisis. This viewpoint was vividly expressed by the Earl of
Halifax, speaking in the House of Lords on February 6, 1957:
"But it seems to me suicidal . . . that we should deliber-
ately, under a mistaken assumption of what is incumbent upon
us, set out to weaken the impact and the power that this
country should have in the world by presenting ourselves as
a people with no unity, torn by discord, and utterly ineffective and leaderless." House of Lords, Debates, Volume
201 (1956-1957), cols. 578-579. There was also considerable
discussion of the Foreign Office's conversion of a commercial
broadcast station on Cyprus (the Near East Broadcasting
Station) to a so-called "Voice of Britain," which roundly
attacked Egyptian President Nasser before and during the Suez
crisis. BBC officials were deeply disturbed by the Foreign
Office's action, which they saw as (potentially) compromising
the integrity of BBC itself. Mohamed Abdel-Kader Hatem, in
Information and the Arab Cause (London: Longmans, 1974),
refers to the activities of this station, which he associates
with the British intelligence service, as "ineffective," due
largely to "positive counter-propaganda by Egypt's Voice of
the Arabs," (p. 184). Hatem also refers to several other

clandestine stations active against Egypt during this period,
including one run by the French and staffed with "Egyptian
turncoats" (pp. 192-193).

19. The Drogheda Report (footnote 15) specifically
recommended such cuts, most of which were carried out in the
late 1950s.

20. The Drogheda Report had recommended that "commercial needs" be taken into account by the External Services.
Summary of the Report, Cmnd. 9138, April 1954, p. 3. BBC
itself had considered "trade propaganda" as one element in
its proposed Empire Service as early as June 1930. BBC, 2nd
Memorandum on Empire Broadcasting, June 1930, p. 16 (unpublished document in BBC Written Archives Centre, Caversham
Park, Reading, England).

21. Some of the response generated by "New Ideas" and
similar programs in the 1970s is covered in "The Ads on the
Air of Araby," Times of London, March 4, 1970, p. 25, and BBC
Handbook 1980, pp. 51-52, and Sir Ian Trethowan, The BBC
and International Broadcasting (London : BBC, February 1981):
pp. 8-9.

22. Both cuts were questioned by Parliament, but to no
avail. House of Commons, Debates, Volume 739 (1966-1967),
col. 161 and Volume 769 (1967-1968), col. 241. There is no
doubt as to the Foreign Office's clear and unquestioned
right to order such cuts. When the dropping of the Albanian
Service was questioned in the House of Lords in 1967, Lord
Chalfont, speaking for the Foreign Office, stated "It is for
the Government, through the Foreign Office, to prescribe
those external services of the BBC which should be carried
out. It is not really relevant that the BBC has offered to
make economies in other fields. It is for the Government to
decide which have a political effect of importance, and which
should be discontinued." House of Lords, Debates, Volume
279 (1966-1967), col. 324. (Italics mine). Lord Carrington,
then Foreign Secretary, repeated that same line of argument
in proposing budget cuts for the External Services in 1981.

23. Report of the Review Committee on Overseas Representation (Duncan Committee), Cmnd. 4107 (July 1969),
Chapter 8. I visited the External Services the year after
the Duncan Report had been released, and found BBC senior
staff still citing examples of various world leaders (e.g.
Egypt's Nasser) who could speak English perfectly well but
preferred to listen to broadcasts in their own national
languages.

24. Peter Hopkirk, "BBC Ends Rhodesian Service," Times
of London, August 9, 1969, p. 3. See also "BBC Accused of
Propaganda," Times of London, August 12, 1969, p. 4.

25. House of Commons, Debates, Volume 623 (1959-1960),
cols. 886-887; "BBC Accused of Bias," Times of London,
May 25, 1971, p. 7. On the other hand, there were specific

commendations of BBC for its role in discomfiting the Eastern
European governments and the government of the USSR. See,
for example, letters to the editor of the Times of London
from Sir John Lawrence (December 7, 1968, p. 9) and K. Baum
(April 3, 1974, p. 15). There were also specific reactions
from the Soviet Union: see Kiril Tidmarsh, "Izvestia Attack
on BBC for 'Spying,'" Times of London, December 17, 1968,
p. 1, and Kiril Tidmarsh, "Russia Accuses Fleet Street,"
Times of London, December 21, 1968, p. 6.
    26. House of Lords, Debates, Volume 279 (1966-1967),
col. 324. BBC staff members were not entirely pleased with
External Service coverage of the Nigerian Civil War, as I
learned in a September 18, 1975 interview with George
Bennett, Head of BBC's African Service. Mr. Bennett felt
that BBC at first relied too heavily on Nigerian Federal
Government handouts. Then Frederick Forsythe, who was
covering Biafra for BBC, became "committed" to the Biafran
cause, and his broadcasts reflected that commitment. Finally
Bennett himself, at that time a senior producer in the
African Service, asked to be sent to Nigeria and was. He
felt that he was able to help restore balance to BBC's
reporting. Coverage of the Nigerian conflict was a problem
for BBC as a whole, and not just the External Services.
    27. There were many articles on the subject in the
British press, of which the following are fairly representa-
tive: Denis Herbstein, "Our Lisbon Lapses--By the Beeb,"
Times of London, July 25, 1975, p. 3; "BBC 'Lapses' in
Portugal Broadcasts," Daily Telegraph (London), August 8,
1975, p. 1; Michael Binyon, "Two of BBC Speakers on Portugal
Dismissed," Times of London, October 21, 1975, p. 3; and
Nicholas Roe, "BBC Man Admits 'Slant'," Sunday Telegraph,
October 26, 1975, p. 5.
    28. George Campbell, "Report on Some Aspects of News
Translation in the External Services," unpublished report,
July 25, 1975.
    29. The Times of London also published some 16 "sup-
portive" letters to the editor between March 28 and April 8,
1974. See also Kenneth Gosling, "Risk to Foreign Language
Broadcasts Feared," Times of London, April 3, 1974, p. 3.
"The Radio War," The Economist, March 23, 1974, p. 8, noted
that the Foreign Office had already cut the External Services budget by almost 400,000 pounds in December 1973;
the article then cited the oft-repeated argument, "If whole
services were to die, it would take years to resurrect them,
and once continuity had been broken it would be a hard
struggle to win back their audience."
    30. Central Policy Review Staff, Review of Overseas
Representation (London: Her Majesty's Stationary Office,
1977), pp. 225-237. (Quotation appears on p. 229).
    31. Robert Taylor, "23 BBC Foreign Services at Risk,"

The Observer (London), August 26, 1979, p. 1. One of the
services the Foreign and Colonial Office proposed to cut was
Turkish. In fact, no language services were cut, and a year
later FCO requested BBC to expand its Turkish language broadcasts presumably because of political turmoil there! According to Deputy Managing Director of External Services,
Austen Kark (interview, September 15, 1981), FCO officials
and the External Services have had several differences of
opinion concerning short-term and long-term strategies for
international radio, with FCO frequently favoring short-term
(cutting, adding and expanding language services as political
conditions seem to warrant) and BBC defending long-term.
      32. See House of Lords, Debates, Volume 420 (1980-
1981), cols. 806-873, "BBC External Services," and "Britain's
Dwindling Voice," briefing paper prepared by the Association
of Broadcasting Staff and the National Union of Journalists
(London: ABS/NUJ, 1981).
      33. Although in theory BBC's Board of Governors has
final power of decision over External Services broadcasts,
just as it does over BBC domestic broadcasts, I have the
distinct impression, based on readings of memoirs and
speeches of former BBC Directors General (Reith, Greene) and
Chairmen of the Board of Governors (Lord Hill of Luton, Sir
Michael Swann), interviews over the period 1967-1981 with
roughly a dozen high-ranking External Services administrators,
and a personal letter from Lord Hill of Luton (August 30,
1975), that the Board concerns itself with program matters
re the External Services very seldom, and then retro-
spectively. The 1974 "Portuguese announcers" incident was
discussed by the Board, because it raised a fundamental
issue of supervisory practices, but it did not result in any
sort of edict being handed down by the Board.
      34. Not long after the new Islamic government had taken
power in Iran, it too was complaining about BBC broadcasts.
Robert Fisk, "Foreign Press Lectured on Why Iran Must Expel
'Times' Men," Times of London, December 18, 1979, p. 5.
      35. Julian Hale, Radio Power (Philadelphia: Temple
University Press, 1975), refers to a "Liaison Officer"
designated by the Foreign and Colonial Office to work with
the External Services. Such a post existed during and again
just after Suez, but a letter from former External Services
Managing Director Gerard Mansell, September 11, 1981, states
that the post was abolished within a few months after Suez.
      36. Interviews with Gerard Mansell, Austen Kark
(Deputy Managing Director), Robert Gregson (Controller,
Overseas Services), Alexander Lieven (Controller, European
Services), Bernard Bumpus (Head of Audience Research) and
Arthur Vann (Chief Accountant) in 1975, 1977, 1980 and 1981
have left me with the impression that External Services
administrators spend a considerable amount of time in

preparing for discussions with the Foreign and Colonial
Office, in part because it is not a simple matter to get FCO
staff to understand the intricacies of international radio,
audience research, etc. In turn, however, various British
Embassy and FCO staff members have told me that they find it
difficult to get External Services staff to even discuss,
much less alter, actual or proposed broadcast practices.
Lord Hill of Luton, who has had much experience in working
with BBC, has stated that "whenever a cut was decided on, the
BBC were not slow to prompt their friends--many of them in
high places, including my Ministerial colleagues--to campaign against it. Even to me, a devoted admirer of the
Corporation, their rigid attitude in negotiation was sometimes hard to take." Lord Hill of Luton, Both Sides of the
Hill (London: Heinemann, 1964), p. 189. See also John
Black, Organizing the Propaganda Instrument (The Hague:
Martinus Nijhoff, 1975), Chapter 5, on External Service
relations with FCO.
        37. Hale, Radio Power, p. 59, notes that there was at
one time a Controller of Output who reviewed the tapes and
transcripts of each language service, but that post was
abolished some time ago, on the grounds that it was, in
Hale's words, "felt to be a waste of time." A September 11,
1981 letter to me from Gerard Mansell, former Managing
Director of the External Services, states that no such
position ever existed, although there was a person who was
frequently commissioned to carry out specific studies of
given language service output during the 1960s. Deputy
Managing Director Austen Kark confirmed in an interview on
September 15, 1981 that a linguist and Talmudic scholar,
Emil Marmorstein, had conducted such studies until his retirement from BBC in 1971. The External Services do have
Controllers for the World Service, European Services and
Overseas Services who keep an eye on programing, but my
observations indicate that most of this is done on an ad
hoc basis and through meetings and corridor conversations.
        38. The External Services share the costs of main-
taining certain correspondents overseas with the BBC domestic
services.
        39. Geoffrey Green, "Russian Sports Fans Tune in to
BBC," Times of London, April 29, 1967.
        40. For some idea of the wide variety of programing
available on the World Service, see BBC Handbook 1981,
pp. 116-119. There are literally dozens of regular and
special series and programs available.
        41. Discussion with staff members, Staff Recruitment
Division, BBC External Services, London, September 23, 1975.
There are "balance" quotas in most BBC language divisions:
so many slots for temporary staff, so many for permanent.
        42. "Comprehension of BBC Broadcasts in English--

Pilot Study of Research Methodology in Lagos, Nigeria,"
Audience Research Unit, BBC External Services, London, 1971
(unpublished study).

43. See, for example, "Soviet Attack on BBC for Resurrecting Orwell," Times of London, January 10, 1974, p. 7;
Mario Modiano, "Greek Regime Warning on Resistance," Times
of London, August 11, 1969, p. 3.

44. BBC Monitoring Service, Summary of World Broadcasts, ME/W 340/B/1, 12 November 1965.

45. BBC Handbook 1981, pp. 55-56, 112-115.

46. In February 1976, the External Services' Audience
Research Department conducted a survey of listener program
preferences by asking all listeners who received the World
Service monthly program guide (London Calling) to indicate,
by marking a condensed version of a typical week's broadcast schedule, which programs they listened to. While newscasts ranked at the top in terms of frequency of listening
and "enjoyment," sports, classical music, comedies and
quizzes, and drama and readings also did quite well in both
categories. Opinions were quite sharply divided where
popular music was concerned. "London Calling Questionnaire,"
Audience Research Division, BBC External Services, London,
1976 (unpublished report). There was a repeat of the survey
in February 1980, but I have not seen its results.

47. Reporters from London and major provincial newspapers are one object of this attention--External Services
officials are very ready to grant interviews and to make
available booklets of foreign and domestic newspaper items
and listener comments supporting BBC--but BBC also broadcasts full and frequent news reports on rumors and declarations of budgetary cutbacks.

48. See "The Times Diary," Times of London, April 26,
1974, p. 18, where in an item entitled "Lobbying," the
writer says, ". . . why should it fall to Britain to bear
the cost and responsibility of keeping the world informed?"

49. Various BBC officials had advocated a jointly-
administered European broadcasting service since the late
1940s. Gerard Mansell proposed such a service in the 1970s.
However, a fresh wave of austerity in Britain, and the decided lack of interest displayed by French officials, spelled
an end to the proposal. Interviews with Mansell, September
23, 1975 (London) and September 11, 1977 (Washington, D.C.).
See also Kenneth Gosling, "European Radio to get Trial Run,"
Times of London, December 1, 1977, p. 1; and "Euradio--
Silenced," The Economist, December 23, 1978.

50. Hale, Radio Power, pp. 61 and 57, criticizes the
External Services for the "democracy vs. totalitarianism"
tone of some of its broadcasts to Communist nations and for
displaying at times a "centrist bias," which "may prove to
have given undue emphasis to the status quo . . ." Two

Soviet authors, Vladimir Artyomov and Vladimir Semyonov, have written The BBC: History, Apparatus, Methods of Radio Propaganda (Moscow: (publisher unknown), 1979), which was summarized and excerpted in translation by David Wedgwood Benn of BBC. The authors state (p. 200ff) that support for the status quo has a propagandistic aim, especially where listeners in Eastern Europe and the Soviet Union are concerned: "The calculation that with the increase in material requirements in the socialist countries the 'virus of consumerism' will spread and that 'an acquisitive instinct will grow' has a bearing on one of the main goals of BBC External Broadcasting. BBC together with other Western radio centres is seeking through its advertisement of the opportunities which capitalist society supposedly offers to everyone, to attract listeners from socialist countries along the path of a consumerist attitude towards life."

51. External Services coverage of a "massacre" of white people in Shaba province (Zaire) in 1978 was criticized by a BBC staff member for concentrating almost exclusively on molestations and deaths of whites during the early days of the disturbances, and almost totally ignoring the far larger number of deaths among blacks. (Graham Mytton, "BBC External Services and the Shaba Story," internal memorandum, May 26, 1978).

Note: A longtime Managing Director of the External Services, Gerard Mansell, is writing a book about the External Services, to be published in fall 1982, on the occasion of the Services' 50th anniversary.

7

A WESTERN ASSORTMENT

BBC and VOA clearly stand out among the Western* international radio stations. They are larger than most, older than many, and more prominent than all others. But the "others" present some interesting variations in the conduct of international broadcasting. Some follow a very definite colonial service approach, others stress certain themes day after day, and still others rely quite heavily on a "personal" approach to reaching listeners. They range in size from Denmark's 12-hour-per-day service in Danish only to West Germany's combined 800 hours per week services in 35 languages; only Ireland, Leichtenstein, San Marino and Iceland have no international services. The five stations I present here should give you some impression of the diversity of the Western operations, and I have concluded the chapter with some generalizations.

DEUTSCHE WELLE AND DEUTSCHLANDFUNK

Although Germany was an early entry in the lists of international broadcasting, with an 8 kW shortwave service in 1929,[1] it disappeared altogether from those lists in 1945. The explanation is simple enough: the Nazi government had made international broadcasting one of its chief instruments of propaganda, and through it carried out campaigns of intimidation and coercion, disseminated misinformation, and encouraged sabotage. Several nations used international

---

*Here including Western Europe, North America, South Africa, Australia, New Zealand and Japan--the last named because of its strong economic and political ties with the West and its espousal of "democratic capitalism."

broadcasting for the same purposes, but it was Germany's misfortune to be on the losing side, and whatever was left of the technical apparatus (the remaining staff had been disbanded or captured by April 1945) was taken over by the occupation forces.[2]

For the next eight years, West Germany lacked its own international broadcast service. There were several reasons for this, including a depressed West German economy, doubt on the part of occupiers and Germans alike as to whether West Germany had much of importance to tell the rest of the world, and a restructured West German broadcasting system with the individual West German states (Länder), rather than the federal government, responsible for broadcasting within their own areas. The federal government was to have no activities in or jurisdiction over broadcasting.

During the late 1940s and early 1950s there was an increasing German interest in "telling the world about Germany." It was accompanied by federal government claims that it, rather than the states, should operate any international station that might be created. But the states won out, and came on the air in May 1953 with the Deutsche Welle ("German wave"), which they operated through their collective broadcasting organization, the ARD.[3]

Deutsche Welle's first broadcasts were in German for German speakers throughout the world, just as the first German international service had been in 1929. One year later, DW added daily five minute newscasts in English, French, Spanish and Portuguese, primarily to reach other European listeners with news about the "new Germany." In 1957, it added German lessons in those four language services. It began its first non-European service in 1959, with 20 minutes daily in Arabic (probably to counter East German broadcasts in Arabic).[4] During that same period, transmitter power increased by leaps and bounds: one 20 kW transmitter in 1953, several transmitters with a total power of over 500 kW by 1960.

But the federal government had not given up its pursuit of an international radio service. It made several attempts to pass legislation establishing a new German language station for listeners in East Germany and elsewhere in Europe, taking DW out of the hands of ARD, and authorizing a second television service. In late 1960, the West German House and Senate passed such a bill. The West German Supreme Court later ruled that creation of a second television service by the federal government was unconstitutional[5] but allowed the other portions of the bill to stand.

The new German language service, the Deutschlandfunk (DLF), and the existing international service, the Deutsche Welle, now were to receive their budgets through annual appropriations voted upon by the West German federal parliament and made available to the stations through the Ministry of the Interior.[6] As was the practice for the state broadcasting stations in West Germany, DLF and DW were to be "controlled" by supervisory councils (<u>Rundfunkräte</u>) made up of people who would be "representative" of the West German citizenry.[7] Since the councils were to meet quarterly[8] day-to-day administration of the stations was to be carried out by station managers (<u>Intendanten</u>), who were appointed and dismissed by the supervisory councils.

In the years that followed, it became apparent that the two international stations were subject to the same wave of politicization that was sweeping West German state radio services.[9] Perhaps the most notable manifestation of that politicization was the "need" to balance political representation within the various administrative and program departments of the stations. For example, if a head of a given department were known to be a member of, or even favorable to, the Social Democratic Party, the deputy head of that department would have to be from an opposing political party.[10] In theory, such a system could lead to politically balanced output from a program department; in practice, it has sometimes led to imbalanced or dichotomized programing.

Deutsche Welle did enjoy notable increases in budgets during the 1960s, and those increases were soon translated into an expansion of language services, transmitter power, and, somewhat later, transmitter location: following in the footsteps of VOA and BBC, Deutsche Welle acquired overseas transmitter bases in Rwanda (1965), Montserrat (1977), Malta (1974) and, together with the BBC, Antigua (1977); it also leased time on a transmitter complex in Portugal. The overseas bases were reinforced by the construction of a 2000 kW transmitter complex in Wertachtel, West Germany (1972). Those overseas locations were made necessary by DW's considerable expansion in both European (e.g. Russian, Polish, Greek, Serbian) and non-European (e.g. Persian, Hausa, Hindi, Mandarin) languages. In all, 26 languages were added to the DW schedule between 1960 and 1970--a rate of growth unmatched by any other international broadcaster during that decade. The operating budget grew from less than two million Deutschmarks in 1960 to over DM 76 million in 1970, and weekly transmitter hours from 315 to nearly 550.

During that same period of time, DLF, which first came on the air with its German service in 1962, added 13 languages, all of them European. It increased its transmitter power from 100 kW (50 kW medium wave, 50 kW long wave) to over 2400 kW (all but 70 kW medium wave, all transmitters located within West Germany). Its broadcast hours rose from 56 to 210 per week, and its budget as of 1970 was 56 million DM. Considered from any angle--operating budget, transmitter power, hours of broadcast or language services

(nine of DLF's languages were also on the DW roster)--West
German international broadcasting clearly had become a major
force in the world of international radio. German language
broadcasts retained their position of prominence: over 80
per cent of DLF's hours of transmission, and roughly 30 per
cent of DW's, were in German.

The rapid growth of DW and DLF during the 1960s was due
to a variety of factors: a desire on the part of the federal
government to reach the peoples of Eastern Europe and the
Soviet Union, often with a strongly anti-Communist message;
a perceived need to combat the broadcasts of East Germany's
Radio Berlin International, especially where listeners in
the developing nations were concerned; a hope of modifying
the negative image of Germany and Germans which had been
developed during the Nazi era; and a wish to develop and
improve trade relations with other nations, since foreign
trade was proving increasingly important to the West German
economy. To those ends, the two stations developed a wide
variety of programs, while carrying others over from the
1950s. News, commentary, music, reviews of the West German
press, features about life and people in West Germany, and
language lessons, were joined by special features about the
West German economy and business and industry, disk jockey
("personality") music shows (some of them encouraging
listener requests), news about the countries and areas to
which DW was broadcasting (DLF stuck to news about Germany),
and regularly-scheduled programs about sports.

The 1970s saw a continuation of most of the existing
broadcast formats, but very little expansion of language
services (DW added Dari, Pushtu and Bengali) and little
increase in hours of transmission. Technical development
continued at a brisk pace, however, with DW's already-noted
expansion of relay bases and construction of the Wertachtel
complex and DLF's installation of two new 500 kW long wave
transmitters. Although the two stations remained separate
administrative entities, they jointly developed plans for a
new broadcasting center. Construction began in 1974, but
DLF did not move into its tower until 1979 and DW until
1981. There was also a "rationalization" of scheduling for
certain European languages broadcast by the two stations;
after 1977, DW produced all programs in Romanian and the
Yugoslav languages, and DLF produced all programs in Polish,
Czech, Slovak and Hungarian, but all of those languages
would continue to be broadcast by DW and by DLF. That move
left both stations in the position of broadcasting as many
languages for as many hours as they had already been doing.

In fact, there is a great deal about the two-station
system that does not seem terribly rational. The federal
government's initial intent appeared to be to create a new
German language broadcasting service for Europe in general

and East Germany in particular. Yet within a few years, DLF
was broadcasting in several European languages, including
some of those already on the DW schedule. Several DW staff
members have told me that the law governing DLF was vague on
the point of additional (besides German) language services,
and that DLF management concerned over a possible need to
justify the station's existence, decided to expand its scope
of operations. DLF staff have pointed out that, where Europe
is concerned, there is a clear technical line of demarcation
between DLF and DW: the latter broadcasts to Europe in
shortwave only, whereas the former broadcasts in medium and
long wave only. There are many similarities in programing:
both stations offer German language courses, both display a
heavy concentration on events and life in West Germany in
their news and feature presentations, both appear to favor a
rather formal style of writing and delivery. By that token,
one might wonder whether listeners know or care which station
they listen to, and if they do not, why two stations are
necessary.[11]

   There are differences, of course, and they are particularly apparent in the German language programing done
around the clock by each station. DLF pays more attention to
events in East Germany but far less to events in its other
target countries than does DW. It also seems less concerned
with the presentation of highly specific detail in newscasts
and features,[12] and it certainly plays much more music: 55
per cent of the schedule, as opposed to 15 per cent of DW's
German program. Most of the music is Western pop or rock or
German popular songs, and it is hard to avoid the feeling
that DLF's German programs are intended as much for listeners
living inside West Germany as for those living outside.

   Most staff members of the two stations with whom I have
talked feel that DW is more conservative in its treatment of
international relations than is DLF. Granted that a far
smaller portion of DLF's broadcast time is taken up with
items and features having to do with international relations,
there are several general and specific instances that staff
refer to in support of this contention. There is the
general allegation that some of the DW language services--
German and Russian are mentioned most often--reflect more of
a "Cold War mentality" in their broadcasts than is in keeping
with West German foreign policy from the late 1960s onward.
That policy has emphasized better relations with the Eastern
European nations, including East Germany and the USSR, yet
some DW broadcasts were referring to the "so-called German
Democratic Republic" as late as the early 1970s, and sarcastic references to the Soviet government continue to be
made, as in this excerpt from a May 14, 1980 DW German
service news analysis:

        Since 1968--thus, since the intervention in
    Czechoslovakia--it is known in East and West that,
    according to the Soviet interpretation, this
    military power [of the Warsaw Pact] also has the
    task of defending the so-called "collective
    achievements" of socialism. Whether and when
    these so-called "collective achievements" are
    endangered is a decision, naturally, for the
    Soviet leadership and the Soviet leadership
    only. (translation mine)

DLF's broadcasts seem on the whole to have less of a
Cold War sound to them, but they are hardly free of such
references. A May 16, 1980 DLF German service analysis on
the same subject seems blunt, rather than sarcastic, but is
no less critical:

        No interference after Soviet interference--
    [that is] the recipe for the [Persian] Gulf region;
    stripping the Mediterranean of NATO's weapons of
    deterrence; and discussion of medium-range missiles
    in Europe only if the Soviet Union's missiles remain
    in Eastern Europe. So simple, so arrogant, so over-
    bearing are the Warsaw Pact's proposals for these
    three regions. (translation mine)

    A 1974 content analysis of VOA, BBC, Radio Liberty and
DW Russian language programing by James Oliver indicated
that DW's negative evaluation score for items and features
about "official" life and events in the USSR was -1.87,
compared with BBC's -1.35, VOA's -.68, and RL's -2.43.
Since DLF does not broadcast in Russian, it was not included in this analysis.[13]
    A more specific instance of alleged DW conservatism is
the attempt made by DW's then director Walter Steigner to
halt DW broadcasts in Amharic to Ethiopia in 1975. DW's
Amharic service had carried news items which the Ethiopian
government judged to be critical of itself, and the West
German embassy in Addis Ababa received an anonymous note
threatening the lives of children enrolled at the German
school there unless the critical news items were halted.
The note was forwarded to Steigner, who travelled to
Ethiopia to assess the situation first hand, then returned
to West Germany and proposed that DW drop its Amharic broadcasts altogether, removing entirely any grounds for criticism by the Ethiopian government. DW's supervisory council
(Rundfunkrat) voted against his recommendation, six to five,
and the service continued, but some DW staff felt that his
move had already served to encourage self-censorship, making
the broadcasts more cautious and conservative in tone than

they had been.[14] There was a similar allegation when Steigner
travelled to Greece in 1972, while the colonels' junta was
still in power there. Upon his return, according to some
staff members, he attempted to persuade DW staff to make a
greater attempt to cover the "more favorable" aspects of the
Greek government and to get the Greek service to be more
neutral in its use of terminology describing that government.[15] DLF staff members have claimed to be free of such
pressures, and several DW staff have spoken enviously of the
"freer atmosphere" at their sister institution.

However, it's difficult for any DW or DLF administrator
to influence the organization as a whole, because those who
head the various program divisions largely function as laws
unto themselves. There appears to be little attempt at
policy coordination in either organization, and it is very
rare that the centrally-prepared commentaries and analyses
MUST be used by the DW and DLF language services, with the
exception of DLF's German service. Likewise, the centrally-
prepared newscasts, although they are supposed to be translated as received from the central newsroom, may come out
sounding differently from one language service to another.
There is little internal review on a day-to-day basis, and
West German labor laws make it exceedingly difficult to
demote or discharge "offending" staff members. Still, most
language services are disposed to accept much, if not most,
of what the central services of the two stations make available to them, if only because it saves extra work and
(perhaps) earns them favor with the central administration.
Thus, any centrally-supported tendency, be it liberal or
conservative, could have some impact.

Aside from the question of possible conservatism, there
is another issue that has arisen during the past decade: how
much emphasis should the stations place on talking about West
Germany and how much on talking about the rest of the world?
The law establishing the two stations states that each of
them is obliged to "present a comprehensive picture of
Germany," and DW is required to "present and explain the
German viewpoint on important questions."[16] However,
roughly four-fifths of DLF's schedule is in German, and the
station's transmitters beam its signal to Europe alone, so
that the preoccupation with Germany displayed in its broadcasts seems entirely logical. Deutsche Welle, on the other
hand, devotes about one-third of its weekly hours of transmission to German language broadcasts, and its signals are
directed all over the world, so one might expect it to be
more "worldly."

It is, to some extent. Particularly in broadcasts to
developing nations, many DW services have sought to cover
non-German news that would be of special interest to Third
World listeners. While DW has no full-time correspondents

overseas, it does have some stringers abroad and a number of
limited contract announcers and writers from those nations
working at its headquarters in Cologne. The Africa service
has worked with some African radio stations on coproductions.
Several of the services solicit listener letters and music
requests. But other services, the German service and the
English service to North America chief among them, concentrate so much of their time and attention on West Germany
that any but dedicated Germanophiles often would be lost,
bored or both.[17] Furthermore, the translations from German
to English sometimes are awkward, and even material prepared
in English may sound antiquated, as in this September 1979
North American Service feature:

> German film star Ingrid Peters . . . tied
> the knot with her manager sweetie Lothar Stein
> last weekend. Well, the wedding day also
> happened to be Stein's birthday, and so the
> bride presented him not only with herself, but
> with a swell camera outfit. Now, what does a
> fella normally do on his wedding night? Well,
> we camera freaks are not normal, and Stein
> spent the night studying the instruction
> manual. 'Nuff said, except to note that the
> bride took it like a sport, saying she'll wait
> and see what (PAUSE) develops.

Former BBC External Services administrator James Monahan was asked by DW to conduct an internal investigation of
the station in 1972. One of his main recommendations was
that DW try to develop a more international approach in much
of its programing. He also wondered whether the station
should be devoting so much of its air time (over 30 per cent)
to German, since it was little spoken outside Europe. DW
administrators felt that Monahan made many sound points, but
his report led to few changes. The present administration
continues to feel that it must, according to the terms of
the law establishing DW, give the German language and coverage
of Germany a prominent place.[18]
Nevertheless, there is evidence that both DLF and DW
have considerable followings. There is a small but quite
active research office within DW (but not within DLF), and
both stations receive research reports from BBC and VOA.
In those parts of the world beyond Europe served by the
three Western international broadcasters, DW usually finishes
behind BBC and VOA, but by increasingly narrow margins over
the 20-year period that it has been in a position to compete
with them at all--and VOA and BBC had a considerable head
start. In East Africa, where DW profits from an excellent
broadcast signal and 150 minutes of broadcasting in Swahili

each day (BBC and VOA have 60 minutes each), surveys have
revealed that the station frequently outdraws its Western
colleagues, sometimes by substantial margins.[19] The station
fares least well in parts of the world where its broadcast
signal is not strong (West Africa, much of Asia), but that
may change as DW secures more overseas transmission sites;
it signed a contract for the construction of a transmitter
base on Sri Lanka with the Sri Lankan government in
November 1980, and existing transmitter complexes may be
strengthened. DLF does quite well when compared with other
international broadcasters serving Western European
audiences--a 1979 BBC survey in France and Belgium revealed
that BBC and DLF French services each had regular listening
figures of just under one per cent in France and about 1.5
per cent in Belgium[20]--but most of its language services
last no more than 30 minutes per day, reducing its potential
impact.
    The future seems to hold little prospect for change for
either DW or DLF, aside from expansion of facilities. Neither
station has added a language service since 1975, and weekly
hours of transmission have shown little variation over the
past decade. The 1980 budgets for the stations--approxi-
mately DM 110 million for DLF, over DM 200 million for DW--
have grown steadily but not spectacularly during the 1970s.*
The federal government appears indifferent to the stations.
One searches almost in vain for indications of close parliamentary scrutiny, of attempts at interference by the
foreign office, or of interior ministry inquiries regarding
the manner in which the budgets are spent.[21] The contrast
with BBC and VOA in this respect is a marked one. Neither
are the stations the subject of much domestic media coverage,
aside from DLF's German service. The supervisory councils
meet too infrequently, and contain too many offsetting
political factions, to exert much influence. Stimulus for
change would have to come from within the stations, but here,
too, offsetting political tendencies seem to have inhibited
much serious consideration of changing roles and tasks. The
aforementioned Monahan report contained many potentially
useful suggestions for change, but few appear to have been
adopted. DW in particular appears to aspire to a stature
comparable to BBC's, and West Germany's prominent role in
world affairs would make the station's ambition a logical
one, but it has not yet been realized.[22]

RADIO NEDERLAND

    From its beginnings in 1927 as privately-operated
station PCJ to its present identity as Radio Nederland, Dutch

---

*However, the government announced a 10 per cent cut in DW
and DLF budgets in mid-September 1981.

international broadcasting has had one constant mission: to
serve Dutch speakers, citizens and expatriates alike,
wherever in the world they might be. In that sense, it has
functioned as a typical colonial service. But from 1928 to
the present, it also has had more broadly international
aims, first with the weekly multilingual broadcasts of Eddie
Startz' "Happy Station" program over PCJ, and later with the
addition of several foreign language services. Until the
Nazi invasion in 1940, the colonial service mission clearly
predominated. The Nazis used the station for their own
purposes, but after the war the Dutch government reestab-
lished it, and in 1947 turned control of it over to an
independent foundation, the Radio Nederland Wereldomroep.

Radio Nederland's financial support came from a share
of the annual broadcast license fee paid by Dutch citizens,
which itself seemed to be a recognition of the station's
colonial service mission; if RN were to have served the
purposes of Dutch foreign policy, then presumably the Dutch
Foreign Office would have paid for it. But RN's early
administrators were also anxious to make a larger portion of
the station's schedule more international, and almost immediately began to add languages: English and Indonesian in
1947, Afrikaans, Arabic, and Spanish over the next several
years. RN chose not to become involved in the Cold War,
and with one minor exception, directed none of its transmissions to Eastern Europe and the USSR.[23] Instead, it concentrated on parts of the world where there were Dutch
citizens and expatriates, on Holland's present and former
colonies (Indonesia and the Dutch West Indies), on the Arab
World (increasingly important to Dutch foreign trade and for
oil) and on the other developing nations, especially in
Africa and Asia.

The station's original transmitter site in Holland
became increasingly inadequate to serve those audiences,
especially as the superpower race got under way, so RN took
its cue from some of the contestants themselves and
established overseas relay bases. The first (1969) was on
Dutch-governed Bonaire, just north of Venezuela; the second
(1970) was on Madagascar. Both relays indicated the particular importance RN attached to reaching the Third World,
partly as an aid to promoting good trade relations and
partly as an aspect of the genuine concern that the Dutch
seem to have for assisting the developing nations--a concern
RN manifests both in its broadcasts and in its training
program for broadcasters from the Third World.

During the 1970s, RN increased its commitment to reaching Third World listeners by adding Portuguese and two West
Indian languages (Papiamento and Sraran Tongo), hiring more
short-term contract staff from the developing nations, increasing broadcast time for English to Africa, and paying

more attention to news and features about and of special
interest to the Third World: tropical medicine, rice growing,
cattle raising, etc. Much of the program material came from
Dutch universities and other public and private institutions,
rather than from RN's own staff, since the station has no
full-time correspondents overseas, the news room receives
little but the standard wire services (Reuters, AP, AFP),
and the number of stringers overseas, although increasing,
remains quite small.

The 1970s also saw criticism of RN from several quarters.
First, it was attacked by a former (temporary) staff member
in a 1974 newspaper article,[24] which was also mentioned and
sometimes quoted in other Dutch newspapers. A "team" of
sociology students from the University of Amsterdam, perhaps
inspired by the article, studied the station in 1975, and
reached some of the same conclusions: RN lacked a well-
defined purpose, did not properly reflect a Socialist (the
ruling party in Holland at the time) philosophy, and had
inadequate information sources for its news and features
writers. The station was suddenly the object of more
domestic public attention than most international stations
ever receive, and a good bit of it was not very positive!

Then it was the government's turn. From 1947 to 1974,
RN had been financed by a portion of the broadcast license
fee money. Some of the domestic stations found this unfair,
especially as RN had become more international and less
colonial, and the government agreed. It began to provide
RN's financial support, and in 1975 released a report on a
special committee investigation of RN's effectiveness. The
report generally was favorable, but a few committee members
wondered whether RN was all that vital to Dutch interests,
and whether it couldn't be reduced in size. Some also
wondered why RN seemed to know so little about its audience.

It's difficult to say whether the budget cut which
occurred in 1977 was made worse by the events of 1974 and
1975. Most governmentally-financed operations were cut
then.[25] But it did illustrate quite graphically what RN had
lost when the financing system was changed in 1974; the
license fee system was not a government appropriation, and
didn't suffer cuts. (RN argued for its restoration almost
from the moment it was taken away, and finally in 1981
managed to convince the Dutch parliament. The "old" system
was to return on January 1, 1982). The cut took about a
tenth of RN's budget, although some of it was restored later.
It resulted in a reduction of broadcast hours for most
languages, the dropping of some medium wave and relay transmission time, and cancellation of the Afrikaans service.
Total weekly broadcast hours went from just over 400 per
week in 1976 to just over 280 per week in 1977, and have
remained there ever since. (Another reason for the

reduction was RN's desire to make better use of satellite relays and to insure that each broadcast be carried on at least two frequencies).[26]

Almost coincidental with the cut was the Dutch post office's announcement that it would no longer maintain RN's antiquated shortwave transmitter site in Holland, because it was "beyond renovation". RN's Board of Governors, which exercises nominal supervision of the station and which is made up of several leading Dutch citizens, felt that RN could not be effective as a worldwide communicator unless it had decent transmitters in Holland; for one thing, they were needed to relay broadcasts to Madagascar and Bonaire. The government ultimately agreed, and by 1984 a powerful new transmitter complex (2250 kW) should be on the air from Holland.

With that vote of confidence (and a little help from its well-placed friends!), RN seems to have weathered its worst storm. Program hours and services are unlikely to increase in the near future, although RN's Programme Advisory Council has suggested that the station add a Russian service, "in the spirit of the Helsinki agreement (CSCE)." But RN is beginning to learn more about its audience; it has stepped up its use of listener panels (see Chapter 12) and its analysis of listener letters, which it solicits often and which it receives in some quantity--about 150,000 per year. Its audience appears to be much the same as audiences for other Western international stations: young to middle-aged, fairly affluent, reasonably well educated, predominantly male.[27] Listeners seem to be attracted by the wide variety of programs, and African listeners in particular praise RN for its coverage of developments within Africa through programs such as "AfroScene" and for its attention to letters from African listeners on programs such as "Club des Amis". RN's newscasts and features receive support for their relative lack of bias, although the station is far from neutral in its coverage of East-West relations:

> The Warsaw Pact still is and will remain a
> tremendous military power instrument of the
> Soviets to preserve order within the socialist
> camp and to intervene whenever this is necessary
> . . . as in 1956 in Hungary and in 1968 in
> Czechoslovakia . . . examples of a way in which
> in the past Moscow protected the so-called
> socialist achievements in the member countries.
> English to Africa, May 14, 1980

Some listeners would like more coverage of Dutch perspectives on world events, and a few wonder why RN should attempt to match the comprehensiveness of BBC and VOA

newscasts. Others consider "Dutch by Radio" a waste of air
time, since (they feel) there can't be that many listeners
who want to learn such an "insignificant" language! But
many listeners very much appreciate RN's numerous informal
programs--the music request shows, "His and Hers" (a casual
"chat" show no longer on the air), and the venerable "Happy
Station," now hosted by Tom Meijer:

> Babette . . . has been promoted to be our
> secretry today. (If it's an American program I
> say "secretAIRy) . . . She's brought along pen
> and ink and she is right now--I cannot see what
> she's doing, but I think she's typing . . . So,
> Babette is typing, Gertie's walking around,
> Jap is laughing. (Jap is our technical genius
> of today) . . .
> Happy Station in English, February 13, 1977

There is no doubt that Radio Nederland is a far more
worldly station today than it was back in 1947. It continues
to place a high priority on serving Dutch speakers--about a
third of the broadcast hours are in Dutch--which probably
helps justify its budget (50 million florins, or about
$20 million, as of 1981). But its chief mission in life
appears to be to reach listeners in various parts of the
world, the Third World in particular, with messages that
will tell them that the Dutch are friendly, good trading
partners, cultured, compassionate, fair and honest.
Sometimes its broadcasts, even the informal ones, sound
terribly formal, and its newscasts cannot match those of
BBC or VOA for completeness. However, it has managed to
maintain its independence from the government (it has no
formal ties with the Dutch Foreign Office), it has not
altered its broadcast schedule to cover crises, and it has
discussed problems in Dutch society frankly. (Its coverage
of demonstrations by housing "squatters" during the inauguration of Queen Beatrix in 1980 earned it some critical
blasts from Dutch citizens for "spoiling" the event). It
seems to be carrying out one major aspect of its program
policy: to contribute to international peace "by supplying
factual information, arrange cultural exchanges but also
provide entertainment in a spirit of friendship" [sic][28]

RADIO RSA

The Republic of South Africa could be considered a
developing country in many respects. Certainly its per
capita income would entitle it to that label, if it were

calculated on the basis of the entire population. But South
Africa is really two countries: one of them white and very
developed, the other black/"colored" and Asian and far less
developed, at least in economic terms. It is largely the
white, developed South Africa that operates and is reflected
through the country's international service, Radio RSA.

South Africa established an international service in
the early 1950s, but it is doubtful that it would have
reached much of an audience. Broadcasts were limited to
relays of the English and Afrikaans services of South Africa
domestic radio, and the two languages were carried on alternate days of the week for nine hours per day, over two 20 kW
shortwave transmitters. The international service introduced
a five-minute newscast in French in 1961, to reach listeners
in the emerging independent nations of Francophone Africa,
but otherwise continued at the same modest level until 1965,
when the million-watt H.F. Verwoerd transmitter station was
dedicated. The growth of the international service from
that point was rapid: whereas the station was broadcasting
for slightly over 80 hours per week in 1965, it was broadcasting for 170 hours by 1970, and English, Afrikaans and
French were joined by Dutch, Portuguese, German and certain
of the Eastern and Southern African languages: Swahili,
Zulu and Chichewa. All languages were on the air daily,
some for several hours, most programing was the product of
the international service itself, and writers and announcers
were of the highest professional quality. Now it was
reasonably competitive with the other major international
broadcasters serving Africa, and its strong signal to Europe
and North America caught the attention of many international
radio listeners in those areas.

The messages received by Radio RSA's listeners were
mixed ones. Newscasts were comprehensive, generally free of
obvious pro-white or anti-black bias, and written and
delivered in a manner highly reminiscent of the BBC World
Service, which itself was something of a model to Radio RSA
staff.[29] Commentaries rarely attacked South Africa's
critics, but they did find some interesting ways in which to
respond to those criticisms, as in this May 8, 1969 broadcast:

> Now there is a new realism, arising to no
> small extent from Black Africa's increasing
> experience in affairs of state. Confronted with
> the realities of government, the more sensible
> Black leaders are coming to realize more and
> more that emotionalism is a heavy burden to
> bear in international relations. Similarly,
> confronted with unmistakable evidence that
> cooperation with South Africa engenders pros-
> perity, it must have become clear to Black

> leaders having the welfare of their people at
> heart, that there is not much to be gained by
> aloofness and animosity, especially not in
> the face of South Africa's consistent willing-
> ness to place its vast knowledge and experience
> at the disposal of the entire continent.[30]

Radio RSA also paid considerable attention to the achieve-
ments of Black individuals and groups within South Africa,
and sometimes by implication, sometimes by direct statement
developed a theme of cooperation and harmony between blacks
and whites. That theme was jarred by the Sharpville "massacre" of 1971, in which a number of black South Africans
were killed and many more injured, and has been jarred still
further by other instances of racial strife during the 1970s,
e.g. the death of Steve Biko in 1977, but Radio RSA passed
over some of those instances in silence and labelled others
as exaggerations or the work of "provocative elements".
Not surprisingly, some of those "elements" were Communist:
the South African government has followed a strongly anti-
Communist policy, and Radio RSA's broadcasts have mirrored
that policy. Military conflict between South African and
SWAPO (Southwest African Peoples' Organization) in the
Namibia-Angola border region, as reported by Radio RSA, has
often sounded like conflict between U.S. and Viet Cong
forces, as reported by VOA in the late 1960s:

> The general commanding the territory force
> of Southwest Africa-Namibia, Major General
> Charles Lloyd, says that the security forces
> are now following a new approach in their
> fight against SWAPO . . . terrorist bases,
> instead of individual terrorists, would in-
> creasingly be the target. General Lloyd
> says the security forces have been instructed
> to follow terrorists to their bases in
> southern Angola, and to destroy the bases.
> . . . General Lloyd said these tactics had
> proven very successful and SWAPO headquarters
> had been thrown into complete disarray . . .
> At the end of the news conference, 21 tons of
> weapons and equipment were displayed to news-
> men. One of the terrorist commanders captured
> was also introduced. He was identified as
> John Awula (?). He said in an interview that
> living conditions of the terrorists were poor,
> and many of them wanted to return to Ovambo.
> News in English to North America, July 13, 1981

When the black "homelands" began to be established in

the late 1970s, Radio RSA treated them as if they were tanta-
mount to independent nations (which they were not), and
covered the ceremonial occasions accompanying their new
status:

> Celebrations to mark the independence of
> the Venda Black State from South Africa were
> attended by thousands of Vendas in the capital,
> Tokoyondo, today. The festivities, which will
> concentrate on sports events over the next week,
> will conclude with the formal granting of inde-
> pendence next Thursday. The new sports stadium
> was opened officially this morning by the chief
> minister, paramount chief Patrick Mapopo. A
> colorful procession of about 2,500 sportsmen
> and women, representing the four Venda districts,
> and a team from areas in urban South Africa,
> paraded at the opening of the flag-bedecked
> stadium.
> Radio RSA in English, September 1979

At times, however, guest experts appearing on Radio RSA
expressed doubts about the viability of the "homelands":

> (INTERVIEWER) Do you think that any of the
> homelands, let's call them national states,
> such as Transkei, after some five years of
> independence, have any of them increased their
> capability in the eyes of the world, or, perhaps
> more importantly, in the eyes of Africa, to any
> extent, to the tiniest degree? Is it possible
> to say?
> (GUEST) Well . . . it's very hard to say, but
> . . . if they have done so, then I haven't seen
> it. . . .
> Strategy for Strength (a weekly feature)
> Radio RSA in English, April 17, 1981

In short, Radio RSA has found itself in a difficult
position. Its major target audiences, in black Africa,
Western Europe and the United States, are likely to be
skeptical of its constant theme of increasing racial harmony
within South Africa, although some listeners would respond
positively to South Africa's anti-Communist stance. The
station has attempted to reduce that skepticism by providing a reasonably straightforward and comprehensive
account of African news, by broadcasting sports events and
other "light" programs which would show South Africa to be a
"normal" nation, by responding to listener letters which
raised points critical of South African policies, and by

airing the views of South Africans who are not in full agreement with government policies. Nevertheless, people with
sharply opposing views, especially if those people are black
or "colored", appear very, very seldom.

Whether the picture will change in the near future is
doubtful. The South African Broadcasting Corporation, Radio
RSA's "parent" organization, was transferred from the Department of National Education to the Department of Foreign
Affairs and Information early in 1981, provoking expression
of fears on the part of some South African opposition
poli'tical leaders that South African radio and television
would be used by the majority Nationalist government to
further its propaganda.[31] Governmental support for Radio
RSA remains strong: although the station's weekly hours of
transmission and numbers of language services have remained
fairly constant throughout the 1970s, new 500 kW transmitters
were added to the existing complex in the late 1970s, and a
new broadcast service to Latin America came on the air in
1981. Audience research conducted by other international
broadcasters active in Africa shows that Radio RSA reaches
almost as many regular listeners as do VOA or BBC in East
Africa, and outstrips the two stations in much of southern
Africa, but it is mentioned rarely in surveys taken among
West African, Western European and North American listeners.[32]
Radio RSA receives and reads on the air many letters of
support from listeners, and the station's New Year's Eve
international call-in show brings many favorable phone calls
from European and North American (and a few African) listeners. Doubtless the station has won over some skeptics and
has reduced the level of skepticism among others, but the
available evidence would suggest that its impact has been
limited.

RADIO JAPAN

At the end of World War II, the circumstances of
Japanese international broadcasting closely resembled those
of Germany. International radio had been an important
propaganda weapon just before and during the war, and Radio
Tokyo's mixture of conciliatory and belligerent programing
won for the station a certain measure of notoriety among the
Allies. Its facilities and staff were largely intact at the
end of the war, but it was dismantled by order of the Allied
occupation authorities.

Japanese domestic broadcasting, however, continued
without a break, and although it was under the control of
the Allied General Headquarters, it remained a national
monopoly. When the Allies removed their ban on international

broadcasting in 1949, it seemed logical that the domestic
broadcasting organization (NHK) should do it. The Japanese
Diet (parliament) approved the reestablishment of an international service, and Radio Japan came on the air in 1952,
broadcasting in English and Japanese for five hours per day
over two 50 kW transmitters. Its announced goals were
". . . to inform other nations of the real situation in our
country, to promote reconstruction of the country with the
understanding of others and contribute to international
amity through cultural exchanges . . ."[33]
     Radio Japan grew rapidly: within five years it had
tripled its broadcast hours and added 14 languages, most of
them Asian and European, which were carried to listeners
over two 100 kW transmitters. By its tenth anniversary,
the station was broadcasting more than 220 hours a week in
20 languages and with six 100 kW transmitters, in addition
to several smaller ones. An NHK history of broadcasting
boasted that ". . . an epoch-making broadcasting system
unprecedented in the world was completed, and Radio Japan's
programmes became receivable at any time and anywhere."[34]
     If that rate of expansion had continued, the statement
would have been correct. Certainly the Radio Japan of 1962
was becoming competitive with all but the largest international broadcasters in number of languages, hours of
broadcast and power of transmitters. NHK had made expansion
of the international service a matter of high priority in its
first five-year plan (1958-1963), and Radio Japan began to
receive a small subsidy from the government in 1959. However,
NHK received its operating revenue through the annual
license fee paid by Japanese listeners and viewers, and
television was claiming more and more of that revenue. The
Ministry of Foreign Affairs seemed indifferent to the
possible uses of Radio Japan as an instrument of public
diplomacy. Few within NHK were prepared to see the station
expand if it were to do so at the expense of domestic radio
and television. By the mid 1960s Radio Japan virtually
ceased to grow. It added services in Malay, Swahili and
Burmese between 1963-1965, increased its broadcast hours to
roughly 250 a week by 1965, and inaugurated two further
100 kW transmitters. From 1965 on, those figures saw little
change in weekly hours of broadcast and none in language
services or transmitters, although beginning in 1979, Radio
Japan leased time from the Portuguese Radio Trans Europe
transmitter complex, in order to improve its signal to Europe.
     In discussions with station staff and in studying
Japanese views on foreign policy, I have detected another
possible barrier to expansion. Japanese are very sensitive
about their image in the world,[35] and see themselves as misunderstood by foreigners or too often judged in light of
their behavior during World War II. At the same time, they

seem reluctant to seek to correct that negative image, at
least through such a public instrument as broadcasting. The
international service appears to be viewed as a necessary
evil: every nation of any size has such a service, and so
must Japan, but let's not let it become <u>too</u> big. As one
consequence of that attitude, Radio Japan's antiquated and
weak (by 1981 standards) transmitters cannot begin to compete with those of the other major international broadcasters active in Asia, let alone with those active in other
parts of the world. It doesn't help matters that the
Japanese company (KDD) which owns and operates the overseas
transmitters used by Radio Japan charges high rates and
seemingly has little interest in modernizing them.36
     That state of affairs seems unfortunate, given Japan's
position of importance in world political and economic
affairs, and given the excellence of much of the station's
programing. English and Japanese services account for well
over half of Radio Japan's broadcast hours, and news and
other informational material for over 90 per cent of all
programing. However, the station does broadcast 45-minute
daily services in Kuoyu (Mandarin) and in Korean, and most
of its remaining language services are on the air for 30
minutes a day, some of them repeated. Its informational
broadcasts contain a wide range of features, as well as some
of the more comprehensive and unbiased newscasts on international radio with special emphasis on news about Asia.
The features tend to concentrate on the more cultural and
personal sides of life in Japan, e.g. in "One In a Hundred
Million," a weekly feature about the daily working and
leisure activities of a Japanese citizen. The station
carries "Let's Learn Japanese" broadcasts in most of the
language services, and attempts to promote Japanese foreign
trade through a weekly "Industrial Report".
     Many of the features are prepared centrally and trans-
lated by various language desks, but most of the translations
are reasonably idiomatic. The picture that emerges is one
of a highly purposeful society, a diverse society, a society
with a strong sense of its cultural past. It is not
ordinarily a picture of a society confronted with serious
political disagreements and scandals (e.g. the Lockheed
"bribery" scandal of the mid 1970s), because Japanese
domestic media usually have seen fit to omit or provide
minimal coverage of such "shameful" acts, and Radio Japan
has followed suit.37 But it can sometimes be a picture of a
society faced with problems such as industrial pollution and
the "workaholic" society:

> (ANNOUNCER) . . . people abroad tend to think of
> the average white-collar worker [in Japan] as
> living a rich and happy life, since he is assured

of a living by the lifetime employment system.
But light and shadow go hand in hand, and the
real situation here is rather different. Many
white-collar workers here suffer from mental
disease and neuroses.
(MALE VOICE) I felt it trying to get up in
the morning. After breakfast, I immediately
returned to bed, but I couldn't go to sleep.
I lay in bed and just brooded over my past
and worried about my future. I felt as if my
fate were sealed. . . . After reproaching
myself for my worthlessness, I felt I was of
no use to the world.
Japan Today, in English, August 1981

Radio Japan appears to have two principal target
audiences in mind: overseas Japanese, especially those
living in South America and along the west coast of North
America, and Asians. For the former, it has relays of some
NHK domestic programs, particularly light entertainment, as
well as news, commentaries and features, with the accent on
life and events in Japan. For the latter, it has newscasts
stressing developments in Asia, Japanese cooperation with
various Asian countries and music from Asia ("Melodies of
Asia"), as well as many features about life in Japan. At
one time, it knew little about its audience, aside from what
listener letters revealed, since it conducted little formal
audience research, but in the 1970s it began to mail out
detailed questionnaires to listeners who had corresponded
with it. Those listeners who responded tended to be young
(teens through thirties), quite well educated, and more
interested in hearing about domestic developments in Japan
itself than about Japan's activities around the world or
Japanese coverage of world news. More random surveys taken
by BBC, VOA and other broadcasters, however, show very small
or statistically nonexistent audiences for Radio Japan, even
in many Asian countries.

If Radio Japan is to increase the size of its audience,
it will have to improve its signal strength and increase the
number of frequencies to which it has access.[38] It would
also help if it were able to program more hours each day in
languages other than Japanese and English. To carry out
those steps, the station would need greater monetary support
than it now receives, but neither of the organizations
chiefly concerned with its financing, the NHK and the
Japanese government, seems disposed to increase that level
of support, which stands at approximately 3-3/4 billion yen
(c. $15 million) as of 1981--a six per cent increase over
the 1980 budget. Various committees and individuals have
been urging increases for nearly two decades,[39] but their

pleas have fallen on deaf ears.* The Radio Japan advisory
council (Overseas Broadcasting Programme Council) a 13-member
group made up of prominent Japanese government officials,
industrialists and others involved with foreign trade and
foreign relations, could be a useful ally in this respect,
but it appears to have been more ceremonial than active.[40]

There is always the possibility that increased financial
support from the government would result in a greater degree
of governmental interference. Radio Japan administrators
meet with officials from the Ministry of Foreign Affairs and
the Ministry of International Trade and Industry, but those
ministries exercise no direct control over the station, and
seem to regard such control as not worth the effort. A more
powerful Radio Japan might lead them to more direct involvement in its programing. But the likelihood of a marked
increase in Radio Japan's budget seems remote, and the
station appears destined to remain a secondary power in international radio, even as Japan grows in international prominence.

RADIO AUSTRALIA

Long distance radio communication was a logical field of
experimentation for Australia, given the size and uneven
population distribution of the continent, and tests of high
frequency equipment starting in the mid-1920s revealed that
broadcast signals were reaching other parts of the world, as
well as Australia itself. But it was not until the nation
entered World War II that an ongoing international radio
service was established, and when it came on the air on
December 20, 1939 as "Australia Calling", the station had a
decided wartime sound: its missions were to reach Australian
military personnel overseas with a mixture of domestic and
specially prepared programing, and to combat Axis propaganda.[41] During the war, it added Japanese, Thai, Indonesian and Mandarin for Japanese military personnel and for
people under Japanese occupation. Control of broadcast
content shuttled between the Department of Information and
the Australian Broadcasting Commission (Australia's public
broadcasting service), ending up with the Department of
Information in 1944.

Following the war, the international service was retained, but received a new title: Radio Australia. In 1950,
control of the service again passed into the hands of ABC,
where it has remained ever since. It is financed by ABC
from its annual appropriations, which are voted by the
Australian parliament. It thus shares a problem with Radio
Japan, namely, that it must compete with Australian domestic

---

*However, in October 1981 a policy research committee of the
ruling Liberal Democratic Party recommended expansion of
Radio Japan, in part to improve Japan's "negative" trade image
abroad. Stephen Cook, "Radio Japan's Bonanza," Manchester
Guardian, October 11, 1981.

radio and television for a share of the same budgetary pie.
It has fared considerably better in that competition than
has Radio Japan in terms of weekly hours of broadcast and
increases in transmitter power. It went from about 180 hours
per week in 1950 to almost 380 hours per week by 1975, then
fell back slightly to its 1981 level of just over 330.   Its
combined transmitter power as of 1950 was approximately
270 kW, from two sites; two decades later, it was nearly
1300 kW, from three sites, including one inaugurated in 1969
near Darwin. The Darwin site was levelled in a tropical
storm five years later, but temporary facilities took up
some of the slack, and combined power as of 1980 was 1130 kW.

The relative stability of language services over most of
Australia's international radio history is partially attributable to the decision made early in World War II to
concentrate on Asia and the Pacific. That decision was
prompted by the war itself, but priorities might have been
expected to change at war's end, or the international service
dropped altogether. Instead, Asia remained the principal
target area, even through a severe cutback in language
services in 1950.[42] In the late 1950s and early 1960s,
services in Japanese, Mandarin and Cantonese, were added or
restored to the schedule and services in Indonesian and Thai
increased markedly in broadcast time.

During the 1970s, Radio Australia added Neo-Melanesian
(Pidgin English) for the South Pacific and Papua New Guinea,
and expanded its Indonesian service to nine hours per day.
By 1975 it was broadcasting nearly 380 hours per week. But
the destruction of the Darwin transmitter in December 1974
very nearly proved disastrous for Radio Australia as a whole.
The ruling Labor Party government appointed a special committee (the Waller Committee) in May 1975 to review the
station, especially in terms of its future needs. Then a
coalition of the Liberal and National Country Parties came
to power, and in April 1976 appointed another committee (the
Green Committee) to examine all of Australian broadcasting.

The Green Committee report reached Parliament before
the Waller report. Its few recommendations on Radio
Australia were positive, and called for the government to
increase its budget and to make separate (from ABC) annual
appropriations for it, even though ABC would continue to
estimate and administer the RA budget and to supervise the
station! The Green report also called for much closer
coordination between RA and the Departments of Foreign
Affairs and Overseas Trade, which would set "guidelines
concerning strategy and target audiences."[43] The Waller
Committee report was just as positive and far more detailed.
It recommended a standing interdepartmental review committee
for RA which would include a member from the Department of
Foreign Affairs, but said nothing about the committee
setting any guidelines.[44]

Parliament discussed both reports, and some MPs (including former Prime Minister Gough Whitlam) wondered whether the government was going to recommend that the station be closed. Finally, in May 1977, Parliament voted an A$10.3 million appropriation for strengthening RA's transmission facilities and reaffirmed ABC control of the station. The interdepartmental review committee never was appointed. Annual budget increases, which had been on the order of five per cent or less in the mid-1970s, moved toward 10 per cent, and the 1980 budget was A$5.75 million (c. US $6.3 million)-- still a low figure in comparison with stations of similar size.

The Waller report had had a good deal to say about the station's principal target areas, and in 1980 a joint review by ABC and the Australian Telecommunications Commission produced the recommendation that Radio Australia's prime target areas be Indonesia, the Peoples' Republic of China, Japan and Melanesia, followed by other Southeast Asian and Pacific nations and areas. One indication of the increasing importance of broadcasts to the PRC was the Australian cabinet's approval in 1980 of an appropriation of A$1.4 million for a special project, "English from Radio Australia for China."

Clearly, Southeast Asia, China and the Pacific, which have always been high on Radio Australia's priority list, now dominate it. More and more of the reports and features deal with events in Asia and events in Australia of special interest to Asian listeners. ABC's staff of overseas correspondents in Asia furnishes much material to RA, either directly or indirectly (through ABC). The weekly ABC radio feature "Report from Asia" has been translated and carried by most of RA's Asian language services since 1978. Some of the services play Asian music. Two have English by Radio programs. Most strongly encourage mail, and the Indonesian and Chinese services, on the air for nine and five hours per day respectively, receive the lion's share of it-- roughly 130,000 letters from Indonesian listeners and almost 200,000 letters from listeners to Chinese language broadcasts in 1980-1981 (12-month period), out of a grand total of over 370,000 letters. Much of the mail is for music requests --heavily promoted by RA--or in connection with the English by Radio programs, but some of it is in the form of questions about Australia, which are answered through the numerous "mailbag" programs:

George had some friends who served in the armed forces during World War Two. His question refers to a time when these friends were stationed in Australia. They talked about primitive people called Fuzzy-Wuzzies. "One of

these Fuzzy-Wuzzies offered to trade his wife
for a wristwatch."
      The Fuzzy-Wuzzies were no doubt Papuans.
These days, New Guinea and Papua are united,
but during the war New Guinea was separate
from Papua, both under Australian control.
The Papuans have what we now call "Afro"
hair styles, hence their name. . . .
      George, it's quite possible that your
friend was offered a wife in return for his
wristwatch. Remember, we're going back 40
years and a lot has happened since then.
. . . almost all children receive primary
education and a very large percentage receive
secondary education. Papua New Guinea is a
Christian country, although many tribal
customs and beliefs still persist, for example
witch doctors. But it's most unlikely that
you'd be able to trade for a wife!
You Asked For It, August 8, 1981

The motivation for RA's heavy concentration on Asia
and the Pacific is not hard to discover. During the 1960s
and 1970s, Australia shed a good deal of its insularity,
including a certain measure of anti-Asian prejudice,[45] as it
sought closer political and economic relations with its Asian
and Pacific neighbors. It took some time for this reorien-
tation to have its full effect upon Radio Australia; when I
visited the station in 1970, its senior administrators still
seemed to be at least as interested in reaching listeners
in Europe and North America as they were in reaching Asians.
However, during the 1970s, most of the new programs and all
of the increased broadcast hours have been for the particular
benefit of listeners in Asia and the Pacific. Broadcast
hours in English have been reduced, mainly through consolidation of separate English language services into a 24-hour
per day service. Asia, the Pacific area, Australo-Asian and
Australo-Pacific relations are major topics of RA current
affairs programs:

      Inevitably in any relationship, and certainly
in one as powerfully important as Australia's
trading partnership with Japan, difficulties arise
from time to time. Japanese companies used to
complain, for instance, at the restrictions on
entry of their consumer goods into Australia,
although of late this has been of less concern.
. . . Australia's complaints have centered
around the attitude some Japanese companies have
taken to price and supply terms in long-term

contracts. . . .
Focus on Australia, January 21, 1981

Government interest in Radio Australia appears to have
increased in the 1970s. The Departments of Foreign Affairs
and Overseas Trade see it as useful to their missions, and
probably had some influence on the 1980 recommendations for
priority areas. However, that interest has not kept RA
from reporting critical comment on government actions within
Australia or among the Asia and Pacific nations, such as
criticism of Australian Prime Minister Fraser's "posturing"
over the North-South economic debate by the Australian
Treasury Secretary, John Stone (July 24, 1981 broadcast of
Australian Insight) and treatment of alleged human rights
violations by Indonesia in Irian Jaya and East Timor.[46]
Radio Australia continues to measure its success in
reaching listeners chiefly through numbers of letters it
receives, as it seems to have done throughout its history.
It has sent out questionnaires on occasion, but hasn't conducted random or stratified sample survey research. BBC and
VOA surveys in Asia have shown that RA, VOA and BBC reach
about the same numbers and types of listeners in many of the
Asian countries, although RA's longer broadcast day, better
transmitter location, many popular music request programs
and thorough coverage of Indonesian events bring it a larger
audience in Indonesia. VOA's listener panel research
(Chapter 12, pp. 324-325) revealed that Malaysian panel
members were impressed by RA's clearly worded and credible
newscasts, liked their emphasis on Asia, enjoyed the sports
coverage, and felt that the station had good balance between
music and spoken word programing. (A 1976 content analysis
of RA's Kuoyu (Mandarin) service supported those observations).[47] In fact, Radio Australia has cultivated a friendly,
relaxed style as a way of attracting and holding listeners,
and its disk jockeys, letterbox hosts and even many of its
reporters contribute to its highly personal image--an image
which many listener letters translate as "warmth". What
this means in terms of the station's contribution to
Australian foreign or trade policies is hard to say, but it
does seem to indicate that RA is helping to dispel the old
image of an Australia with no interest in its Asian and
Pacific neighbors.

                        SOME GENERALIZATIONS

The five cases I have presented here are not perfectly
representative of all Western international stations, but
my years of listening to various stations and my conversations with staff members from most of them lead me to feel

confident in offering the following general observations.

First, the vast majority of Western international stations came into existence to reach their citizens and
expatriates living and working abroad. Many of the stations
became more truly international during World War II. Most
continued to be international after World War II, although
few dropped the colonial service approach completely, and
most retain it to this day. Most of the stations suffered
budget cuts just after the war, but experienced considerable
growth in the 1950s and 1960s. The Cold War, the advent of
independence for developing countries (some of them former
colonies) and the increasing importance of international
trade helped to promote that growth. Very few stations
expanded during the 1970s, and little growth is expected in
the 1980s.

Second, there is cooperation and coordination among the
Western stations, most of it in technical matters and
audience research. BBC, VOA, DW, Radio Nederland and Radio
Canada International (RCI) have annual meetings to coordinate
frequency usage to their best mutual advantage, and several
stations (notably BBC, VOA, DW and RCI) share transmitter
facilities.[48] BBC, VOA and DW exchange audience research
data and cooperate on some research projects. RCI, RN,
Radio Sweden and Swiss Radio International exchange information about operating procedures and even have a short-term
exchange of staff. Radio Japan exchanges staff with several
of the other Western broadcasters. But programing seems to
involve very little exchange of information, and there is no
evidence of coordination of themes among the stations,
although the nearly universal use of the same three or four
wire services (AP, UPI, Reuters, AFP) often makes their newscasts sound remarkably alike.

Third, while BBC and VOA have responded to certain
crises by expanding existing language services (both
increased Portuguese in the mid-1970s) or adding language
services (both did so to Central Asia in the period 1979-
1981), few other Western stations exhibit such behavior,
whether because they choose not to, as officials at RN and
Swiss Radio International have told me, or because they don't
have the necessary budgetary, technical or production
resources to do so.

Fourth, few of the Western nations have engaged in clandestine broadcasting, other than during World War II. The
United States has been the major exception, followed by Great
Britain and France (both active during the mid-1950s vis-a-
vis Egypt). There is no evidence that the "official" international broadcasting services of those countries had anything to do with the establishment or operation of the
clandestine services, and specific evidence to indicate that
BBC deplored their creation by the British Foreign Office.[49]

Fifth, several of the Western stations make every attempt to reach a worldwide audience, and have exchanged transmission facilities with one another, erected transmitters in other parts of the world, and leased transmitter time from still other nations (e.g. from Portugal and Sri Lanka). But many appear content to reach a largely regional audience (e.g. Spain to Latin America) or an audience with specific characteristics (e.g. Radio France International to French speaking listeners throughout the world).

Sixth, several of the Western stations engage in survey research, with VOA and BBC leading the way, followed by DW and RCI. Radio Japan, Radio Australia, Radio Nederland and Swiss Radio International have shown increasing interest in research involving mail questionnaires, but many Western stations still rely heavily upon numbers and content analysis of listener letters as their chief measure of effectiveness.

And finally, foreign ministries and other governmental departments display varying degrees of interest and involvement in the Western international radio services, ranging from seeming indifference (Japan) to sporadic interest (Australia) to continuing involvement (France). On the whole, the Western stations attempt to maintain an arm's length relationship with their respective governments; some are quite successful, especially when they are aided by "sheltered" (from government control) financial resources or institutional structures, but others are more or less at the mercy of the government.

NOTES

1. Heinz Lubbers and Werner Schwipps, "Der Deutsche Weltrundfunksender: Kurzwellenrundfunk für Auslandsdeutsche," in Mit 8 kW Rund um die Welt (Berlin: Haude and Spenersche, 1969), pp. 11-31.

2. Werner Schwipps, "Wortschlacht im Äther" and Gerhard Goebel, "Fernkampfwaffen im Rundfunkkrieg," in Wortschlacht im Äther (Berlin: Haude and Spenersche, 1971); and Willi Boelcke, Die Macht des Radios (Frankfurt: Verlag Ullstein, 1977), Chapters 2-4 are helpful sources of information on the wartime period.

3. Rolf Steininger, Langer Streit um Kurze Welle (Berlin: Haude and Spenersche, 1972), offers a very detailed account of the debates over the reestablishment of a German international radio service. Several individuals who had been connected with West German radio activities during the 1950s have told me that they had the impression that the Allied High Command supported the reestablishment of the service in part because it might serve a useful purpose in

the Cold War, but I have been unable to find specific evidence for this. See also Anita Mallinckrodt, <u>Die selbstdarstellung der beiden deutschen staaten im Ausland</u> (Köln: Verlag Wissenschaft und Politik, 1981), pp. 55-59.

4. Hanns Werner, <u>Das Provisorium</u> (Berlin: Haude and Spenersche, 1976), pp. 51-53. Werner also notes the interest of the federal government in an Arabic service as an instrument for achieving closer diplomatic ties with the Middle East.

5. For a fuller account of this complicated issue, see Arthur Williams, <u>Broadcasting and Democracy in West Germany</u> (Bradford, U.K.: Bradford University Press, 1976), pp. 20-31; and Gerard Braunthal, "Federalism in Germany: the Broadcasting Controversy," <u>Journal of Politics</u> 24 (August 1962): 545-561.

6. DLF also receives approximately one-third of its annual operating budget from license fee revenues collected from West German listeners and viewers for the West German domestic broadcasting stations.

7. DW's <u>Rundfunkrat</u> is by law made up of 11 members: two each are elected by the two houses of the Federal parliament, four are appointed by the Federal government, and three are nominated by religious organizations: Catholic, Protestant and Jewish. Its membership is far from representative of the West German society in any institutional sense, although members are encouraged to approach their deliberations in a broad-minded way! DLF's <u>Rundfunkrat</u> has 22 members, but its composition is almost identical to DW's.

8. The Administrative Councils (<u>Verwaltungsräte</u>), which are appointed by the <u>Rundfunkräte</u>, may meet more often. They supervise the conduct of each station's budgetary and administrative affairs.

9. There are many sources of information on the politicization of West German broadcasting; two of the best, and most accessible, are Williams, <u>Broadcasting</u>, and Alfred Grosser, "Federal Republic of Germany," in <u>Television and Political Life,</u> Anthony Smith, ed. (New York: St. Martin's Press, 1979), Chapter 4.

10. When a new editor-in-chief was to be appointed to DW in 1975, one apparently strong candidate, Gustav Trampe, allegedly withdrew his name from consideration because DW director Walter Steigner, himself nominally a Social Democrat, was giving in to Christian Democrat pressure and placing such restrictions on the job that Trampe would be discouraged from taking it. "Die SPD schiesst auf den eigenen Mann," <u>Süddeutsche Zeitung</u>, August 19, 1975, p. 6.

11. These observations were made in the course of meetings I had with DW staff in September 1975 and April and May 1980, and with DLF staff in April 1980.

12. I became particularly aware of differences in level

of detail when monitoring the broadcasts and reading scripts
of newscasts and features from the two stations for the
period May 11-15, 1980. On the issue of Warsaw Pact arms
strength, for example, DW commentaries and reports would
often go into very specific detail as to weapon types, exact
numbers of weapons, etc., whereas DLF tended to use generic
names (e.g. "long-range missiles" instead of "SS-20 missiles")
and round off its figures.

13. James Oliver, "Comparison of the Russian Services
of the Four Major Broadcasters (VOA, BBC, DW, RL),"
Washington, D.C.: U.S. Information Agency, Office of Research,
Report R-8-75 (July 28, 1975), pp. 20-22.

14. Interviews with DW staff, September 1975; "Deutsche
Welle in Dammerung," Stern, Nr. 15, April 3, 1975.

15. Interviews with DW staff, September 1975; memo,
Redakteurausschuss der Deutschen Welle "to all DW editorial
colleagues," Köln, July 21, 1972. According to this memo,
Steigner said that he had discussed his visit to Greece with
the West German foreign office--a rare occurrence, because
DW usually has as little contact with the foreign office on
policy matters as possible. He also indicated that he did
not have in mind any specific prohibitions that would change
the character of DW's Greek service, but he was concerned
about the use of terms such as "junta" or "military government". He was not convinced that the situation in Greece
was as bad as DW's Greek service seemed to portray it,
especially with respect to political prisoners. A high
ranking DW official told me in September 1975 that, following
Steigner's return from Greece, the Greek service did receive
closer scrutiny, and its head, a Greek who was certainly not
in sympathy with the military government in Greece, was
eventually demoted.

16. "Gesetz über die Errichtung von Rundfunkanstalten
des Bundesrechts," November 29, 1960. Cited in Bundesgesetz-
blatt, Jahrgang 1960, Teil 1, nr. 61, p. 863.

17. I base this observation on my own monitoring of DW
over approximately 15 years and on conversations with shortwave listeners in several parts of the world, but especially
the USA and Canada. I understand German fairly well, lived
there for over a year, and have visited West Germany several
times, yet I find many DW features and commentaries too
detailed for easy comprehension and too parochial in nature
for any but dedicated Germanophiles. Mallinckrodt,
Selbstdarstellung, p. 98, reaches the same conclusion.

18. I discussed this subject with most of the top-
level DW administrators when I visited the station in April
and May 1980. All felt the way I have stated.

19. A BBC-commissioned survey done in Kenya in September and October of 1978 revealed that DW's Swahili
service obtained a regular (once a week or more) listening

figure of 10.8 per cent of the rural and urban population,
whereas BBC had a figure of 2.5 per cent, and VOA's figure
was even lower. BBC Handbook 1980 (London: BBC, 1979), p. 58.
       20. BBC Annual Report and Handbook 1981 (London: BBC,
1980), pp. 61-62. Radio Canada International and Radio
Moscow were far behind. VOA does not broadcast in French to
France. The DLF and BBC figures are reasonably high when
compared with figures obtained by any international broadcaster transmitting to Western Europe; those figures seldom
rise above two or three per cent for regular listening to
any given station.
       21. Both Conrad Ahlers, Director of DW (since deceased)
and Jürgen Reiss, Head of European Services, DLF, told me in
April 1980 interviews that they would appreciate more
attention from the federal government, both as an aid to
budget requests and as an antidote to a morale problem faced
by both stations: staff frequently feel that no one knows
or cares about what they do. Dr. Otto Busch, head of DW's
central newsroom, told me in an April 1980 interview that
DW's virtual invisibility within West Germany hindered
attempts to recruit well-qualified journalists for the newsroom.
       22. Julian Hale, Radio Power (Philadelphia: Temple
University Press, 1975), p. 63, states that the then Managing
Director of BBC External Services Gerard Mansell "fears the
competition offered by DW more than any rival" because of
West Germany's relative lack of a colonial past and West
German prominence as a "spokesnation" for Western Europe as
a whole. My own conversations with Mansell in 1975, 1977
and 1980, revealed no trace of that "fear"; while he respected
DW, Mansell also could see its limitations. My own discussions with some three dozen DW staff members in 1967,
1975 and 1980 also revealed a strong tendency for DW staff
to compare themselves with the BBC--an organization almost
all of them had listened to regularly, many had visited, and
a few had worked for. None felt that they were yet up to
BBC's standard of presenting news and features. Some saw
themselves as improving, others not.
       23. Milton Hollstein, "Tiny Holland's Mighty Radio
Voice," Journalism Quarterly 51 (Autumn 1974):487, quotes
then program director H.J. Van Eijndhoven as saying that RN
regarded Eastern Europe and the USSR as already "saturated"
with British and U.S. broadcasts. In my visits to the
station in September 1972, September 1975 and May 1980,
administrators indicated that they had little interest in
broadcasting to the Communist nations of Europe; broadcasts
to the developing nations had higher priority, and the
introduction of services in Russian, Polish, Hungarian, etc.
would almost certainly be regarded as a propaganda move.

There was a French service to Eastern Europe in 1953;
according to Bert Steinkamp, RN's program director, the
Dutch foreign office asked the station to initiate it in
order to reach Eastern European intellectuals, many of whom
were thought to speak French, with a service they might
accept more readily, since it didn't come from one of the
major Western powers and wasn't in any of their own national
languages. It was dropped because there was very little
evidence that it was listened to. Interview, Steinkamp,
Hilversum, the Netherlands, September 12, 1975.

24. Paul Brennan, "Radio Nederland," Vrij Nederland
(November 29, 1974), pp. 2+. Brennan was especially hard on
the station for its lack of a reference library; such few
books and magazines as existed were usually old, and anyone
turning to them for assistance in writing a feature or news
item was almost certain to be disappointed. When I visited
the station in 1975, staff members were still furious about
the article, mostly because they felt that Brennan hadn't
worked for the station long enough to become an informed
critic, but some staff agreed that he had at least a few
valid points, especially about the "reference library".

25. Bert Steinkamp told me in May 1980 that the
Ministry of Culture, under which RN is located for budgetary
purposes, had nothing against the station, but that its
head (who didn't know much about the station, either) was
anxious to protect various social services from cuts, and
was willing to sacrifice part of RN's budget for that
purpose.

26. Bert Steinkamp, letter to me, May 26, 1981.

27. I gathered information on RN's audience through
interviews with several RN program staff members in 1972,
1975 and 1980 from several RN audience research reports on
the results of listener panel projects in Africa, North
America and the Pacific, and from various comments made by
shortwave listeners writing to the Review of International
Broadcasting. Many of the comments appearing in RIB were
critical of what the writers saw as too much informality,
to the point of idle and meaningless chatter, on such
programs as "The Happy Station".

28. From Programme Policy, Hilversum: Radio Nederland,
no date (1978?), p. 2. The same policy states that RN
"cannot . . . adopt a neutral position" with respect to such
basic Dutch values as freedom to express one's opinion and
ideology.

29. C.D. Fuchs, then Director of Programming for the
South African Broadcasting Corporation, told me in a May
1967 interview in Minneapolis that most Radio RSA staff were
regular listeners to the BBC External Services, and regarded
them with something approaching veneration. A few RSA staff
had worked for the BBC External Services at one time or
another.

30. Vernon Mackay, "The Propaganda Battle for Zambia,"
Africa Today 18 (1971):18-26, contains this and other excerpts from RSA's broadcasts, as well as an overall appraisal
of the station's news service, which Mackay found generally
free of bias.
31. "SABC Switch Stirs Propaganda Fears," World Broad-
cast News 3 (February 1981):1.
3 2. A survey conducted by the University of Zambia
Institute for African Studies in 1971 showed that 13 per
cent of the (urban) sample listened to Radio RSA. Graham
Mytton, "National Mass Media Audience Survey: The Major
Towns," Zambian Broadcasting Services Research Project,
Research Reports and Papers No. 2 (mimeographed), Lusaka:
University of Zambia Institute for African Studies, 1971. A
BBC survey in Kenya in September and October 1978 showed
Radio RSA English broadcasts had a regular listenership of
2.5 per cent, the same figure that BBC's English service
registered. BBC Handbook 1980, p. 58.
3 3. The History of Broadcasting in Japan (Tokyo: NHK,
1967), p. 289. This work contains considerable information
about the early years of Radio Japan; see especially pp. 288-
295.
3 4. Ibid., p. 291.
35. The Silent Power: Japan's Identity and World Role
(Tokyo: The Simul Press, 1976) (edited by Japan Center for
International Exchange) is a rich source of information on
this subject.
3 6. Interview with Chosei Kabira, Administrative
Controller, NHK, in Strasbourg, France, September 9, 1981.
37. I discussed this lack of coverage with a high administrative official in the NHK News Division in September
1976. He said that the tradition of Japanese journalism
does not really include investigative reporting, and,
furthermore, that political scandal is considered to be
something of a disgrace to the nation as a whole, particularly if the official is elected, rather than appointed, to
office. Failing to cover a political scandal, or covering
it minimally, could be seen as respectful to the public in
its shame. (How the public is supposed to learn about a
scandal in order to feel ashamed in the first place is
another question!) This administrator disagreed with that
philosophy, and knew many other journalists who shared his
views, but saw the philosophy as representing majority
opinion. However, Japanese media were extremely critical of
Prime Minister Suzuki following his disclosure in May 1981 of
the fact that several Japanese governments, including his
own, had allowed U.S. nuclear-powered ships to enter Japanese
harbors.
3 8. Japan's status as a defeated nation, and its absence
from international broadcasting between 1945 and 1952, left
it in a very poor position to acquire good broadcast

frequencies for Radio Japan.

39. Seiki Sakiyama, "The International Broadcasting of
Japan," Studies in Broadcasting (Tokyo: NHK, 1965), p. 23.
Sakiyama's article provides many details on the founding of
Radio Japan.

40. Interviews with Radio Japan staff in April 1970 and
September 1976. Sakiyama, "Japan", p. 32, comes to the same
conclusion regarding the Council's potential usefulness and
actual behavior.

41. The British government was anxious to see Australia
develop a shortwave broadcasting service in case BBC facilities should be destroyed or damaged in a bombing raid, and
therefore assisted the Australian government in the technical
development of the news service. "The Constant Voice,"
Melbourne; Radio Australia, 1964, p. 31.

42. The Australian cabinet directed ABC to reduce
Radio Australia's budget at the time ABC resumed control.
While the station was not threatened with extinction, neither
was it a particularly high priority item for the government.

43. Parliament of the Commonwealth of Australia,
Australian Broadcasting, Canberra, ACT: Parliamentary Paper
No. 358/1976, p. 135.

44. Parliament of the Commonwealth of Australia, Radio
Australia, Canberra, ACT: Parliamentary Paper No. 97/1977.
The Waller Committee report reproduces a great deal of
information on the importance and effectiveness of international broadcasting in general. Most of the claims are not
particularly well documented (although some BBC surveys are
quoted), but the thrust of the report is that Radio Australia
remains important because international broadcasting itself
remains important.

45. Donald Horne, in The Lucky Country (London:
Angus and Robertson, 1966) and in Death of the Lucky Country
(Ringwood, Aust.: Penguin, 1976), presents a thorough, well-
balanced picture of modern Australia, and of its co-
operation with but suspicion of other Asian and Pacific
nations. J. Hyde, Australia, the Asia Connection (Malmsbury,
Aust.: Kibble, 1978), presents a more detailed picture of
Australian-Asian relations.

46. In 1980, the Radio Australia Officer for Jakarta,
Indonesia was refused a visa by the Indonesian government,
apparently on the grounds that RA's coverage of the country
in its Indonesian language service displayed a "negative
tone". Australian Broadcasting Commission, 48th Annual
Report, 1 July-30 June 1980, p. 11. I monitored RA broadcasts to Asia in the course of a research project in 1970,
and found that news items containing material critical of
the U.S. role in Vietnam were quite frequent.

47. James Oliver, "Comparison of the Mandarin Services
of Four Major Broadcasters to the Peoples' Republic of
China," Washington, D.C.: U.S. Information Agency, Office of

Research, Report R-11-78 (March 10, 1978). Oliver concludes
that RA's primary audience at that time was the Asian overseas Chinese community, and not listeners in the PRC itself.
The latter audience seems to have increased in importance in
recent years.

    48.   However, not all requests for cooperation are
honored. For example, an Australian committee was unrecep-
tive to a Canadian request for time on Radio Australia transmitting facilities in the mid-1970s, on the grounds that it
could open the door to more such requests, some of them
presenting potentially serious policy problems. Radio
Australia, (footnote 44), p. 12

    49.   This was made especially clear to me by Asher Lee,
then head of the Audience Research Department of BBC's
External Services, in an interview in London in August 1967,
and reaffirmed in an interview with Gerard Mansell, then
Managing Director of BBC External Services, in London in
September 1975. See also Chapter 6, footnote 18, p. 183.

8

RADIO MOSCOW AND
OTHER SOVIET VOICES

The sheer physical power and linguistic scope of Radio
Moscow are awesome to behold: millions of kilowatts of
transmitter power broadcast to the globe daily in well over
80 languages. The station is also one of the oldest international broadcast operations: it was formally inaugurated
over 50 years ago, in October 1929. Over the years, it has
put together a talented staff of announcers, writers and
reporters, and placed at their disposal a wealth of information, including airmail editions of newspapers and
periodicals from throughout the world. Furthermore, the
Soviet Union has been one of the two or three major world
powers since World War II, and is certainly the leading
Communist power, so what Radio Moscow has to say ought to be
of some interest to the world. With this combination of
strengths, Radio Moscow should be a dominant international
broadcast voice. In many respects it is, but it also faces
some major problems, as will become evident later in this
chapter. First, however, we'll consider its history.

Foreign broadcasts from the Soviet Union date back to
at least 1926, when the USSR engaged in a propaganda campaign against Romania, as it agitated for the return of
Russia of the then-Romanian but once Russian province of
Bessarabia. Radio played a small role in this propaganda
campaign; its use was tactical and very brief.[1] Radio also
played a role in the celebrations marking the tenth anniversary of the Bolshevik Revolution in 1927. Honored guests
from foreign countries were invited to address listeners in
their homelands by means of shortwave broadcasts from
Moscow. When the celebrations ended, so did the broadcasts,
but they doubtless served as inspiration for the eventual
creation of Radio Moscow.

Radio Moscow's growth following its inauguration in 1929
was steady: four languages at first (Russian, German,
French, English), not all of them on a daily basis, growing
to 11 languages by 1933 (almost all of them European). Its

early programs were designed for the most part to explain
what the Revolution had accomplished, how the country was
progressing toward Communism, how the workers and peasants
were benefitting, etc. News and features predominated; the
latter might include such fare as "Life in a Moscow Boot
Factory" or "Leningrad's Hermitage Museum". Music--Russian
folk music in particular--also played an important role.
Relatively little programing in those early years consisted
of direct attacks on opposing ideologies. However, Germany
was a frequent target of Soviet criticism at that time, in
part because Karl Marx had held it to be the logical birth-
place of Communism, and the Soviet Union seemed quite
determined that it at least follow the USSR as soon as
possible.[2]

The coming to power of the Nazis in Germany changed
Radio Moscow's approach quite dramatically. The Nazis
quickly and clearly showed that the Communists were their
arch enemies, as revealed by attacks on the Soviet Union
over Germany's Deutschlandsender. That touched off a no-
holds-barred radio war between the two countries until 1939,
when the German-Soviet Friendship Treaty was signed. "Peace"
came immediately, and the two radio stations began to play
music by each other's most prominent composers as a token of
good relations between the two nations.[3]

WORLD WAR II

Violation of the treaty by Germany in June 1941 caused
an abrupt about-face. World War II now began for the Soviet
Union, and RM and Deutschlandsender were once again on the
attack against each other. In addition to the more con-
ventional sorts of broadcast attacks through news and commentary, Radio Moscow also employed the services of a
"Comrade Ivan", who spoke fluent German. Ivan's job was to
listen to the domestic (German language) service of the
Deutschlandsender, and, when the announcer paused after a
story, quickly add a comment in German, such as "That's a
pack of lies," or, if the German item had concluded with a
line such as "The victorious German army marches on," Ivan
would add ". . . to their graves." Radio Moscow was beaming
a strong signal to Germany on the Deutschlandsender's long
wave frequency, and many German listeners could hear Ivan's
voice almost as clearly as that of the Deutschlandsender
announcer.[4]

Much as BBC had done during World War II, Radio Moscow
made heavy use of exiles in its various European language
broadcasts. When the German army invaded many of the
European nations, political and labor leaders who left the

country generally fled in one of two directions: left-wing
socialists and Communists were more likely to head for
Moscow, while other types of socialists, as well as center
and right-wing adherents, more often sought refuge in London
or the United States. Many of those individuals subsequently
found themselves broadcasting over the BBC or Radio Moscow
(or, less often, VOA), and in some cases carrying on their
own propaganda wars with each other, bidding for the loyalty
of listeners in their homelands.[5]

The foreign broadcasts of the Soviet Union during World
War II were generally more hard-hitting and even reckless in
terms of urging people in the occupied areas to risk their
lives for the overthrow of the Nazis than those of the other
Allied nations. A broadcast to France, for example, said:

> French workers, sabotage everything you can!
> Wreck production! Make unusable all aeroplane
> parts and other pieces of machinery for tanks and
> war weapons. Explode the munition depots and all
> stores, derail trains and impede every means of
> transport![6]

Radio Moscow devoted a good deal of effort to strength-
ening the will to resist and survive among Communists in
occupied Europe and within Germany, particularly by reporting
the successes of their comrades in acts of sabotage or
escape from work camps. It also stressed the particular
hostility, but also the ultimate ineffectiveness of the Nazis
in dealing with Communists.[7] Captured German soldiers were
interviewed frequently, and Axis disunity, particularly in
Italo-German and Hungarian-Romanian relations, were played
up heavily (see Chapter 3, p. 69).

There is some anecdotal evidence that Radio Moscow's
German-language broadcasts had a considerable following in
Europe, and were feared by Nazi officials.[8] The station's
impact on American and British listeners during the war was
probably less profound, in part because of the basic difficulty the Soviet Union had in giving much credit to the
United States and Great Britain for the role they were playing in the war, in part because of an apparent need to re-
interpret anything that smacked of capitalism:

> . . . we realize [Independence Day] to be no
> capitalist feast but a genuine expression of a
> progressive people which has now allied itself
> with Russia.[9]

INTO THE COLD WAR

When World War II had ended, Radio Moscow, unlike BBC
or VOA, reduced its broadcast activities very little. In
fact, Communist (if not specifically Soviet) international
broadcast activity increased, as the Soviet Union assisted
the various peoples' democracies of Central and Eastern
Europe in establishing their own international broadcast
services. Since they were coordinated with Radio Moscow,
they were able in certain respects to serve as extensions of
it.[10]

Radio Moscow broadcasts after World War II continued
with much the same variety and number of languages that had
been employed during the war, which meant that Europe, North
and South America, the Middle East and certain parts of Asia
(especially China) remained as prime target areas. Broadcasts in English formed a very important part of Radio
Moscow's daily schedule worldwide, but each geographic
region--the North American Service, the service for the
British Isles--had a different staff of announcers. Quite
often, those announcers had lived in England, the United
States, India or wherever, and might even have been citizens
of those nations at one time. Their English was fluent and
their knowledge of life in the various target areas reasonably sound. This heavy concentration on English reflected
the Soviet view that, in order to reach many of the world's
"elite", broadcasts in English were a necessity.

Tensions produced by the Cold War in the late 1940s rose
as the Korean War began in 1950. While Radio Moscow continued to broadcast a large amount of positive material--the
quality of life in the Soviet Union, the excellence of Soviet
culture--the United States came under increasing attack as
the leading capitalist nation.[11] This January 3, 1951
excerpt from a North American Service broadcast talk
(written by Soviet author Ilya Ehrenberg) couches the attack
in highly colorful terms reminiscent of some World War II
broadcasts and uses the theme "your leaders are misleading
you".

In Korea, the soldiers were abandoning
their arms, while in Washington, the senators
were brandishing the sword. Senator Knowland
wanted bombs dropped on Chinese territory.
Senator Ferguson and others insisted upon the
immediate use of the atom bomb. They were
backed by Stassen, one of the leaders of the
Republican Party. Senator Pepper declared
that it would be stupid to be too fastidious.
Mr. Dewey, Governor of New York, shouted that

America was waging a desperate fight, and could
not afford to be over-scrupulous. Finally,
Senator Morse jumped up and demanded petulantly
for the Soviet Union to be atom-bombed without
delay. The people who have not lost their
reason will ask, "What's the matter? Why are
the American rulers, losing a small war, striv-
ing to unleash a big one?" It is difficult to
answer this question. Here, there is no logic
--only signs of mental disorder.[12]

And since the Soviet Union was experiencing a sort of
"cult of personality" in the early 1950s, a number of Radio
Moscow features presented Soviet leader Joseph Stalin in
glowing colors, as in this excerpt from a November 1951
broadcast on the North American Service:

A storm of applause greeted the announcement that Comrade Stalin had given his consent
to stand for Deputy in that district. The
representatives of the factory workers who
nominated and supported the candidacy of the
leader said how proud they were that the
electors of the district would be fortunate
enough to cast their ballots for the great
Stalin. There was a prolonged ovation in the
hall in honor of the inspirer and organizer
of the Soviet peoples' victories, the standard
bearer of peace, Joseph Stalin.[13]

In most of its English-language broadcasts through the
mid-1950s, there was a good deal of formality to Radio
Moscow's newscasts and features, as in the excerpt just
cited. Lack of skill on the part of individual translators
could be one reason for that formality, although many of
Radio Moscow's translators are very skillful. But a factor
of equal if not greater importance would be that translators apparently were allowed to deviate very little from
the precise language of centrally-prepared news items and
features. Since much of this centrally-prepared material
was itself highly formal in tone, the translators generally
followed suit.[14]

By the late 1950s, however, some changes were evident,
at least in the North American Service. Colloquialisms,
slang and shorter sentences became more and more common,
especially in programs in which North American Service
announcer (since 1941) Joe Adamov made an appearance. This
was particularly evident in the weekly "Moscow Mailbag", a
show in which listeners' questions were answered. "Moscow
Mailbag" during this era was one of the more carefully

calculated programs offered by any international broadcaster
in its careful attention to the ordering of questions and
the manner in which they were answered. The three Radio
Moscow staff members involved in "Mailbag" would often inter-
rupt one another and even occasionally disagree with one
another. Furthermore, the program was structured in such a
way that "heavy" and "light" questions were skillfully
balanced, and the program usually concluded with a "light"
item.[15] This three-person approach disappeared by the
mid-1960s, although Joe Adamov has continued to host the
program.

RESPONDING TO A CHANGING WORLD

The 1960s saw a tremendous increase in Radio Moscow
broadcasts to Africa, many of them in languages seldom used
by other international broadcasters: N'debele, Shona, Zulu
and several others, most of them spoken by groups living in
the troubled areas of southern Africa. India too received
increased attention, perhaps because of the Sino-Soviet
dispute, and again in many languages used by a few other
international broadcasters. But the most radical change in
Radio Moscow's schedule came in the early 1960s, as the
Peoples' Republic of China and the Soviet Union began to go
their separate ways. Broadcasting became an immediate symbol
of this separation, as Radio Moscow was soon beaming a 24-
hour-a-day service in Kuoyu (Mandarin) to the Peoples'
Republic[16] and receiving just about as many broadcasts in
Russian from Radio Peking. Aside from its Russian language
services for sailors, expatriates and others capable of
following broadcasts in Russian, Kuoyu took up more hours
of the RM broadcast schedule between 1967 and 1978*than any
other language. (Introduction of a 19-hour-per-day World
Service in English late in 1978 pushed English ahead of
Kuoyu).[17]
The use of so many languages to so many parts of the
world could serve as a gauge by which to measure the USSR's
interest in influencing public opinion in specific parts of
the world. In some respects, it could be a fairly accurate
gauge. There is a heavy concentration on languages spoken
in the racially-troubled parts of southern Africa, and RM's
obvious interest in reaching listeners in India (12 Indian
languages plus English) is predictable in light of Soviet
foreign policy in South Asia over the past 20 years. However the gauge is far from infallible, for one simple reason:
once RM has added a language service, very rarely is it
dropped (although small services in Lingala and Catalan were
dropped in the late 1970s).

---

*It became a 24-hour-per-day service in April 1980.

A close examination of hours of programing broadcast to
various parts of the world is perhaps more useful as a gauge
of Soviet interests. Sub-Saharan Africa did not even appear
as a target area for Radio Moscow broadcasts until 1956.
Starting in 1960, however, it increased rapidly over the
next ten years, going from just over 40 hours per week in
1960 to 165 hours per week by 1970, after which it levelled
off at the present figure of approximately 170 hours per
week. By contrast, the "non-Arab Middle East" had risen to
prominence as a target area in the 1950s, and changed very
little during the 1960s, moving in a narrow range of between
158 and 165 hours per week during the decade. North America
likewise remained stable during that period, whereas broadcasts to Latin America and to East Asia and the Pacific
enjoyed three- and four-fold increases, respectively.
Western Europe started and ended the 1960s prominently (256
hours per week in 1960, 273+ hours per week in 1970), but
suffered a drop in 1964 (186+ hours) and 1965 (190+ hours),
which coincides nicely with a period of relative relaxation
in relations between the USSR and a number of Western
European countries.[18]

The 1970s brought much the same sort of stabilization
for Radio Moscow as they did for most major international
stations. Aside from a sharp increase in broadcasts in
Portuguese to Portugal during the mid-1970s, when several of
the major Eastern and Western stations did the same, expansion of language services and broadcast hours was slight.
Creation of the World Service in 1978 was really more an
assemblage of existing English language services to different parts of the world, e.g. Australia and New Zealand.[19]
At the end of the decade, there was a major increase in
broadcast hours in Dari and Pushto for Afghanistan, in connection with the entry of Soviet military forces there;
combined hours rose from 21 hours per week in September
1979 to nearly 60 hours per week by April 1980 with some
of the increase being handled by Radio Dushanbe in the
Tadzhik S.S.R.

PROGRAMING

As is the case with its two major rivals, BBC and VOA,
Radio Moscow attempts to provide a wide variety of programing designed for a wide variety of potential listeners.
News and commentary (the latter often drawn from material
written by TASS correspondents or taken directly from Soviet
newspapers and magazines) predominate, at least in the sense
that they lead off the schedules of the various language
services. The typical newscast contains several items about

events in the Soviet Union, a few items about events in or
concerning Eastern and Central European socialist states,
and anywhere from one or two to several items about events in
developing and capitalist nations. A worldwide network of
TASS and NOVOSTI correspondents,[20] plus airmail subscriptions
to many of the world's leading newspapers and periodicals,
make it possible for Radio Moscow to present generally up-
to-the-minute news and to quote directly from Western
sources, although "sensitive" items such as the illness of
the Soviet head of state or the crash of a Soviet airliner
may be held back for several hours to several days, or
simply go unmentioned.[21] Live reports from overseas correspondents almost never appear; instead, their reports
usually are read by studio announcers from scripts.

Music also is prominent, sometimes appearing in clearly-
labelled program formats (Music At Your Request, Music From
Moscow), sometimes used as "filler" in half-hour blocs of
news and commentary. Russian music predominates, and a
fair share of it comes from the various Soviet republics to
better illustrate the diversity and unity of the USSR.
Rarely are more than one or two sentences used to describe
the music, its composers, artists, origins, etc., and it is
not unusual for it to be played with no identification at
all, or for it to be cut off partway through.

Features about various aspects of Soviet life are
plentiful on the larger language or geographic area services;
the North American Service, for example, includes one or
more of these each evening: What is Communism?; The Soviet
Way of Life; Vladimir Posner's Talk (Mr. Posner's personal
reflections on assorted aspects of Soviet life, including
such potentially negative topics as alcoholism in the Soviet
Union). Features usually last for 15 or fewer minutes, and
sometimes include interviews with Soviet citizens and with
foreign visitors. There are both "heavy" and "light"
features; the World Service's weekly Round About the Soviet
Union portrays Soviet regions and cities, such as Vladivostok:
". . . a port town where men and women in seafaring apparel
are at the dockside, for practically every second person
waits for their beloved ones from a faraway sea" (Broadcast of
October 26, 1981). "Moscow Mailbag" and similar programs on
other language services present replies to listener questions about life in the USSR, Soviet foreign relations, etc.
Radio plays, broadcasts of sporting events, readings from
short stories or novels, etc., are largely absent from the
schedule.

The smaller language services--and Radio Moscow carries
several of 30 minutes per day (e.g. Shona, Zulu)--concentrate
much more heavily on news, commentary and current affairs,
and are almost exclusively "serious" in tone and highly
topical in content. Broadcasters for these services usually

are recruited directly from the target countries, although
they also may be enlisted from among the ranks of foreign
students attending universities in the Moscow region.

While there is considerable variety in the types of
programs offered over many Radio Moscow language services,
there is less variety in the tone of those broadcasts. With
the exception of the station's English language services to
Great Britain and to the United States, where announcers
often are quite informal and may even have regional (e.g.
Scots) accents, the general style of announcing is clear,
correct, and quite formal. While that could be due to the
nature of the copy itself, as I have suggested earlier, it
may have as much to do with a more "old-fashioned" view of
appropriate radio style, and an even more deep-seated
Russian trait of feeling more comfortable with formality in
many social settings where an American would speak more informally.[22]

Radio style also may be affected by the nature of the
audience Radio Moscow hopes to reach. A broadcast service
which is ideologically oriented, as is Radio Moscow (and as
are most international stations, to greater or lesser
degrees), faces a choice-cum-dilemma: does it preach to the
converted, and, if so, does it concentrate on sustaining them
in their faith, when few around them may share it, or does
it emphasize material that will enable them to convert
others? Or does it concentrate on attacking opponents,
stressing their internal weaknesses, the failures of their
alliances, the inevitability of their decline? Or does it
deal chiefly in messages calculated to display the country's
peaceful intentions to skeptics or neutral parties? There
are many variations and refinements to these elements, and
any one program may certainly serve more than one purpose,
as many programs doubtless do in the many hours offered each
week in Russian, Kuoyu and English.[23]

But there are choices to be made, and the balance will
most often end up clearly in favor of one approach or another.
It well may be that the World Service, as it develops, will
be a way for Radio Moscow to reach a different sort of
audience than it might choose to do with its North American
Service.[24] Based on nearly 20 years of listening to the
latter, I would say that it is intended primarily for a
reasonably intelligent, curious, "worldly" listener, who
neither despises nor worships the United States or the
Soviet Union. Even when a potentially thorny subject such
as belief in the existence of life after death is brought
up, as it was by an American listener in a 1965 "Moscow
Mailbag", Joe Adamov's reply was full of conviction, but
still managed to include at least one reference that would
be congenial to American listeners:

We certainly do not advocate that there is
an existence after death. We do not believe
that there is a spirit or a soul apart from the
natural body. Therefore we do not believe in
life after death, any more than we believe in
the existence of ghosts. But we do firmly believe
that man can make a life of happiness, a life of
plenty, right here on earth for everybody. And
we believe in the immortality of human beings--
in the immortality of human thought, not of the
soul. We believe in the immortality of such
men as Washington and Lincoln. We believe in
the immortality of men like Beethoven and
Tschaikovsky, of Marx and Lenin.

With enough listening to Radio Moscow, one becomes aware
of a heavy and continuing concentration on certain themes,
almost as if a sort of credo were being recited. One of the
strongest elements in this credo is "the workers and peasants
are the foundation of the Soviet Union and of any true
socialist state". It appears in this excerpt from an
episode of What Is Communism on the North American Service
(August 1979):

There are no privileged categories of
people who are elected to the different governing
bodies. Out of a total number of more than two
million members of different governing bodies,
more than half are factory workers and farmers,
and almost one-half of the members of our governing bodies are non-Party people.

Other themes are nearly as prominent in Radio Moscow
broadcasts: the importance of young people and women in
Soviet society; the economic strength of the USSR; the
nation's desire for peace but readiness and ability to
defend itself in time of war; the importance, popularity
and accessibility of culture in the Soviet Union; the high
esteem in which the Soviet Union is held by foreign visitors
and observers; the inevitable triumph of world Communism,
hopefully through peaceful means; the aggressive intentions
but increasing weakness (as revealed by strikes, inflation,
rising unemployment, etc.) of the capitalist nations. No
newscast or feature fails to work in at least some of these
themes.[25]
There is, in short, a certain feeling of repetitiousness about most Radio Moscow programing, with almost predictable words and phrases appearing on an almost predictable
schedule. Certain announcers, such as Joe Adamov and
Vladimir Posner, appear to have the freedom and/or ability

to treat these themes in a "looser," more colloquial manner.
Most Radio Moscow staff members do not, or are less skilled
in exercising that freedom, and the resultant formality of
written and oral style can make the station's broadcasts
somewhat tedious to the uncommitted but curious listener.

                          THE AUDIENCE

     In sharp contrast with BBC and VOA, Radio Moscow does
little formal audience research. That may be the result of
what appears to be a widespread Soviet distrust of survey
research, which is still held in certain circles to be
"bourgeois" and even unnecessary in a society where people
and State are synonymous.[26] The station does actively
solicit listener letters, in the forms of asking for specific
comments on Radio Moscow programing, promising answers to
questions sent in by listeners, playing music upon request,
furnishing verification of reception (QSL) reports to DXers
from throughout the world who request them. There also are
contests in which listeners must answer a few simple questions (e.g. What is the place of Communism in the development
of world society?) in the hope of winning prizes ranging from
commemorative stamps or phonograph records to all-expenses-
paid trips to the USSR.
     Given the variety of listener mail soliciting devices
employed, one would expect that a station as large as Radio
Moscow would receive considerable listener mail each year.
The station rarely releases precise figures, although a
May 6, 1981 broadcast stated that there had been 300,000
listener cards and letters received in 1980.[27] Nor does it
release any summative figures on the composition or geographical distribution of this audience, or its comments on
Radio Moscow programing, although it does refer to listeners
by name, city, country and even street address when answering questions or playing musical requests--a practice which
also reveals clearly that many of the same listeners write
to "Mailbag" time and again! The station also uses contest
replies in subsequent programing, reading excerpts from
these replies to illustrate the variety of listener response
to such questions as "Where did you first hear of Lenin?"
and "What does the name of Lenin mean to you?" (both asked in
a 1970 Radio Moscow contest). This is part of a reply from
an Australian listener for the 1970 contest:

          It was during my school days that the name of
     Lenin first came to my attention. As I learned of
     the revolution of the people of Russia against
     the oppressive regime of the czars, the concept
     of this one man leading people out of the slough

of imperialistic domination captured my
imagination. The dry pages of the history books
came to life, and I was able to see that the
thoughts and actions of this one man had changed
the course of mankind. I learned more of Lenin,
and the more I learned, the more impressed I
became.

Radio Moscow also attempts to get TASS and NOVOSTI correspondents stationed abroad to send back reports on clarity
of signal and any random listener reactions to its programs
that these correspondents might chance to hear. However,
Radio Moscow staff members have told me that few correspondents go about this task seriously or systematically.

While Radio Moscow has conducted few if any survey
research studies on its audience, several other international
broadcasters have done surveys which have revealed something
of the size and composition of RM's audience and occasionally
the station's relative credibility.[28]

These data often are fragmentary, and their validity
might be contested on the grounds that Western nations were
responsible for the surveys, which, if this were suspected
or known by respondents, could lead to a reluctance to disclose listening to Radio Moscow. Making such allowances,
there appears to be generally lower listenership to Radio
Moscow as compared with VOA, BBC and certain regionally
important international stations, such as RFE and Radio
Cairo's Voice of the Arabs. The RM audience seems predominantly composed of university students in many countries,
although again BBC and VOA often attract three to four times
as many such listeners, while in Eastern Europe listeners
with primary and secondary educations appear to predominate
in the Radio Moscow audience. It is rare to find any survey
in which listening to Radio Moscow once a week or more is
done by more than 20 per cent of any one segment of the
population, whereas this figure has been reached and even
doubled or tripled by VOA and BBC in numerous surveys, again
for individual segments of the population. On the few
occasions when listeners have been asked about the reliability or credibility of various international radio
stations, VOA and BBC usually have come out ahead of Radio
Moscow, sometimes by margins of two or three to one.

Those figures should not be taken as a sign that Radio
Moscow's audience is insignificant in size or unimportant
in composition, or that its listeners distrust it. They
show only that Radio Moscow does not fare as well in those
terms as do its chief competitors. It's quite possible, as
I suggested earlier, that the station seeks to reach rather
different audiences than do BBC or VOA. Analysts of Soviet
propaganda techniques have long claimed that Radio Moscow

by and large serves those already committed to the cause of
world Communism, and that its audiences will for that reason
alone be small.[29]

One very specialized study has indicated that individuals (in this case, Americans) might be agreeably surprised
by Radio Moscow's programing once they had the opportunity
to hear it. Donald D. Smith, then a sociologist at Florida
State University, exposed 122 F.S.U. students to Radio
Moscow broadcasts over a 2½ month period. Smith administered
before and after tests of attitudes toward the Soviet Union
and toward Radio Moscow. The overall results showed a
general shift of opinion in favor of both, and several nar-
rative comments indicated that students even thought that
"they were really trying to reach us," "(it) makes you
realize they're average people like us who don't want a
war," etc.[30]

It is quite possible that one of Radio Moscow's greatest
barriers to "popularity" is that many people don't know that
it exists or don't realize that it broadcasts in languages
other than Russian.[31] Radio Moscow sometimes has advertised
in local newspapers, but seems to have done little else to
publicize itself. However, it has supported the concept
of "radio clubs" (groups of Radio Moscow listeners, largely
in the developing countries), and does pay some attention to
their activities in its broadcasts. Formality of style,
repetitiousness of thematic content and one-sidedness
(rarely is there criticism of anything in Soviet society,
and never of the government, while Western governments are
seldom treated in favorable terms) may reduce its attractive-
ness, too.

TECHNICAL SERVICES

Radio Moscow has one advantage over every other international broadcast station where transmissions are concerned:
its great land mass, which enables it to locate transmitters
at a variety of sites in order to reach a variety of targets.
Dozens of transmitters with a total power of several thousand
kW are scattered throughout the eastern, southern, central
and western sectors of the Soviet Union. Sub-Saharan Africa
and Latin America generally have been less well served by
clear, powerful signals than has the rest of the world,
although the latter has benefitted from the relay of Radio
Moscow World Service broadcasts by Radio Havana since 1979.

Aside from the Radio Havana relay, Radio Moscow has
relied very little on this means of bringing its signal
closer to its target audiences. There are relay stations in
the GDR and in Bulgaria, in order to better reach parts of

Western Europe and the Middle East, but for the most part
Radio Moscow has avoided placing too much reliance on relays,
partly because they are unnecessary and partly because they
are unreliable (as will be evident through the experiences
of Radio Tirana and Radio Peking when I cite them in the next
chapter).

As is true of other major international broadcast
stations, Radio Moscow employs a large number of frequencies
simultaneously in order to reach some of its chief targets.
Broadcasts to the Peoples' Republic of China have been
carried at times on as many as 25 frequencies simultaneously; broadcasts to North America often are carried on as
many as 14. Parts of Europe, the Middle East and Asia
receive Radio Moscow broadcasts on both short and medium
wave. When broadcasts change frequencies from one hour to
the next, RM informs listeners as to the best meter bands
to use in order to continue to receive the broadcasts.[32]

Radio Moscow also has attempted to place tape recordings of some of its programs--those dealing with Soviet
culture in particular--with radio stations throughout the
world. On occasion, broadcast stations have initiated the
request, although in most instances RM itself appears to
have taken the initiative; and on occasion the program
material has been more informational than cultural, as when
Sterling, Illinois radio station WSDR decided to carry
"Moscow Mailbag" in 1979.[33]

FUTURE PROSPECTS

I have already pointed out that Radio Moscow's expansion of program hours and languages slowed down during the
1970s, and increased at the end of the decade only because
of the situation in Afghanistan. This levelling off could
be due to budgetary factors, but that seems unlikely. While
there may have been a shift in the direction of a more con-
sumer-oriented Soviet economy in the 1970s, it has not been
great enough, nor Radio Moscow's apparent share in the
national budget large enough,[34] to make this the likely
cause. It is just as possible that the Central Committee of
the Communist Party, which provides regular policy direction
for Radio Moscow and other Soviet media through its Agita-
tion and Propaganda Section, feels that the station has
reached its logical limits in terms of effectiveness. (The
Soviet Foreign Ministry also maintains contact with RM, but
the station may not always follow the foreign policy "line"
of the Ministry).[35] It is also possible, but less likely,
that the Committee on Radio Broadcasting and Television,
within which Radio Moscow is included, wishes to invest more

of its overall budget in domestic broadcasting, and has thus
adopted a "hold the line" budget policy for Radio Moscow.

It's unlikely that Radio Moscow will undertake any
radical shifts in programing policy during the 1980s. There
may be a few more moves in the direction of informal styles
of program presentation and of more self-criticism, but
large-scale shifts of this sort seem improbable. It appears
to be difficult for Russians to behave informally outside
their own particular societal groups, and domestic radio
style also tends to be formal. Nor are Russians much given
to criticizing their own society, much less their government,
in front of strangers,[36] which means that the generally uncritical and even highly laudatory approach followed by Radio
Moscow in its items and programs about the Soviet Union is
likely to continue, whatever its effect on credibility.

Radio Moscow probably has been slower to change its
program schedules and its basic approaches to program content than have most major international broadcasters. The
major share of Radio Moscow's North American Service schedule
looked the same in 1980 as it did in 1970 and even in 1960,
built as it is and has been around news and commentary and
such recurring features as What Is Communism?, Science and
Engineering, Spotlight on Sports and Moscow Mailbag. This
could mean either that Radio Moscow's directors feel that
they have a winning formula and are unwilling to tamper with
it or that there is considerable resistance to change within
the organization, which may or may not be related to overall
resistance to change within Soviet and Russian society.
Whatever the reason, Radio Moscow is quite likely to sound
much the same in the 1980s as it has for the past 20 or more
years.

                        THE OTHER SOVIET VOICES

Considerably less varied in their approaches, and therefore easier to analyze, are three other types of international broadcast activity carried out by the Soviet
Union: the services operated by the various Soviet
republics; a service operated by Radio Moscow but ostensibly
administered by a public organization; and various clandestine
radio stations. All appear to have specific, coordinated
roles to play in Soviet international radio.

                        The Republics

While they sometimes carry attacks on the USSR's ideological opponents (Radio Tashkent frequently berates China),

the republic stations more often serve to reinforce Radio
Moscow's more positive messages regarding the strength of
the USSR and Communism. They also reflect some of the
diversity of the Soviet Union by highlighting what occurs in
their own areas, which are often quite different in tradition,
geography, etc. from what most listeners would think of as
"Russian". Sometimes this touch of local color is quite
entertaining and enlightening, but quite often the "local-
ness" of the message is lost in the apparent need to stress
some more dominant national theme, as in this excerpt from
an August 1979 feature carried on Radio Vilnius' (Lithuania)
North American Service. While trade unions in Lithuanian
factories is the specific subject, the basic theme is part
of the credo: the primacy of the workers in a socialist
country.

> This is characteristic not only of this in-
> dustrial enterprise but of Lithuanian trade
> unions in general. We cannot imagine our lives
> without trade unions--without their constant
> care for the working people. That is why the
> majority of our working people belong to the
> trade unions of Lithuania.

The effectiveness of such broadcasts is sometimes
further reduced by a rather weak signal and a stiff and
formal style of writing and delivery. Still, these services
certainly add something in volume to overall Soviet broadcast output: the nine republic stations active in international broadcasting beam a sum total of roughly 315 hours
per week, in 17 languages, to overseas listeners.

Radio Peace and Progress

Even larger is Radio Station Peace and Progress, sub-
titled "The Voice of Soviet Public Opinion". Developed in
1964 to serve as an additional broadcast voice in the radio
war between Moscow and Peking, it was soon enlarged and made
more diverse. It is operated allegedly by Soviet public
organizations (e.g. Union of Journalists, Union of Soviet
Composers, Soviet Peace Committee) for the purpose of promoting "mutual understanding and trust among nations."[37]
It uses the same transmitters and some of the same announcers as does Radio Moscow. It broadcasts in 11
languages, with Kuoyu (Mandarin) clearly in the lead,
followed by English, and is on the air for roughly 160 hours
per week, going to most parts of the world with North
America as a notable exception.

If the announcers and the transmission facilities come from Radio Moscow, one might wonder whether the casual listener could detect the difference, aside from station identification. That's relatively easy, given Peace and Progress' heavy concentration on two major themes: the evils of China's leaders and the evils of the Western powers. The following excerpts are typical:

> . . . [China] has actually played the role of
> a major supplier in the undeclared war against
> the Afghan people in the interests of U.S.
> imperialism in order to help those counter-
> revolutionary scum invade Afghan territory via
> neighboring Pakistan. This has made the
> Chinese people pay a heavy price of several
> billion yuan.
> RPP in Kuoyu, June 16, 1981
> FBIS Daily Reports 3 (Soviet Union), No. 116, June 17,
> 1981, B3

> The decision to keep Namibia as their neo-
> colonialist appendage forces the West to provide
> all-round aid to South Africa. The racists
> are continuing to receive NATO arms, and there
> are mercenaries from among the imperialist powers
> in the ranks of the South African armed forces.
> There is recent reason to believe that the
> secret services of the Western countries are
> involved in working out a racist plan for the
> annihilation of 200,000 indigenous Namibians,
> replacing them with white settlers.
> RPP in English, August 1979

Radio Peace and Progress also broadcasts items and features which support independence movements and newly independent socialist nations in the Third World. However, negativism is such a dominant feature of the station's programing that it is highly doubtful that anyone but a supporter of the Soviet viewpoint--and a strong supporter, at that--would find RPP's broadcasts at all congenial as a steady diet. For such a listener, there would be the added problem of tuning to the station in time to hear it, since most of the broadcasts last no longer than 30 minutes, although some are repeated.

Clandestine Stations

The various clandestine stations broadcasting from within the USSR frequently serve as outlets for exile groups.

One of them, Radio Free Spain, lasted from 1941 to 1977, but many have had either shortlived or on-again, off-again existences, as relations between the Soviet Union and the target country or area waxed and waned. Iran and Greece, for example, have been intermittent targets of such broadcasts. Most of the clandestine stations transmit over equipment located in other Eastern and Central European countries, although none identifies its location in its broadcasts. The illusion to be sustained is that these stations are operated from within or very near the target country, and represent the threat or the promise (depending upon one's political preferences) of impending revolution. In keeping with this, the broadcasts are often couched in revolutionary terms. A December 1978 broadcast from the National Voice of Iran referred to the "Shah's blood-shedding regime" and concluded by saying: "The day is not far away when the army men, by fully joining the ranks of the people, will cast the heads of this blood-shedding regime and its criminal generals into the trash can of history." (FBIS Daily Reports 5, No. 249, December 27, 1978).

Similarly revolutionary messages have been carried over such clandestine stations as Voice of the People of Malaysia, Our Radio (for Turkey) and Sparks (for the Peoples' Republic of China), to mention a few.[38] Not all of these operations are actually based on Soviet territory, but most of them appear to be administered by Iranian, Malaysian, Turkish, dissident Chinese and other pro-Soviet Communist Party members working in or directed from Moscow.

Clandestine broadcasting seems to be intended for two audiences: those in the target area who are committed to the causes supported by the station and tune to it for sustenance or guidance, even to the point of picking up slogans from the broadcasts and then using them in pamphlets, wall posters, street banners, etc.; and the various broadcast monitoring stations around the world, who listen in hoping for clues to shifts in domestic and foreign policy on the part of the clandestine station operators and their hosts.[39] For example, the Soviet Union clearly meant to signal its readiness for better relations with Greece when, following the restoration of parliamentary democracy there in 1974, the Soviet supported Voice of Truth (to Greece) ceased its broadcasts.

The clandestine stations play a definite but probably limited tactical role in Soviet international broadcasting. They bear little resemblance to most other international stations, either in format (they broadcast little else besides news and commentary) or in style (their announcers usually speak with little polish but lots of conviction, and the vocabulary tends to be polemical). Their effectiveness may be hampered by the limited number of frequencies to

which they have access and by their brief broadcast time.
If they are to sustain the illusion of being "secret", then
it won't do for them to be on the air for several hours at a
time, over several frequencies! (Radio Free Spain was a
major exception--it was on the air for 80 hours a week until
shortly before its demise--but 30 minutes of less per day is
the average). A listener wishing to hear them must have an
accurate watch and a good receiver, plus good receiving
conditions, to have much hope of success.

* * * * *

When one adds up the broadcasting done by the three
"other" categories of Soviet international radio, they come
to well over 500 hours per week. In other words, the Soviet
Union devotes as much time to this overall category of programing as do all but the largest international radio
stations in Eastern Europe. To be sure, each category of
service appears to fill a specific role in the conduct of
public diplomacy, and those roles may well be mutually
exclusive, but together they serve as a large and important
complement to Radio Moscow, and therefore as a potentially
important element in Soviet foreign policy.

NOTES

1. "Russia and Romania Engage in Radio War," New York
Times, September 26, 1926, p. 3.
2. Several articles deal with these attacks: "Soviet
Radio Talks Resented in Berlin," New York Times, July 11,
1930, p. 10; "Reich May Combat Soviet With Static," New
York Times, July 15, 1930, p. 7; "Soviet Broadcasting
Arouses Ire in Germany," New York Times, March 15, 1931, 3,
p. 4. Programs frequently began with exhortations such as
"Police and soldiers of Germany, remember you are prole-
tarians," and "Remember in Germany, too, the October
[Revolution] way is the right way. Long live the German
Soviet Republic." The Soviet Union claimed that these were
domestic broadcasts, intended for German-speaking citizens
living in the Volga region, while German Communists answered
the German Government's complaints by pressing a counter-
demand that the Pope be told to confine broadcasts over
Radio Vatican to Latin or Italian! Wladimir Ostrogorski,
"50 Jahre Auslandssendungen aus Moskau," Beiträge zur
Geschichte des Rundfunks (Berlin: DDR Rundfunk) 13 (1979),
pp. 26-48, also covers this period.
3. Willi Boelcke, Die Macht des Radios (Frankfurt:
Verlag Ullstein, 1977), pp. 32-33; Charles Rolo, Radio Goes

to War (New York: G. Putnam, 1942), pp. 200-205, also describes Radio Moscow broadcasts during this period. Both
Harold N. Graves, Jr., War on the Short Waves (New York:
The Foreign Policy Association, 1941), p. 48 and E. Tangye
Lean, Voices in the Darkness (London: Secker and Warburg,
1943), p. 213, speak of Radio Moscow's "reserve" in broadcasting items about Russo-German cooperation.

4. Ivan's activities, and a number of similar efforts
from the Soviet Union and elsewhere, are treated by several
authors, among them Rolo, Radio, pp. 201-205; and Don Jensen,
"The Strange Saga of Ivan the Terrible," Electronics Illustrated 14 (November 1971):29-31+.

5. See Ostrogorski, "Moskau", pp. 38-41.

6. Cited in Lean, Voices, p. 214.

7. Henning Hagen, "Rufe in die Nacht, 2 Teil: Das
Echo," Beiträge zur Geschichte des Rundfunks (Berlin: DDR
Rundfunk) 12 (1978), pp. 41-52.

8. Hagen, "Rufe", p. 52. Radio Moscow programs to Nazi
Germany frequently featured interviews with or brief talks by
German prisoners of war. Gestapo officials feared that these
would both undermine German morale and contribute to more
listening to Radio Moscow, since "prisoner" broadcasts often
gave details on who were alive and in what condition--details
rarely available through official German channels.

9. Rolo, Radio, p. 208.

10. Anthony Leviebo, "Our Voice May Be Lost in World's
Radio War," New York Times, April 27, 1947, 4, p. 10. The
Soviet Union did establish relay transmitters in Poland,
Romania, Bulgaria and the German Democratic Republic at one
time or another, to strengthen Radio Moscow's signal to
Western Europe. Those in the G.D.R. and Bulgaria are still
in use.

11. The Soviet Government claimed that Radio Moscow was
responding to U.S. attacks on the Soviet Union over VOA, as
well as U.S. "distortion" of its own economic situation; see
"Hungary Denies Seizing Listeners," New York Times, July 23,
1948, p. 2.

12. Broadcast monitored and taped by Professor William
Howell, Department of Speech-Communication, University of
Minnesota, and part of his personal collection.

13. Ibid.

14. These observations on the practices of translators
and the central news room were confirmed in a conversation
I had with Joe Adamov, announcer for Radio Moscow's North
American Service, in Minneapolis, Minnesota on November 26,
1979.

15. William S. Howell, "The North American Service of
Radio Moscow," Quarterly Journal of Speech 46 (October 1960):
262-269. See also Edna Clapham Sorber, "An Analysis of the
Persuasion Used in Radio Moscow's North American Service,"

unpublished Ph.D. dissertation, University of Wisconsin, 1959 for a detailed description of Radio Moscow news and features during the period 1957-1958.

16. Robert Trumbull, "Chinese Say Russia Jams Their Broadcasts on Rift," New York Times, March 2, 1963, p. 1+; "Soviet Gives Signs of Easing Radio Drive Against West," New York Times, September 26, 1964, p. 2. The most comprehensive account I have found on the early phases of this "radio war" is contained in "The Sino-Soviet Radio War," China Topics YB 459, January 29, 1968.

17. If one calculates on the basis of "transmitter hours"--that is, numbers of hours of programing multiplied by numbers of transmitters carrying it--it well may be that Kuoyu remains the second most prevalent language in the Radio Moscow schedule, since there have been times when it has been broadcast to China over literally dozens of transmitters, employing a host of frequencies. Jamming of signals coming from Radio Moscow and Radio Peking to each other's respective nations is intense, and this "saturation" technique is used by both sides to enhance the possibility of at least a few transmissions passing through the jamming network.

18. These statistics are drawn from External Information and Cultural Relations Programs: Union of Soviet Socialist Republics (Washington: United States Information Agency, Office of Research and Assessment, April 1973), p. 127.

19. There is an excellent account of the founding and early programing practices of the World Service in "The World Service of Radio Moscow," Summary of World Broadcasting (London: BBC Monitoring Service, December 20, 1978), SU/5999/C/1.

20. TASS and/or NOVOSTI have correspondents or stringers in some 80 countries around the world; Moscow Radio and Television has its own correspondents in roughly a dozen of these countries.

21. Unfavorable news about foreign political leaders with whom the USSR is friendly also may go unmentioned on Radio Moscow, as did news about Nixon and Watergate in 1973-1974. See James Oliver, "A Comparison of VOA and Soviet Media," Washington, D.C., U.S. Information Agency, Office of Research, Report R-11-75, August 29, 1975, p. 4-5.

22. I discussed this matter with several Radio Moscow staff members, including correspondents, in my visit there in April 1970. Joe Adamov made many of the same observations when we talked about Radio Moscow in the course of his visit to Minneapolis, November 26-30, 1979.

23. Many of those hours are repeat programs. Even Radio Moscow can't provide 24 hours a day of original programing, in Kuoyu or in English! The North American Service of Radio Moscow is on the air for six hours each evening,

but "original" programing accounts for only 90 minutes; the
remaining time is taken up by repeat broadcasts.

24. The World Service has already introduced a few
features which have no exact counterparts on the other Radio
Moscow services. An example would be "ear ticklers", which
are "four minutes of oddities gleaned from the 8,000 newspapers and 5,000 magazines in the Soviet Union." One item
started off: "A talking magpie by the name of Chita an-
nounces the numbers during concerts by an all-bird choir in
Soviet Belorussia. The choir includes 60 birds of all
kinds."

25. This summary of themes is derived in part from my
own listening to Radio Moscow in various parts of the world
over a period of nearly 20 years. It is corraborated, by
and large, in Frederick Baarghorn's Soviet Foreign Propaganda (Princeton: Princeton University Press, 1964); John
Clews, Communist Propaganda Techniques (New York: Praeger,
1964); Overview of External Cultural and Information Activities of Communist Countries in (year--appears annually, under
slightly different titles) (Washington: Office of Research,
United States Information Agency) (after 1978, U.S. International Communication Agency), Sorber, "Analysis" and
Oliver, "Comparison". See also Baruch Hazan, Soviet Propaganda: A Case Study of the Middle East Conflict (Jerusalem:
Israeli Universities Press, 1976) for a somewhat tendentious
but quite thorough discussion of the role of Radio Moscow
and other Soviet media of communication vis-a-vis Israel
during the 1960s and early 1970s. A brief treatment of one
of the more effective Soviet international propaganda
campaigns is provided in "Soviet Propaganda: The Neutron
Bomb," The CIA and the Media, Hearings before the Subcommittee on Oversight of the Permanent Select Committee on
Intelligence, House of Representatives, 95th Congress, 1st
and 2nd Sessions, December 1977-April 1978.

26. See Mark Hopkins, Mass Media in the Soviet Union
(New York: Pegasus, 1970), pp. 310-314. Gayle Durham
Hannah, Soviet Information Networks (Washington: Center for
International and Strategic Studies, Georgetown University,
1977), notes the uses made of public opinion polling as "an
outlet for public sentiment," but observes that polling is
not based on accepted research techniques (p. 18). There
are recent signs that survey research is becoming much more
acceptable to Soviet authorities and much more rigorous in
approach and techniques. I attended a convention of the
International Association for Mass Communication Research in
Warsaw, Poland in September 1978, and heard several interesting and comparatively "progressive" papers on the role of
research in a socialist (Communist) society. The work of
Boris Firsov, a sociologist at the University of Leningrad,
is especially noteworthy in this respect.

27. Cited in <u>World Broadcasting Information</u> (BBC Monitoring Services), Edition No. 19, May 14, 1981, p. 19/A3. BBC received 330,000 letters in 1979.

28. There is a useful summary of USIA and other studies between 1973-1980 in "Audiences to VOA, BBC and Radio Moscow," Washington: USICA Office of Research, January 1981. Various of the BBC Handbooks also contain references to research studies which reveal the relative size of Radio Moscow's audience in certain countries where the BBC has conducted surveys. See also "Listening to Radio Moscow and Radio Peking in Czechoslovakia, Hungary, Poland and Romania," Munich: Radio Free Europe, Memorandum, March 28, 1978. Given the limitations of Radio Free Europe's conditions of research, these data should be regarded as no more than suggestive.

29. Donald Dunham, <u>Kremlin Target, USA</u> (New York: Ives Washburn, Inc., 1961), p. 90; also Clews, <u>Propaganda</u>, <u>passim</u>. My University of Minnesota colleague William S. Howell, who has visited Radio Moscow in 1958, 1968 and 1978, and has discussed the matter of target audiences with Radio Moscow staff members, has come to the same conclusion, although he feels that certain specific services, e.g. the North American and World Services, are intended in large part for somewhat less committed listeners. Baarghorn, <u>Propaganda</u>, pp. 283-284, questioned the effectiveness of Radio Moscow broadcasts to North America as of 1960, finding them too tendentious, although he added that they were per- haps intended for "communists and fellow travellers" rather than average Americans.

30. Don D. Smith, "Mass Communications and Inter- national Image Change," <u>Journal of Conflict Resolution</u> 17 (March 1973):115-129.

31. Over the past 18 years, I have asked various students in classes in international broadcasting about their own listening habits. Most of them had never listened to international broadcasts before enrolling in the course; one common reason given was that they had assumed that stations broadcasting from the USSR, Albania, West Germany, etc., would be doing so only in their own national languages.

32. Information on Radio Moscow technical facilities is difficult to come by, since the station shares a limited amount of this information: its own program guides often fail to list specific frequencies, and even meter bands are not always indicated. Over-the-air announcements are generally confined to meter bands only. The annual <u>World Radio-Television Handbook</u>, is of some help in this respect, and <u>External Information and Cultural Relations Programs</u>, has a useful section (pp. 28-29) on the subject. Radio Moscow also follows the increasingly common practice of broadcasting on a number of "out-of-band" frequencies.

33. Few figures are available on program exchanges,
but according to one report, there are over 400 radio stations in the United States on the Radio Moscow distribution
list, although it is doubtful that all of them receive pre-
recorded programs (many probably receive schedules and other
printed information only). See Bill Richards, "For Farm
Fans, A Russian After Reagan?", Washington Post, January 27,
1979, D1. WSDR dropped the rebroadcasts following the
Soviet entry into Afghanistan.

34. No specific budget figures for Radio Moscow and
associated international stations are available. U.S.
Information Agency analysts, working from known Soviet
budget data and extrapolating from these data, estimated a
budget of 70 million rubles as of 1971. See External Information and Cultural Relations Programs, pp. 21-23.
Working from this admittedly tenuous base, it is quite
likely that the present figure is in the neighborhood of
110-120 million rubles annually. At a 1980 exchange rate of
c. $1.60=1 ruble, this would result in an annual budget of
$175-200 million, or just about the same as the current
combined budgets for VOA, RFE and Radio Liberty. The USIA
report uses a different basis for calculating the real value
of dollars and rubles; on their basis, the current budget
for the USSR would be closer to $270 million. The network
of jamming transmitters operated by the Soviet Union is a
separate cost, which could be anywhere between $100-300
million annually.

35. An October 5, 1979 UPI report from Moscow by
correspondent Douglas Stanglin indicates that there is some
room for policy initiative on the part of Radio Moscow
executives, and that in at least one case of disagreement
between the Foreign Ministry and Radio Moscow (over the
issue of commentaries on SALT II, which the Ministry wanted
to suspend while "delicate" negotiations proceeded, but
which Radio Moscow wanted to continue), Radio Moscow prevailed.

36. Hedrick Smith, The Russians (New York: Random
House, 1976), offers many such observations on Russian
and Soviet society.

37. From a "DXClub" broadcast on Radio Moscow to Great
Britain and Ireland, 2000 GMT, October 23, 1977, as reported
in BBC's Summary of World Broadcasts, SU/5649/A1/9, October
25, 1977.

38. Following the deposal of the Shah, the National
Voice of Iran remained on the air, presumably because the
Soviet Union was uncertain about the foreign policy of the
new government. It continues to be critical of what it sees
as "pro-Western" figures such as Iranian president Bani-Sadr,
who was forced out of office in mid-1981.

39. See Lawrence Magne, "Broadcasting Stations of Clandestine, Exile, Intelligence, Liberation and Revolutionary Organizations," How to Listen to the World 7 (1972), pp. 133-134, where the author mentions the change in postmark on QSL cards as one indication of a change in the political coloration of Radio Free Spain.

9

THE OTHER VOICES
OF COMMUNISM

BBC's annual Handbook contains a listing of most of the leading international broadcast stations, ranked according to their totals of weekly hours of programing. While most of the stations appearing in the list are affiliated with specific countries, one group--the Warsaw Pact nations-- appears as a collective entity, followed by individual figures for its six members, excluding the USSR. (Up until publication of the 1974 Handbook, figures were furnished for the collective entity only). This is but one manifestation of a tendency to view international broadcasting from the Warsaw Pact nations, and indeed from the "Communist world" in general, as some sort of monolith. While that view is not without some measure of historical and contemporary justification, there is a great deal of diversity in the programing of the Communist stations, and some of that diversity is quite meaningful in political and cultural terms.

It is true that at one time the Soviet Union exercised great influence over the other Communist stations, and one could speak of them in terms of a "Red chorus". Most of the stations received some measure of Soviet technical assistance at their inception, although few of them installed powerful transmitters before the early 1950s, and most received advice on programing. Broadcast schedules, choice of foreign languages and programatic themes were, and for the Warsaw Pact nations still are, the subject of annual or more frequent collective deliberation in a forum where the USSR appears to call the shots.[1] But total cooperation and coordination ended in late 1961-early 1962 as Albania, followed by the Peoples' Republic of China, introduced broadcast services in Russian and began to attack the Soviet approach to Communism.

Since that time, the ideological struggle among certain of the Communist nations has become more intense, some of them jamming each other's broadcast signals, some such as

Cuba having attempted at times to maintain neutrality between
the major ideological combattants, a few such as Poland
broadcasting as little ideological material as possible, and
one (Albania) adopting a position of "a plague on both your
houses" in its broadcasts to and about China and the USSR.
The monolith clearly has disappeared, and it is most unlikely
that it will reappear in the foreseeable future.

At the same time, it is evident that most Communist
countries attach considerable importance to international
broadcasting. Eight of them hold places in a BBC list of
weekly program hours for the 30 largest international broadcasters, and four of them--the USSR, China, North Korea and
Albania--hold places in the top ten. Transmitter power is
more difficult to determine, but most stations appear to
have access to a range of short wave transmitters running
from 100 to 240 kW, while a few have 500 or even 1,000 kW
transmitters at their disposal, some of them medium wave and
long wave. Some of the stations claim to furnish services
for most or all parts of the world, most broadcast in eight
or more languages, all but Cambodia broadcast in their native
language(s), and all broadcast in English and French. Individually, however, they show many interesting differences.
I present six of them here, selected to give some indication
of their variety of purpose and approach.

RADIO TIRANA (ALBANIA)

The Albanian international service started during World
War II, when Albanian partisan forces operated a low-powered
transmitter. Its initial languages (English, French, Serbo-
Croat, Greek, Italian) clearly revealed that Europe was its
principal target. The service continued after World War II,
but in 1953 the station began to use Bulgarian transmitters
to broadcast to listeners in the Americas, as its own transmitters, most of them 3 kW, were too weak to do the job.
Radio Tirana's growth during the 1950s was slow, and by 1960
it was only on the air for seven hours per day in seven
languages. Although it offered Albanian music and talked
about the rapid growth of the Albanian economy under the
leadership of Communist party chairman Enver Hoxha, there was
nothing to distinguish it in any fundamental way from the
other Communist international broadcast services; it attacked
the West and praised the Soviet Union, decried colonialism
and spoke warmly of the fraternal brotherhood of the Communist nations.

That state of affairs changed abruptly in 1961. In
September, Bulgaria withdrew the use of its transmitters,
bringing a halt to Albania's broadcasts to the Americas.

The service reappeared in November, relayed by Radio Peking
transmitters. In October, Radio Tirana halted its rebroadcasts of Radio Moscow programs in Albanian, and in November
it recommenced its Russian language service (it had offered
such a service for a short while in the mid-1950s).   In
December, Radio Moscow's home service began broadcasting
over two new frequencies which happened to match those used
by Radio Tirana's international service, in the obvious hope
of overpowering the latter. That started the radio war among
the Communist nations--a war which has expanded in volume
ever since.[2]
     Albania's entry into international broadcasting had been
made possible with technical and financial aid from the
Soviet Union; now the Peoples' Republic of China stepped in
to help complete some unfinished Soviet-backed transmitter
construction and to add further facilities. Albania stepped
up its broadcast activities , nearly doubling its weekly
transmission hours from 1964 (112 hours) to 1966 (c. 200
hours) and introducing or restoring to its schedule services in all of the Eastern and Central European languages
save Romanian[3] between 1962 and 1966. Those services carried messages of praise for China and Albania and condemnation of the Soviet Union and the Warsaw Pact. Stalin was
still invoked on occasion, and in laudatory terms.
     Radio Tirana, even as it was expanding, seemed content
to leave certain parts of the world largely unserved. There
were no broadcasts in native African languages, and only one
in an Asian language: Indonesian. Most parts of the world
received broadcasts in Albanian and English, and there was
a fairly large Arabic service from 1957 on (although some of
it seemed to be a relay of Radio Peking's Arabic service),
but Europe was clearly Tirana's major target area, with the
vast majority of its language services directed there.
Fifteen of its 17 languages as of 1970, 17 of 22 as of 1980,
were Eastern and Western European tongues, although some
were used in other areas of the world as well. If it was
becoming a major international broadcaster, it was major in
regional rather than global terms.
     During the latter part of the 1970s, Radio Tirana's
broadcasts revealed yet another shift in political cur-
rents: having initiated its criticism of the United States
in the late 1940s, and having added the Soviet Union to that
company in 1961, it now began to include the PRC in its
attacks. It had said very little about the Chinese-American
rapprochement in the early 1970s, but by 1978 Albanian
political leaders apparently decided that the PRC was beyond
redemption, because Radio Tirana both ceased to function as
European relay base for Radio Peking and began its own
Kuoyu language service to China. Chinese leaders were chas-
tized for having deviated from the principles of Marxism-

Leninism, especially in terms of cohabiting with the capital-
istic United States and its allies:

> In the talks between the envoy of the
> Chinese social imperialists, Huang Hua, with
> the reactionary leaders of Thailand, it was
> stressed that the relations between the two
> countries should continue to strengthen. On
> this occasion, Prem Tinsulanon, the chieftain
> of the reactionary regime, stressed that both
> countries should collaborate because China
> and Thailand are good friends. For his part,
> the Chinese envoy was very pleased to extend
> to this servant of American imperialism a
> cordial invitation to visit China at the earliest
> possible time.
> English to Europe, May 11, 1980.

As of 1981, Radio Tirana was broadcasting just over 550
hours a week in 22 languages; roughly 40 per cent of its
transmission time and 10 of those 22 languages were directed
to other Communist countries. Albania no longer has any
acknowledged allies in the Communist world, and Radio Tirana
makes something of a boast of that independence. Operating
such an ambitious international service must be a considerable drain on the national budget, and after the 1978
rupture with China it became Albania's burden alone. Likewise, China was no longer there to provide assistance with
the more exotic language services such as Indonesian or
Arabic, yet Radio Tirana has continued to provide them in
undiminished quantity, though the source for the necessary
talent is a mystery.[4]
     Over the years, there have been two constant elements
in Radio Tirana broadcasts: style of presentation and Enver
Hoxha. Its style has won for the station an unenviable
reputation as one of the two (Radio Pyongyang is the other)
"most difficult to listen to" international stations so far
as shortwave listening clubs such as the Association of North
American Radio Clubs are concerned--an evaluation that is
consistent with my own experience. This excerpt from an
April 27, 1980 broadcast shortly after the abortive U.S.
hostage rescue mission in Iran should give you some sense of
the turgidity of Tirana's prose, although it cannot convey
the overly precise, monotonous delivery:

> In the meantime, the Soviet social imperialists
> have established themselves all over Afghanistan,
> and have encircled Iran from the north, eastern
> and southern parts. The Iranian people, who have
> coped with the numerous pressures and threats of

American imperialism with their courage and
bravery which characterize them, were able to
cope with this aggressive act, too, and to
stand unflinching in the possession of their
just rights.

The second constant element, Enver Hoxha, is notable for
two reasons: first, few Communist political figures have
enjoyed such long and unrivalled terms of power, and second,
few have been so glorified by their nations' domestic and
international media. Josef Stalin, Mao Zedong, Kim Il Sung,
and perhaps Ho Chi Minh would be comparable examples, but
Enver Hoxha has outlived all except Kim. Listeners to Radio
Tirana have been able to count on hearing something about or
by him every day at least the past three decades.
      Radio Tirana's broadcasts of Albanian popular music have
served as leaven for the station's newscasts, commentaries
and frequent readings from Enver Hoxha's works. There are
also features about Albanian history, traditions and folk-
lore. Listeners are encouraged to write to the station, to
enter the occasional contest, to ask questions about Albania,
or to comment on its programing. Tirana does not disclose
the numbers of letters it receives each year, but it is quite
possible that it has a devoted audience which agrees with its
view that all three superpowers (the USSR, the U.S. and
China) are imperialist. Curiously, it may owe its sheer
magnitude to all three: to the United States as the eternal
enemy, to the USSR for having built it up to combat that
enemy, and to the PRC for having built it up still further in
order to combat the U.S! Its Chinese-built 500 kW medium
and shortwave transmitters enable it to be heard clearly
throughout Europe and further afield, but the effect of its
messages remains uncertain.

RADIO PEKING (PRC)

      Much like Albania, the Peoples' Republic of China began
its international broadcast activities before it became a
sovereign state. The Communist Party had operated a domestic
radio service sporadically during the civil war, and even
broadcast in English on occasion.[5] In September 1945, the
Party set up a 300 watt transmitter in a small temple near
Yenan. Radio Peking traces its birth to that date, although
the miniscule transmitter would have made reception beyond
China's borders highly improbable. Kuoyu (Mandarin) was its
first language, English followed in a little over a year,
then Amoy, Cantonese, Chaochou and Japanese in 1949 and
Korean, Hakka, Indonesian, Burmese, Thai, Mongolian, Tibetan

and Vietnamese in 1950. That complement of services remained
stable until 1956, when Cambodian and Lao were added, probably
because of increasing French problems in Indochina, but
Mongolian and Tibetan dropped. For the first ten years of
its existence, Radio Peking assumed the role of regional
international broadcaster. It acted as advocate of peoples'
liberation movements, particularly in Indochina; as champion
of international Communism, with the USSR as acknowledged
leader; as enemy of imperialism, particularly the U.S.
variety; and as portrayer of progress in the PRC, under the
leadership of Chairman Mao.

Radio Peking took on a more international role as it
began to broadcast to Europe, the Middle East, Africa and
South Asia in 1956, at first in English and Spanish, then in
Arabic, Persian, Turkish and various Chinese languages for
overseas Chinese beyond Southeast Asia. Weekly hours of
transmission more than doubled from 1955 (c. 160) to 1957
(c. 320), and it was increasingly clear that Radio Peking
was to play a part in the Communist international radio
array second only to Radio Moscow's.

Radio Peking had assumed a special role with respect to
the Republic of China (Taiwan) some years earlier. Ever
since the Communists had taken control of the mainland in
1949, they had directed a special broadcast service to Taiwan,
at first through the radio station in Shanghai, then starting
in 1954 through Radio Peking itself. In 1958, the Fukien
Front Station of the Peoples' Liberation Army began to broadcast to ROC military personnel stationed on the offshore
islands of Quemoy and Matsu. Between them, the two broadcast services soon were transmitting well over 100 hours per
week to Taiwan and the offshore islands, and by 1972 that
figure had more than doubled. Broadcasts attacked the
Kuomintang government, but also attempted to convince listeners that progress on the mainland was great, and that a
number of Chinese from Taiwan and the offshore islands had
discovered that fact for themselves by defecting. Some of
the defectors came on the air to tell their own stories.[6]
Peking's broadcasts also attacked the America "paper tiger"
as unreliable and decaying:

> Although U.S. imperialism has always boasted
> about the "wealth" and "prosperity" of the United
> States, it is unable to cover up forever the
> worsening ulcer of the decadent U.S. social
> system, nor the poverty of the great masses of
> U.S. workers, farmers and Negroes. Unemployment
> and poverty are the incurable diseases of U.S.
> society. Thousands upon thousands of U.S. workers
> have been rendered unemployed . . . In every
> major U.S. city, there are unemployed workers

roaming the streets without food.
Broadcast in Kuoyu to Taiwan, February 24, 1965[7]

Even as Radio Peking gained strength during the late
1950s, cracks were beginning to appear in Sino-Soviet
solidarity, and they became very evident by 1960. In the
following year, Albanian-Soviet relations soured, and for
several months Radio Tirana became a surrogate for the
Chinese point of view, as it carried denunciations of Soviet
leadership and ideology. In 1962, Peking introduced its own
Russian language service in a major way: 31½ hours per week.
By 1969, that figure had increased to 162 hours a week, and
this virtual 24-hour-a-day service was made even stronger
through the use of some 28 shortwave and five medium wave
transmitters (not all at the same time, to be sure), in an
attempt to penetrate Soviet jammers.[8] The attacks often were
exceptionally virulent:

> You have worked hand in glove with the
> United States in a whole series of dirty deals
> inside and outside the United Nations. In close
> coordination with the counter-revolutionary
> "global strategy" of United States imperialism,
> you are now actively trying to build a ring of
> encirclement around socialist China. Not only
> have you excluded yourselves from the inter-
> national united front of all the peoples against
> United States imperialism and its lackeys, you
> have even aligned yourselves with United States
> imperialism, the main enemy of the people of
> the world, and established a holy alliance against
> China, against the movement and against the
> Marxist-Leninists.
> New China News Agency, March 23, 1966[9]

Russian listeners were Radio Peking's major target in
the Communist world, but language services for the Warsaw
Pact nations were added to the schedule in 1967-1968, and
the new services frequently were relayed through Radio
Tirana's facilities. By that time, Radio Peking was broadcasting over 1,150 hours per week, closing in on Radio
Moscow's weekly total of nearly 1,500 and was carrying 36
different language services, compared with Radio Moscow's
62.[10]
But languages and hours of transmission do not tell the
whole story and, as Radio Peking entered the 1970s, it was
beginning to suffer from increasingly outmoded transmitting
equipment. Breakdowns were more frequent, and the transmitter "superpower" race was leaving China behind: Radio
Peking's largest transmitters in the early 1970s appear to

have been 120 kW, enough to reach the rest of Asia but hardly
adequate for more distant lands. Use of facilities in
Albania helped, but they consisted of only three shortwave
transmitters and one medium wave transmitter as of 1971.[11]
Nor was it easy to continue to expand language services,
particularly for the non-Asian tongues, following the turmoil of the Cultural Revolution in the late 1960s. Foreigners
particularly if they were not Asian, did not find it easy to
live in Peking during that period,[12] and although the PRC
had made strong efforts to expand training in foreign
languages for its own citizens, the disruptions of the
Cultural Revolution made that task more difficult, too.

The early to mid-1970s saw relatively little change in
Radio Peking's broadcasts, aside from a marked expansion of
broadcast hours for Taiwan and the offshore islands in 1975.
Few new languages were added, weekly broadcast hours increased very little, and program content remained much the
same. The Soviet Union and the United States continued to be
denounced as enemies of the people; Mao Zedong's wisdom was
quoted daily (sometimes repeated two or three times at
dictation speed); China's progress was noted in every newscast and in many features, such as In the Peoples' Communes;
Chinese "revolutionary" music could be heard daily, most of
it with a strongly anti-imperialist and some of it with a
specifically anti-Japanese (World War II) flavor; and
Listeners' Mailbag provided responses to (alleged) questions
from Radio Peking listeners around the world, although seldom
were those listeners identified by name or even location.

However, following President Nixon's visit to China in
1972 and U.S. disengagement from Vietnam in 1975, there was
a notable improvement in U.S.-Chinese relations, and Radio
Peking moderated its criticism of the United States. It
even began to praise its former foe for technological
prowess, although it continued to criticize the U.S. on
ideological grounds. The Soviet Union was treated as
harshly as ever, especially for the military threat it
allegedly posed, not only to China, but to other Asian
nations.[13] Chinese-Vietnamese relations worsened in the late
1970s, and finally erupted in a series of border skirmishes,
which saw Chinese troops enter Vietnamese territory (and
vice versa) in 1979. Broadcast attacks on the Soviet Union
as Vietnam's supporter intensified, while RP castigated
Vietnam itself regularly:

> Over the past few years, the Hanoi authorities
> have further tightened their fascist grip on the
> people. A Vietnamese refugee said: the Viet-
> namese people's daily ration is becoming in-
> creasingly smaller, meanwhile the Vietnamese
> army and police forces are larger than ever and

more and more prisons are being built.

However, historical forces prove that dictators can never maintain their fascist rules with bayonets. Despite the Hanoi authorities control and repression and clamor for stronger measures to maintain political security, they certainly cannot quell the discontent and opposition among the Vietnamese people. On the contrary, their acts only prove their weakness and panic.

Radio Peking in Vietnamese to Vietnam, March 24, 1981
FBIS Daily Report, PRC 1, No. 058, March 26, 1981, E3

The improvement in relations with the United States marked a more general "opening to the West" and an increase in tourism. As a result, Radio Peking broadcasts placed greater stress on features concerning the more traditional aspects of China, and took greater care in the preparation and delivery of scripts. Up until the mid-1970s, scripts had sounded as if they had been translated by people with adequate textbook knowledge of languages, but no sense of spoken languages. Now they began to display more natural language, and announcers sounded livelier when delivering them. To aid in the process, Radio Peking began to place some of its staff members with other international radio stations such as the Voice of America, which received several of Radio Peking's English language staff in spring 1980.[14]

In addition to its official international services, the PRC has operated several clandestine stations for the benefit of various exile groups and its own foreign policy, and to the discomfiture of several of its neighbors. In the usual manner of clandestine stations, some of them have come and gone, but as of 1980-1981, several were still functioning: the "Voice of the People of Burma", the "Voice of Democratic Kampuchea (Cambodia)", and the "Voice of the Malayan Revolution" (reportedly off the air as of July 1, 1981, and possibly replaced by a "new" station: the "Voice of Malayan Democracy"). The "Voice of the People of Thailand", perhaps the longest-running of the PRC-based clandestine stations, began in 1962 and went off the air in 1979, probably because China's conflict with Vietnam made it expedient that the PRC be less hostile toward Thailand. Although no one station's rhetoric is typical of them all, this excerpt from a Voice of Democratic Kampuchea broadcast on January 30, 1981, should serve as an example of their general tone and approach:

On 26 January, the Hanoi Vietnamese clique summoned the Vientiane puppets and the Phnom Penh lackeys to meet in Saigon, South [sic] Vietnam, in order to find a so-called solution

to the tension in Southeast Asia . . . Compared
with the meeting they held in Vientiane in July
1980, this conference was most revealing, as
between then and now the foul smell of Vietnamese
Indochina federation has been spreading all over
the world . . .
FBIS Daily Report, Asia and Pacific 4, No. 021,
February 2, 1981, H11

Radio Peking's growth since the mid-1950s has been
phenomenal: just under 160 hours per week and 13 languages
in 1955, roughly 1,400 hours per week and 43 languages by
1980. However, its emphasis remains heavily on Asia and the
other Communist nations. The loss of the Albanian relay
transmitter has decreased its ability to cover the Middle
East and Europe with a strong signal, not to mention its
negative effect on broadcasts to North and South America.
It has modernized its transmitting facilities over the past
few years, which has helped to make up for the Albanian
relay, but it appears to be content to maintain the status
quo on its languages and hours of transmission.
        Radio Peking is mentioned rarely by listeners in most
surveys conducted by VOA, BBC and DW and when it appears at
all, it is apt to be in a country where nearly all international broadcast listening is minimal. A USIA survey
taken in Mexico in 1972 showed that Radio Peking came in
eighth among international broadcasting stations, with .4
per cent of listeners stating that they listened to it once
a week or more. Its listenership among its few immediate
neighbors where surveys can be taken or pro-Peking responses
freely given show somewhat better, but not spectacular,
results: a USIA survey done in urban Thailand in 1973
showed 1.4 per cent claiming to be regular (once a week or
more) listeners (BBC drew 4.1, VOA 3.4 and Hanoi's Voice of
Vietnam 1.4), while a BBC survey done in the Indian state of
Tamil Nadu in late 1977 showed that about three per cent of
the population listened to Radio Peking's Tamil service once
a week or more (BBC Tamil broadcasts drew four per cent).
        Peking probably does not expect to attract large
quantities of listeners, even with its now somewhat warmer,
more personal style in some of its language services. It
remains the conveyor of a certain form of Marxist-Leninist
ideology, and is for the moment an implacable foe of the
Soviet Union. A listener who was willing to listen select-
ively could enjoy Chinese music and could learn a great deal
about Chinese historical and contemporary life through Radio
Peking's broadcasts. However, the heavy diet of continued
and repeated insistence of the ills and evils of the Soviet
Union and its allies, especially Vietnam, of the disservice
that Soviet political leaders were performing where world

Communism was concerned, and of the threats posed by the USSR
to world peace and stability, could wear thin in short order.

RADIO HABANA (CUBA)

Shortly after taking office in December 1959, Cuban
Prime Minister Fidel Castro turned to radio and television
to help consolidate political power and encourage economic
reform. In some of those early broadcast speeches, Castro
referred to Cuba's readiness to "export revolution", so it
was hardly surprising to see his government develop an international radio service as soon as it did. On May Day, 1961,
Castro dedicated a 500 kW transmitter complex for the new
Radio Habana Cuba, stating that it would "bring his truths
to the four corners of the world".[15]
Actually, it was clear from the beginning that one cor-
nor of the world would receive more attention than any other:
Spanish to Latin America was on the air for 11 hours per day,
outstripping the combined total for the other two services
(English, French). Cuba also created a special service for
the Caribbean area, transmitted in Spanish (and since
February 1980, English) over the medium wave La Voz de Cuba.
Many Latin American exile groups such as the Peruvian Anti-
Imperialist Struggle Movement and the Nicaraguan Unity Front
used Habana's facilities. But Cuba's neighbor to the north,
with whom relations had gone from "correct" to non-existent
during Castro's first year in power,also received attention
in the form of a two-hour-plus-per-day English language
service. Going one step further, Cuba added a special
service for U.S. Blacks in October 1962; "Radio Free Dixie",
a one-hour program broadcast through the facilities of a
50 kW medium wave station in Havana, was a mixture of commentary and jazz, with occasional uses of satire.[16] Its
basic message was that U.S. Blacks were being exploited by
the white power establishment, and as the conflict in Vietnam
grew, being exploited by the U.S. military as well. The
service appears to have been dropped in the very early 1970s.
Radio Habana remained a regional service, to all intents
and purposes, for nearly 20 years. It added a few languages
during the 1960s, Creole, Quechua and Guarani for the Caribbean and Latin America, Arabic for North Africa, but transmitter power, with a maximum of 100 kW per transmitter
(shortwave), made reception outside the Americas problematic.
With the escalation of the war in Vietnam, however, the
station began to play a larger role in the overall picture of
Communist broadcasting. On occasion, it was used to relay
broadcasts to the Americas from other more distant Communist
stations, e.g. from North Korea in 1968, when the North

Koreans brought the USS Pueblo into a North Korean port.
During the period 1968-1973, Radio Habana staff members
read scripts prepared in North Vietnam for a "Voice of
Vietnam" English language program to North America. Attacks
on U.S. actions in Vietnam were a feature of every program,
but they sometimes appeared in unusual settings, as in this
Mother's Day 1973 broadcast:

>   Dear friends: As mothers, we should have
> the right to acquire a happy life together with
> our dear children. However, imagine the grief
> and horror encountered by the South Vietnamese,
> Laotian and Cambodian mothers during the meddling
> military operations and bombardments by B-52s.
> If you ever heard the heartbreaking shrieks of
> distressed mothers before the dead bodies of their
> children and saw the parentless and homeless
> children, certainly you would be overwhelmed
> with grief, and would feel a great indignation
> toward the Nixon administration and its henchmen
> for having continued the war . . .
> Voice of Vietnam in English, May 13, 1973

Radio Habana had always played selections of Cuban music
but began in the late 1960s to broadcast regular music
requests shows and more non-controversial feature material.
"P.O. Box 7026" served as forum for replies to listener
letters, which were solicited every evening. "Cuban
Profile" portrayed the accomplishments of individual Cuban
citizens. One of the more unusual "soft" features was
"Philately in Cuba", with news of stamp collecting around
the world.[17]
Most of that schedule has remained intact. Still, even
with the large amounts of "soft" material--roughly half of
the English service schedule--the station does not hesitate
to take strong political stands where those who oppose Cuban
and Soviet policies are concerned. It stayed clear of the
Sino-Soviet conflict until the early 1970s, but when it
finally became involved, it did so in no uncertain terms.
In its attacks on China during the February 1979 China-
Vietnam border conflict, Chinese Vice Premier Deng Xiaoping
was called a "clown" and "a Fascist apprentice". Even then,
however, Radio Habana pointed out that Deng, who had just
visited the United States, must have received encouragement
from the U.S. government to undertake "aggressive action"
against Vietnam. For the United States government remains
Habana's number one target of criticism, especially where
U.S. activities in Central America are concerned, but wherever Cuba sees evidence of U.S. opposition to national
liberation movements:

It's pretty plain that what Reagan and his
advisors really mean by "international terrorism"
are national liberation movements everywhere.
During the Carter administration, the big p.r.
campaign was about human rights, but not many
people fell for that one, either . . . Reagan
and his people are falling all over themselves
to give more loans and credits to reactionary
regimes around the world, while at home they've
jacked up the military budget to over $122
billion. The new administration claims it's
responding to Soviet threats. Washington is
dragging this excuse out of the 1950s history
books (to justify?) its meddling in other
countries' affairs. It's also lifted restrictions recently on arms sales to countries like
Argentina, Chile, Paraguay and Uruguay. . . .
Washington already has money, arms and advisors
committed to El Salvador; it'll probably do the
same in Guatemala. (Elsewhere?) it's backing
Israel and Egypt to the hilt, in hopes that those
two countries will continue to act as its policemen in the Middle East. In Africa, Reagan and
company are moving closer to Pretoria. And what
all this adds up to is a very serious threat to
world peace. If a major flare-up does take
place, Washington will have no one to blame but
itself.
Radio Habana to North America in English, July 15, 1981

Radio Habana expanded its effective broadcast reach
beyond the Western Hemisphere in 1979, when Radio Moscow
began to relay its broadcasts through Cuba and repaid Cuba
in kind by arranging for the relay of Radio Habana broadcasts in French, Portuguese, Spanish and Arabic from the
USSR. Radio Habana's weekly hours of broadcast and numbers
of language services had remained largely unchanged throughout the 1970s, and stood at just over 325 hours per week and
eight languages at the start of 1979. One year later, thanks
to the Soviet relay base and Habana's consequent increase in
its broadcast hours in French, Portuguese and Spanish, total
weekly hours had risen to over 380, although the number of
language services remained the same.[18]
Radio Habana is one of the few Communist stations aside
from Radio Moscow to make a significant showing in polls and
surveys conducted by other international broadcasters. (It
does no surveys of its own, although it does solicit listener
mail and holds frequent contests where listeners answer
questions or write brief essays about events in Cuban history).
BBC and USICA-VOA surveys in Latin America frequently show

Radio Habana in the number one, two or three position among
Spanish language international broadcasters to the region[19]
--a level of popularity aided by widespread Latin American
curiosity regarding Cuba and by the provision of a 19-hour-
per-day service in Spanish, usually on several different
frequencies. Its production staff is quite skilled, in contrast with the frequently unprofessional quality of many
Latin American domestic radio services, and its coverage of
anti-government activities in various Latin American
countries should win it an audience which receives little of
this material through its own media.

RADIO BERLIN INTERNATIONAL (GDR)

     Last on the international broadcasting scene of the
Warsaw Pact nations, East Germany (GDR) has risen to a
position of leadership in short order. The official service,
Radio Berlin International, grew with amazing speed, going
from two languages (English and French) and nine hours per
week in 1955 to ten languages (largely European, but also
Arabic and Swahili) and over 300 hours per week a decade
later! The growth of clandestine services was almost as
rapid, starting with Freiheitssender 904 (Freedom Station
904) in 1956, for members of West Germany's outlawed Communist Party. 904 was joined by Deutsche Soldatensender
([West] German Soldiers' Station), Voice of the Turkish
Communist Party, Our Radio (also for Turkey), the Voice of
Greek Democrats Abroad, the Voice of the Immigrant (Italy)
and others from time to time, including a Radio Vltava to
Czechoslovakia in 1968-1969. (The Greek, Turkish and
Italian services seemed to be intended primarily for "guest
workers" in West Germany).
     The various clandestine stations "tend to appear, dis-
appear and reappear with the shifting sands of political
fortune,"[20] and those associated with East Germany are no
exception to the rule: the normalization of relations
between East and West Germany brought about the demise of
Freiheitssender 904 in 1971 and of the Deutsche Soldatensender in 1972,[21] while the Voice of Greek Democrats Abroad
disappeared shortly after the Greek colonels' junta was
removed from power in 1974. Nevertheless, East Germany
remains a major center for this sort of activity, which can
include some very uncompromising broadcasts, containing
attacks on more than one country:

          Let us recall the May Day incidents of 1977
     in which 34 patriots were killed. This bloody
     plot was the work of MIT. [Turkish intelligence

organization]. It is the experts of MIT who are
now conducting all the tortures on detained
progressives, socialists and communists. MIT
is linked to NATO and is directly run by it.
The junta government has refrained from taking
any action against MIT. Thus policemen as well
as U.S. and FRG [West German] agents that have
infiltrated into the organization are freely
conducting their activities.
"Our Radio" in Turkish, January 17, 1981
FBIS Daily Report, Western Europe, 7, No. 015,
January 23, 1981, T2

Aside from clandestine activities, East Germany's Radio
Berlin International is a formidable station in its own right.
It broadcasts in 11 languages and over 370 weekly transmission hours as of 1980, and attempts to serve most areas
of the world with an array of short and medium wave transmitters, some of them running as high as 50 kW. Its Arabic
service is large by any standards: roughly six hours per
day, or about the same as West Germany's Deutsche Welle. It
is the only Warsaw Pact country, aside from the Soviet Union,
to broadcast in Hindi. Swahili is on the air for 90 minutes
per day. RBI has encouraged the formation of "RBI Listener
Clubs", chiefly in the developing countries, and talks about
their activities on the air and in the quarterly, multi-
language magazine "RBI Journal".
RBI's broadcasts present the healthy state of the East
German economy, the relative decadence and neo-Naziism of
West Germany, the collective strength of the "socialist"
nations (the Warsaw Pact and certain of the Asian Communist
nations), the warmongering of the United States, and East
Germany's cooperation with the developing nations. There
are frequent reminders, too, that East Germany is first and
foremost a workers' state:

At the Furstenwalder tire works, for
instance, a setter operator named Karl Heinz
Huebner has been keeping notes since last
December of the daily waiting time of his
machine. Due to insufficient labor organization, this waiting time amounted every day
to between 70 and 80 minutes. This has been
overcome. The consequences: labor produc-
tivity has increased by 14 per cent, not
through the use of more muscular strength,
but through the better use of technology, and
Karl Heinz Huebner's monthly wage has also
increased, by 70 marks. Asked why he drew
attention to his notes concerning the plan,

he replied, "Who else is to implement our
economic policy if not in the first place we
workers?
RBI in English to North America, August 1979

The device of personalizing its broadcast messages by
emphasizing that they are the beliefs and acts of specific
individuals is a common one on RBI, but its effectiveness
is hindered somewhat by the station's frequent use of a
highly formal prose style and an equally formal manner of
reading copy. Furthermore, despite its powerful array of
transmitters, its signal in the Americas, Asia and parts of
Africa is weak, and my conversations with RBI staff members
in Berlin in 1972 and 1980 have revealed that they see their
chief target areas as Western Europe, North and East Africa,
the Middle East and South Asia. Anything beyond that happens
more or less by chance and hard work on the listener's part.

RADIO BUDAPEST (HUNGARY)

Along with Czechoslovakia, Hungary shares the dis-
tinction among Eastern European Communist nations of having
had an international radio service even before World War II.
This earlier version of Radio Budapest had come on the air
in 1937 with broadcasts in Hungarian, English and Spanish,
and added French, German and Italian over the next few years.
Those language services have continued to the present day,
and were joined by Esperanto and Russian shortly after the
war, then by Serbo-Croat and Slovene as Yugoslavia broke
away from the other European Communist circle in 1948.
Greek and Finnish came along in 1950, Turkish in 1951.
Radio Budapest's rate of growth from the late 1940s
through the mid-1950s compared favorably with that of most
of the other Communist international stations, rising from
86 hours per week in 1950 to nearly 115 hours by 1955. The
1956 Hungarian uprising changed that picture abruptly. The
year-end figure for 1956 was just under 50 hours per week,
and although it climbed back up over 100 hours within a
year, it has hovered between 100 and 130 hours since 1960.
The total number of broadcast languages has dropped to
seven, all of them European.[22]
As Eastern and Central European international broadcasters go, Radio Budapest is at the bottom of the pile in
terms of numbers of languages and hours of transmission. Its
programing is quite varied and relatively relaxed and
personal, and it is possible that its German, Greek,
Italian and Turkish services reach a fair number of listeners
(although I have never seen Radio Budapest mentioned in a

BBC, VOA or DW survey), since those languages are on the air
for an hour or more each day over several frequencies simultaneously, including medium wave and with transmitters up
to 250 kW. Such listeners would hear newscasts which provide items about Hungary's progress and the unity of the
Warsaw Pact nations, but which feature less condemnation of
the United States, other NATO members and China than is
usually the case with the Communist international stations.
They would also hear of Hungary's desire to increase tourism,
already an important source of "hard" currency:

> [The Forum Hotel] will be another luxury
> hotel, with swimming pool and saunas, but guests
> there will find this hotel less expensive, for
> it will not have its own restaurant, and, if they
> want to, they can go to the Intercontinental
> Hotel [also in Budapest] for breakfast. As a
> result of the link-up between the two hotels,
> guests will be able to enjoy two [words indistinct]
> for the price of one. However, as you and I are
> unlikely to make a stampede for this type of
> hotel, I should add that there are less expensive
> hotels in both Budapest and the countryside,
> with a full range of services, including restau-
> rants, coffee shops, room service, and so on,
> and are much cheaper. For those who want some-
> thing more down to earth, and are perhaps making
> a holiday by car, there are the motels, which
> provide only accommodation, but with directions
> to all the low-cost restaurants for meals. But
> for those who want to see how the locals live,
> the best bet is to take a room through the "Paying
> guest" service . . .
> English to Europe, April 21, 1980

It is difficult to escape the conclusion that Hungary's
independent action in 1956 and more pragmatic approach to
economic policy in the 1960s and 1970s have had a negative
effect on the growth of Radio Budapest. Its services for
listeners outside of Europe are smaller than those of any
other Warsaw Pact international station. While it supports
Warsaw Pact policies in its broadcasts, it appears to spend
less time on such material than do its Pact colleagues.
Hungary's activities in clandestine broadcasting, never
large, ceased in 1968. In short, it does not appear to
occupy, and perhaps does not desire, a position of high
trust within the circle of Warsaw Pact international broadcasters.

RADIO PYONGYANG (NORTH KOREA)

Radio Pyongyang was born shortly before the Korean War
began, with a Korean language service which came on the air
in January 1949 for South Korea. The war itself saw the
addition of English and Japanese services (both in 1950),
but when the war ended the English service was dropped, not
to be resurrected until 1960. The Japanese and Korean
services remained Pyongyang's sole offerings until 1960, but
it was clear where the station's priorities lay: Japanese
got seven hours a week, Korean 134! English, Kuoyu and
Esperanto joined them in 1960 (the only year Esperanto
appears to have been on the schedule) and other languages
have been added since: French, Russian, Spanish and Arabic.
Korean, however, has remained its principal language service,
and Korean affairs its principal preoccupation; its closest
rival among Communist broadcasters in terms of chauvinism
has been Radio Tirana, with which it shares a number of other
characteristics, formality of style and dullness of presentation among them.
    The extensive Korean language service--well over 200
hours a week, as of 1980--is intended primarily for Koreans
in South Korea and in Japan, although much of it is available in theory to Koreans throughout the world. North Korea
has had some success in getting expatriate Koreans to return
to their homeland and settle in the North, whether they or
their ancestors came from there or not. The Japanese service
is Radio Pyongyang's second largest, and has increased from
one hour per day in 1962 to over ten hours per day in 1980.
Japanese-Korean relations are important to North Korea for
several reasons: attempting to keep Japanese-South Korean
relations from becoming too cordial, promoting trade, and
reaching that portion of the Korean minority in Japan which
has forgotten its native tongue. Pyongyang's Kuoyu and
Russian services symbolize the two major powers with the
greatest direct influence over North Korea's policies and
economy. Arabic, first introduced as a one-hour-per-day
service in 1970, had grown to over five hours per day by
1980, in part it seems because of a desire to thwart South
Korea's attempts to develop closer ties with the Arab World.
English, German and French go chiefly to listeners in Europe
and Asia, Spanish to Europe and Latin America.
    North Korea finds itself in a difficult position with
respect to the two Communist superpowers. It is the only
Communist nation, save Mongolia, to have borders with both.
At the same time, under its leader Comrade Kim Il-Sung, it
practices a form of Communism that is more doctrinaire and
even Stalinist than do either the USSR or China. Radio
Pyongyang and its associate, "Voice of the Revolutionary

Party for [Korean] Reunification" (66 hours a week in Korean,
seven in English) generally avoid mentioning the Sino-Soviet
dispute, and do not even say that much about each nation as
an individual entity. They do say a great deal about South
Korea and the United States, whose governments and leaders
are often treated as the common enemy of the people. There
have been times when the attacks have lessened in intensity,
especially when the two Koreas have engaged in peace talks,
but more often the stations employ terms such as "warmonger",
as in this VPRP report on the attempted assassination of
U.S. President Reagan in March 1981:

> Observers attributed this [attempt] to the
> fact that Reagan surpasses his predecessors in
> warmongering and violating human rights. This
> punishment is clearly deserved by a warmonger
> and a strangler of human rights. The shooting
> incident clearly shows that those who like fire,
> not peace, will be burned to death.
> VPRP in Korean, March 31, 1981
> FBIS Daily Reports, Asia and Pacific 4, No. 061,
> March 31, 1981, D1

Like Albania's Enver Hoxha, North Korea's Kim Il Sung is
the subject of daily attention, and his writings and sayings
are quoted liberally. Even his son Kim Chong-il receives
praise as a model of behavior:

> When the old woman heard that the kind and
> grateful young man who carried her coal bucket
> was none other than the son of the great leader,
> she was awed and did not know what to do. This
> person held the hands of the old woman, who asked
> pardon for letting him carry the heavy buckets,
> repressing the tears swelling in her eyes. He
> said to her very gently: Do not mention it, old
> woman. I also am a son of the working people.
> I will not spare any efforts for them. Nothing
> is more wonderful than to work for the people.
> VRPR in Korean, March 22, 1981
> FBIS Daily Reports, Asia and Pacific 4, No. 056,
> March 24, 1981, D3

Unlike Radio Tirana, most of the music played by Radio
Pyongyang is revolutionary music, and traditional music is
rare. To add to its narrowness, the station's announcers
read most of their foreign language material in a monotonous
or oddly-inflected manner. It is one of the least favorite
stations of DXers, and members of monitoring services have
told me that it ranks alongside Radio Tirana as their most
unpopular station to monitor.

SOME GENERALIZATIONS

Although all of the stations covered in this chapter can be called "Communist" because of the form of government in their host countries, they and the other Communist international broadcasters exhibit some interesting similarities and differences.

First, some of the stations grew very quickly, while others were slow to develop, but the majority reached something close to their present dimensions by 1970 and have changed little during the past decade. Few have added or dropped language services in the 1970s.

Second, the Warsaw Pact stations have shown some interesting patterns of response to crises within Eastern and Western Europe. The Hungarian revolution of 1956 saw notable increases in Hungarian language broadcasts only from the USSR and Romania. The 1968 Czech uprising saw initiation of service or notable increases in Czech and Slovak language broadcasts from East Germany, Hungary, Poland and the USSR (Radio Moscow went from seven hours per day in 1967 to 84 hours per day in 1968 and 1969!) Political instability in Portugal in the mid-1970s brought increases in Portuguese broadcasts from most of the Pact stations, seemingly in an integrated fashion (see footnote 1, this chapter).

Third, there appears to be a high degree of similarity in the content of Warsaw Pact station newscasts. It may be that the Soviet official news agency, TASS, has some influence on that similarity (much as Western news agencies appear to do for Western stations), since all of the Pact stations receive it. One example of this similarity is a series of stories concerning one Emelda Veret, who left the employ of NATO and went to East Germany in April 1980. No other Western or neutral news source appears to have carried the story of her "defection" and subsequent revelation of NATO plans to target nuclear missiles at various Eastern and Central European cities, but almost all Warsaw Pact stations carried it over several days and with much the same detail. Also, although Veret entered East Germany in late April and held a press conference then, the story was not used by most of the stations until two weeks later, when the NATO foreign ministers were meeting in Brussels.[23]

Fourth, with the exception of Radio Moscow, none of the Warsaw Pact stations has correspondents or stringers stationed abroad. Although some of them are able on occasion to use a report filed by a correspondent from one of their domestic media, their newscasts mostly consist of a straightforward (and often monotonous) reading of translated wire service copy. Newscasts also are quite predictable; they frequently lead off with major declarations or activities of political

leaders. I have sometimes had the impression that Australia
could sink into the Pacific Ocean and the event still would
be reported after items on the activities of the Czech,
Soviet or North Korean heads of state! There also is a lack
of timeliness in some newscast items, whether because release
is held up pending clearance by someone higher up or because
it suits the purposes of the stations to withhold items so as
to make them coincide with upcoming events. However, station
administrators and editors seem more sensitive to the need to
be timely than they once were.[24]

Fifth, several Communist nations have or once had clandestine stations, while others never have engaged in that
activity. Why some of them take it upon themselves (or are
asked to do so) while others do not is not altogether clear,
although the presence of exile groups in some countries,
physical proximity to the target audience, ideological
affinity and trustworthiness (the USSR being able to depend
upon another country to get the job done right) all may have
some bearing on the selection.

Sixth, apart from Radio Moscow and Radio Peking, most
of the Communist stations cater largely to audiences in their
own geographic areas. Attempts to reach listeners in more
distant parts of the world are minor for most of the stations.
Very few of the Warsaw Pact stations broadcast in the indigenous languages of the developing nations, perhaps because they lack ready access to a dependable supply of
writers and announcers, lack the necessary transmitter
power, or do not have the USSR's blessing on such enterprises,
to the extent that the USSR may influence such decisions.

Seventh, while I have been unable to obtain budget
figures for the Communist stations, I can state that they do
not seem to be terribly well endowed. For example, staff
members of Polish, East German, Romanian and Soviet stations
have told me that they would very much like to visit some of
the countries to which they broadcast, in order to have a
more concrete picture of what those listeners and their
countries are like. Restrictions on such travel appear to
be monetary rather than political. Staff members also have
told me that it's not always easy to obtain the "hard"
currency necessary for subscriptions to magazines and newspapers published in the countries they attempt to reach.
Without such subscriptions, broadcasters are under a further
handicap in terms of having a timely, concrete picture of
life in the target areas.[25] (The privilege of being allowed
to read magazines and newspapers not available to the general
public is, I understand, one of the "perks" of working for a
Communist international station!)

Finally, although most stations solicit listener letters,
none conducts formal surveys. There were ideological barriers
to conducting survey research at one time--it was considered

"bourgeois"--but most of those barriers have fallen. Lack of
"hard" currency with which to pay for surveys may be a
stronger reason, as may the wish to avoid embarrassment over
what probably would be low figures for listenership. However,
there are some relatively sophisticated forms of mail solicitation and analysis available, yet even those go largely
unused.[26] Most administrators talk about desiring large
audiences, but they seem more interested in reaching the
ideologically committed, and less interested in determining
whether they've reached that larger body of listeners which
would be open to diverse viewpoints but which might be a bit
skeptical of the stations' generally unselfcritical fare.[27]

NOTES

1.   Interview with Karel Jedzinsky, Radio Free Europe,
Munich, September 1975. Mr. Jedzinsky had been a staff
member at Radio Prague in the 1960s and attended several coordinating conferences. Gerard Mansell, then managing
Director of BBC External Services, told me in September 1977
about a study BBC had done of Warsaw Pact radio broadcasts
to Portugal in the mid-1970s, during the political turmoil
there. That study showed careful coordination of schedules
so as to form an almost continuous Portuguese language
service. "Communist International Radio Broadcasting--1975,"
Washington, D.C.: USIA Office of Research, Report R-18-76
(October 4, 1976), pp. 5-6, indicates that Warsaw Pact
broadcasts in Portuguese increased markedly in 1975, rising
from just over ten hours per week in late 1974 to just under
55 hours per week in late 1975. (BBC went from about 5½ to
7 hours per week over the same period; VOA, which had dropped
Portuguese to Europe long since, resumed a 30-minute daily
service in May 1976).
2.   "Developments in Communist Bloc International Broadcasting in 1961," Washington, D.C.: USIA Office of Research,
February 7, 1962.
3.   Romanian had been on Tirana's schedule between 1946-
1948 and was restored in 1969 shortly after Romania's refusal
to join Warsaw Pact forces in Czechoslovakia.
4.   Mehmet Biber, "Albania, Alone Against the World,"
National Geographic 158 (October 1980) paints a picture of a
people highly suspicious of foreigners and of a lifestyle
which would have few appeals for non-Albanians.
5.   "Chinese Communist Tells of Civil War," New York
Times, September 24, 1944, p. 28.
6.   "The External Information and Cultural Programs of
the Peoples' Republic of China," Washington, D.C.: U.S.
Information Agency, Office of Research, March 1973, pp. 102-

103. See also Irving Fang, "The Chinese-Chinese Psywar,"
Gazette 25 (1979):46-57.
     7. Cited in Daniel Lyons and Stephen Pan, eds., Voice
of Peking (New York: Twin Circle Publishing Company, 1967),
p. 3. I heard a Radio Peking broadcast in English in 1964
which featured a dramatization of Albert Maltz' short story
"The Happiest Man on Earth". The story is a grim and tragic
portrayal of the plight of the poor in depression-era
America, but the station presented it as if it were a contemporary event!
     8. In a further effort to combat the jammers, Radio
Peking has sometimes played broadcast tapes backward, which may
or may not have deceived the Soviet jammer operators. It would
have been possible for Russian listeners to tape the broadcasts and then reverse the tapes for playback, since many
Russians own tape recorders. See "The Sino-Soviet Radio
War," China Topics, YB 459, January 29, 1968, pp. 8-9. China
appears to have made little effort to jam broadcasts from
Radio Moscow or Radio Peace and Progress, perhaps because
not many Chinese citizens own radio receivers (The 1981 World
Radio TV Handbook estimate is 12,000,000).
     9. Lyons and Pan, Voice, p. 315. NCNA (New China News
Agency) materials are relayed regularly by radio and are often
rebroadcast by Radio Peking.
     10. Figures are for "official" broadcasts, and do not
include clandestine services, Radio Peace and Progress, or
China's service to Taiwan and the offshore islands. They
come from several USIA and USICA Office of Research annual
reports on Communist broadcasting and from several World
Radio TV Handbooks.
     11. "The External Information and Cultural Programs of
the PRC," p. 94.
     12. See Colin Mackerras and Neale Hunter, China Observed
(London: Thomas Nelson, 1967).
     13. See Robert Scalopino, "Chinese Media Treatment of
the United States and the Soviet Union," Washington, D.C.:
USIA Office of Research, Report R-12-78 (March 22, 1978);
also T. Rama Murthy and Andrea Ngai, "Radio Peking: What it
Says About the U.S. and the USSR," paper delivered at annual
convention of the Association for Education in Journalism,
August 1979.
     14. Not all Western broadcasters were receptive to Radio
Peking's overtures. Deutsche Welle staff members told me in
April 1980 that they were asked to receive Radio Peking
staff as "intern visitors", but declined because they valued
their staff exchange relationship with the Voice of China
(Taiwan).
     15. Cited in James Monahan and Kenneth Gilmore, The
Great Deception (New York: Farrar, Strauss and Company,
1963), pp. 178-179. The authors are vehemently anti-Castro.

They quote several interesting excerpts from broadcasts made
over Radio Habana by various Latin American exile groups.
See also "The External Information and Cultural Programs of
Cuba," Washington, D.C.: USIA Office of Research, 1972,
especially pp. 5-6. Strangely, given Brazil's size and
importance in Latin America, broadcasting in Portuguese has
not been a high priority for Radio Habana. It was not among
the station's initial language services and it remains well
behind Spanish, English and French, with two hours of broadcast per day to Brazil (1980).

16. Tad Szulc, "Radio Free Dixie in Havana Praises
Negro Revolt," New York Times, October 8, 1962, p. 15.

17. Jerry Ray Redding, ""Castro-ating" the Media,"
Educational Broadcasting Review 5 (June 1971):40-42, gives
a brief account of Cuban international broadcasting during
its first decade.

18. There were brief periods during the mid-1960s when
other languages appeared on Radio Habana, such as Aymara
(South American Indian) and Swahili, but they did not last.
Weekly hours of transmission in various languages may be
particularly misleading for Radio Habana: the five-hour-per-
day English service to North America consists of the same
90-minute bloc repeated at different times over different
transmitters. Richard Snitkey, "Radio Habana Cuba's World
News Roundup: A Content Analysis," unpublished M.A. thesis,
University of Minnesota, 1974, pp. 13-14.

19. BBC surveys in 1978 in Mexico City (adults from
upper and middle socioeconomic groups) and Colombia (adults
in cities of 100,000 or more) showed "regular listenership
(once a week or more) of 9.7 for VOA, 9.3 for BBC and 4.8
for Habana in Mexico City, 5.6 for Habana, 5.5 for VOA and
4.3 for BBC in Colombia.

20. Lawrence Magne, "Broadcasting Stations of the
Clandestine, etc. Organizations," in How to Listen to the
World, 7th edition (1973), p. 126.

21. See Fred Casmir, "Two Unusual East German Radio
Stations," Journal of Broadcasting 12 (Fall 1968):323-326,
for further details on these two stations.

22. Radio Budapest carried an Arabic service from 1960
to 1966 but rarely for more than an hour per day. It resumed
broadcasts in Esperanto, a language that appears to have
fascinated most of the Communist stations, in 1966 but dropped
the service in 1969.

23. As further evidence of coordination, a Radio Moscow
report on the 1981 general assembly of the OIRT (International Television and Radio Organization, which is made
up largely of the East European nations and the USSR) stated
that there was discussion of the propagation of Soviet
President Brezhnev's recent peace proposals, and "stress was
placed on the need for coverage of the fulfillment of

decisions of party congresses." BBC Monitoring Service, World
Broadcasting Information, Edition No. 21, May 28, 1981,
p. 21/A2. It is likely that this discussion was intended to
guide the national and international broadcast policies of
most OIRT members.

24. Technological advances, such as a satellite link
(1980) between the USSR and Cuba, also have helped them to
do so. One example of the problems of earlier days remains
particularly vivid to me: when Soviet Communist Party
Chairman Nikita Khrushchev was deposed in 1964, the major
Western stations picked up the report and, after satisfying
themselves that it was genuine, broadcast it. Radio Moscow
said nothing about it until many hours after the Western
stations broadcast the report. Radio Prague said that
Khrushchev was vacationing along the Black Sea (and, in
truth, he was there when he was deposed). Radio Habana had
him at a Moscow airport, greeting arriving Cuban President
Dorticos, where he would have been if he hadn't been deposed! My observations are drawn from my monitoring of the
stations. For an explanation of the Communist viewpoint on
the practice of journalism, see Vladimir Hudec, Journalism--
Substance, Social Functions, Development (Prague: International Organization of Journalism, 1978).

25. Every Communist international station staff member
I have talked to over the past ten years has mentioned that
she or he listens to broadcasts from other countries,
primarily Western, on a regular basis. BBC and VOA head the
list, with DW not too far behind. Some have mentioned
listening to Radio Free Europe and Radio Liberty. In contrast, very few staff members of the Western stations have
mentioned listening to Communist stations, at least with any
regularity.

26. I was told by a former staff member of the Romanian
radio and television service that Radio Bucharest attempted
to conduct a content analysis of its listener mail in the
mid-1970s. However, as the solicitation of that mail by the
station had not been very specific or directive, few of the
letters yielded useful data.

27. A conversation with a Radio Berlin International
news editor in April 1980 on this point was quite revealing.
When I mentioned the difficulty of receiving RBI in North
America, he said, "Yes, we're aware that our signal is weak
in many parts of the world, but we assume that our audience
is willing to go to considerable effort to listen to us."

10

THE THIRD WORLD SPEAKS

Despite some controversy over the precise meaning of the term, and certain instances of denial that it has any meaning whatsoever, there is fairly widespread agreement that "Third World" includes those nations which are not members of Western or Eastern military and economic alliances, such as NATO, the Warsaw Pact, the European Economic Community or Comecon. Often, the Third World nations are less well developed economically than are the Western and Eastern nations, although several of the Arab nations have high per capita incomes. Africa (except for the Republic of South Africa), the Middle East, South and Southeast Asia, much of the Far East (except for Japan), Latin America, the Caribbean, and most of the Pacific island nations are generally thought of as comprising the Third World. In other words, much of the world belongs!

Most of the Third World nations that have international broadcasting* have initiated it within the past 20 years. Since most of them were colonies or protectorates through the first half or more of the 20th century, their colonial masters rarely saw the need to provide them with international voices. With the wave of independence during the 1950s and 1960s, there was a consequent wave of activity in international broadcasting, which seemed to become as much a badge of nationhood as a national airline or a new national currency. These new stations found themselves at a tremendous initial disadvantage: the frequency spectrum was already crowded with the international services of the Western and Eastern nations, and there was little room left for much more than regional broadcasting activity. As a consequence, many had to confine themselves to reaching their more immediate neighbors.

---

*I have excluded from consideration here the many international religious stations and overseas relay stations operating from within the Third World.

Lack of frequency spectrum space was far from the only problem faced by the Third World nations. Few of them manufactured the necessary transmitting and production equipment; consequently, most of it had to be imported from Western countries and paid for out of scarce "hard" currency reserves. "Home grown" talent capable of speaking foreign languages was often gobbled up by governments and business enterprises needing to deal with foreign countries, and there was little left over for international broadcasting. Domestic news gathering services often were inadequate, leaving the international stations in the position of being unable to say much about events in their own countries or neighboring areas, and relying heavily on the large international wire services.

Most of the Third World international stations got off to a slow start, but a few managed to attain regional if not worldwide importance quite rapidly. Those few were for the most part in countries headed by charismatic, diplomatically active leaders, such as Gamel Nasser of Egypt and Kwame Nkrumah of Ghana. But the three or four languages, 100 to 200 kW international station is the rule in Third World countries even today. What they lack in size they make up in sheer numbers, so I've chosen in this chapter to provide brief accounts of international broadcast activity within geographical areas, with more detailed descriptions of four Third World stations.

SUB-SAHARAN AFRICA

Some 20 stations broadcast from the nations of sub-Saharan Africa. Aside from the international service of the Belgian-run International "Goodwill Station" (OTC) in the Belgian Congo, Radio Brazzaville (French Congo--established during World War II by the Free French government in exile), the international commerical service of Radio Lourenço Marques in Mozambique (run by and for South Africans) and ELWA, an international religious service in Liberia (supported by an American evangelical organization), there were no international radio stations active in sub-Saharan Africa before 1960. In the early 1960s, Ethiopia, Nigeria, Ghana, Guinea, the Ivory Coast and Senegal came on the air with what were generally small stations. By the end of the decade, they had been joined by Somalia, Tanzania and the former Belgian Congo (whose international service was an on-again, off-again proposition). By 1980, all of those services, with the exception of Radio Lourenço Marques and Zaire (former Belgian Congo) were still on the air, and had been joined by Angola, Cameroun, Comoro, Gabon, Liberia

(a government-run station in addition to ELWA), Madagascar,
Malawi, Mozambique (a government-run station), Swaziland (a
commercial station), Uganda and Zambia. There were also
various religious and other international services or relays
of services operated by foreign governments and organizations.
    This rapid increase is impressive, but few of the inter-
national services in Africa reach beyond the continent, and
many reach little more than the immediately surrounding
countries. The largest of the stations broadcast in six or
seven languages, but most manage only two or three. Few
have more than one or two hundred kilowatts of transmitting
power for their international broadcasts. Only Nigeria
broadcasts for more than 100 hours per week, and it had
broadcast for less than 70 hours per week up until the late
1970s. Many of the stations suffer frequent equipment
breakdowns, and, since there is rarely any backup equipment
available, certain language services or even stations as a
whole may disappear from the air for hours or days at a time.
    Most of the African international stations have fairly
similar program schedules, featuring domestic and some
international news, features about life in their countries,
and indigenous music. The larger stations have listeners'
letterboxes, but few of the smaller ones do. The quality of
writing and announcing varies a good deal; some of the
stations translate and read from government press releases,
which are often long and formal, and announcers sometimes
sound as if they haven't laid eyes on the copy before
broadcast time! None of the stations engage in survey
research, although a few have sought to analyze listener
mail and have sent out questionnaires on occasion. Surveys
conducted by or for other international stations occasionally have revealed fair-sized listenership figures for a few
of the African international services (Nigeria, Ghana,
Tanzania) among their immediate geographical neighbors, but
it is rare to find them mentioned at all in surveys conducted outside of Africa.
    Since part of the target audience for many of the
African international stations consists of their own citizens
abroad, as diplomats, businesspeople and students, one would
not be surprised to note the absence of mentions of the
stations in the surveys conducted outside of Africa. Nevertheless, certain of the stations show great interest in
reaching listeners in the Arab world, Western Europe and
North America--the Nigerian international service broadcasts
for 90 minutes per day in Arabic, and several other stations
have 30 to 60 minute Arabic services, while six or seven
stations broadcast in English and French to Europe and/or in
English to North America. The fact that most of these
stations broadcast their services to other continents on one
frequency only, and on transmitters of low power by today's

international standards, probably hinders their chances of
reaching many listeners outside of Africa.

Nigeria

Nigeria introduced its international service shortly
after gaining independence. The Voice of Nigeria came on
the air in 1962[1] over four 100 kW transmitters in English,
French, Hausa, Swahili and Arabic. But rarely did it broadcast for more than 60 hours per week, and rarely did it make
much of a showing in surveys of international broadcast
listening in West Africa, much less anywhere else in the
world.

The Nigerian Civil War in the late 1960s apparently
brought home to the federal government just how little
Nigeria was understood in the rest of the world, and how
easy it was for secessionist Eastern Nigeria (Biafra) to
appeal to world public opinion on its own behalf.[2] That
state of affairs provoked discussion among federal government
officials, who decided that it would be useful to increase
the transmitter power of the Voice of Nigeria.[3] Several
years passed before anything was done, but in 1979 a substantial increase in power took place with the installation
of a 250 and a 500 kW transmitter. Nigeria's oil money had
helped, but the country was also very aware of its leading
position among African nations, and was more anxious than
ever to bring itself to the attention of a larger public.
At the same time that Ghana's international service was
almost disappearing from the airwaves, Nigeria's was growing,
not only in transmitter power, but in weekly hours of broadcast: in 1978, 63 hours per week, in 1980, almost 160 hours
per week.

Language services have remained relatively constant
through the Voice of Nigeria's history: English, French,
Hausa, Arabic and Swahili (which was dropped in the late
1960s but restored in 1979), with German being added in 1979.
From its early days, the station has sought to present
information on Nigeria and Africa, but its presentation of
that information has become much more professional in tone
in recent years, and its news reports manage, at least some
of the time, to avoid the "uncritical government handout"
tone so characteristic of many international radio stations:

> A survey of juvenile beggars is to be carried
> out in Bauchi State to find out the exact position
> (?) of the problem. The First Deputy Governor . . .
> made it known at the conference on child welfare
> in the state capital. He [words indistinct]

problem noted by government workers in child
development in the area regarding the traditional
practice whereby parents assigned their children
to Koranic schools for religious education. He
said that it became evident that such children
were not cared for, as a result of which they
had to feed themselves by begging.
Voice of Nigeria in English to West Africa,
March 1, 1981

It remains to be seen whether Nigeria will maintain its
new-found interest in international radio. It is unlikely
that the Voice of Nigeria will add many language services to
the existing six; recruiting difficulties (Lagos, where the
Voice of Nigeria is located, has an exceptionally high cost
of living) and the apparent lack of desire to serve as
broadcast host for the various African political opposition [4]
movements or to enter the East-West confrontation make it
impractical and/or unnecessary for the station to present a
wide array of language services. Its presentation of a
variety of programs about life in Nigeria and its newscasts,
which emphasize coverage of events in Nigeria and Africa,
will probably bring increased listenership now that the
station is more powerful and broadcasts for longer hours, but
the years of relative neglect of international broadcasting
probably will mean that the Voice of Nigeria will face an
uphill battle in establishing itself as a major international
broadcasting voice, in Africa or elsewhere.

Clandestine Services

Africa has seen a host of "liberation movements" over
the past two decades. Some have been short-lived affairs,
while others have existed for years. Some have found continued support from other American countries, while others
have seen support come and go with almost equal rapidity.
One common form of support has been in the form of facilities
for clandestine broadcasting. Although the liberation
movements themselves may differ widely, their use of radio is
remarkably similar in physical terms: programs are brief
(15-30 minutes), are often in a number of African and
European languages spoken in the target area, and are broadcast over low-power transmitters and on one or two frequencies.
A few dozen African liberation movement clandestine
broadcast services have existed during the 1960s and 1970s,
from Zaire and Congo (Brazzaville) to Angola, Libya to Chad,
etc. Activities of such services as of the early 1970s

have been neatly summarized by James Kushner,[5] and a few of
those services, such as SWAPO to Namibia from Tanzania,
remain on the air. Most have disappeared, but fresh services
have arisen. SWAPO now broadcasts from at least four
locations (Brazzaville, Luanda, Lusaka and Dar-es-Salaam),
and the liberation movements active in Eritrea have increased
their broadcast services to three or four, operating under
different names, e.g. "Voice of the Tigre Revolution" and
"Voice of the Eritrean Revolution," and emanating from
different political factions.

It is difficult to determine the effectiveness of these
stations. Listening to them can be dangerous, and few who do
so would be willing to report the fact in a survey. Most of
them are difficult to receive. Their typically polemical
tone would be attractive to their supporters, but that tone
would probably not be very appealing to anyone other than a
"true believer". Finally, the fact that some of the liberation movements broadcast over facilities provided by foreign
governments means that portions of their broadcasts sometimes must be devoted to covering causes and events in which
their hosts are interested, as appears to be the case with
the "Voice of the Eritrean Revolution" broadcasting from
Iraq.[6]

The Future

If clandestine broadcast activity has slackened over the
past decade, "legitimate" international broadcasting has not.
The 1980s show every prospect for growth: Gabon's new "Africa
No. One" international service, with its four 500 kW shortwave transmitters, should be clearly audible throughout the
continent, although its staple of disk-jockey hosted popular
music programs and commercials for such products as Marlboro
cigarettes might not have much influence on African listeners'
images of Gabon. Kenya has plans for an international
service to be on the air by 1983, while Zimbabwe may in-
augurate such a service even sooner. But most of the services,
present or anticipated, seem destined to remain confined to
the African continent by their relatively low power transmitters and often unfavorable frequency allocations, making
it difficult for the rest of the world to hear about Africa
from an African perspective.

NORTH AFRICA AND THE MIDDLE EAST

The oil wealth of many of the North African and Middle
Eastern nations has raised their per capita incomes to the point

where it may be difficult to think of them as part of the
Third World. Yet most consider themselves to be politically
unaligned with either the United States or the Soviet Union.
Furthermore, Egypt's one-time president, Gamel Abdul Nasser,
is thought of as a founding father of the Third World movement, and certain other political figures from this general
geographical area, e.g. Khomeini of Iran, Qaddhafi of Libya,
have achieved a certain prominence or notoriety as Third
World leaders.

North Africa and the Middle East have exhibited a pattern
of international broadcast development similar to sub-
Saharan Africa's. Many of the countries there did not become
independent until the late 1950s or early 1960s, and international radio stations were few in number before 1960.
Egypt, Israel and Saudi Arabia initiated their international
services during the late 1940s and early 1950s, and Morocco,
which had served as "home" for various international
stations (Tangiers-based Radio International and Pan American
Radio) and relay transmitters (VOA) during the 1950s, began
to use time on the VOA transmitters for its own international
service in 1959. The 1960s saw international services com-
mence in Tunisia, Algeria, Sudan, Jordan, Syria, Iran, Iraq,
Kuwait and Lebanon. These were joined in the 1970s by
Libya, the United Arab Emirates, Dubai and Qatar. In short,
almost every nation in the area has an international service,
and thanks in part to oil wealth, more and more of them are
turning to high-power transmitters of 250, 500, 1,000 and
even 2,000 kW to bring their stations to a wider audience.[7]

Why this high degree of interest in international broadcasting? Part of it may be attributable to a general love
of and reverence for the spoken word throughout this part of
the world. Arabic in particular, with its highly emotional
oral and literary qualities, lends itself well to presentation
via radio. At the same time, there has been a longstanding
tradition of mistrust of those in authority, and that mistrust has often been attached to the domestic radio services
as well, so there is a widespread habit of tuning to foreign
radio stations, some of which began broadcasting from Europe
(Italy, Germany, Great Britain) to the Arab world in Arabic
in the late 1930s. Illiteracy is widespread, making radio
particularly attractive to the masses. And finally, coups,
armed incursions and war have been common within and among
the nations of North Africa and the Middle East, with conflicting ideologies as one of the root causes of the disruptions, and with radio as one of the chief transmission
belts to bring those ideologies to the attention of a wider
listenership.

In contrast with sub-Saharan Africa, international radio
stations in North Africa and the Middle East are often on
the air for several hours per day, and broadcast to Europe,

sub-Saharan Africa, and, less frequently, North and South
America and South Asia. Only Israel broadcasts expressly to
Eastern Europe and the Soviet Union, and a few of the Arab
stations broadcast to Moslem nations in Southeast Asia.
Arabs vacationing, working or studying in other parts of the
world are a frequent target audience; most of the programing
directed to them consists of relays of domestic services.
The vast majority of the stations are run by the governments
of the respective countries, although a few of them carry
commercial advertising. (Radio Monte Carlo's Cyprus station
appears to be particularly popular with Arab listeners in
the Middle East, who admire its neutral newscasts and enjoy
its "intimate" disk jockeys). And finally, because religion
is so important a factor in most of the countries, most of
the stations carry religious programs, and three nations--
Libya, Saudi Arabia and Egypt--have stations that carry
nothing but religious programing (see Chapter 11).

Egypt

Up until the time of the so-called colonels' revolt in
1952, Egypt had a reasonably well-developed domestic radio
service, but no international station. Within a year of that
revolt, the country established an international service
that was to become one of the more prominent stations in the
annals of international broadcasting. One of the colonels
who led the revolt, Gamel Abdul Nasser, saw radio as a way
of reaching the rest of the Arab world with a message that
would hasten the downfall of colonial and "reactionary"
governments and would lead to a resurgency of Arab pride.
He also saw international radio as a valuable weapon in the
struggle with Israel and in the liberation of sub-Saharan
Africa.
Nasser's interest in accomplishing those tasks stemmed
in part from his vision of himself as leader of the Arab
world and enemy of colonialism, but he also saw that Egypt,
at the same time an African and an Arab nation, was particularly well suited to reach out to listeners in both
areas. His chief communications advisor, Mohamed Abdel-
Kader Hatem, may have proposed the idea of an international
service, but it was Nasser's enthusiastic support that
allowed the station to develop as rapidly as it did.[8] From
its inaugural broadcast on July 4, 1953, the first Egyptian
international service, the Voice of the Arabs, developed
swiftly, becoming a 24-hour-per-day Arabic language service
by the end of the decade. It was soon joined by an International Service broadcasting in Arabic and, in short order,
Hebrew, English, French, German, Portuguese, Spanish, Sudanese

Arabic, Kurdish, Turkish, Amharic, Somali, Swahili, Urdu, Benga
Malay and Indonesian within the next five years. Most of
these services were on the air for 30 to 45 minutes per day,
few were repeated during the day, and all went out on one
frequency only with a maximum transmitter power of 100 kW,
which became increasingly inadequate as the years passed.

However, there was more than enough transmitter power
to reach North Africa and the Middle East, Nasser's primary
area of interest. Various independence and opposition movements, most of them exiled from their homelands, came on the
air to broadcast to their followers and others in Algeria,
Tunisia, Iraq and other countries. The Voice of the Arabs
added its own reports and comments, sometimes calling for the
overthrow of colonial or pro-Western governments (e.g. Iraq),
sometimes calling for the removal of Western advisors to
Arab governments (e.g. Jordan), constantly criticizing Israel
as an "alien presence" in the Middle East. Further afield,
broadcasts frequently took the same shape: in 1957 a clandestine Swahili service began to attack British colonial
rule in Kenya and to support the "terrorist" Mau-Mau movement
there, and sometimes attacked British colonial policy in
general:

> The [British] suckers of blood and squeezers
> of nationals' lands are determined to impose their
> policy of overlordship on East, South and Central
> Africa. The British bwana wants all people who
> are not white to be slaves.[9]

In most of their broadcasts, the Voice of the Arabs and
other Egyptian international services enjoyed some special
advantages: in addition to serving as vehicles for Nasser's
prestige and Egypt's demonstrable anti-colonialist policy,
the stations were often the clearest and loudest receivable,
and sometimes the only station with programs in certain
languages. In addition, the Arabic broadcasts featured the
talents of some of the most beloved entertainers in the Arab
world, such as singer Oum Khaltoum. The central propaganda
points delivered by the Egyptian stations were drummed home
constantly; as one British observer who served for years in
the Federation of South Arabia pointed out, "'Say anything
a hundred times to simple, unsophisticated folk and say it
well, and they will believe you' seemed to be Cairo's axiom.
And as I moved about the countryside, I began to realize
that they [the people] did."[10]

The Voice of the Arabs enjoyed what some have called its
greatest triumph in its broadcasts to Yemen, where those
broadcasts were widely credited with helping to bring about
the collapse of the royalist government in 1962, chiefly
through calls for armed uprising coupled with reminders of

various injustices and restrictions imposed by the royalist
government.[11] Five years later, the Voice of the Arabs
suffered its greatest setback, when its announcers proclaimed
non-existent Arab victories over Israel in the so-called
six-day war. Listeners felt that they had been deceived, and
the Voice's chief announcer, Ahmed Said, who had been regarded as a hero for his skillful propaganda campaign against
Yemen, now resigned in disgrace.

The Voice continued its attacks against Israel until
well after Nasser's death in 1970, but its attacks on other
Arab governments almost ceased, perhaps because Saudi Arabia,
a frequent target of those attacks before 1967, was one of
the few nations able to help Egypt recover financially
from the disastrous 1967 war. The attacks against Israel
ceased in 1975, as Egypt and Israel commenced serious discussion of a peace treaty--a move which itself brought
increased broadcast attacks on Egypt from other Arab radio
stations, and led Egypt to attack those nations in its broadcasts!

> The Libyan authorities are contracting a
> number of international terrorists and members of
> the Mafia for liquidating the Libyans opposing the
> regime of Colonel al-Qadhdafi abroad, according
> to a statement issued here [Paris] today by the
> Libyan Free Officers. The Free Officers said
> that Colonel al-Qadhdafi (declared?) that he will
> pay 100,000 pounds sterling for the assassination
> of any of his political opponents. The statement
> said that these terrorist accords are coupled with
> the actions of the gangs of the revolutionary com-
> mittees (that?) pursue and assassinate any opponents
> to the tyranny of al-Qadhdafi.[12]

Even as the Voice of the Arabs was enjoying its period
of greatest glory in the late 1950s and early to mid-1960s,
Egypt's other international services were expanding. Perhaps
the most notable expansion was in broadcasting to sub-
Saharan Africa. Egypt had announced the creation of a "Voice
of Africa" service in 1955, at first using Swahili only, but
later adding English, French, Portuguese and a variety of
African languages, most of them spoken in the southern part
of the continent (e.g. Zulu, Shona, Ndebele). Within ten
years, the Voice of Africa went out in 14 languages, ten of
them African. By 1970, five more languages had been added,
most of them spoken in West Africa (e.g. Ibo, Wolof), and
Dankali joined the list in the early 1970s.

Most of the African languages were chosen for one or
both of two reasons: to encourage anti-colonialist and
anti-neo-colonialist movements or factions, and to reinforce

Islam. Most of the languages were broadcast for 45 minutes, once each day, and over one frequency. Writers and announcers frequently came from exile groups or from the ranks of African students studying at one or another of Cairo's universities. Those sources of supply were not particularly dependable, however, and broadcasts in some of the languages would cease at times because of the unexpected departure or indisposition of the one or two individuals responsible for them.

The other special international services, for Sudan, for Israel, for the rest of the world, the Middle East commercial service, and the Voice of the Holy Koran, all grew rapidly during the 1960s and by 1970 the collective international services included some 35 languages and were on the air for roughly 540 hours--a figure which did not include the hundreds of hours of Egyptian Home Service broadcasting in Arabic which could be heard throughout much of North Africa and the Middle East.[13] But transmitter power continued to be inadequate to bring signals to listeners beyond the Middle East and North Africa. Also, Egypt's preoccupation with Israel probably wore out its welcome with many European, American, Asian and sub-Saharan African listeners, although its stations continued to provide a varied diet of Arab music (as well as Asian, for Asian listeners, and European, for many others), had numerous features about ancient and contemporary Egypt and the Arab world and, since 1966, lessons in Arabic. Surveys taken in the Middle East and North Africa showed high levels of listenership for the Voice of the Arabs and moderate ones for the Middle East commercial service, but surveys elsewhere rarely showed regular listenership levels of more than two or three per cent of the population, and often less.[14]

There seems little doubt that Egypt's external broadcasting services during the period since Nasser's death have become far less important in terms of serving as instruments of Egyptian foreign policy. Anwar Sadat, who succeeded Nasser in 1970 and who was assassinated in 1981, made ample use of radio and television within Egypt, but did not appear to see himself as unifier and rejuvenator of the Arab nations and Arab nationalism, or as champion of anti-colonialism or anti-neocolonialism in Africa, as did Nasser. As a consequence, the external services stabilized during the 1970s, experiencing a slight decline in number of language services (Njanya, Sesuto and Persian were dropped), a growing and then declining number of weekly broadcast hours (540 in 1970, nearly 640 in 1974, just over 540 in 1979), and little change in transmitter power. In 1976, new 250 kW transmitters were installed, but most of the language services continue to be broadcast over one frequency only. The vast majority of its broadcast hours are still intended

for listeners in the Middle East, North Africa, and, to a
lesser extent, sub-Saharan Africa. Despite its still-
substantial number of broadcast hours, then, Egypt's international services are nowhere near as "worldly" (worldwide)
as BBC, VOA, Radio Moscow, DW or Radio Peking, and show
little likelihood of becoming more so in the 1980s.

Clandestine Services

Because of the political turbulence that has characterized this part of the world since World War II, clandestine
broadcasting has flourished. It's safe to say that no
country in the area has escaped being a target of clandestine
broadcasts at one time or another. Several Arab and Jewish
clandestine stations were active during the Palestine war;[15]
when it ended in 1948, most of the Arab stations went off
the air, while the Jewish ones became part of the official
Israeli broadcasting service. During the 1950s, Egypt aided
various North African liberation movements, particularly
those of Tunisia and Algeria, by providing them with air time
over Radio Cairo's facilities. Egypt itself became the
target of several British and French clandestine stations
just before and during the 1956 "Suez Canal War", the
British government-backed Sharq al-Adna playing a particularly prominent if inglorious role. During the 1960s, the
civil war in North Yemen and fighting between Kurds and
Iraqis were accompanied and encouraged by clandestine stations, as were disagreements between Egypt and her Arab
neighbors, Iraq and Syria in particular. During the 1970s,
Iraq and Syria themselves frequently served as bases of
operation for clandestine stations directed against one
another, Saudi Arabia, Egypt and Iran. The Peoples' Democratic Republic of Yemen (South Yemen) set up an anti-Oman
clandestine station in late 1973.

Many of those stations have continued on into the 1980s,
while others have disappeared and sometimes reappeared as
political alliances have shifted. Algeria established an
anti-Moroccan clandestine station in 1980, and the coming to
power of the new government in Iran in 1979 led to the development of three or four anti-Khomeini clandestine stations
shortly thereafter, as active in their way as had been the
various anti-Shah clandestine stations in the 1960s and
1970s. The civil war in Lebanon in the late 1970s led to the
creation of several clandestine stations representing various
factions, one of the most colorful being the Lebanese
Christian "Voice of Hope";[16]

Whenever the jug hits the jar or whenever the Israeli planes hit the saboteur's positions, there is a hue and cry in Lebanon. Dr. Al-Huss becomes excited and Fu'ad Butrus rise to the occasion. The Butrus palace casino [presidential palace] opens its doors to receive the ambassadors of the great states. After this, orders are sent to Ghassan Tuwayni to play a tragicomic scene at the theater of the United Nations and the Security Council. A complaint to the Security Council is a right reserved by the virgin girl [Lebanon] to be compensated for the loss of her honor.
FBIS Daily Reports, Middle East, No. 189, September 27, 1979, G5

As with clandestine stations throughout the world, those in the Middle East tend to come and go without warning, tend to suffer from limited broadcast time and frequency availability, and tend to serve as tools of the host governments, rather than expressing purely independent viewpoints. The various Palestinian clandestine stations display all of those problems: appearing and disappearing from the airwaves as one or another country favors or disfavors whichever Palestinian faction desires air time, the various Voices of Palestine have led an uncertain existence since their debut in 1954.[17] The effectiveness of most of the clandestine stations is something of an unknown quantity, although surveys conducted in some of the Middle Eastern countries with large Palestinian populations have revealed widespread listening to PLO broadcasts. It is quite possible that, in common with their counterparts in other areas of the world, most of them are intended more for reception by monitoring services than by actual listeners in their target areas.

The Future

There is no indication that the 1980s will bring any reduction of interest in international broadcasting in the Middle East and North Africa. The area remains conflict-ridden, and the presence of oil wealth has virtually insured that most of the nations able to afford it will be investing in more and more powerful transmitters, if they have not done so already. But transmitter power does not insure popularity, and the enormous Libyan and Saudi Arabian transmitter expansion projects of the 1970s do not appear to have brought much increased listenership. Perhaps it is because so many of these international stations have relatively little variety in their programing; perhaps it is because few of them have been able to assemble truly professional

foreign language staffs. Whatever the reason, most of them
seem destined to remain each other's best customers for some
time to come, with little impact on public opinion in the
rest of the world.

ASIA AND THE PACIFIC

International broadcasting in Asia and the Pacific
started before World War II, but few of the services came
from sovereign nations, since most of the area was under
various forms of colonial rule at the time. Japan, as
already noted, employed international broadcasting to reach
overseas Japanese and to justify its own expansionist
policies in Asia. China countered Japanese broadcasts as the
Japanese invaded China. The Japanese introduced international broadcasting services in some of their conquered
territories, e.g. Thailand and Indo-China. Australia
started its international service as a direct result of the
war, and most of the major Allied and Axis powers broadcast
to Asia during the war, often in major Asian languages (e.g.
Mandarin, Urdu, Hindi).

After World War II, the independence movement swept
through Asia. First came India, Pakistan, Burma, the Philippines and Indonesia, and then in the 1950s and 1960s most
of the other Asian countries. Some developed international
stations almost immediately, others such as the Philippines
waited a while to do so, and a few haven't gotten around
to it yet; as of 1981, Burma, Sikkim and Bhutan have no
international stations. Most of the stations are of re-
spectable size, with two to several transmitters in the
100-250 kW range, six to 12 languages (mostly Asian, but
often English and French, too) and weekly totals of broadcast hours ranging from 40 (Bangladesh) to nearly 400 (India).
Most of the stations concentrate on reaching Asian listeners,
and few even attempt to serve audiences elsewhere. Aside
from Australia and New Zealand, no Pacific Island nations
operate international services, although some serve as relay
bases for religious stations.

India

Just as India is a dominant force in non-Communist South
and Southeast Asia by reason of size and population, as well
as leadership in the non-aligned movement (Indian prime
minister Nehru was one of its originators), India's international broadcast service is the largest in the area, with

25 languages, just under 400 broadcast hours per week, and a
large array of transmitters, including some of 1,000 kW (not
for the exclusive use of the external services).

India is one of the few nations in the world to have
had a reasonably well-developed international service at its
disposal at the time of its independence. The British administration put a Pushto (for Afghanistan) service on the
air in October 1939, less than a month after war had broken
out in Europe.[18] Other languages, most of them South and
Southeast Asian, were added to the schedule; there were 22
by the end of the war. The British administration cut the
external services by more than half between 1945 and 1947,
which still left enough to get the new Indian government off
to a fast start in 1947.

From the time of that second beginning, the external
services have had two primary target audiences: Indians
living and working overseas, primarily in other parts of
Asia and in East Africa; and listeners in most of the
countries in Asia, many of which were still under colonial
rule in 1947, and some of which looked to India for leadership in the struggle against colonialism. Many of the
appropriate language services were already on the air, and
the 1950s saw relatively little expansion of either languages or broadcast hours. Transmitter power was adequate
to reach a radius of perhaps a thousand miles, which left
most of Europe, most of Africa and all of the Americas
essentially unserved. Broadcasts emphasized India's cooperative spirit and rich culture, but also contained
attacks on neighboring Pakistan, especially regarding the
disputed territory of Kashmir.

The greatest period of growth came during the period
1965-1975, when weekly hours of transmission rose from 175
to just over 325. A few language services were added
(Russian, Bengali, Sindhi, Baluchi), and transmitter power
increased by several thousand kW through the installation of
new 250 kW shortwave and 1,000 kW medium wave transmitters,
though time on them had to be shared with various Indian
domestic services. (The external services have been a
division of All India Radio since 1947). That growth may
have been due in part to India's border conflict with China
in 1962, when India perceived that world public opinion,
which may not have favored the Chinese, was nevertheless far
from enthusiastically supportive of the Indian case either.
Similarly, a major conflict with Pakistan in 1971 once
again brought to India's attention the "need" for more
effective international communication of its viewpoint.[19]
Language services which had previously been offered once or
twice a day now began to appear three or four times a day,
and on more frequencies.

The external services have continued to grow, and by

1980 were on the air for 389 hours per week, but there has
been no increase in language services and little in transmitter power over the past several years. The program
schedule continues to emphasize Indian culture (music in
particular, both classical and popular), science and
industry, and news and commentary (roughly 15 minutes per
hour) with a heavy emphasis on developments in India and
South Asia. Broadcasts in English account for nearly 30
per cent of the total broadcast time, and although announcers'
accents are sometimes a bit difficult to understand if one
is unaccustomed to Indian English and if signal interference
is heavy, some of the features are quite interesting, com-
bining as they sometimes do both cultural and political
messages:

> (FEMALE VOICE) In one of Nabin's famous poems
> which means "The Wind Spoke to me," distinguished
> like the rest of his poetry by felicity of
> expression and freshness of treatment, the
> wind, summing up, says to the poet:
> (MALE VOICE)
> One is the slogan of the gardens.
> Kashmir is ours, and Kashmir's bright future is ours.
> (FEMALE VOICE) Typical of the simple poet that
> he is, Nabin says that he will not chant soft
> and tender songs until Kashmir is well off,
> happy and free.
> All-India Radio in English to Europe, September 1975

The external services have sent out questionnaires to
listeners who had written to the station previously, but
they do not conduct survey research. BBC, VOA, and DW
have done little survey research in the countries immediately
surrounding India, partly because the national governments
would discourage it, but surveys done farther afield, in the
Middle East and East Africa, rarely turn up listeners who
claim to listen to the station, regularly or not. The
broadcast signal to the more distant target areas is not
particularly strong, most of the more powerful transmitters
being devoted to serving South Asia; the unabashedly pro-
government slant of news and features wears thin rather
quickly; and the manner of presentation of material, with
its emphasis on factual detail, and its highly formal
delivery, would not encourage listeners who were not already
deeply interested in India.

Clandestine Services

Various Communist nations, especially the Peoples'

Republic of China, have been active in clandestine broadcasting in Asia (Chapter 9), and CIA was involved in it
during the war in Vietnam (Chapter 5) and possibly following
the Soviet incursion into Afghanistan (1979-). Aside from
those activities, most of the non-Communist nations have
left one another alone where clandestine radio is concerned.
However, an anti-military government station was reported
in or near Burma in the early 1970s, there was a Khalistan
Radio directed against India and perhaps backed by Pakistan
or the PRC during 1972, and South Korea has engaged in clandestine broadcasting to North Korea at various times. An
anti-government clandestine station broadcasting to Afghanistan (possibly from Egypt) and calling itself first Radio
Mojahedin and later Voice of the United Muslim Fighters of
Afghanistan came on the air in 1980. Other anti-Afghan
government stations have joined it; a "Radio Free Kabul"
and a "Radio Free Afghanistan" reportedly came on the air in
August 1981, allegedly with the financial support of a
European human rights group for the former and an Italian
film executive for the latter.[20] Finally, Radio Maubere, a
clandestine station operated by an East Timor political
opposition group, has been on and off the air from mid-
1975. It reappeared most recently in November 1980. Its
staff claimed that it had broadcast from Darwin, Australia
during one period of its life.[21]

                        The Future

        Several Asian nations (e.g. Malaysia and Pakistan) have
shown steady increases in broadcast hours and some expansion
of language services during the 1970s, but most Asian
international broadcasters continued to be hampered by weak
transmitters (most are no more than 100 kw) and, as a consequence, cannot be heard with any reliability outside of
Asia, even though many of the broadcasters appear to be
interested in reaching African, Middle Eastern, European and
American listeners. A few, such as Bangladesh, are planning to invest in more powerful equipment, but there is still
a very real question as to whether the programs themselves
will attract listeners, once they can be heard clearly.
Some of the services do not sound particularly professional,
and most feature a dull, "recitation of facts" manner of
presenting material. Their own citizens and expatriates
living or temporarily working abroad probably will remain
the major targets of the stations in the 1980s.

LATIN AMERICA

There are few parts of the world which can match North
America's emphasis on commercial radio, although Japan, the
Philippines and South Korea all make strong showings in that
regard. But Latin America, if anything, outdoes its northern
neighbors in its widespread dedication to commercial broadcasting, to the point where strong public or other forms of
government-financed stations are rarities. While there are
other possible explanations for the general absence of international broadcasting from and within Latin America--isolated
geographical position, relative non-involvement in World War
II-the aggressively commercial nature of Latin American broadcasting has probably served to inhibit the development of
international radio there. Since almost every country already
had dozens of commercial stations, an international commercial
station à la Radio Luxembourg or Radio Monte Carlo made
little sense. And since almost every country featured a high
degree of governmental instability, whichever government was
in power seemed content to influence the existing stations,
rather than create its own, domestic or international.
    Aside from Cuba (see Chapter 9) and Argentina, no Latin
American country has had a strong and continuing commitment
to international broadcasting, although several have dabbled
in the field,[22] and one--Brazil--now may be ready to involve
itself in a more substantial way. The Argentine international station started in 1949, mainly for the purpose of
publicizing the accomplishments of the Peron government and
countering attacks on it.[23] When its new 100 kW transmitters were installed in 1950, the station appeared ready
to take its place alongside all but the largest international
broadcasters. It had six language services (English, French,
Portuguese, German, Italian and Spanish) and beamed several
hours a day to the Americas and to Europe. Thirty years
later, it has the same transmitters, the same language
services (plus Japanese) and little increase in broadcast
hours (14 per day as of 1980), although it made substantial
programatic revisions in 1979. Peru's private La Voz del
Altiplano had a one-hour daily service for Peru's neighbors
in the late 1950s, and Radio Nacional del Peru had brief (15
minute) two-or-three-day-per-week services in English, French,
German, Spanish and Japanese during the early 1960s, but each
vanished within a few years. More recently, Uruguay and
Venezuela have shown some interest in international broadcasting (Venezuela began a service in 1974, and had a 4½-hour-
per-day schedule in five languages, including Arabic, as of
1980), and Chile's international service, active during the
1970s, went off the air "temporarily" in 1980, allegedly
because of the tight economic situation there. Following the

accession to power of a revolutionary government on the Caribbean island of Grenada in 1980, Radio Free Grenada began
broadcasting to North America and Europe. Guatemala and
Nicaragua initiated small international services (Spanish
only, although English may be added later) in 1981.

Brazil

     Brazil's international station, Radio Nacional do
Brasil, illustrates many of the problems in Latin American
international broadcasting. Two Brazilian domestic commercial stations had offered miniscule international services
in the 1950s, but they did not last. A government-backed
international service was rumored during the 1960s, and
finally came on the air in 1972. By 1973 it was broadcasting in six languages--English, French, German, Spanish,
Italian and Portuguese. By 1974 the station had access to a
250 kW transmitter and was on the air for four hours per
day. By 1977 it was off the air (reportedly an economy
measure).
     In 1979, the station returned, but in English only and
for one hour per day. It added 15 minutes daily of Portuguese in 1981. Its staff did manage to put together a
fairly ambitious program schedule, with Brazilian popular
music almost every night (and usually with announcer comment
on it) and nightly features on sports, literature, the arts,
business and economics in Brazil--the last-named doubtless
due to Brazil's growing industrial importance and increasing
exports. The general tone of presentation is quite formal,
but a few of the announcers and writers have managed to
develop a tongue-in-cheek style: in one program about the
unsuccessful attempt of an Italian soccer club owner to
recruit a suitable Brazilian player, the final comment was
"he had to return home empty-handed to face the ire of his
fellow citizens."
     But if listeners expect to receive comprehensive, ob-
jective coverage of Brazilian or Latin American news from the
station, they will be disappointed. There is little of it.
Where Brazil itself is concerned, coverage is usually uncritical
The station is financed through a governmental grant to its
parent corporation, Radiobras, and operates under a very
tight budget, with every expenditure approved by Radiobras,
and there are only eight program and administrative staff!
In other words, Brazil's commitment to international broadcasting, as with Latin America in general, has been neither
constant nor strong.

Clandestine Services

Aside from CIA involvement in broadcasting to Guatemala
in 1954 and to Cuba in the 1960s (Chapter 5), and possibly
Cuban involvement in Bolivia in the late 1960s, Latin America
remained relatively free of clandestine radio until the late
1970s. At that time, fighting in Central America, mainly in
Nicaragua, El Salvador and Guatemala, saw the birth of
numerous clandestine stations. Most of them probably operated with the assistance of Cuba or the United States (CIA).[24]
Most of the stations connected with the Nicaraguan war have
gone off the air or have become "official", as did Radio
Sandino. However, new stations have sprung up, including
Radio Quince de Septembre (opposing the Sandinista government
in Nicaragua) and Radio Venceremos (the station of the Fara-
bundo Marti National Liberation Front in El Salvador). There
also have been several stations operated by Cuban exiles,
most of them from transmitter sites in Florida and bearing
such titles as Radio Cuba Libre. Most of the clandestine
stations emphasize news and revolutionary music; the following excerpt from a January 1981 Radio Venceremos broadcast is quite typical of their rhetoric:

> The statements of the new U.S. secretary
> of state, the murderer Alexander Haig, approving
> Yankee aid to the dying genocidal military junta
> of El Salvador are clear proof of not only the
> total desparation, but also of the open imperialist
> intervention in the domestic affairs of our country.
> FBIS Daily Reports, 6, No. 013, January 21, 1981, P16

The Future

There is little prospect for increased international
broadcast activity from and within Latin America in the 1980s,
aside from clandestine stations. Few governments are willing
to invest in it in the first place, perhaps because they
doubt that they'll be around long enough to reap any benefits
such a service might bring. Latin America appears destined
to remain a receiver, rather than sender, of international
broadcasts for some time to come.

SOME GENERALIZATIONS

International radio broadcasting has spread through the
Third World rapidly, but not equally. Latin America remains

relatively dormant, roughly half of the sub-Saharan African
nations do not have it, and it is absent among the new
Pacific island nations. It should be obvious that not all
Third World nations consider international broadcasting to
be a necessity. I have indicated that the presence of a
national leader with international ambitions and philosophies
often seems to lead to the creation or expansion of an
international radio service; clearly this was the case in
Ghana, Egypt and Argentina. But many nations without such
leaders have developed international radio, and some, such
as Malaysia and Nigeria, have developed it quite extensively.
A closer examination shows that most Third World international
services have come into being for one or more of the following reasons: to respond to a neighboring nation's broadcast attacks, to initiate attacks on a neighboring nation,
to "liberate" countries under colonial rule, and to communicate with one's citizens and expatriates overseas.
Seldom does a desire to let the rest of the world know what
life is like in the country, for whatever diplomatic or
commercial gain that might bring, seem to have been a
primary reason for the founding of those services. Because
of their sheer number and the great ideological diversity of
the nations operating them, it is hard to provide summative
statements about international broadcasting in the Third
World, but the following may be of some help.

First, almost all of the stations are financed by their
respective governments, and operate as part of the national
broadcasting service, which itself often operates under a
Ministry of Information or similar government agency. Thus,
most are subject to government control, and usually show it
in terms of the uncritical coverage afforded that government.
However, few of the stations seem to be subject to day-to-day,
program-by-program supervision of their broadcasts; few of
them seem to be considered suitably vital or important to
governmental foreign policy to warrant such attention.

Second, the program schedules of most of the stations
(except for clandestine operations) lean heavily in the
direction of "soft" features and cultural material. The
musical culture of the broadcasting nation almost always
accounts for the largest single share of the cultural portion
of the schedule: it is the least expensive and most readily
available way to fill out the schedule.

Third, stations appear to have a strong preference for
employing their own country's citizens, naturalized or not,
as announcers and writers. Whatever the reasons for that
preference, it would seem to limit the number of language
services the station can offer; there is a decided shortage
of people with foreign languages and skills in most Third
World countries, and many government agencies and businesses
compete for them. If international radio is a low priority

item, as it often appears to be, the announcers and writers
it can employ may be less professionally skilled than their
counterparts at Western and Communist stations.

Fourth, survey research is non-existent among Third
World international broadcasters, as far as I can discover,
and very few broadcasters send out listener questionnaires.
Most of them seem very receptive to comments made in listener
letters perhaps because it's the only form of feedback they
receive, since few of their staff members ever get to travel
to target areas.

Fifth, despite widespread increases in transmitter power,
most Third World international stations continue to suffer
from inadequate allocation of "good" frequencies, so that,
even if they wished to reach listeners half a world away (and
many do not so wish) and had adequate transmitter power, they
would be hampered in their efforts. The fact that transmitting equipment is often poorly maintained simply adds to
the problem.

Despite the expense of international broadcasting, which
is magnified for most Third World nations because of their
own poverty and the need to spend their hard-won "hard"
currency on equipment and maintenance, and despite the lack
of evidence of listenership, much less influence, for most of
the stations, expansion of the activity seems destined to
continue. However, it's questionable whether it will ever
become widespread in Latin America, and it may be some time
before it gains a prominent position in the Pacific Island
nations and through the Caribbean area, due to the miniscule
size and small national incomes of most of those countries.

NOTES

1.   Ian Mackay, Broadcasting in Nigeria (Ibadan:
University Press, 1964), pp. 85-91, documents Nigerian hesi-
tency in initiating the service. He indicates that the
Federal government was "pressured" into taking action because
two Nigerian political parties made it a campaign issue. The
government then acted "conscious of what was already being
accomplished in other African countries" (p. 86).

2.   John de St. Jorre, The Nigerian Civil War (London:
Hodder and Stoughton, 1972), Chapter 13, "The War of Words".
According to the author, neither side did much with international radio, and Biafra's inaugural international broadcast contained some incorrect information (pp. 352-354).

3.   Olajide Aluko, "The Civil War and Nigerian Foreign
Policy," Political Quarterly 42 (London, 1971):177-190.

4.   But when Nigeria's president dedicated a new Voice of
Nigeria transmitter complex in June 1981, he stated that the

station "must increase its programs designed to assist the liberation struggle in Namibia and South Africa." Cited in World Broadcasting Information, BBC Monitoring Service, Edition No. 25 (June 25, 1981), p. A5.

5. James Kushner, "African Liberation Broadcasting," Journal of Broadcasting 18 (Summer 1974):299-309.

6. "World Broadcasting Information (BBC Monitoring Service), Edition No. 7, February 19, 1981, p. 7/A6.

7. See Douglas Boyd, Broadcasting in the Arab World (Philadelphia: Temple University Press, 1982), Part 3 for a thorough description of the international services of Arab nations.

8. Hatem has described his collaboration with Nasser in Information and the Arab Cause (London: Longman, 1974).

9. "Voice of Venom," Time 71 (March 3, 1958), pp. 28-29. "External Information and Cultural Relations Programs: The Arab Republic of Egypt," Washington, D.C.: U.S. Information Agency, Office of Research and Assessment, May 1973, contains a useful compilation of information about Egypt's many informational activities, including radio.

10. Sir Kennedy Trevaskis, Shades of Amber (London: Hutchinson, 1968), p. 58. It is possible that an American "propaganda expert" had something to do with Egypt's choice of propaganda techniques. Miles Copeland, in The Game of Nations (New York: Simon and Schuster, 1969), p. 100, mentions that a U.S. citizen, Paul Linebarger, was "lent" to Egypt for consultation on the subject by "U.S. diplomatic interests".

11. Edgar O'Ballance, The War in the Yemen (London: Faber and Faber, 1971), passim, but especially p. 63 and p. 209. See also Douglas Boyd, "Egyptian Radio: Tool of Political and National Development," Journalism Monographs No. 48 (February 1977). Boyd feels that the Yemen campaign was not particularly successful in terms of achieving Egypt's long-term aims. His monograph offers an interesting account of the growth of Egypt's broadcast services.

12. Cairo MENA in English, January 12, 1981, cited in FBIS Daily Reports, Middle East and Africa, January 13, 1981, 5, No. 008, D6.

13. Another problem in calculating numbers of languages and hours of transmission is that Egypt has a foreign language service for foreign diplomats, tourists and business personnel in Egypt, but this service also may be intended for listeners in Israel, Lebanon and other Middle Eastern nations.

14. A number of surveys done for USIA in sub-Saharan Africa between 1972 and 1974 revealed low levels of listening to Radio Cairo's international broadcasts, although an urban-only survey of adults in Nigeria showed regular listening to Cairo by 14 per cent of the respondents. More

typical were figures for Senegal (just over one per cent, and
no reports of regular listening in Wolof, although Cairo is
one of a handful of stations to broadcast in it), Tanzania
(0.6 per cent) and Cameroun (1.3 per cent). Most samples
were urban-only, and it's possible that Cairo might do better
among rural listeners, but an urban-rural survey in Kenya
(1973) showed 0.8 per cent claiming to be regular listeners.
A 1972 survey in Lebanon (urban-rural) showed 27 per cent
regular listenership. A 1978 survey done for BBC in Israel
showed regular listening figures of four per cent for Cairo's
English service and 8.7 per cent for the Arabic service.
Surveys done by the McCann organization in some of the Arab
Gulf states in 1979 (adults, urban, and in one case--Oman--
men only) showed that from four to nine per cent of the
respondents in the various states had listened to Cairo's
"Voice of the Arabs" at some time within the past seven days
(of being surveyed). The Egyptian international services do
not conduct surveys, and engage in only occasional and rudi-
mentary analysis of mail.

15. Menachim Begin describes some of the Jewish clandestine activity in The Revolt (New York: Nash Publishing
Company, 1951), pp. 332-335. Boyd, Broadcasting, passim,
describes various clandestine stations active in the Arab
World.

16. The Voice of Hope is supported by a U.S. fundamentalist Christian organization. It was to be joined in
1981 by a television station called "Star of Hope". Both
stations are something of an embarrassment to the U.S.
government; see R.H. Boyce, "U.S. Church Draws Lebanon
Static," Pittsburgh Press, February 15, 1981.

17. See my article, "The Voices of Palestine: A
Broadcasting House Divided," The Middle East Journal
29 (Spring 1975):133-150.

18. G.S. Awasthy, Broadcasting in India (Bombay:
Allied Publishers, 1965), p. 136. Awasthy covers the
External Services up to 1964, and offers some interesting
critical comment, especially on what he perceives as the
slowness of the news department in responding to important
developments (pp. 136-148).

19. The Indian Minister of Information and Broadcasting
at that time, Inder Gujral, told me in a conversation in
Strasbourg, France in September 1981, that it had been very
difficult to convince the Indian government of the need to
strengthen External Service transmitters, but that messages
from Indian embassies abroad mentioning the need for a
"louder" presentation of India's policies helped to win
special appropriations for more powerful transmitters.

20. Several issues of World Broadcasting Information
have mentioned clandestine broadcasts to Afghanistan,
especially editions 25 (1980) and editions 26, 32 and 35
(1981).

21. From South and East Asia Report, No. 974 (February 25, 1981), cited in Review of International Broadcasting, No. 54 (August 1981), pp. 2-3.

22. Richard Wood, "Shortwave Broadcasts Span the Hemisphere," Americas 27 (October 1975), states that Argentina, Brazil and Chile all broadcast on shortwave in the 1930s. While their broadcasts were received abroad, it isn't certain that they were intended for foreign listeners or that they were regular (continuous).

23. A New York Times article, "U.S., British Broadcasts are Barred in Argentina," March 28, 1951, p. 15, refers to a weekly broadcast from Venezuela to Argentina of news and music as having been "prohibited" without stating how the Argentinian government planned to do so. Argentine president Peron made the inaugural broadcast over the Argentinian international station in 1949. He said that he didn't mind not being heard, but he hated being "malevolently interpreted." Virginia Lee Warren, "Peron Institutes Shortwave Talks," New York Times, April 12, 1949, p. 23.

24. Glenn Hauser, "Revolution by Radio," Popular Electronics 16 (November 1979), pp. 104-107 discusses speculation regarding Radio Sandino's possible Cuban or Costa Rican "home" during the Nicaraguan civil war.

11

THE VOICES OF FAITH

Anyone who is familiar with the history of U.S. domestic broadcasting will know that stations operated by religious groups and organizations have been a part of American radio from the early 1920s. Most of these stations were intended to serve as one element in a program of missionary outreach, directed particularly toward those with no specifically professed faith. It seemed only a matter of time before some organization would seek to extend this activity to other parts of the world, where Christians were in the minority or even altogether absent. And, because few other countries had broadcasting stations operated by religious organizations, it seemed logical to expect that the first international religious station would be American.

It very nearly was. Station HCJB--the call letters signify Heralding Christ Jesus' Blessing--was established by a U.S. evangelical organization, the World Radio Missionary Fellowship, albeit in Quito, Ecuador, and began broadcasting on December 25, 1931.[1] However, Vatican Radio had come on the air in February 1931, from Vatican City, and with enough transmitter power to guarantee that its signal could be heard at least in neighboring countries, if not worldwide, whereas HCJB had only 200 watts at its disposal.

There was a fundamental difference in the programing policies of the two stations. Vatican Radio attempted to serve Catholics wherever they might be, but particularly in remote locations, and the program schedule was dominated by talks, masses, etc., that would help make up for the absence of a Catholic church or priest. HCJB, on the other hand, was interested in reaching both the converted and the unconverted, the latter in particular. Thus, its program schedule was rich in evangelizing messages, religious music and specific examples of conversions to Christianity on the part of listeners.

Both remained the only stations of their kind until after World War II; they were joined in 1948 by another

station founded by a U.S. evangelical organization.[2] And
again, as with HCJB, the organization chose a foreign
location: Manila. The Far East Broadcasting Company (FEBC)
began its transmissions to the Philippines in 1948, but
quickly expanded to include much of the rest of Asia, particularly following the Chinese Communist Party's assumption
of control in mainland China in 1949.

The next two decades saw a great expansion in international religious broadcasting, particularly within Africa
and Asia, but also from the United States. Most of the new
stations were backed by U.S. evangelical organizations,
although a few derived their financial and administrative
support from European sources. ELWA, or Eternal Love
Winning Africa, came on the air from Liberia in 1954, as
did the Voice of Tangier from Tangiers. Team Radio began to
broadcast from South Korea in 1956, and station KGEI, The
Voice of Friendship, took over an old General Electric international station near San Francisco and was formally inaugurated in 1960 as part of the FEBC operation. In the 1960s,
it was Trans World Radio, which superceded the Voice of
Tangier and began (or recommenced) its broadcasts in 1960
from Monte Carlo, Radio Cordac, from Burundi in 1963; Radio
Voice of the Gospel, from Ethiopia in 1963; WINB, or World
in Need of the Bible, from Red Lion, Pennsylvania in 1962;[3]
Radio Veritas, a Catholic international station near Manila,
in 1969; and WYFR, Family Radio, originally transmitted
from Scituate, Massachusetts[4] and now from Okeechobee,
Florida, in 1973. The Far East Broadcasting Association, or
FEBA, came on the air from the Seychelles Islands in 1969,
at first as an offshoot of FEBC. It is now essentially
independent of its "parent", and is financed by a British
group.[5]

This growth in numbers of stations is impressive, but
doesn't tell half the story. All of the stations except
Vatican Radio began life modestly; now, at least four of
them--Vatican Radio, FEBC, HCJB and Trans World Radio--would
rate places among the top 20 international broadcasters in
terms of numbers of broadcast hours per week. Furthermore,
several of them broadcast in ten or more languages, and claim
something close to worldwide signal coverage. That is not
an idle boast: it is not uncommon for the larger stations
to possess transmitting capacities of several hundred
thousand to well over a million watts, and to have transmitter sites in more than one country. And, while most of
the major secular international broadcasters held steady in
terms of broadcast hours and numbers of languages during the
1970s, international religious broadcasting grew rapidly.
For example, FEBA began test transmissions with a handful of
languages in 1969; by 1980 it was broadcasting in 21
languages for approximately 120 hours per week.

There also has been a tremendous growth in placement of
pre-recorded religious programs on transmitters located in
other countries. U.S.-based Adventist World Radio (AWR) is
perhaps the most spectacular example of this: starting in
1971 with one program in one language on one transmitter, by
1980 it was placing programs in 24 languages over six transmitter sites (Portugal, Luxembourg, Andorra, Malta, Sri Lanka
and Macau). AWR pays the various national authorities for
the broadcast time it uses--in one case as little as ten
minutes--and supports this missionary work through contributions it receives. Not only are those contributions
enough to support a growing placement effort; AWR is also
constructing its own transmission facilities in Guatemala.
A Swedish organization, IBRA Radio AB, is nearly as active;
as of 1980, it prepared programs in 25 languages and placed
them on transmitters in Portugal and Malta. Most of the
programs prepared by AWR and IBRA are brief (10-30 minutes),
and many languages come on the air only once or twice a week,
but the growth of this sort of activity is nonetheless quite
impressive.

This growth comes at considerable expense. Religious
organizations themselves are one of the main sources of
financial support: Vatican Radio is financed by the Catholic
church, Radio Voice of the Gospel was supported by the
Lutheran World Federation and the World Association for
Christian Communication until the Ethiopian government
closed it down in 1977, and Radio Veritas receives its support through the Catholic church in the Philippines, although the Catholic church in West Germany helped to obtain
money for its initial costs. But there are other sources at
least as important: solicitation of contributions by direct
over-the-air appeals, and the sale of air time to various
Christian organizations which desire to broadcast individual
programs but don't care to, or can't afford to, operate
their own stations. Often, these individual programs contain their own appeals for funds or "sales pitches" for
books, as in this example from a WINB broadcast in August
1979:

> The main book "Get All Excited, Jesus is
> Coming Soon," "Those Remain," "The Destiny of
> America" and the Time Line Chart that tells you
> what all is happening and the order of events in
> which it will happen . . . the Destiny Chart
> Package, just ask for the Destiny Chart Package,
> over 100 news items on Bible references on that
> chart and the three books. Just send $15.00 to
> "Today in Bible Prophecy," or send $20.00 for the
> cassette inquiry instructions for "Those Remain".
> God bless you, we want you to know that which is
> going on.

The main source of financial support for an international religious station generally will dictate the character of its program schedule. A station which sells large amounts of air time to others will have a schedule that is broadly evangelical or fundamentalist in character, but the messages and styles will show considerable variation. A station which produces most, if not all, of its own programing is likely to have a more specific religious orientation and greater uniformity of style; it is also far more likely to broadcast programs which reflect something of the life of the country in which the station is located.

The broadcasting of programs on host country life is not dictated by financial considerations, but by a combination of perceived need to remain in the good graces of the host government and the very real need to conform to binding legal agreements made between the station and the country. As part of its agreement with the government of Ecuador, for example, HCJB must provide coverage of Ecuadorian events; as one clause of the agreement states, the station is required "to intensify the cultural, social and touristic propaganda of the nation, to the benefit of its integral development, in all bands of the [radio] system and in diverse idioms."[6] The original agreement between ELWA and the Liberian government stated that broadcasts "will include Government broadcasts such as non-political programs and Presidential proclamations."[7]

Self-censorship or governmental censorship of the news may also be a condition of continued existence for these stations. After the revolutionary government had taken over from Ethiopian Emperor Haile Selassie in 1974, the copy for Radio Voice of the Gospel newscasts had to be approved prior to each broadcast.[8] ELWA, according to one of its then staff members, was very cautious in preparing its newscasts: "News broadcasts are never critical of the government or of its leadership. Special care is taken in reporting Liberia's position in international relations. ELWA has adjusted to the realities of the local political scene in order to carry out its total program."[9]

In certain respects, then, the stations become instruments of the domestic and foreign policies of their hosts. To some extent, this is true of secular broadcasters with transmitters on foreign soil, although their agreements are more likely to take the form of time sharing on the transmitter. Furthermore, if the secular broadcaster and the host government come to a fundamental disagreement, the broadcaster can at least consider the possibility of doing without the transmitter, rather than compromising on principles, inasmuch as other transmitters remain available. For several of the religious broadcasters, however, this would mean the loss of their only, or principal, base of operation.

Although all of the stations have different characteristics, an examination of four of them--TWR, HCJB, Vatican
Radio and ELWA--should provide a reasonably well-rounded
picture of the varied nature and scope of international
religious broadcasting.

TRANS WORLD RADIO

TWR came on the air in 1960, although its founder, Paul
Freed, had operated a similar station, the Voice of Tangiers,
from 1954 to 1959. When that station was closed by order of
the Moroccan government, Freed sought another transmitter
location, and found one in Monaco--a facility erected by
Germany during World War II. Some of the program material
came from the United States, and was produced by various
U.S. religious organizations; however, more of it had to be
produced in studios in Europe and the Middle East, since
TWR broadcast in Arabic, Hebrew, French, German, Italian,
Portuguese, Spanish, Russian, and several Eastern European
and Scandinavian languages, as well as English.

TWR's headquarters is in New Jersey, and Freed attempted
to establish a transmission base to reach the Western Hemisphere soon after he founded the Monaco station. He petitioned
the Federal Communications Commission for a construction
permit for a location on Puerto Rico in 1963, but the FCC was
unwilling to consider it because it had imposed a temporary
freeze on the licensing of international radio stations.
Nothing daunted, Freed secured the approval of the Netherlands government for a transmission base on Bonaire, in the
Netherlands Antilles, which came on the air in 1964. Since
then, he has added transmitters in Sri Lanka, Swaziland and
Guam, and has arranged to lease one hour per day from Radio
Monte Carlo's Cyprus station.[10]

Thanks to its worldwide array of transmitters, TWR is a
very attractive "buy" for religious organizations wishing
to bring their messages to one or many parts of the world in
one or many languages. These organizations pay TWR for the
use of air time, and this is one of two principal sources of
income for the station. The other comes in the form of
donations from individual listeners, in response to requests
contained within programs or during intervals between programs. Unlike many religious stations, TWR is not connected
with a specific denomination, preferring to operate under its
own corporate title, International Evangelism, Inc. This
leaves it free to accept programs from whomever it wishes,
but deprives it of any advantages that might accrue from
affiliation with a particular denomination--and churches can
serve as very effective fund-raisers for religious stations.

If one is to judge from the scope of its broadcasts,
however, TWR is in sound financial shape. Not only did it
rise from one transmitter site to six in a little over 15
years (Guam came on the air in 1976), but it also rose from
20 languages to more than 60 over the same period of time,
and broadcasts in 75 as of 1981. Most of the foreign
language broadcasts are prepared in overseas studios, some
operated by TWR, others by other religious organizations
(e.g. Norea, in Oslo, Norway). Productions are rarely
elaborate; few feature more than one voice per program.
Most are brief, as well, with many of the language services
available in 15 or 30 minute blocs which may or may not be
repeated and may come on the air once, twice or three times
a week. Because of this brevity, and because of the overseas production of many of the programs (often done by
dedicated staff members who accept low rates of compensation),
TWR is able to keep costs relatively low.

Broadcasts are almost 100 per cent religious. Some
programs seek to reinforce those who are already Christian,
while others seek to convert those who are not. There is a
small amount of music and news on some of the language
services (particular English and Spanish to the Caribbean
and Latin America), but religious talks predominate.
Listeners are encouraged to write to TWR, and many do: in
1976 (the last year for which it has reasonably accurate
figures), the station received between 300,000 and 350,000
letters. Some letters expressed appreciation for a specific
program, others attested to conversions. Letters are TWR's
evidence of effectiveness, since the organization does not
conduct surveys.

                               HCJB

The programing practices of HCJB form a strong contrast
to those of TWR. HCJB broadcasts from one location only,[11]
but with a powerful array of transmitters placed high in the
Andes, and it carries programs in 14 languages. Most
language services are available for periods of anywhere from
30 minutes to 24 hours a day, and all but one (Danish) are
available daily. There is a fairly wide range of music,
including but not limited to religious, there are several
feature programs, and newscasts are frequent and quite detailed, with some material gathered by HCJB staff.

Furthermore, HCJB takes a serious interest in audience
research, and appears more than willing to alter its lines
of approach if evidence suggests that the present formula is
not working. The station will not compromise its basic
Christian principles, but it is willing to follow more than

one path to better implement them. Like most Christian international broadcasters, HCJB tries to reach both the converted,
with messages of sustenance, and the unconverted, with
messages of salvation. Since the same appeals are not likely
to be of equal effectiveness with these two groups, programs
for them are more apt to be clearly for one or the other than
to be attempting to reach both at once.

Conversion itself must be understood in a particular way
where HCJB is concerned. It includes conversion of already
practicing Christians as well as those who have other faiths.
Catholics are one target audience--logical enough, given the
station's Latin American location--and there is some specific
if limited evidence of such conversions, although HCJB's role
in the process is rarely that obvious. A great deal of
effort also goes into producing broadcasts that will sustain
Christians in countries where there are assumed to be
restrictions on freedom of worship: Czechoslovakia, Romania
and the USSR. And finally, because of the aforementioned
clauses in the agreement between Ecuador and the station,
many programs deal with Ecuador itself. HCJB may mention
strikes and political opposition within Ecuador, but generally
supports the country's foreign policy:

> Ecuador's new Minister of Foreign Relations,
> Luis Valencia Rodriguez, today reaffirmed the
> traditional foreign policy of this South American
> nation. The Minister told a news conference in
> Quito that the most transcendental problem that
> the country faces is in the area of the terri-
> torial controversy with Peru. The Ecuadorian
> official reiterated that his nation has a constant
> invitation to Peru to start negotiations that
> would lead to a just and definite solution to
> the problem, but added that Ecuador would con-
> tinue to maintain the necessity of its rights to
> the Amazon, and would make sure that such rights
> are recognized.
> Passport (News About Latin America), November 5, 1981

HCJB carries a limited number of broadcasts from other
Christian groups, for which it receives compensation. An
unusual source of income (c. five per cent) is the hydro-
electric station it operates just outside Quito. The station
generates power for HCJB and its ancillary activities (including a hospital), with enough left over to sell to Ecuador.
The World Radio Missionary Fellowship, with headquarters in
Opa Locka, Florida, also conducts fund raising drives on
behalf of the station. Most station staff are volunteers who
have arranged for their own sponsorship through church groups
in the United States, further reducing operating costs. HCJB

appears to be in good financial shape, if one is to judge by
the fact that an elaborate and expensive steerable antenna
system was just installed in 1979.

VATICAN RADIO

The vast majority of international religious stations
must depend upon the sale of air time to other religious
organizations and/or the solicitation of donations. Vatican
Radio, thanks to the total support of the Vatican itself, has
no need to concern itself with such matters. It is the oldest
international religious broadcaster, and would be older still
if Vatican officials had been able to work out an agreement
with the Italian government in late 1923-early 1924.[12] When
it finally did come on the air in 1931, it benefitted from
the latest studio equipment, a 10 kW transmitter (large by
contemporary standards) and technical advice from the "father
of radio," Marconi, who introduced the Pope in the inaugural
broadcast.

From the beginning, the station was regarded as a vehicle
to permit the Pope to communicate with Catholics around the
world, and papal speeches, messages, the celebration of the
Mass from St. Peter's and news from the Vatican made up the
broadcast schedule. Some of this material was translated
into European, Asian and African languages, although that
depended very much on the availability of priests, brothers,
etc., who were capable of translating Latin or Italian into
French, Amharic, etc. Little music was transmitted, and
newscasts were nonexistent.

World War II brought the special service of carrying
messages to and from prisoners of war, refugees, etc., and
some criticism of fascism (see Chapter 3, footnote 10, p. 88)
but the program schedule remained basically unchanged until
the late 1940s, when concern over restrictions placed upon
the practice of the Catholic faith in Central and Eastern
Europe caused Vatican Radio to step up its attempts to reach
listeners in those countries with more religious programs.
The station increased its transmitter power, thanks in part
to donations received from Catholics in various countries,[13]
and soon began to experience jamming as a "reward" of sorts
for its increased efforts.

However, its services to the rest of the world changed
little until the late 1960s, when its administrators
decided that the station should make greater efforts to reach
young people. Experiments with the broadcasting of popular
music in a religious context began in 1968; the Director of
Vatican Radio observed that "Beat music--on which we suspend
artistic judgement for the moment--represents nevertheless an

ideal bridge toward the young who understand also 'through
songs, the value of the spirit.'"14
    The station also reconsidered the nature of its broad-
casts of news about the Catholic world, and decided that,
much as it had done during World War II, it should not hesitate to deal with controversial matters that were more
traditionally a part of the secular world than of the religious
such as the Vietnam War:

> Stating that he did not agree with President
> Nixon on the expansion of the war into Cambodia,
> Father Hesberg [then President of Notre Dame
> University] observed that most young people do not
> see America's brightest future identified with
> this military venture.
> Vatican Radio in English, May 12, 1970

    Yet Vatican Radio was coming in for a fair amount of
criticism in the early 1970s, most of it concerning the unprofessional quality of much of its broadcasting, which in
turn seemed to be connected to lack of an overall program
policy, shortage of qualified staff, and administrative
rigidity and unwillingness to undertake or permit critical
evaluation.15 Most listeners would find to this day that
much of the station's programing is uninteresting and/or
incomprehensible to any but theologians. Programs sometimes
are made even less palatable by speakers' monotonous delivery
and heavy accents. Even the simpler messages often have an
abstract quality:

> St. Paul tells us of the presence of the
> spirit in our lives. And he suggests that it is
> precisely in the gift of God's spirit that we
> come to realize many of our weaknesses. This
> does not mean that Paul denies the inherent
> goodness that each human person possesses. Rather,
> he is saying that, placed within the light of
> God's holy spirit, our own fragile nature is made
> more visible . . .
> Vatican Radio in English, July 19, 1981

    Furthermore, although there is considerable ferment and
controversy within the Catholic church today, Vatican Radio
reflects little of it in its broadcasts. The Pope's pronouncements on birth control appear, but not the disagreements with that policy voiced by certain Catholic theologians
and laypersons. Vatican criticisms of "liberal" theologians
such as Father Schillebeeckx are broadcast by the station,
but his defense of himself is not.16 Because the station is
directly responsible to the Vatican Secretary of State,

although it is operated by the Jesuit order, that situation
is not likely to change in the near future, and Vatican
Radio's 30 broadcast languages almost certainly will continue
to speak in the name of Catholic orthodoxy.

Radio Veritas, which broadcasts to Asia from Manila, is
considerably more open, experimental and ecumenical than
Vatican Radio. It is operated and financially supported by
the Catholic archdiocese of the Philippines, with the help of
contributions primarily from European Catholics. It broadcasts on medium and short wave in ten languages. Its program
schedule includes world and regional news, music, news about
the Catholic church, and information about conferences,
festivals and other events taking place in Asia. It is as
apt to present a description of a Buddhist festival or Shinto
observance as it is a Catholic or other Christian feast day
or solemn occasion, and there is no indication that one faith
is superior to another.

ELWA

The establishment of radio station ELWA (Eternal Love
Winning Africa) was characterized, as is usually the case
with the fundamentalist international radio stations, by
persistence, faith, and not a few seemingly miraculous occur-
rences.[17] And, like many of those stations, once it had been
established, it displayed a remarkable capacity for growth:
English and a handful of Liberian languages for its inaugural
broadcasts in 1954 had grown to include several West, Central
and East African languages (Hausa, Kikongo, Swahili, etc.),
French, Portuguese, and Arabic within five years. The
addition of a 50 kW transmitter brought a strong signal to
most of Africa, especially in comparison with other shortwave
services operating there at the time.

ELWA's program philosophy has remained constant throughout its existence: to bring the gospel message to believers
and unbelievers throughout the continent. There is nothing
in this philosophy that differentiates the station from HCJB,
FEBC or most other fundamentalist stations, but the implementation of it is quite different. Like most other stations,
ELWA offers religious music, but only music of impeccably
fundamentalist religious character. By this token, selections
by such artists as Johnny Cash (seen as a born-again Christian)
would be acceptable, while those by Tennessee Ernie Ford
(seen as a profit-seeker) would not. Divorced artists, no
matter how Christian, are unacceptable. Music is not to be
used as "bait" to attract listeners.[18] Few programs are
accepted from other religious organizations; "Back to the
Bible" is a rare exception. ELWA produces most of its

foreign language (i.e., other than English and Liberian
languages) programs in production centers operated by itself
or by missionaries of the Sudan Interior Mission, ELWA's
"parent".

ELWA includes newscasts in several of its broadcast
services, most notably English, although most of the news
items are culled from other news broadcasts by domestic and
international stations, and some VOA newscasts are relayed
directly by ELWA. The station also carries certain sporting
events (e.g. soccer and basketball), which is something of a
rarity among international religious broadcasters, but which
is seen as a way of showing God's interest in the "whole
person".

Like those of most other "multilingual" international
religious stations, many of ELWA's language services,
especially those for West and Central Africa, are brief (15-
30 minutes) and on the air once or twice a week. Most of
those services also promote mission centers operated by the
Sudan Interior Mission, and listeners are urged to visit the
missions if they would like to know more about Christianity
as portrayed by the broadcasts. The station has little
interest in developing cooperative links with other missionary
organizations, although it has worked together with the Far
East Broadcasting Association (Seychelles) to reach the
Arab world.

ISLAMIC BROADCASTING

The vast majority of international religious broadcasting
is done by Christian organizations. The only other religion
to have established stations for this purpose is Islam, and,
since there is no separation between religion and state in
Islamic society, the stations are operated as part of the
national broadcasting authorities. The oldest of these
stations is the Voice of the Holy Koran, which came on the
air from Egypt in 1964. It broadcasts on medium wave (60 kW)
and short wave (100 kW), and is on the air for 17½ hours daily,
although much of the material is repeat broadcasts. Arabic
alone is used, and programing consists largely of readings
from the Koran, discussions of Koranic texts, and lectures
from mosques. Green claims that the service appeals mainly
to older listeners,[19] while Boyd feels that it may have been
established to remind Arabs that, despite Nasser's "close
identification with the Soviet Union . . . Egypt had not lost
its religious orientation."[20] It is part of the Arab Republic
of Egypt Broadcasting Corporation, and as such receives
direct support from the State, so that it has no need to
worry about listener donations or sale of air time.

Saudi Arabia's Holy Koran Broadcast originated in 1972.
There are actually two services, one in Riyadh and one in
Mecca, the former for 18 hours per day and the latter for 16.
Both emphasize Koranic readings, lectures, and discussions
of religious texts. Libya's Holy Koran Program, which
started in 1975, is on the air for 12 hours per day from
transmitters on a ship anchored in Tripoli harbor. It, too,
emphasizes readings from the Koran and lectures and discussions on religious texts. One Libyan source notes that the
station tends to attract a preponderance of older listeners.[21]

None of the Islamic stations is intended to convert
listeners; all attempt to reinforce and deepen the faith of
believers. And despite the many internal frictions of Islam,
such as those between Sunnis and Shiites, not to mention the
political conflicts between Egypt, Libya and Saudi Arabia,
the stations appear to avoid religious and political controversy.

THE AUDIENCE

As I already have noted, audience research is a variable
practice for international religious stations. KGEI, FEBC
and HCJB have conducted quite a bit of relatively sophisticated audience research,[22] primarily through questionnaires
mailed to listeners who have written to the stations. This
method of selection is not truly random, of course, and
pretty well eliminates illiterate listeners, but if the
questions are phrased in an unbiased manner and cast in
specific terms, they can elicit much useful information on
signal quality, preferred times of listening, programing
strengths and weaknesses, and demographic data.

Most international religious stations, however, content
themselves with analyses of listener mail, some of it spontaneous, some of it encouraged or solicited by the stations.
Much of the mail that I have seen on my visits to some of
these stations consists of DXer requests for confirmation of
reception (QSL cards), although listener requests for specific
selections of religious music or other forms of programing
also are plentiful. Letters attesting to how the station's
programs have strengthened a listener's faith or brought
about a religious conversion are far less numerous, although
most stations get at least a few each day.

Occasionally a station will attempt to analyze letters
to see what they reveal about the nature of the listener,
the success or failure of programs, etc., but more often
stations appear to limit themselves to counting total numbers
of letters and perhaps categorizing them as to country or
continent of origin. And, while few station staff I have

talked with believe that these letters can be taken as representing listener opinion as a whole, they do tend to take
them very seriously.

Studies conducted by KGEI, FEBC, HCJB and in its time
RVOG, reveal that the audiences for these geographically
distant stations are remarkably similar in many respects.
This may be because the stations follow roughly the same
programing practices (a wide variety of material, much or
most of it produced by the stations themselves), because they
subscribe to roughly similar religious beliefs (all are
Protestant and evangelical, although perhaps not as fundamentalist as TWR, WINB, Family Radio or ELWA), or because
they broadcast mainly to much the same sorts of countries:
developing nations with rapidly urbanizing populations and
Communist nations.[23]

These studies have indicated that the respondents are
predominantly male, comparatively young (under 40), moder-
ately educated by local standards (the average listener has
an upper primary-lower high school education) and urban. It
is more difficult to discern predominant religious beliefs,
but in Latin America non-Protestants have made up from 30 to
75 per cent of those who have chosen to state their religious
beliefs, while a 1974 study for FEBC of audiences in India
reportedly revealed that well over half of the respondents
considered themselves to be Christians. When program preferences have been elicited, listeners appear to favor news
broadcasts and religious music (hymns in particular).[24]

Given the practice followed by most international
religious stations of broadcasting religious programs produced
by a variety of sources, with an attendant variety of accents,
wordings, production practices, etc., one might assume that
some of the stations would have an interest in determining
whether listeners could comprehend the broadcasts--the more
so because many of them are in English, which is not the
national language of most of the nations to which these
stations broadcast. As far as I can determine, only one such
study has been conducted--for FEBC in the Philippines, in
1974--and it revealed that certain speakers (e.g. Billy
Graham) and certain texts (e.g. the King James version of the
Bible) were difficult to understand for listeners of modest
educational backgrounds.[25]

Given the high cost of field research or even questionnaire mailing and analysis, and given the small budgets of
many of these stations, perhaps it is not surprising to find
that few of them conduct systematic research. Money
probably is not the only reason, however: as studies by King
and Kushner have revealed, certain stations see their work as
divinely inspired and guided, so that research is unnecessary,
while others seem more interested in providing a transmission
facility for still other religious broadcasters, who, if they

wish to know more about their listeners, should go to the
expense and effort of doing so themselves.[26]

When random or stratified sample studies have been conducted by or for secular international broadcasters in
regions or countries where religious stations also can be
heard, the results have been mixed. Certain stations, such
as ELWA in West Africa, RVOG in Kenya, FEBC in the Philippines, HCJB in Brazil, have often placed somewhere in the
middle of the secular international broadcasters, although
both generally have finished well behind the major national
station(s) and, if there is one, the major national station
of a neighboring country with the same language(s) and traditions. Certain others, such as Family Radio, WINB, Radio
Vatican, rarely if ever appear in the lists of the stations
mentioned by respondents. When volume of listener mail is
compared, however, some of the largest religious stations,
such as TWR, FEBC and HCJB, claim figures very much in line
with those for the largest secular stations: 200,000 to
350,000 letters per year.

INTERNATIONAL RELIGIOUS STATIONS AND FOREIGN POLICY

I already have mentioned that stations with studios and/
or transmitters based on foreign soil attempt to maintain
good relations with their hosts, often by broadcasting favorable material and/or refraining from broadcasting unfavorable
material about them. HCJB does so for Ecuador, FEBC and
Radio Veritas for the Philippines, Team Radio for South
Korea, ELWA for Liberia, and, until each was closed in 1977,
Radio CORDAC for Burundi and Radio Voice of the Gospel for
Ethiopia. The stations thus become identified to some degree
with the government of the day in those countries. There
have been a few vivid demonstrations of such identification:
Radio CORDAC's American staff members saw some of their Hutu
staff killed by the minority, but politically dominant, Tutsi
in the course of a bloody "ethnic conflict" in 1972, yet the
station had to avoid doing anything that might seem critical
of Tutsi policy.[27] FEBC was one of only a half dozen
stations allowed to stay on the air following a declaration
of martial law in the Philippines on September 23, 1972, a
mark of unusual favor,[28] and ELWA came back on the air almost
immediately following the 1980 coup in Liberia.[29]

Because many of the religious stations are supported by
organizations located in the United States, there is always
the possibility that listeners could view their broadcasts
as a manifestation of American approval of the particular
national government. However, few of the stations publicize
their American connections. There is also the possibility

that the organizations supporting the stations will turn to
the United States government for assistance in procuring
foreign bases of operation or in addressing problems encountered by the stations vis-a-vis host governments.

There is evidence that the U.S. military has become
involved directly in supporting the activities of certain of
the international religious stations. The construction of
FEBC's transmitter site on Okinawa was made much easier
through the assistance of the U.S. Marine Corps, which
levelled the site free of charge.[30] Given the strongly anti-
Communist bent of most international religious stations, it
is not surprising that the U.S. military would favor their
establishment, and certain of the countries where stations
are located are also countries with a U.S. military presence:
the Philippines, South Korea, and, at one time, Okinawa (for
FEBC).

A potentially more serious issue is the broadcasting of
material which has bearing on the conduct of foreign policy--
American foreign policy in particular. Three of the religious
stations broadcast from the United States, while two have
transmitters on American-administered territory: TWR on
Guam, FEBC on Saipan. A number of the programs they rebroadcast were made for U.S. audiences and feature strongly-
worded statements on matters of U.S. domestic and foreign
policy, as in this August 1979 rebroadcast by WINB:

> They [the U.S. government] can conduct an
> entire nuclear war from that plane, or from any
> of three planes exactly like it. They can con-
> duct an entire nuclear war, and that plane is in
> the air 24 hours a day, around the clock, at all
> times, always on the move. Just in case Russia
> strikes first, we'll have a plane someplace,
> somewhere, that can command our missile supply,
> and our submarines can release that which is in
> them that can make a cinder out of Russia . . .
> bless your hearts, we've got 11,000 nuclear war-
> heads aimed at them.

A foreign listener hearing this broadcast might be
excused if she or he were to experience some confusion over
U.S. foreign policy, since its threatening tone is not likely
to bear much resemblance to any VOA broadcasts. Yet few
nations have more than one international broadcast service,
and when one does those further services are likely to be
operated by the government, as well. Thus, most international broadcast listeners are quite likely to assume that
all international stations reflect official viewpoints, to
some degree.

CONCLUSION

If there is a "growth industry" in the field of international broadcasting, clearly it is religious broadcasting.
While some of the major religious stations appear to have
levelled off in terms of numbers of languages broadcast,
transmitter power continues to grow. It is difficult to
foresee any limitation to this growth, unless it would be
in the form of shortage of frequency spectrum space; and
even here, thanks to a combination of persistence and resourcefulness and to the practice on the part of many
organizations of leasing air time over existing transmitters,
the possibilities seem almost limitless.

Many members of short wave radio listeners' clubs
criticize international religious stations on several grounds:
because they take up frequency space that could be used for
"normal" sorts of international broadcasting, because they
rebroadcast material which is available already over domestic
radio, because they have a self-righteous tone, and because
there's not much evidence that anyone listens to them. There
is some truth to these accusations, but the accusations themselves are highly subjective, for the most part. Letters
attesting to conversions or praising the work of the stations
come in by the tens and even hundreds of thousands every year.
The self-righteous tone of much of their broadcasting finds
its secular echo in the broadcasts of many of the more
political international stations. Rebroadcast material is a
small portion of the overall schedule for most of these
stations, and it is not available over the domestic services
of most countries.

At the same time, there is little doubt that the stations
do have real or potential political impact, particularly on
U.S. foreign policy and relations. Several of the countries
where the stations were or are located have had problems with
human rights; the Philippines, Liberia, Burundi, and South
Korea are all cases in point. How does the presence of the
stations affect listener perceptions of the U.S. government's
position on human rights? How do the stations deal with
that issue from a Christian perspective? How does the anti-
Communist stance of most of the stations fit in with U.S.
foreign policy? In what ways do the stations support their
host governments? We have partial answers to these questions,
but they merit further study, particularly in view of the
seemingly continuous expansion of this form of international
broadcasting.

NOTES

1. Clarence Jones, Radio: The New Missionary (Chicago: The Moody Press, 1946) gives a detailed account of the founding of HCJB. Jones was one of the founders of the station, but his description of many events in "miraculous" terms makes it harder to determine fact.

2. A U.S. evangeligal organization called "Pillar of Fire" applied to the FCC for a construction permit for an international shortwave station station in May 1938. Frequencies were available on a "shared time" basis only, and the organization was not interested in sharing time. Jerry Ray Redding, "American Private International Broadcasting," unpublished Ph.D. dissertation, The Ohio State University, 1977, pp. 232-234.

3. See my article "WINB: A Private 'Voice of America'," Journal of Broadcasting 16 (Spring 1972):147-157.

4. The WYFR Scituate transmitter beamed WRUL's broadcasts to Europe and Latin America starting in the mid-1930s. A subsequent owner of the WRUL facilities, the Bonneville International Corporation (the Mormon Church), could be added to the list of international religious broadcasters, except that the station, by then WNYW, devoted very little time to religious programs, Mormon or otherwise, during the nine year period (1964-1973) of Corporation ownership.

5. Reg Kennedy, "The Missionary Broadcasters," World Radio-TV Handbook, 33rd edition (Hvidovre, Denmark: J. Frost, 1979):71-76, provides a brief description of FEBA and several of the other stations.

6. Government of Ecuador, Registro Oficial, Numero 664, Octubre 22, 1974, p. 4, "Obligaciones . . .," Section d). (Translation mine).

7. Letter from John L. Cooper, Commissioner of Communications and Aeronautics, Republic of Liberia, to President, West African Broadcasting Association, Wheaton, Illinois, February 14, 1951. Cited in James Kushner, "International Religious Radio Broadcasts in Africa," unpublished Ph.D. dissertation, University of Minnesota, 1976. The basic agreement contained in the 1½ page letter remained unaltered even after the coup led by Sergeant Deo in April 1980. Letter to me from David Schult, Broadcasting Director, ELWA, August 4, 1981.

8. Kushner, "International", pp. 175-178.

9. Richard Reed, "The Interaction of Government, Private Enterprise and Voluntary Agencies in the Development of Broadcasting in the Republic of Liberia from 1950 to 1970," unpublished M.A. thesis, Temple University, 1970, p. 82.

10. TWR has assisted in financing transmitter construction in Monaco, and constructed them in Sri Lanka, but

in effect leases time on both from the host governments.
Kennedy, "Missionary," pp. 72-74, also letter to me from
William Mial, Assistant to the President, TWR, July 21, 1981.
James C. King, "A Survey and Analysis of the Major Inter-
national Evangelical Shortwave Broadcasters: TWR, HCJB and
FEBC," unpublished Ph.D. dissertation, University of Michigan,
1973, contains much useful information on TWR and the other
stations.

11. HCJB's parent organization, the World Radio Mis-
sionary Fellowship, also operates AM and FM stations in
Panama City, Panama, and provides a "home service" for
Ecuador.

12. "Vatican May Use Radio," New York Times, December
25, 1923, p. 3, and "Vatican Denies it Will Broadcast," New
York Times, January 1, 1924, p. 2.

13. Camille Cienfarra, "Vatican to Expand Broadcast
Range," New York Times, September 24, 1950, p. 42.

14. "Vatican Radio Admits Mixed Blessing of Pop," Los
Angeles Times, May 31, 1968, Part V, p. 16. Certain of the
older priests were opposed to the introduction of pop music,
but the station manager saw it as a necessity if younger
listeners were to be reached.

15. Robert R. Holton, "Vatican Radio," The Catholic
World (April 1970):12; James J. Onder, "The Sad State of
Vatican Radio," Educational Broadcasting Review 5 (August
1971):43-53. Both articles contain details on Vatican
Radio's history.

16. Henry Tanner, "Theologian Describes the Vatican's
Inquiry," New York Times, December 16, 1979, p. 3.

17. Jane Reed and Jim Grant, Voices Under Every Palm
(Grand Rapids: Zondervan Publishing House, 1968). Similar
accounts, each emphasizing hard work and miraculous occur-
rences, are available for TWR in Paul Freed's Towers to
Eternity (Waco: Word Books, 1968) and Let the Earth Hear
(Nashville: Thomas Nelson, 1980); for FEBC in Gleason
Ledyard's Sky Waves: The Incredible FEBC Story (Chicago:
Moody Press, 1968); and for HCJB in Jones, Radio.

18. Kushner, "International," passim, but especially
p. 98, makes several references to these policies, and his
appendices include both the ELWA program standards and music
standards. ELWA did broadcast rock music from late 1970
until early 1972, but it led to a protest resignation by two
staff families and a flurry of protesting letters. (Kushner,
pp. 95-96).

19. Timothy Green, "Egypt," in Sydney Head, ed.,
Broadcasting in Africa (Philadelphia: Temple University
Press, 1974), p. 22.

20. Doublas Boyd, "Egyptian Radio: Tool of Political
and National Development," Journalism Monographs No. 46
(February 1977):19-20.

21. Mohamed Sweidan, "The People's Revolutionary Broadcasting Corporation," 1976, cited in John Gartley, "Broadcasting in Libya," Middle East Review 12 (Summer-Fall 1980):37.

22. Radio Voice of the Gospel had a Department of Audience Research and Planning from 1970 until the station went off the air in 1977. Much of its research, according to Kushner, was quite sophisticated, and it even "bought into" a commercially-developed research study on radio listening in Kenya in 1972. Kushner, "International," p. 221.

23. Both FEBC and HCJB also devote a portion of broadcast time to reaching listeners in Japan, and HCJB also broadcasts in German, Swedish, Norwegian and Danish. The two stations began to cooperate on audience research in 1974, when HCJB turned to FEBC for assistance in setting up its own research program in Latin America. Attachment, April 1974, p. 3, to letter from William E. Haney, Research Officer, FEBC, Manila, the Philippines, to Dr. Harold Niven, Executive Secretary, Broadcast Education Association, Washington, D.C., August 28, 1974. By the time I visited HCJB in February 1977, the research effort was well under way, and several surveys were being conducted each year. However, a letter to me from Phillip Sandahl, Audience Research, HCJB, Quito, October 28, 1980, indicated that the pressure of other activities and a shortage of personnel had temporarily reduced the scope and the "academic rigor" of the station's research effort.

24. See Haney, letter to Niven and attachment; Haney, "An Idea Whose Time Has Come," International Christian Broadcasters Bulletin (Second Quarter 1974):3+; Kushner, "International," Chapter 6; King, "Evangelical," pp. 260-266. The 1974 India survey was conducted by Anne Ediger and its results reported in highly summarized form in Haney, letter and attachment.

25. Dennis Lowry and Theodore Marr, "Closentrophy as a Measure of International Communications Comprehension," Public Opinion Quarterly 39 (Fall 1975):301-312.

26. See footnotes 7 and 10 for full citations of Kushner and King.

27. Kushner, "International", p. 62. Kushner told me that, in his own conversations with the U.S. staff at CORDAC, he learned that the conflict had been a severe test of faith; they witnessed the deaths of some of their Hutu colleagues without being able to intervene.

28. From U.S. Foreign Broadcast Information Service (FBIS), "International Broadcast Activities," October 1972.

29. ELWA was off the air for several hours on the day of the coup, but then resumed its Liberian language services upon request of "someone" in the new government. The international services came back on the next day. Letter, Schult.

30. Ledyard, Sky Waves, pp. 163-165.

12

WHO LISTENS AND
HOW DO WE KNOW?
AUDIENCE RESEARCH

Winston Churchill once stated that the Soviet Union was "a riddle wrapped in a mystery inside an enigma." The same could well apply to audiences for international broadcasting. Citizens of most of the industrialized nations have grown accustomed to seeing articles in newspapers and magazines which disclose how many people listen to radio or watch television, which particular stations and programs they like, whether certain programs are more popular with men or with women, with young or with old, etc. There are even occasional articles which disclose or purport to disclose why people like or dislike certain programs, or which state the harmful or beneficial effects certain programs are likely to have on audiences.

All of this comes about because most industrialized nations are very research-conscious: large numbers of organizations and people want answers to questions regarding size and composition of audiences, reasons for watching, effects, etc., and are willing to pay for those answers. The results may be used for decisions on advertising, creation of new programs, need for further government regulation, and a host of other purposes. Audience research, as a result, is a large and sophisticated enterprise, and, in the United States alone, millions of dollars are spent on it each year.

A very large share of the world, the developing nations in particular, has no comparable "need" for audience research, and has not developed the capacity to conduct it. Still another group of nations--the socialist states of Eastern Europe and the Soviet Union--has developed some capacity for audience research (Poland, Hungary and the GDR are leaders in this regard), but researchers there often are in no position to ask questions that many in Western nations would take for granted, because of their potential political sensitivity; nor are the results of this research made public all that often.

This creates a peculiar situation where audience research

for international broadcasting is concerned. It is generally
assumed that audiences for international radio will be
smallest in those countries which are already well served by
the mass media in both quantitative and qualitative terms.
Yet those are precisely the countries where audience research
is likely to be most sophisticated. Thus, we are able to
learn more about audiences which may be less interested in
international broadcasting in the first place, and audiences
which many, if not most, international stations are least
interested in reaching!

The relative inaccessibility (for research purposes) of
some audiences has led certain international broadcasters to
devise ingenious methods of overcoming the various barriers
to research that exist. Some of the methods are simply
specialized applications of standard research techniques,
which themselves will be immediately recognizable; others
represent some highly specialized research techniques which
are compromises between scientific objectivity and what is
possible under the circumstances. In no necessary order,
they are:

RANDOM SAMPLE SURVEYS

Commonly used throughout the industrialized world, they
involve the selection and questioning of a scientifically-
derived random sample of the total population, or a designated segment of it. Such surveys are most feasible in
industrialized nations, where there will be sufficient data
to permit selection of a scientifically-derived random
sample and where the concentration of a majority of the
population in urban areas lowers the cost of gathering data.
Data may be gathered by face-to-face contact, mailed questionnaires or telephone calls, although the poor state of the
postal system and the telephone service in many countries
makes these means of data collection less feasible than
face-to-face contact (which, however, is more expensive).

While the cost of conducting random sample survey
research on international broadcast listening is a major
inhibiting factor in its use--a moderate-sized (N=1000)
survey can easily cost $25,000 to $50,000--there are several
other problems. Many developing countries do not have
survey research firms, so outside firms must be brought in,
adding to the expense and risking "outsider bias", although
most firms will attempt to employ local surveyors. Many
governments do not care to have survey research teams
travelling around the country asking questions about what
their citizens listen to and why. And, since most international stations do not attempt to reach a mass audience, a

random sample survey may well see nine out of every ten
survey contacts "wasted" because the respondent doesn't
listen to international radio.

Even with those deficiencies, several of the major
international stations make some use of survey research. BBC
does so on a continuing basis, VOA's use of it has been almost
continuous, DW does so less often, and smaller stations such
as Radio Canada International have commissioned it on occasion
"Commissioned" is the correct word in almost every instance,
since the stations feel that the credibility of the survey
results would be called into question if the stations were to
conduct the research themselves. Stations will also "buy
into" surveys that have five or six different participants.
Such a survey might have a set of questions dealing with
readership patterns and practices for local newspapers,
another set of questions on domestic radio listening and
television viewing, another set on attention paid to advertising, and yet another on international radio listening.
This lowers the cost of the survey for each participant, but
raises questions as to the amount of attention each respondent
pays to any given portion of the questionnaire.

There also are occasional surveys of specialized
audiences, particularly those known to be regular listeners
to international broadcasts, such as members of radio
listening clubs. Surveys by Hall and McDaniel and by
Elliott[1] have produced evidence that such listeners may be
more typical of audience members in general than had been
supposed previously.

ANALYSIS OF LISTENER MAIL

Most international radio stations ask their listeners to
write to them, and some have contests designed to encourage
listener mail. A large international station will receive
200,000 to 350,000 letters each year, which should constitute a fair basis for determining something about the
station's listeners. In fact, much of this mail consists
of requests for broadcast schedules or for selections of
popular music, and tells the station little more than the
listeners' names and where they were when they wrote their
letters. Contest mail is more useful in that as a condition
of entering the contests, writers usually must indicate
name, address, age, sex, occupation, program on which the
contest announcement was heard, quality of reception, and
perhaps something about general listening habits with respect
to the station hosting the contest.

Some stations go a bit further and require contest
entrants to write a short essay on a particular topic. Radio

Moscow and several of the international stations in central
and eastern Europe have followed this practice for many
years, and the prizes are sometimes considerable: free one
or two week trips to Poland, the USSR, etc. The stations in
turn hope that the essays will give them some more specific
indication of who their listeners are and of whether various
points made in the broadcasts seem to have taken root with
these listeners, to the extent that one can assume that the
appearance of those points in an essay would "prove" that
listeners in fact obtained them from the broadcasts,
accepted them as valid, etc.

The essays are useful in a non-research manner as well.
Stations often use extracts from them as program material,
in the sense that the essays are quoted on station broadcasts. The 1970 centenary of Lenin's birth was the occasion
for a major listener contest on Radio Moscow, and it drew
thousands of replies, according to station officials.[2]
The station then used the essays thus generated as part of
its program material for the various listener mail programs
it broadcast, as in the instance already cited in Chapter 8
above (page 234).

DXer requests for confirmation of reception (QSL cards)
form an important category of listener mail for many international stations, some of which broadcast programs specifically designed to attract such requests. Information thus
generated is likely to be of most use to the stations'
engineering departments, since the requests usually indicate
the quality of the broadcast signal received by the listener.

Even if one is able to live with the obvious deficiencies of listener mail--the need for literacy, the costs of
postage[3] and materials, and the uncertainty of the mails, all
contribute to the non-representativeness[4] of this form of
research--there are still other problems. First, it is not
likely that most people who write to a station will be
critical of it, unless that is specifically requested of
them, and analyses of listener mail conducted by various
international stations reveal only small amounts of criticism.[5] Second, the act of writing to a broadcasting station
in another country can itself attract the unwelcome attention
of police and other internal security officials in some
countries, if the station is judged by the authorities to be
"hostile". Third, there is no simple way to verify whether
letters are genuine, and there is some evidence to indicate
that some letters may in fact emanate from "disinformation"
departments that wish to mislead station officials as to
listner reactions.[6] Fourth, there are certain categories of
listeners which are generally very important to international
stations but which rarely appear in the ranks of letter
writers, perhaps because these listeners are busy or don't
wish to express their views in this form of communication;

they would include government officials, businessmen and
-women, and teachers.[7]

LISTENER PANELS

The assembly of a panel of listeners to advise a station
on various aspects of its broadcasting has been little practiced by domestic broadcasters. However, BBC's External
Services have used listener panels since just after World
War II, and several other international broadcasters, including VOA, Deutsche Welle and Radio Nederland, have
adopted various versions of them in succeeding decades.

Actually, there are several different types of listener
panel, each with certain advantages and disadvantages. One
type, the "expert" panel, has been developed to deal with
those situations in which the station wishes to learn more
about probable audience reactions to its programing when
certain of its listeners live in "closed" societies, where
mail may be censored and where there is little or no survey
research allowed, especially on behalf of another nation.
The Voice of America, Radio Free Europe and Radio Liberty all
have made use of such panels, for programs directed to
audiences in Eastern Europe and the Soviet Union.

Expert panels are made up of people who are thoroughly
familiar with both the language and the customs of the
"closed" society, and who probably have spent some time living
there themselves. Panel members are asked to listen to a set
of tapes of programs recently broadcast to the country in
question. They are asked to judge the broadcasts in terms
of how they think the intended audience would have reacted to
them. In other words, panel members are asked to role-play,
and their reactions represent a highly sophisticated form of
guesswork. Some panelists are apparently able to immerse
themselves in the character of their listeners; others seem
to encounter some difficulty in doing so.[8]

Evidence gathered by expert panels is particularly useful in bringing to light outmoded language, overuse of
certain terms or phrases, and failure to take into account
changing tastes and trends in the "closed" society. A 1980
VOA expert panel on the station's Russian language broadcasts
had several specific recommendations to make on language
employed in the broadcasts, but it was more concerned with
the need for more background to major news items, since
panel members felt that many well-educated Russian listeners
would be unable to understand certain news items, especially
those about development in Western nations, without more
background information on them--information that was not
likely to be readily available in the USSR. They also spoke

favorably of "personality" broadcasting, and recommended
that broadcasts on current affairs not shy away from conveying a point of view, since otherwise the United States
might sound "wishy-washy" to its Russian listeners.[9]
    Since the method generally followed in expert panel
research involves each panel member listening to a pre-
selected set of tapes, then writing a report, then convening
with other panel members to discuss reactions to the material,
there are potential flaws in the system. The station,
knowingly or inadvertantly, may have selected an unrepresentative sample of tapes; the experts may be operating on
the basis of biased or dated opinion and knowledge of the
country and its people; the panel discussion may be dominated
by one or two individuals who do not reflect majority
opinion, etc. However, the checks and balances inherent in
the "individual-plus-panel" reactions to the programing, as
well as the likelihood that at least one panel member would
detect an unrepresentative sampling of programing, make the
system fairly reliable, within its admittedly unscientific
limits.
    The "lay audience" panel is a more common form of
listener panel research. Until the 1970s, only the BBC used
it regularly, but now Deutsche Welle, VOA, Rādio Nederland,
Swiss Radio International and others employ versions of it,
as well. The system works as follows: a station selects a
sub-sample from among the letters received by a specific
language service, then contacts those listeners to ask them
whether they would be willing to serve on a listener panel
for that language service. They are told that, if they do
so, they will receive questionnaires from time to time, in
which they will be asked for their reactions to specific
broadcasts, types of broadcasts, broadcast practices, etc.
Questions may deal with pace of delivery, comprehensibility
of material, possible bias or lack of thoroughness in covering subjects, etc. Panelists serve for a limited number of
years, and panelists who agree to serve but then fail to
return questionnaires over a period of time are dropped.
    This form of panel research has the obvious limitation
of being not only non-random, but even highly selective, in
that the vast majority of listeners who write to the stations
and who agree to serve on panels will be disposed favorably
toward the stations. The stations themselves acknowledge
this deficiency, but feel that they are able to obtain a
quality and quantity of specific reaction to programing that
is not available through other forms of research. Most of
them realize that the reactions they receive will represent
the views of a segment of the audience which is comprised
largely of their most faithful and often more intelligent
listeners. But if those listeners report moderate difficulty with a given announcer's accent or pace, or with

comprehension of a given program, most of the stations will
take this as an indication of a still more serious problem
where the "non-panel" listener is concerned.

Not all lay audience panels operate in the manner described. The BBC appears to adhere most strictly to this
model, but some stations apply it more loosely, selecting
a fresh panel each time a questionnaire is mailed, employing
non-scientific means of selecting the sub-sample, etc. Such
procedures may or may not bias results, but they do make it
more difficult to get others to accept the results as valid
indicators of problems.

The Voice of America developed a very different approach
to panel research in the mid-1970s. With the assistance of
U.S. Information Service posts, it established listener panels
in Kuala Lumpur, Lagos, Medellin (Colombia), Kuwait and
Abidjan. There were actually two listener panels in each
city, one made up of people who claimed to listen to VOA, the
other of people who claimed to listen to other international
broadcasters but not VOA. A local interviewer was provided
with a list of questions (the same for all locations); he
or she then convened the panel and had its members engage
in discussion of each question. The discussions were recorded
and later transcribed for the use of VOA staff. Each panel
met six times, and the questions covered a wide range of
topics: why panelists began listening to foreign radio
broadcasts, what they considered to be the distinguishing
characteristics of various stations, whether they felt that
news broadcasts from various stations were reliable or
unreliable and why, etc.

This type of listener panel had certain advantages,
chief among them the stimulation of specific reactions
through group discussion, but it operated on the basis of a
very small sample of the audience, and if choices of panel
members were not carefully made, the results would be
virtually meaningless. A participant who completely dominated
discussion, for example, would have transformed a group
evaluation into a one-person evaluation. A group leader who
forgot or did not care to ask certain questions from the list
would remove the possibility of subsequent comparative
evaluation of data from all the panels for those questions.
Those and other problems occurred during the 2½ years that
this panel system was used (October 1975 to March 1978).
Cost of the project was high, and many staff members within
VOA had doubts as to the validity of the data gathered,
since the panels were small (attendance might run as low as
five or six in some sessions).[10]

However, USIA and VOA did find the panels useful in
certain respects. They highlighted various aspects of programing practices that could be built into survey research
studies in the future and they gave a clearer picture of
certain qualitative dimensions of programing than had been

available from other research data. For example, panelists
emphasized the importance of first-hand ("on the spot")
reporting by one's own correspondents in establishing the
credibility of an international broadcast news operation and
some of them criticized VOA for a lack of timeliness, and,
to some degree, relevance, in its newscasts.[11] There was also
considerably more data on comparisons between VOA's broadcasts and the broadcast practices of other international
stations than had generally emerged in other research
studies. Further panel research projects of this sort were
being carried out in 1981 in Washington, D.C. with foreign
nationals.[12]

CONTENT ANALYSIS

Although it is not audience research in the strictest
sense of the term, content analysis of international broadcasts is intended to give program makers and supervisors
some indication of themes, phraseology, etc. that are being
presented to listeners, which may in turn serve as a basis
for inferring listener reactions. The assumption is that
those involved with day-to-day production and supervision
may lack perspective on their broadcasts, may be "unable to
see the forest for the trees". Content analysis should
serve to present a more abstract picture of broadcast content,
since it is generally based on an examination of programing
over a period of time: a week, a month, a year. Often it
is conducted by someone from outside the station who has
some knowledge of the area to which the broadcasts are
directed.

Few international broadcasters have commissioned content analyses of their programing; it appears to be regarded
by them as having limited value in program decision-making
and review. The Voice of America has been the subject of it
on several occasions, however, generally for broadcasts to
"closed" societies. For example, USIA's Office of Research
commissioned Dr. James Oliver, a political scientist at the
University of Maryland, to undertake a comparative content
analysis of Russian language broadcasts by VOA, BBC, Radio
Liberty and Deutsche Welle (1974)[13] and of Mandarin language
broadcasts by VOA, BBC, Radio Australia and Deutsche Welle
(1976).[14] These analyses revealed that the four stations
covered many of the same events and in much the same way,
but with differing approaches to the inclusion and presentation of "positive" and "negative" material. Content
analysis by Martelanc, et al. and by Lindahl, et al. formed
the basis of two studies on the nature of international
broadcasts directed to Yugoslavia and to Sweden.[15] The

analyses disclosed that there were considerable differences
in newscast content and style between the stations, some
being more "neutral" in their choice of language than others,
some including news from a greater number and variety of
countries than others.

Content analyses of international radio broadcasts sometimes have a fault that may compromise results: many of
them are based on examination of broadcast scripts, rather
than the actual broadcasts. While this practice makes the
coding of words, themes, amounts of time per story, etc.
much simpler, it removes a dimension which could give a coder
a very different impression of a news item or feature than
might be derived from the script alone. Consider, for
example, a content analysis of the scripts for the BBC
Portuguese language service in mid-1975 (see Chapter 6,
pages 167-168 above). The biases injected by the newsreaders
would not have been noted by anyone who had only the scripts
to analyze, since their insertions were ad lib and their
negative references often conveyed through tone of voice.
All the same, this form of research can be very useful in
revealing patterns and practices that program staff are not
aware of. As USIA's Office of Research put it in summarizing
Oliver's 1974 Russian language study: "Conclusions presented
in the study provide materials for possible discussion of how
programing directives are implemented in VOA's broadcasts,
whether the selection of content and the allocation of
programing time are commensurate with the objectives set
forth for VOA, and how VOA compares in content with three
other major broadcasters."[16]

EXPERIMENTAL RESEARCH

Very few international broadcasting stations have conducted experimental research on possible audience perceptions,
attitudes, etc., toward specific programs or programing in
general. Such research, which has been quite frequently
conducted with respect to domestic broadcasting in industrialized nations, usually involves the manipulation of
one or more variables. For example, a person may be tested
for his or her level of aggression, then shown any one of
several program excerpts, some "violent", some not, then
tested again for level of aggression, or placed in a situation
where there is an opportunity to behave aggressively. In
theory, this should help to determine whether the program
excerpt helped trigger or increase aggressive tendencies.

Such manipulation would not be practical for most
international stations, since it is very expensive to conduct
this type of experimental research and since so few countries

would be likely to permit it within their own borders. However, it would be possible to do pre- and post-testing of audience reactions to or comprehension of specific broadcasts, since this type of experimental research is simpler in design and lacks any specifically manipulative features. One example of such a research study is BBC's investigation of the comprehensibility of its English language broadcasts in urban Nigeria (Chapter 6, page 175), but it lacks any pretesting. A study which did feature pre- and post-testing was conducted by Professor Don Smith (Chapter 8, page 236). However, few international stations seem to have much interest in this sort of research.

DOMESTIC MEDIA REACTION

"If the other side yells, we must be hitting where it hurts" would be one way of describing the underlying premise of this form of research. It is little practiced at present, but it was quite prevalent in the 1950s among Western stations broadcasting to the "Soviet bloc," Radio Free Europe, Radio Liberty, RIAS and VOA chief among them. The research technique consisted of analyzing newspapers, magazines, radio and television broadcasts within the target countries, to see how often, in what manner, and for what apparent reasons, broadcasts from "the West" were mentioned, either by name or in terms of a campaign one or more of them might be conducting. If the domestic media were reacting frequently or strongly to the "Western" broadcasts, this was a good indication that the broadcasts were touching some sensitive nerves and probably reaching an influential and even perhaps sizeable audience.[17]
Such research is largely inferential, and rarely is it based on rigorous procedures of selection and content analysis of domestic media content. Furthermore, media silence does not necessarily mean that international broadcasts are not reaching their targets or touching sensitive nerves; by the same token, media reaction does not necessarily mean that international broadcasts are effective. It is quite possible that media reaction, far from being spontaneous, could be designed to give international broadcasters the impression that their programs are effective when in fact they are not. This might serve to divert attention from more crucial problems and could cause the international broadcaster to waste time, energy and money. However, analysis of media coverage can reinforce other forms of research. A sudden decrease in listener mail coupled with a sudden increase in media attacks on a given international broadcaster and a sudden increase in anecdotal reports of

public interest in broadcasts from that station would probably
signify that the station was having enough effect that the
domestic government was compelled to take strong measures
against it, such as increased censorship of mail, in addition
to criticizing it. Again, this is inferential, but the
inferences may gain strength with additional forms of data.

ANECDOTAL MATERIAL

     Most international stations receive anecdotal material
from first-hand observers: members of their countries'
diplomatic corps, reporters from their domestic media,
professors visiting or residing temporarily in other
countries, etc. There is no set form for this material, and
it cannot be collected on a regular basis, so it does not
lend itself to scientific analysis. However, much like
domestic media reaction from target countries, it can be
used in conjunction with other data. Some first-hand
observers, reporters in particular, are adept at gathering
bits and pieces of evidence on listening to international
radio broadcasting, while others are far less thorough or
less reliable. As I mentioned in Chapter 8 above (page 135),
Radio Moscow had some difficulty in obtaining reports on the
effectiveness of Radio Moscow broadcasts from TASS and NOVOSTI
correspondents stationed abroad, and I know from first-hand
experience that VOA has not had much more success in getting
reports from U.S. diplomatic personnel.
     Interviews with refugees might also be considered as
anecdotal material, in that the flow of refugees is itself
uncertain and their reasons for leaving their countries
varied, but at least the material sometimes can be collected
in a reasonably scientific manner, with standardized questionnaires. Deutsche Welle, VOA, RFE, Radio Liberty and RIAS all
have engaged in such interviews. Much of the information
thus gathered can be quite useful, especially if it deals
with the media habits of friends and acquaintances of the
refugees who remain in the target country. However, there
may be a strong tendency for refugees to tell interviewers
what they think the interviewers would like to hear, perhaps
because it symbolizes their break with their former country.
Refugees also represent a special category of the population
--those who disliked their living conditions enough to do
something quite drastic about it--so their perceptions of
media habits, attitudes toward international radio programing,
etc. for themselves as well as their neighbors and associates
may not be particularly representative.
     A 1973 Deutsche Welle report on interviews conducted
with refugees from the Soviet Union (N=366) included

questions that are commonly found in such research projects:
did you watch television, listen to radio, how often and at
what times, did you listen to any of these foreign stations
(a list was provided), when did you ordinarily listen, how
credible did you find their news items about Russia, etc.
Negative comments on the broadcasts of the "Western"
stations rarely appeared; for example, no more than two per
cent of those interviewed found the broadcasts of DW, BBC,
VOA or Radio Liberty "not believable."[18] Still, specific
evidence as to preferred times of listening, reception conditions, etc., are valuable information when little else is
available. Any negative reaction to program practices on
the part of members of such a positively disposed segment
of the population probably would be worth heeding, although
it's always possible that some refugees are sent out to
spread misinformation.

COMPUTER SIMULATION OF AUDIENCES

In the late 1960s, certain social scientists, particularly at the Massachusetts Institute of Technology, began to
develop computer-based analyses of audiences for international
broadcasting in closed societies. This system was further
refined during the 1970s, and in 1980 the individuals who
had developed and/or refined it produced a projection of
some of the demographic characteristics of audiences for
international broadcasting inside the Soviet Union. The
projection was based on data that had been gathered over a
four-year period (1974-78) from interviews of visitors
coming from the Soviet Union to Western Europe. Most segments
of the population were represented among the visitors, but
some, particularly the less educated and the rural dwellers,
were present in numbers far smaller than would be truly
representative of their strength in the national population.
A mathematical projective technique called "Mostellerization"
was applied to these data in order to develop a more accurate
estimate of the audience for international (in this study,
Western) broadcasts in the Soviet Union.

As is the case with most audience research on listening
in closed societies, the results of this study must be
treated with caution. The raw data upon which the projection
is based may itself be unreliable, for a variety of reasons.
Visitors from the Soviet Union to Western Europe represent
something of a privileged class, as Hedrick Smith has
pointed out,[19] and their radio listening habits may not be
typical of other segments of the population. Since it is
difficult to supervise the work of interviewers in these
particular circumstances, and impossible to check back with

interviewees to see whether and how the interview was actually
conducted, some of the data might be false or erroneous, even
though Radio Liberty, under whose auspices the interviews were
conducted, claims to be able to spot deviations in interviewing.[20] The mathematical projective technique itself may
not be as accurate as its users claim. Nevertheless, it is
another piece of information that can be added to other
pieces of information about audiences in the Soviet Union,
and it has in fact accorded quite closely with the little
Soviet research on audiences for radio that is available outside the USSR.[21]

THE AUDIENCE FOR INTERNATIONAL BROADCASTING

     Given the advanced state of computer technology, it
should be possible to combine information from the many
studies that have been conducted on audiences for international
radio and arrive at a composite picture of that audience.
In practice, that would be extremely difficult: the nature
of the data varies a great deal, most of it has been gathered
under less than random conditions, and there is no uniformity
to most of the categorizations, such as age groups or occupations. Nevertheless, and without benefit of computeriza-
tion, I have attempted to summarize the several dozen
studies of various types that I have read over the last 20 or
so years; this is what they yield.
     There is great geo-political variation to the extent of
listening. The industrialized countries of the West seem to
have the lowest percentages of regular listeners (once a week
or more) to foreign broadcasts: there are few of these
countries where it exceeds five per cent of the population,
and many where it is lower. Japan may be an exception, but
mail analyses and surveys have revealed that the majority of
listeners there are teenagers, who have been encouraged to
listen to international broadcasting thanks to vigorous sales
campaigns conducted by Japanese manufacturers of shortwave
sets. Central and Eastern Europe and the Soviet Union appear
to represent considerably higher levels of regular listenership, ranging from 25 to 50 per cent. The developing nations
show even greater variation, running from five to 50 per cent
of the population; since so few random sample surveys have
been conducted in countries falling into either of these last
two categories, those figures are not terribly firm. "Crisis
listening" is not figured into these estimates; the little
research evidence I have seen on it indicates that major
world crises will have a considerable temporary effect on
listenership, often doubling the usual audience figures.[22]
     Audience composition is somewhat more consistent from

one part of the world to another, if the studies are to be
believed. Audiences for international radio appear to be
predominantly male, predominantly urban, predominantly
younger (under 40), predominantly well-educated (a relative
term--an eighth grade education may be a considerable ac-
complishment in many countries), and predominantly middle-to-
upper income (again, a relative term). There are undoubtedly
many reasons for this profile, among which amount of leisure
time, curiosity about the rest of the world, ability to
afford a halfway decent shortwave receiver, and some rigid
attitudes about the "proper" interests of men and women, may
all play a part. The forms and practices of research themselves may well have some effect, too; in many countries, it
simply is not the practice to ask women or poor people their
opinions, and even if a researcher were to attempt it, she or
he might well be met with stares of incredulity or mumbled
apologies for being unable to answer.[23]

The physical aspects of listening also appear to be quite
consistent. The average listener probably devotes less than
an hour to this activity each time she or he performs it.
Listening is most often done in the evening hours, with early
morning hours as the second most prevalent period and early
afternoon hours third, particularly for countries with a
siesta tradition. The average listener will tune to three or
four different stations in a given week, and perhaps one or
two others on a less frequent basis.

It is extremely difficult to determine whether certain
stations are preferred over others, partly because the
question is not posed in most audience studies and partly
because it's such a "loaded" question: if the respondent
feels that an honest response is likely to cause her or him
subsequent problems with local authorities, or if the respondent thinks that the interviewer or station hopes for a
certain response, then the data will be valueless. Such data
as will allow for a global comparison shows BBC and VOA as
"most widely listened to" stations, with others assuming considerable regional importance (e.g. Radio Cairo's "Voice of
the Arabs" in the Middle East, Radio Habana in much of Latin
America, Radio Australia in Indonesia, Radio France International in Francophone West Africa). Determining why some
stations are more popular than others is even harder, since
very few studies pose this question. Answers provided
generally include clarity of signal, duration of broadcast,
choice of language (English may be a universal language, but
Tanzanians appreciate being able to listen in Swahili and
Brazilians in Portuguese), variety of programing, and perceived truthfulness and accuracy. There is a good deal of
evidence, most of it from listener panels and listener mail,
to indicate that listeners do compare international stations
--their treatment of the news in particular--quite regularly.

Preferred programing is easier to determine, since this question is often asked, and the question is answered with remarkable consistency. News is the clear leader, although some listeners feel that too much time is devoted to it. Popular music places second, and musical request programs are especially in demand. Commentaries and analyses, particularly of political issues, often finish at or near the bottom of preference lists. Language lessons, for English in particular, are very popular in developing countries.

It is also interesting to consider some of the questions that are rarely, if ever, asked but that would seem to be important to international stations. What attracted listeners to a given station in the first place? What caused them to continue to listen to it or to drop it? Do listeners discuss what they hear on these stations with others? If so, who do they talk with and what do they discuss?[24] What are the most important elements in the ease or difficulty of understanding a program?[25] If the listener were to attempt to describe a country in terms of the image she or he thinks it presents over its international radio service, what would that image be?

Why don't stations ask these questions? I have already suggested cost as one reason. Many of these questions would have to be asked in face-to-face surveys, through listener panels, or, in some countries, over the telephone. Then the answers would have to be collected together, analyzed and categorized--a process which is far more time-consuming than noting numbers of yesses or nos, or check-marks. Answers to such questions tend to ramble, as my examination of the transcripts of the VOA five-country listener panel project revealed, and it isn't always clear that the question has in fact been answered. Yet if such data are to be of any value to program staff, they must be condensed and organized into meaningful patterns, e.g., how many people seem to have difficulty understanding a given announcer and did many of them agree as to the reasons for that difficulty? In other words, program staff will want to know whether they're dealing with one complaint, however well expressed, or with several; and they'll want to know whether there are corresponding compliments, because one obviously cannot please every listener. And if analysis and categorization of these data is time-consuming and expensive when done in the broadcasting country's own language, imagine the expense and time involved in doing it for a foreign language.

Still, given the perceived need for effective communication that must be the ultimate goal of most, if not all, international stations, the expense and time would seem to be worthwhile. There may be other reasons for not conducting such research. One reason may be the generally low regard in which audience research seems to be held by program staff.

Producers, announcers and writers generally think of themselves as professionals who have a "feel" for what "their"
audience wants, needs, likes and can understand. Often this
"feel" has been acquired through years of experience in the
broadcasting nation's domestic radio or television services,
and program staff may consider that experience to be just as
valid for audiences in other countries. Many program staff
members were born and raised in other countries, which in
theory should give them an even better understanding of
foreign listeners. Still others have worked in other countries
as overseas correspondents, embassy personnel, etc., and rely
upon that experience to help them judge the needs and desires
of their listeners. In light of that experience, and given
the uncertain nature of most audience research, why should
more time and more money be invested in still more research?
As one USIA researcher observing practices in the BBC's
External Services put it,

> The distinguishing characteristic of BBC
> programmers was an anything-but-understated
> confidence that they knew their audiences.
> This was expressed in several ways, ranging
> from comments like "Our listeners don't have
> any competing loyalties" to outright national
> stereotypes: "The Arabs are incredible hypo-
> chondriacs, so we give them lots of medical
> features.[26]

This line of reasoning on the part of program staff is
far from being wrong, but it is awfully narrow; nor do all
program staff subscribe to it. The great advantage to well-
conducted audience research is that it focusses questions on
certain specific matters and attempts to insure that a wide
variety of people respond to them. Also, researchers should
be able to pose questions and analyze responses in an un-
emotional way, whereas program staff are apt to be emotionally
involved in them. There is much to be gained from listening
to the voice of experience and the voice of research, and
neither can or should stand alone as the "truth". In most
stations at present, however, the voice of experience appears
to have the upper hand, and audience research generally is
understaffed and underfunded, if it exists at all.

THE PURPOSES OF RESEARCH

My assumption throughout most of this chapter has been
that research exists to tell the program staff what sorts of
audiences they reach, with what sorts of program, and, more

rarely, whether and why programs are successful or not.
Ideally, all audience research should serve this purpose,
and hopefully researchers and programers will understand each
other well enough to agree upon what they want to discover
and how to go about doing so in a manner that each will find
acceptable. As I have just indicated, that is not easy.

It may be made even more difficult when, for various
reasons, research studies have to be designed to serve other
needs. In some stations, administrators ask for studies of
audience size, composition, etc. in certain countries because
they anticipate that they will be asked to justify broadcasts
to those countries by foreign ministries, congresses, parliaments, etc. In still other cases, research studies may be
designed to elicit data that will raise the fewest indications
of problems and bring the most favorable responses, especially
in budgetary support, from supervising and financing bodies.[27]
Still other research projects have been carried out because
"they've always been done that way," whether they seemed
useful any longer or not; in other words, bureaucratic inertia
had set in.

If the goal of audience research is to enable the program
staff to communicate more effectively whatever it is that the
station and its various language services are supposed to be
communicating--and sometimes this itself is not very clear
or not very realistic, which further complicates the task of
the researcher--then it seems evident that more needs to be
done to bridge the gaps between researchers, administrators
and programers. No station has managed this very well, although some do better than others: the Audience Research
Department of the BBC External Services is far and away the
largest and best-financed research unit in international
broadcasting; that alone has given it more time to work with
program staff and administrators in order to better coordinate
audience research projects with overall policy priorities and
specific program practices. The Voice of America, in contrast, must turn to the Office of Research of its administrative "parent", USICA, for research projects, since its one
research officer (when the position is actually staffed,
which it sometimes is not) is responsible for liaison with
the Office of Research and a certain amount of research on
internal practices, and does not conduct audience research.

There is little doubt that, if top-level administrators
are unsympathetic or indifferent to audience research, whatever meaningful research might be done will have no ultimate
impact on programing. And if station programing policies
are unclear, little meaningful research can be done. Interviews and discussions with several dozen members of audience
research units in BBC, DW, VOA and other international
stations over the past 15 years have led me to conclude that
strong support for audience research from top administrators

has been very rare, except for BBC. Both VOA and DW have
experienced long periods of administrative indifference, and
VOA experienced something worse in that regard during much of
USICA Director John Reinhardt's term (Chapter 4, page 115).
The status of research also could be enhanced if it were used
as part of a formal program review process, but few stations
have such a process.

Audience research, especially of the sort that would be
useful to program decision making, is in even shorter supply
for other stations than it is for BBC, DW and VOA, although
Holland, Canada, Switzerland, Japan and two of the religious
stations, FEBC and HCJB, increased their efforts during the
1970s. Much of this increased effort appears to be intended
more to satisfy the stations' various supervisory and
budgetary masters than to guide program decisions.[28] There
is little doubt, however, that far more is known about
audiences for domestic radio throughout the world than is
known about audiences for international radio, and there seem
to be few prospects for a change in this situation.

NOTES

1. James Hall and Drew McDaniel, "The Regular Shortwave
Listener in the U.S.," Journal of Broadcasting 19 (Summer
1975):363-371; Kim Andrew Elliott, "International Radio
Broadcast Listening in the United States," unpublished M.A.
thesis, University of Minnesota, 1977.
2. Discussion with a "roundtable" of Radio Moscow
English language services staff, Moscow, USSR, April 30,
1970.
3. Several international stations have established
local addresses in foreign countries, often through their
nations' embassies, cultural centers, etc. This reduces
the cost of postage considerably, and sometimes speeds
delivery of listener letters, which may be forwarded through
diplomatic pouch.
4. "VOA Target Group Contestants and Listeners in India:
A Comparison," Washington, D.C.: U.S. Information Agency,
Office of Research and Assessment, Report R-6-71, April 29,
1971, contains a very interesting comparison of results
obtained from analyses of listener mail in response to a VOA
contest and a personal interview survey conducted among
"target" groups in the population (e.g. students, government
officials). Among the more revealing results were these:
contestants tended to favor lighter VOA programing, while
interviewees spent more time on news and current affairs
broadcasts; students and professionals were over-represented
among contestants, while government and political leaders,

businessmen, labor leaders, professors and media executives
were underrepresented.

5. A content analysis of over 15,000 letters received
by VOA in and prior to 1974 revealed that criticism of VOA
programing appeared in roughly one per cent of all letters,
and that some of those critical letters also contained
favorable remarks about programing. "A Content Analysis of
VOA Audience Mail," Washington, D.C., U.S. Information Agency,
Office of Research, Report E-25-76, December 28, 1976.

A Radio Moscow World Service listener contest held on
the occasion of the 50th anniversary of Radio Moscow apparently turned up much the same lack of criticism, because one
of the announcers for the World Service "Listeners' Forum"
observed in one broadcast, "You know, your favorable comments do make us feel good, but we realize that there's room
for improvement in our broadcasts, and we'd like to hear
from you more critical remarks and suggestions." Transcript
of broadcast undated, but probably early October 1979, contained in Radio Nederland, "Worldwide Communication: The
Role of International Broadcasting," Hilversum, The Netherlands: Radio Nederland, 1980, p. 144.

6. Ladislav Bittman, in The Deception Game (Syracuse:
Syracuse University Research Corporation, 1972), pp. 148-149,
describes the activities of Hungary's "disinformation department", which as of 1965 (he claims) both screened letters from
Hungarians to Radio Free Europe and generated its own false
letters to mislead RFE as to Hungarian reactions to its programing. Bittman goes on to claim that none of the other
Eastern European countries had imitated the Hungarian
practice, because it "seemed too tedious".

7. "VOA Target Group Contestants".

8. These conclusions emerge from my examination of the
transcripts and final reports of VOA expert panel research
and my many discussions with Fred Collins, VOA Research
Officer, Emery Keeri-Santo and Henry Hart, Audience Analysis,
Radio Free Europe, and various members of the Audience
Research Division, Radio Liberty.

9. "VOA Russian Listeners Panel," Washington: USICA,
Research Memorandum, January 26, 1981.

10. Several VOA staff members and one present and one
former member of USICA's Office of Research discussed the
panels and their problems with me on a number of occasions,
from shortly after their inception until well after their
termination. James Kushner, former member of the Office of
Research, and the person chiefly responsible for supervision
of the panel project, was especially helpful.

11. See especially "Radio Audience Perceptions of Treat-
ment of News and News Analysis by VOA and by Other Major
International Broadcasters," Washington, D.C.: International
Communication Agency, Office of Research, Report R-17-78,

August 2, 1978. This was one of six reports issued by USICA on the panel deliberations.

12. Telephone interview with Peter Janicki, USICA Office of Research, Washington, D.C., October 21, 1981.

13. James H. Oliver, "Comparison of the Russian Services of the Four Major Broadcasters," Washington, D.C.: U.S. Information Agency, Office of Research, Report R-8-75, July 28, 1975.

14. James H. Oliver, "Comparison of the Mandarin Services of the Four Major Broadcasters to the Peoples' Republic of China," Washington, D.C.: U.S. Information Agency, Office of Research, Report R-11-78, March 10, 1978.

15. Tomo Martelanc, et al., "External Radio Broadcasting and International Understanding," Reports and Papers on Mass Communication No. 81 (1977), UNESCO (Paris); Rutger Lindahl, Broadcasting Across Borders (Göteborg, Sweden: CWK Gleerup, 1977).

16. Oliver, Report R-8-75, p. 3.

17. I have cited examples of this research in "The History and Programing Policies of RIAS," unpublished Ph.D. dissertation, University of Michigan, 1961, Chapter 9 and pp. 312-314. Malcolm Toon, former U.S. Ambassador to the Soviet Union, used domestic media reaction as evidence of effectiveness when he appeared on National Public Radio's "Communique" on March 27, 1981. He said, "The real indication of the Soviet concern about the impact of foreign radios on their people was the fact that whenever something was said on the radio which they felt represented a disturbing development to them, they would blast the radio in their press and on other media."

18. Deutsche Welle, "Befragung russicher Ausiedler in Grenzdurchgangslager Friedland, 1973" (Köln: DW Hörerpost/ Programmbeobachtung, 1973).

19. Hedrick Smith, The Russians (New York: Ballentine Books, 1976), Chapter 19.

20. Interviews with staff members of Radio Liberty and Radio Free Europe Audience Research Department/Division, Munich, Germany, September 1975.

21. The study is summarized in R. Eugene Parta, John Klensin and Ithiel de Sola Pool, "The Short-wave Audience in the USSR: Methods for Improving the Estimates," unpublished paper, summer 1980. The comparison with Soviet domestic research appears on pp. 4-5.

22. One of the few such studies I have seen is "The Performance of Western and Domestic Radio During the Polish Crisis," Munich: Radio Free Europe, East European Area, Audience and Opinion Research, March 1981. Because of sampling problems, there is a high range of error, and most of the study deals with which stations were most listened to, did the best job of covering the crisis, etc., but there is

an indication (page 3) that listening to Western radio increased markedly in most Eastern European countries (save
Bulgaria) during the period August-November 1980.

    23. See William O'Barr, David Spain and Mark Tessler,
eds., Survey Research in Africa: Its Applications and
Limits (Evanston: Northwestern University Press, 1972) for
an indication of some of the problems faced by those attempting to conduct survey research in developing countries.
Curiously, the book does not deal with mass communication
research per se.

    24. A small-scale study by Elliott indicates that, of a
sample of 29 U.S. listeners who had identified themselves as
listeners to BBC's World Service, 23 said that they did
discuss programs heard on shortwave broadcasting with others,
although such discussions were not all that frequent, and
political information was only one of several subjects discussed. Five respondents felt that they might have influenced someone else by such discussion. Kim Andrew Elliott,
"An Alternative Programing Strategy for International Broadcasting," unpublished Ph.D. dissertation, The University of
Minnesota, December 1979, p. 179.

    25. Evidence gathered through BBC listener panels has
revealed that those listeners seem to find that clear diction,
good vocal variety and a moderate rate of speaking all help,
as does a display of interest and "life" on the part of the
speaker. Criticisms center around over-complex phraseology,
speakers who sound as if they're lecturing, and heavy accents.

    26. David Gibson, memo to Daniel Garcia, Chief, Media
Research, U.S. Information Agency, Subject: Activities and
Impressions of an Exchange Researcher at BBC, March 26, 1978.

    27. I have spoken with more than 40 members of audience
research departments and other units carrying out research in
some two dozen stations over the past 15 years. Most of them
have indicated that at least some of their research projects
were designed for one or both of these purposes.

    28. When I visited Radio Nederland in September 1975,
it seemed apparent that lack of audience research, aside
from some analysis of listener mail, had hindered the station
in its attempts to favorably influence members of the Dutch
parliament. Since parliament had just assumed the responsibility for appropriating RN's annual budget, this was a
matter of no small importance. In fact, RN suffered a
rather substantial budget cut in 1977; although inadequate
audience research was not the sole cause of the cut, it
certainly did not help. RN increased its research effort in
the late 1970s, and when I visited it in May 1980, it had
prepared several studies, most of them based on mailed
questionnaires.

13

LOOKING BACK AND LOOKING AHEAD: CONCLUSIONS, SPECULATION, AND SUGGESTIONS

At the end of the first chapter, I said that with all of the potential problems surrounding international broadcasting, you might wonder why anyone would bother to engage in it. I had already discussed some of the probable reasons for doing so, and the next ten chapters provided plenty of specific examples. Those examples should have shown clearly that reasons vary (and that they may not be particularly evident), just as do practices. If there's agreement upon anything, it's the belief that international broadcasting continues to be worth doing, for whatever reasons. But very few stations know or seem to care to know how <u>well</u> they're doing.

I begin this chapter with a brief consideration of five factors (excluding technical and legal matters) that appear to have a major bearing on any given station's effectiveness in influencing its listeners, and follow that with a consideration of what we know about that influence. I then look at the likely future of international broadcasting, and I conclude by attempting to enlist your help in studying a few as yet little-studied aspects of the "limitless medium".

FACTORS IN EFFECTIVENESS

When I spoke of the common concerns of international radio stations in Chapter 1, I did so in the context of opportunities and limitations. Now that we have seen how stations evolved and what they do, I think it appropriate for us to consider those opportunities and limitations from another perspective--one which takes into account stations' objectives, strategies, programing practices, supervisory practices and uses of research. I single out those five factors because I feel that any station which considers each and every one of them carefully should stand an excellent chance of effectively reaching and influencing listeners.

Objectives

Many international radio stations appear to have little understanding of what they wish to accomplish or why they wish to accomplish it. It may be that some of them had clear objectives at one time, especially during World War II or during the "colonial era," but after the war had ended and the colonies had become independent, those objectives were no longer quite so relevant. It may be that the day-to-day pressures of operating the station keep staff members from standing aside and reassessing objectives. It may be that they question the wisdom or feasibility of setting objectives in a rapidly changing world.

Whatever the reason(s), few stations that I have visited or read about have displayed much interest in setting and pursuing objectives. Quite often, the impetus to do so, where it has appeared, has come from outside the broadcasting organization itself, such as the various special committees that have looked at the BBC External Services or the U.S. Comptroller General (GAO) reviews of Radio Free Europe-Radio Liberty. While a station can function without objectives, their absence makes it very difficult to develop strategies and, in turn, purposeful programing.

Strategies

Just as stations may or may not have objectives, they may or may not have strategies, and the absence of the one does not necessarily preclude the presence of the other. It would be unusual for a station to think in terms of strategies without having ultimate objectives in mind, but those goals might be nothing more than seeing whether the strategies work! Again, the day-to-day press of churning out program material may mean that staff members cannot develop the practice of standing aside from what they're doing and considering other ways of doing it.

When they do examine strategic approaches to effective communication, they may think in terms of short-term and/or long-term strategies. Judging from my own experiences with international stations, short-term strategies predominate, when there are any strategic considerations at all. This may be a legacy of World War II where, as you have seen, there was frequent use of international radio as an instrument of psychological warfare, and where tactical strategies, with a concommitant need for rapid adjustment to changing circumstances, were quite common, but it is further encouraged by pressures from foreign offices, legislative bodies, etc. for "quick action".

Short-term strategies are appealing for another reason: if they work, those who developed them will know it immediately, and can derive immediate satisfaction from their successes. Those successes also form excellent justification for the continuation of the broadcasts when station administrators appear before parliaments, congresses and other financing bodies. Finally, if coordinated with other forms of action, such tactical broadcast activities can be quite effective, as several episodes in World War II and the Cold War seem to show.

But other episodes, such as Radio Cairo's broadcasts during the 1967 Mideast War, show one of the limits of short-term strategies: if such broadcasts are not carefully coordinated with other information and specific forms of action, the broadcasts will not be accepted by listeners, and the station itself may suffer a loss of credibility that will be difficult to recover, even as did Radio Cairo. And if a short-term strategy takes the form of suddenly adding, expanding and taking away language services, there is the danger, as I have suggested in Chapter 1 and elsewhere, that some listeners may resent such evident manipulation.

I believe that there is a place in international broadcasting for short-term strategies, but that they should not exist in the absence of long-term strategies. Those strategies may bring a station into conflict with its government or supporting organization, but the ability to provide listeners with long-term consistency in at least some matters should help to enhance a station's credibility, as BBC's World War II and Suez experiences seemed to do.

Programing Practices

As you have seen, there is considerable variety to programing for international radio. As a rule, the more hours a given language service is on the air, the greater the variety. For the vast majority of stations, informational broadcasts are the "main freight," and entertainment broadcasts, especially music, generally serve the purpose of "bait" to attract listeners who hopefully will stick around for, or eventually be attracted to, the heavier fare. Yet few station staff have any evidence that entertainment serves this purpose. Even if such evidence existed--and the largely anecdotal evidence on the matter both supports and rejects the theory that entertainment attracts "serious" listeners--there is a question of balance: how much of each element is the right amount? Given the variety of purposes for which stations exist, and the variety of listener tastes,

there can be no one correct answer, but programers might
enhance station effectiveness if they would think more often
about program balance in terms of goals and strategies.

Program style also displays great variety, running along
a continuum from extremely informal to extremely formal.
Although informality has become more common over the past 20
years, formality still predominates. Perhaps it should:
listeners may expect stations to sound authoritative, which
in turn seems to demand a certain amount of formality. However, radio is remarkably effective at conveying one human
voice to individual listeners. Most international radio
listening is done by individuals, not by groups. The human
voice is a marvelous instrument for conveying a sense of
personality. International broadcasters often fail to take
advantage of that instrument, hobbling it with scripts more
appropriate to courts of law or treaty-making bodies than to
communication by one ordinary human being with other ordinary
human beings. Even stations which have programs designed to
"humanize" the broadcasting nation sometimes fail to see
that the manner in which the humanizing message is presented
will have a great deal to do with its effectiveness in winning
over the listener.[1]

Supervisory Practices

Even with carefully devised goals and strategies, and a
suitable program format and style, there is always the possibility that the station's effectiveness will be impaired
because its administrators don't know what its writers and
announcers are doing. This may be a particular problem in
the larger multi-lingual stations, where the presence of so
many exotic languages makes it difficult to monitor, much
less fully comprehend, everything that goes over the air.
A few stations monitor their own foreign language output
very systematically, but most lack the money and/or personnel
to do so. A few stations, notably RFE-RL, VOA, DW and Swiss
Radio International, have formal internal review systems,
but some of their language services are reviewed every other
year or even less. The head of each language service is
responsible for day-to-day supervision, but she or he may
lack the ability to pick up the nuances of a given language,
especially where intonation and inflection have a lot to do
with the meaning of words. While it is out of the question
to check out every minute of broadcast time, it is surprising
to note how very few stations do examine their broadcast
output with any care or regularity.

As we have seen with VOA, RFE/RL and BBC, lack of tight
and/or careful supervision can lead to problems. Yet

supervision cannot be too tight if writers and announcers
are to feel that they are being treated as professionals and
if the news in particular is to be timely: translation of
news items takes long enough, and if newscasts had to be "back-
translated" for verification of accuracy before going on the
air, the delay would be considerable. Still, I sometimes
have the impression that the broadcasts of some stations,
especially those with large amounts of program content dealing with international relations, constitute a sort of walking
time bomb, where a future broadcast could easily insult or
anger another nation to the point of hostility because of a
translation error or willful misconduct on the part of a
writer or announcer. The speed with which broadcasts are
sent and received adds to the hazardousness of the situation.
Admittedly, the good reputation of many of the stations helps
to offset the potential dangers, since most listeners would
probably be able to place the "offending" broadcast within
the overall context of a station's broadcasts, but the right
combination of elements could still prove disastrous.

Uses of Research

In view of what I've already said in Chapter 12, it
should not come as any surprise that I regard lack of audience
research, whether of all sorts (as it is for some stations)
or of particular sorts (as it is for most) as an important
consideration where effectiveness is concerned. But if a
station does not have carefully considered goals and strategies, then research is not likely to do much to make the
station more effective as an agent of international communication, however much it may serve to show the station's
financial supporters that there are listeners out there.
Perhaps one problem is that international broadcasters
feel that research techniques are too crude to permit investigation of the more psychological aspects of broadcast
effectiveness, or that, because they themselves direct most
of the research, whether independent firms execute it or not,
it must remain confined largely to the tried and true techniques, so that results can be measured against an acceptable
standard. One solution might be for a group of international
broadcasters to commission an independent research organization to conduct a number of small-scale "psychology of
listening to international broadcasting" studies, leaving it
largely to the research organization to develop the appropriate
research techniques. That could be a significant step in
drawing back the veil of ignorance surrounding the fundamental
question in international broadcasting: how can a station
bring a listener to attend to, understand, believe, and perhaps
even accept (be persuaded by) its broadcasts?

Few stations appear to have considered specific factors
of effectiveness. Perhaps they are unwilling to concede
that present practices may be outdated or even misbegotten,
and that is not an easy concession to make. However, there
are stations which seem to be more effective than others in
more or less measurable respects. BBC's External Services
seem, on the basis of the limited evidence we have, to draw
more listeners in times of crisis than do most other stations.
They also receive high marks for overall quality of service
from various radio listener clubs and organizations. They
receive more listener mail than all but a very few stations
year after year. They have been imitated by Radio RSA, Radio
Moscow's World Service, and several other international
stations. Staff members from Western, Communist and Third
World international stations speak of them in highly compli-
mentary terms. Although BBC administrators and staff may
not consider with equal care each of the five factors I've
covered here, they do consider them. It may be too much to
claim that this is why they're successful, but I feel that
it has a lot to do with their success.

INFLUENCE

In spite of its considerable history, we know very
little about the ultimate influence of international broadcasting. Perhaps broadcasters don't really know what to
look for. Perhaps they're afraid to ask because the results
might be disappointing. Perhaps the listeners themselves
couldn't answer such questions, either because they hadn't
yet considered their listening in that light, or because
they find it difficult to single out international radio
from among a host of different sources of information on
international events. As I've mentioned in the previous
chapter, listener letters and anecdotal reports from diplomatic personnel and media correspondents, and the occasional
direct evidence of an action taken as a result of an international broadcast, provide the bulk of evidence that
listeners attribute some importance to what they hear.
There is further, somewhat more direct, evidence relating
to the importance of international broadcasting, but it is
not plentiful. A series of polls was conducted for the U.S.
Information Agency in France, West Germany, Italy and Great
Britain in the late 1950s to mid-1960s. Known collectively
as the Project XX series, one poll (1960) in the series
contained a question asking respondents to examine lists of
possible sources of information on the United States and
then indicate which of them were "important"--a term for
which no definition was provided. The Voice of America

generally drew a lower percentage of mentions than did the
other U.S.-produced media (newspapers, books, magazines,
television, personal acquaintance) and always ran well behind
each country's domestic media. One must bear in mind that
VOA was not broadcasting to Europe in Italian, French or
German at the time, although it had done so up until a few
years earlier; even so, for citizens of those countries who
claimed to speak English well, the relative ranking of VOA
showed little change, although the percentage of mentions
did increase. Even in Great Britain, where language should
not have been a factor, only three per cent of respondents
cited VOA as an important source of information about the
U.S., somewhat behind American newspapers (four per cent),
books (seven per cent), magazines (14 per cent), and well
behind American TV (33 per cent) and the British media. It
is probable that VOA would fare considerably better in
countries where the media were in shorter supply and/or more
closely supervised by the government, but that is speculation.

A 1958 Project XX survey in the same countries asked
respondents to assess the effect on their countries of five
American "media"--newspapers, servicemen, tourists, students
and VOA--in terms of whether each was very good, more good
than bad, more bad than good, very bad or of no influence at
all/don't know. VOA received the highest number of don't
know/no influence responses, ranging from 52 per cent in
Italy to 71 per cent in France, and fewer favorable mentions
than all but American newspapers, but fewer unfavorable
mentions than all but students.

One problem may be that many people are not terribly
interested in international affairs, and would probably have
little interest in international broadcasting, either. A
1964 Project XX survey asked respondents how interested they
were in international affairs; when the responses "a little
interested", "not at all interested" and "don't know" are
clustered, they produce the following figures: France, 54
per cent; Italy, 78 per cent; West Germany, 53 per cent; and
Great Britain, 55 per cent. The better educated and those
in the major target groups scored considerably higher in
levels of interest, but the overall results seem to support
the contention of many international broadcasters that their
stations are not likely to attract the masses under most
circumstances, for the simple reason that the masses don't
care to be attracted![2]

Karl Deutsch and Richard Merritt subjected some of the
Project XX and other Western European data, as well as public
opinion studies done in the United States, to analysis of a
different sort: they attempted to discover whether various
types of events, which they labelled spectacular, cumulative
and shifts in governmental and mass media policy, would have
any long term effect on peoples' attitudes toward other nations

and international affairs. Despite the obvious limitations
of the data base (only five countries, all of them Western;
questionnaire items dealing largely with Cold War issues;
most recent survey undertaken in 1963), their conclusions
appear to support the findings of the 1964 Project XX survey
as noted above:

> Almost nothing in the world seems to be able
> to shift the images of 40 per cent of the population
> in most countries, even within one or two decades.
> Combinations of events that shift the images and
> attitudes of the remaining 50 or 60 per cent of the
> population are extremely rare, and these rare
> occasions require the combination and mutual re-
> inforcement of cumulative events with spectacular
> events and substantial governmental efforts as well
> as the absence of sizable cross-pressures.[3]

Most students, businesspersons, tourists and military
personnel who return home from trips abroad and talk with
their friends about the trip have probably experienced much
of the same indifference to things foreign that these data
seem to suggest. And if individuals, with all of the persuasive powers at their command, meet with indifference,
how likely is it that the majority of the people in any
country will go to the trouble to seek information about
other countries through internatonal radio broadcasts?
    However, international radio does not meet with universal
indifference, either. As I have indicated in previous chapters
certain stations do succeed in attracting a considerable
number of regular listeners, and appear to attract still more
when there is a major event of international, or even
regional, importance. But what we do not know, aside from a
few pieces of anecdotal and inferential evidence, is how the
listeners may be influenced by what they hear. The BBC
External Services are able to point to numerical evidence of
their success in getting listeners to write to British manufacturers to request further information on or to place
orders for products they have heard about over "New Ideas",
but such direct evidence of the persuasive power of international broadcasting is very rare.
    Many scholars have conducted studies of decision-
making with respect to international affairs. Most of those
studies explore the climate within which decisions are made
and who participates in them, but very few examine the sources
of information used by decision-makers, and even fewer
attempt to assess the relative importance of those sources to
the decision-makers. In the few studies I have seen where
sources of information are cited, international radio broadcasting does not appear in the lists.[4] That may be because

the studies are conducted in the media-rich Western countries, where international radio may be less important or harder to recall among the many media sources. One might predict--and anecdotal evidence appears to support the prediction--that it would be more important in closed societies and media-poor countries. It also is possible that decision-makers fail to recognize international broadcasting as the primary source of information they may receive at second hand, through monitoring service reports or through their own domestic media or in briefing papers prepared for them by subordinates who have made use of international radio.

It appears that, for many people who even care to follow what goes on in the rest of the world, international radio is one of a number of sources at their disposal. Listeners in Communist societies and Third World Nations may have fewer alternate media sources, but even there things appear to be improving, sometimes as a result of international broadcasts! If international radio is to retain and possibly increase whatever influence it has at present, I think it will be best equipped to do so if it applies programatic themes and practices that don't necessarily change every time there's a change in national political leadership, if it indicates a willingness to view events from more than one perspective, if it strives for the greatest possible accuracy, if it reminds itself that foreign audiences may need more background information than do domestic ones, and if it can use radio for its "humanizing" quality--people talking with people.

THE FUTURE

Sydney Head has pointed out that the media of mass communication has undergone several adjustments in their relatively brief histories, and most of us are familiar with the evolution of highly specialized magazines, radio programing formats and movies.[5] Head indicates that the development of television, although not the sole cause, had much to do with "redirection" of the other media. If international television, especially through direct broadcast satellites, should enjoy similar development, what would happen to international radio? Would some stations disappear? Would others revise their formats?

International television would have some obvious advantages over international radio. Its ability to show as well as tell would allow its programers to present audiences with explicit images of tourist attractions and new industrial products. Dramas and documentaries would be seen as well as heard. Language lessons could be illustrated. But none of these program types is a mainstay of any current international radio station, although many stations offer them. Furthermore, none (with the possible exception of language lessons) commands anything like a mass audience, even by the standards of international broadcasting. The news, commentary, press roundup and musical programing which makes up the bulk of the schedule for most international radio stations would appear to have little to fear from international television, although newscasts might evolve into little more than headlines (many stations already follow this practice in presenting some of their news material) or into a more highly detailed presentation of fewer items (a few stations already do so for certain of their newscasts).

International stations also would seem well suited to withstand the onslaught of international television, should it ever materialize, for certain psychological reasons. In more or less closed societies, the act of exposing oneself to "hostile" propaganda (or information, depending on one's perspective) still entails various risks and disadvantages. While few countries throw their citizens in jail for such acts, that has happened in the past and could happen in the future. Even more important to the individual may be the social ostracism, from associates, friends and even family, that may accompany such exposure. The more visible the exposure, the greater the risk of ostracism. A radio set is highly "neutral", private and concealable, while a book or magazine, once printed, cannot change itself into something else, and miniaturized television receivers are unlikely to be abundant for a few decades to come.

It would be satisfying to be able to conclude that international radio is well equipped for future survival. In some respects, it is: while many stations seem to me to be very poor investments for their respective governments or other supporting organizations in terms of their effectiveness, there are many others that seem to do a relatively good job of informing, entertaining and possibly influencing listeners. When all is said and done, international radio can be of tremendous aid and comfort to the internationally-minded individual. It is considerably cheaper than books or magazines or newspapers, and far cheaper than travel, if not as enjoyable! Within one radio set, it is possible to discover more information about a wider assortment of cultures and a greater diversity of viewpoints than any other medium of communication offers, and at a fraction of the cost. While the numbers of internationally-minded listeners may be a small minority in most countries, and may not grow much in years to come, they are likely to remain among the most influential members of their respective societies.

Whether those listeners will be able to hear their favorite stations as clearly in the future as they do at present is another question. The "superpower" race and the crowding of the frequency spectrum make it problemmatical that they will. Although most listeners to international broadcasts are willing to put up with a certain amount of static, fading and other technical uncertainties, one assumes that there must be a limit to their toleration. Monitoring services may be prepared and equipped to comb through a jungle of overlapping and fading signals, but few ordinary listeners are, and they remain, and should remain, the primary target for international radio. Monitoring services form a very uncertain retransmission belt, and their reports are available to few potentially interested parties. Other rebroadcast arrangements are little more certain.

Direct broadcasts to listeners, then, will remain the primary means by which international radio stations reach their audiences. But the most effective use of the frequency spectrum depends upon international cooperation and goodwill. Because many nations see other nations as using international radio to sow discord, develop ill will and misinform or fail to inform listeners about the "true" situation in other countries (especially in the Third World), it isn't surprising that the International Telecommunications Union has done a less than perfect job of regulation. Despite adjustments made in the course of the 1979 World Administrative Radio Conference (WARC), there has been little improvement in the overall situation. Direct broadcasts from many stations, especially the less powerful ones, will likely become more difficult to receive in the years ahead. Present experimentation with satellite transmission of radio signals that would be receivable on ordinary radio sets may result in success, but how many international broadcasters will be able to afford satellite technology?

To add to those difficulties, financial support for international radio may be in shorter supply in the future. Many of the international stations that are linked administratively and budgetarily with domestic broadcasting services seem to be finding it more and more difficult to maintain present levels of service, much less expand, in the face of the tremendous financial requirements of television. Stations receiving budgetary support through direct appropriation from legislatures appear to have fared slightly better on the whole, although they are more vulnerable to sudden cuts, or threats of cuts, as various experiences of VOA, BBC, RFE-RL and Radio Nederland have shown.

However, the fact remains that very few international stations have cut back their services, that almost none of the "legitimate" (as opposed to clandestine) stations have gone off the air completely, and that new stations, not to mention new transmitters for old stations, are going on the air each year. Fundamentalist Christian international stations are expanding their services; to a lesser degree, so are international commercial stations. While bureaucratic inertia may have served to prolong the lives of some stations, many of them seem to have the support of their budgetary masters and the endorsement of some of their countries' political leaders. Whatever the limits of the limitless medium, growth does not appear to be one of them.

A FEW REMAINING QUESTIONS

My main purpose in writing this book has been to interest more people in international radio. If I have succeeded, there should be at least a few of you who will conduct studies of your own. Every chapter of the book fairly bristles with unanswered or incompletely answered questions, which I hope will serve as inspiration for further studies. Three further questions occur to me, and I mention them here because I think that they are crucial to our further understanding of why international broadcasting exists and how it functions.

First, I would like to see more examination of the decision-making process surrounding the introduction of an international radio station in general and of a new language service in particular. My one thorough examination of this question, not yet published, concerns the introduction of foreign language broadcasts to the BBC Empire Service in the late 1930s. It has revealed a fascinating melange of public policy, personal pride, financial considerations and overt and covert consultation, to the point where I am not sure just whose purposes were best fulfilled by the ultimate decision. Jack Nargil's study of the Armenian service of VOA raises some of the same questions,[6] although much of the data needed to answer them was unavailable to him. If we had a better understanding of how (for what reasons) a station or language service was introduced, it should be easier to understand and assess its objectives. That in turn should give us a clearer picture of how international broadcasting fits in with overall policy-making, whether by a government or a religious organization.

Second, I would like to see more examination of the day-to-day process of decision-making, particularly with respect to news and current affairs. Again, I have conducted an investigation of this subject, and again, it is not yet published as I complete this book. It dealt with the newsroom operations of eight international stations, all but one of them Western. It revealed a high degree of dependency on the wire services and the domestic media of each originating country in setting the newscast lineup, although overseas correspondents played important roles for BBC and VOA (the only stations of the group to have their own overseas

correspondents). It did not reveal the presence of a pre-
scribed plan or set of guidelines which dictated what sorts
of stories should be carried or how they should be slanted
for any of the stations; whatever ideology the newscasts
conveyed appeared to emerge from within each society as a
whole, and was already part of the psychological makeup of
reporters, editors, etc. before they joined the station.
But we have much yet to learn about decision-making within
stations, especially those in closed societies (often the
hardest to study), which would allow us to assess the degree
and manner of utilization of international radio stations as
"instruments" of persuasion.

And finally, we very much need research comparing the
broadcast content of the various language services within
stations. I have often heard people in various countries
complain that, while Station X's English language service
may sound non-threatening or non-critical with respect to a
given country or political system, its Russian or Kuoyu or
Spanish or whatever other service(s) are very threatening or
very critical. Given what I said earlier about lack of
supervision, it's entirely possible that such differences
exist, but if they do, it may be for any number of reasons:
exile politics, a foreign policy that "speaks out of both
sides of its mouth," or carelessness in translating material.
Whatever the reasons, the first step is to determine that
there are real differences. And if those differences turn
out to be a matter of the nature of story treatment, rather
than the selection of items, those undertaking such comparative studies would have to be very well equipped to
understand the meaning of those languages within their own
societies, and not just the dictionary definitions of terms.

NOTES

1. Harold Lasswell, in "The Future of World Communication and Propaganda," Chapter 14 of Harold Lasswell, et
al., Propaganda and Communication in World History,
Volume III: A Pluralizing World in Formation (Honolulu:
University of Hawaii Press, 1980), offers some interesting
thoughts on style in international communication, as he discusses the merits and demerits of "opulent" and "parsimonious"
styles (pp. 525-528).
2. Some of these studies, as well as a few others
bearing on the same subject, are cited in Daniel H. Willick,
"Public Interest in International Affairs: A Cross-
National Study," Social Science Quarterly 50 (September 1969):
pp. 272-285.

3.   Karl Deutsch and Richard Merritt, "Effects of Events on National and International Images," in Herbert Kelman, ed., _International Behavior_ (New York: Holt, Rinehart & Winston, 1965), p. 183.

4.   Some of the more recent studies of international decision-making are: Robert Jervis, _Perception and Misperception in International Politics_ (Princeton: Princeton University Press, 1976); Robert Axelrod, ed. _Structure of Decision: The Cognitive Maps of Political Elites_ (Princeton: Princeton University Press, 1976); Irving L. Janis and Leon Mann, _Decision Making: A Psychological Analysis of Conflict, Choice and Commitment_ (New York: Free Press, 1977).

5.   Sydney Head, _Broadcasting in America_, 3rd Edition (Boston: Houghton-Mifflin, 1976), pp. 481-485.

6.   Jack Nargil, "The Voice of America as an Instrument of American Foreign Policy: A Case Study of the Armenian Service," unpublished M.A. thesis, The George Washington University, 1976.

APPENDIX A: INTERNATIONAL BROADCASTING PROGRAM CATEGORIES

I. Information: News and Commentary

Newscasts--length and content vary, but almost all
stations carry them. Some feature primarily domestic
news, some feature foreign news, most present a mixture
of the two. BBC carries a weekly feature consisting solely
of reports from its overseas correspondents.

Commentary--sometimes by station staff, sometimes by
outside experts or journalists, sometimes taken directly
from domestic and foreign media.

Editorials--drawn largely from the domestic media,
as in "roundups" of editorial opinion. Editorials
written and delivered by station staff are very rare.

Discussions and interviews--often rebroadcast from
domestic radio and television, e.g. AFRTS' rebroadcast
of ABC's "Issues and Answers".

I. Information: Features (for particular audiences on
particular subjects)

Business and industry--usually straightforward
reports on domestic developments. However, BBC and VOA
have special programs to directly promote British and
U.S. products.

Agriculture--much the same as for Business, but no
promotional programs.

Science--sometimes reports, sometimes interviews,
occasionally lectures, speeches, etc.

Medicine--much the same as for Science, but usually
with heavier emphasis on interviews and lectures.

Religion--usually talks, sermons and interviews, the
latter frequently on "non-denominational" subjects. Also
religious services. (Religion could also be considered
under "Cultural Propaganda". It all depends on your
point of view!)

353

Military--very rare as a feature category, but
certain AFRTS programs dealing with armed forces activities can be included here.

Women--few stations have specific feature programs
for women, but several include such programs as occasional
elements within a program bearing an "umbrella" title,
such as Radio Berlin International's "The Land We Live
In."

Youth--much the same as for Women, but a few
stations, e.g. Radio Moscow, carry features such as
"The Younger Generation" which deals with the accomplishments of "young people".

Problems in society--if treated at all in features,
they usually appear as a series of broadcasts (a number
of weeks) within an "umbrella" program.

Ideological--explanations and/or applications of a
political or religious ideology. Fairly frequent in the
schedules of Communist and religious stations. Rare in
Western and Third World broadcasting.

II.   Entertainment and Cultural Propaganda

Popular music--sub-categorization might be helpful
here (e.g., folk, jazz), but it is very difficult
because of the ambiguity of those terms when applied at
an international level. One subcategory worth mentioning,
however, is the practice followed by certain stations of
playing music of some other country or region, and certain
stations devote specific programs to this (e.g., Radio
Cairo's Music of India, Radio Japan's Melodies of Asia).

Classical music--if understood in a truly international sense, most stations broadcast such music, often
with accompanying commentary about the composer, the
artist, etc. This is less often the case with popular
music, but such commentary is not altogether absent there.

Cultural heritage and life--often includes interviews with painters, composers, architects, etc. A
sub-category here is book reviews, which are done by
several international stations on a continuing basis.

Documentaries and drama--usually done as part of an
ongoing series (e.g., VOA's Studio One, BBC's World
Theatre). May be written and produced by the international
operation itself, or may be taken directly from the
domestic service.

Sports--as handled by most international operations, this would appear to be a mixture of entertainment (when a game or contest is broadcast), cultural propaganda (when a "portrait" interview of an athletic is broadcast), and straight "news" (roundups of baseball, cricket, soccer scores). Programs within this category often appear to be intended as much for expatriates as for truly "foreign" listeners.

Light entertainment--includes quiz shows (e.g. BBC"S Brain of Britain) and variety shows. These are almost always taken directly from a domestic station, and are intended primarily for the expatriate audience, but they probably serve as cultural propaganda for certain overseas listeners. A particular sub-category here--and one that is produced by the international operations themselves--is the modified disk-jockey format used in VOA's Breakfast Show and by numerous other international stations. These programs have hosts (and at times, hostesses) who sometimes converse with each other between records, occasionally answer listener mail on the air, play a good deal of popular music, but also "take time out" for brief features, newscasts, etc. These programs are more than just light entertainment, but their mixtures of elements makes them difficult to classify, and the underlying mood is certainly light.

Everyday life--often in the form of "portraits" of individuals in society (thus serving to "humanize" the nation), but also collections of brief reports on life in the nation's capital, principal cities, etc.

III. Formal Instruction

Languages by radio--virtually all of the government sponsored international broadcast operations offer at least the beginning level of instruction in their own national languages(s), and a few (e.g. Radio Cairo, BBC) offer more advanced work. Radio Cairo has even carried a regularly-scheduled program in which it answered specific questions from listeners relating to the learning of Arabic.

Aspects of language instruction--intended primarily for teachers in other countries who are teaching "your" language. Pedogogical tips, background information, etc. Very rare.

IV. Inducing Listeners to Write (and to Listen to Other
     Programs)

     Listener request programs--listeners are specifically
invited to request their favorite songs, which in turn
are played within a specific "listener request program".

     Answers to listener mail--most international oper-
ations feature at least one such program weekly; sometimes there are several, subdivided by areas of the
world from which the requests come and to which broadcasts are beamed. Occasionally, these questions are
answered by "experts", but generally they are handled by
staff members.

     "Contest" and promotional announcements--done
almost universally.

     DX programs--designed to facilitate exchange of
reception information among hobbyists, but also to get
them to send reception reports to the station.

APPENDIX B: LANGUAGE SERVICES ADDED [AND DROPPED] BY SIX MAJOR INTERNATIONAL BROADCASTERS--1960-1980

	1960-1965	1965-1970	1970-1975	1975-1980
Radio Moscow	Amharic, Somali, Hausa, Bambara, Nepali, Sinhalese, Thai, Zulu, Lao, Lingala, Malagasy, Malayalam, Cambodian, Marathi	Punjabi, Czech*, Afghan, Telugu, Kannada, Ndebele, Shona, Assamese, Gujerati, Fulani, Oriya		[Lingala, Catalan]
Radio Peking	Serbo-Croatian, Swahili, Russian, Tamil, Hausa, Esperanto, Tagalog, Mongolian*	Urdu, Romanian, Czech, Polish, Albanian, Bengali	Nepali, Foochow, Quechua, Pushto	Bulgarian, Hungarian
Voice of America	Swahili, Cambodian, Thai, Lao	[Japanese, Tamil]	Uzbek	Dari, Hausa, Azeri** Farsi*
Deutsche Welle	Persian, Turkish, Polish, Czech, Slovak, Hungarian, Serbo-Crotian, Russian, Swahili, Bulgarian, Romanian, Hausa, Indonesian, Greek, Italian, Hindi, Urdu, Mandarin, Amharic	Sanskrit, Maghrebian Arabic, Macedonian, Japanese, Pushto, Dari	Bengali	
BBC	Thai*, Portuguese*	[Hebrew, Albanian]		[Sinhala]
Radio Cairo	Thai, Lingala, Njanja, Fulani, Sesuto, Zulu, Shona, Ndebele	Ibo, Yoruba, Hindi, Bambara, Wolof, Afar	Russian, Dankali	[Nyanja, Farsi, Sesuto]

[] indicates services which were dropped
* indicates services which were reinstated after being suspended for five years or more.
** VOA's Azeri service was announced in 1980. However, it had not come on the air yet as of November 1981.
Note: I have included in this table only those language services actually broadcast by the stations. Many of the international broadcasting stations also furnish transcription services in various languages, designed for local placement. Data on the month or even year of introduction of a language service is not always readily obtainable. I have used the World Radio-TV Handbook as my primary source of information, and have supplemented this with specific information from Deutsche Welle, VOA and FBIS.

357

APPENDIX B (cont'd)
ESTIMATED WEEKLY BROADCAST HOURS FOR SOME LEADING
INTERNATIONAL RADIO STATIONS

	1950	1960	1970	(December) 1979
USSR (Radio Moscow Radio Peace and Progress and Republic stations)	533	1,015	1,908	2,020
United States	497	1,495	1,907	1,845
Voice of America	497	640	863	828
Radio Liberty	–	411	497	462
Radio Free Europe	–	444	547	555
Peoples' Republic of China	66	687	1,267	1,390
Federal Republic of Germany	–	315	779	798
Great Britain	643	589	723	712
North Korea	–	159	330	597
Albania	26	63	487	557
Egypt	–	301	540	542
India	116	157	271	389
Cuba	–	–	320	382
German Democratic Republic	–	185	274	371
Australia	181	257	350	333
The Netherlands	127	178	335	287
Japan	–	203	259	259
Czechoslovakia	119	196	202	254
Spain	68	202	251	242
Bulgaria	30	117	164	233
Portugal	46	133	295	210
Romania	30	159	185	198
Israel	–	91	158	184
Italy	170	205	165	170
Nigeria	–	–	62	170
South Africa	–	63	150	166

These figures* are taken from the BBC Handbook 1981 and do not
include international commercial or religious stations or
international stations in South Korea, Taiwan or Vietnam.
Based on figures in the 1981 World Radio TV Handbook, all
three stations would rank well up in the BBC's list: Radio
Hanoi broadcast for approximately 300 hours per week, as did
Radio Korea, while Taiwan's "Voice of Free China" broadcast
for about 340.   A few of the religious broadcasters, such as
HCJB, broadcast for 400 or more hours per week.   Clandestine
stations are not included in the BBC's figures.

*Used here with kind permission of BBC.

APPENDIX C
SIX MAJOR INTERNATIONAL BROADCASTERS AND THEIR SERVICES
IN SOME OF THE WORLD'S MAJOR LANGUAGES

	Radio Moscow	Radio Peking	Voice of America	DW and DLF	BBC	Radio Cairo
English	MM	MM	MM	MM	MM	MM
Russian	MM	MM	MM	MM	MM	M*
Kuoyu (Mandarin)	MM	MM	MM	M	M	-
Arabic	MM	MM	MM	MM	MM	MM
Spanish	MM	MM	MM	MM	MM	M
French	MM	MM	MM	MM	MM	MM
Japanese	MM	MM	-	M	M	-
Indonesian	MM	MM	MM	M	M	M
Portuguese	MM	MM	MM	MM	MM	M
German	MM	MM	-	MM	MM	M
Italian	MM	M	-	m	m**	M
Persian (Farsi)	MM	M	MM	M	M	-
Swahili	MM	M	M	MM	M	M
Hindi	MM	MM	M	m	MM	M
Hausa	MM	MM	m	M	M	M
Korean	MM	MM	M	-	-	-

Source: World Radio TV Handbook, 1981

Key: MM = two hours or more daily
     M = one to just under two hours daily
     m = less than one hour daily
     - = no service in that language

Note: This table does not take into account the fact that
repeat broadcasts probably help to swell the total hours for
many of these language services, and it is based on collective figures for each language, e.g. all BBC broadcasts
in Portuguese, whether to Latin America or to Europe.

* Cairo's Russian service is on medium wave only, and is
  intended for "the Palestine area"

**October 1981 budget cuts have made it likely that BBC's
  Italian service will be abolished by 1982

359

A SELECTIVE BIBLIOGRAPHY

I assume that any reader wishing to pursue specific points will use individual footnotes for guidance on further sources of information, but I also assume that guidance on more general or comprehensive sources of information would be help-ful, and have provided the following bibliography to that end.

General--the U.S. Foreign Broadcast Information Service Daily Reports and the BBC Monitoring Service Summary of World Broad-casts, either or both of which should be available in the libraries of the larger public and private universities in the United States and in the national libraries of some other countries, provide excerpts from domestic and foreign news and other informational broadcasts, and can be a useful, if non-comprehensive, source of information on broadcast styles and themes. The BBC Monitoring Service's weekly World Broad-casting Information (available by subscription from the Monitoring Service in Caversham Park, Reading, England) con-tains much information on the activities of domestic and international broadcasting stations.

Very few books deal solely with international broad-casting. Willi Boelcke, Die Macht des Radios (Frankfurt: Verlag Ullstein, 1977) is quite good on international radio before World War II and very thorough on German international radio during World War II, but has scant coverage of most other aspects and periods of international broadcasting. Julian Hale, Radio Power (Philadelphia: Temple University Press, 1975) has a more all-embracing treatment of the sub-ject, but it is not very detailed, source citations are few, and there is a fairly marked anti-VOA bias. David Abshire's International Broadcasting: A New Dimension of Western Diplomacy (Beverly Hills: Sage Publications, 1976) (The Washington Papers, No. 35) covers very little history and generally restricts itself to international broadcasting between Eastern (Communist) and Western nations. Richard Wood, Shortwave Voices of the World (Park Ridge: Gilfer Associates, 1969) provides a useful account of technical aspects of shortwave listening, and includes a few details on programing practices of various stations.

Several newsletters and periodicals deal with current practices in international broadcasting. Many listeners' clubs distribute monthly, quarterly or yearly newsletters to their members. A monthly publication called Voices--The Guide to International Radio (Box 226, Helsinki 17, Finland) contains

a considerable amount of broadcast schedule information and
some interesting portraits of international broadcasters, but
not much else. The Review of International Broadcasting (Glenn
Hauser, ed., University Radio WUOT, Knoxville, Tennessee 37916)
receives information and comments from listeners all over the
world, provides considerable scheduling information, and is
clearly organized by country of broadcast origin.

There are no bibliographies devoted entirely to international broadcasting, but Lawrence Lichty's World and International Broadcasting, A Bibliography (Washington, D.C.:
Association for Professional Broadcast Education (now Broadcast Education Association), 1971) contains a lengthy section
on books, articles, theses and reports on the subject from
the early 1920s through 1969. Most of the references are to
U.S. publications, but a few foreign sources are also listed.

Language services and times of broadcast, as well as
frequencies used, appear in two publications: J. Frost's
World Radio TV Handbook (annual) (Hvidovre, Denmark); and
Internationales Handbuch fur Rundfunk und Fernsehen (annual)
(Hamburg: Hans Bredow Institut). The aforementioned World
Broadcasting Information (BBC Monitoring Service) also contains two to four schedules (times, languages and some overall
program categories) per weekly issue for domestic and international radio stations.

For technical and legal regulation, the following are
particularly helpful: George Codding, The International
Telecommunications Union (Leiden: E.J. Brill, 1952); George
Codding, Broadcasting Without Barriers (Paris: UNESCO, 1959);
Delbert D. Smith, International Telecommunications Control
(Leyden: A.W. Sijthoff, 1969); L. John Martin, International
Propaganda: Its Legal and Diplomatic Control (Minneapolis:
University of Minnesota Press, 1958); and David M. Lieve,
International Telecommunications and International Law (Leyden:
A.W. Sijthoff, 1970). All of these works are somewhat to
considerably dated, but all provide fair and comprehensive
treatments of international regulation. For psychological
aspects of programing and audience receptivity to inter-
national communication, Herbert Kelman, ed., International
Behavior (New York: Holt, Rinehart and Winston, 1965), is an
excellent collection of original articles by some of the best
social scientists in the field, e.g. Pool, White, Deutsch,
Merritt and Janis, while Harold Lasswell, et al., Propaganda
and Communication in World History, Vol. III: A Pluralizing
World in Formation (Honolulu: University of Hawaii Press,
1980) also contains several good articles (Pool, Martin,
Lasswell) on international communication. Maury Lisann's
Broadcasting to the Soviet Union (New York: Praeger, 1976)
is a good case study of the politics of jamming.

Specialized collections of materials--most international radio

stations do not keep particularly comprehensive or well-
organized records of their past activities, although VOA, RIAS,
RFE-RL, BBC and DW all have collections of historical
materials, generally including scripts, program schedules,
reports, audience research studies and sometimes even internal
memos. Not all of this material is available for public inspection, although scholars may be permitted access to the
"non-public" documents. BBC's Written Archives Centre in
Caversham Park (near Reading), England, has an extensive and
carefully catalogued collection of material about the BBC
External Services, but one must reserve space at the Centre
months in advance, due to its limited seating capacity.
Furthermore, due to the Official Secrets Act, many materials
dating from any time within the past 30 years will not be
available for inspection; this particularly affects inter-
office memos and confidential reports.
     There are also collections of materials on international
broadcasting before and during World War II in the National
Archives (Motion Picture and Sound Division), the Library of
Congress, and the National Association of Broadcasters (Broadcast History Collection), all in Washington, D.C. (The
National Archives and the Library of Congress collections
contain many recordings of World War II broadcasts, both Allied
and Axis). The Sarnoff Library at Princeton University contains many speeches, memos, etc. by David Sarnoff concerning
U.S. international broadcasting.

Legislative hearings and station annual reports--several
international stations are subjected to annual legislative
hearings, for budget if nothing else, and the hearings are a
rich source of information on current activities and problems,
especially for BBC, VOA and RFE/RL. In addition, VOA activities are described in the annual USIA/USICA "Report to Congress" (pre-1972 reports are called "Review of Operations"),
and, up until 1977, in the annual reports to Congress of the
U.S. Advisory Commission on Information. The Board for International Broadcasting (RFE/RL) also makes an annual report to
the President and to Congress. BBC External Services
activities are reported each year in the BBC Handbook, while
Deutsche Welle publishes a DW Handbuch every two (even-
numbered) years, and Radio Nederland issues an annual
jaarverslag.

Communist stations are the subject of annual reports by the
USIA/USICA Office of Research. Those reports list changes
in language services and broadcast hours, but rarely deal
with program content. The Foreign Broadcast Information
Service's weekly "Trends in Communist Media," published since
1947, covers domestic media far more thoroughly than international, but its comparisons of themes and modes of presentation of various subjects is helpful in explaining variations

in approach among Communist international broadcasters. BBC's
World Broadcasting Information notes changes in technical
services, hours of broadcast and languages, but rarely treats
program content. Radio Free Europe and Radio Liberty both
prepare numerous reports on international broadcast developments within the Communist countries. A few of the Communist
international stations have been the subject of articles
appearing in Beiträge zur Geschichte des Rundfunks, a quarterly
publication of DDR Rundfunk (the broadcast service of the
German Democratic Republic).

Third World stations are more difficult to research, but the
BBC World Broadcasting Information is of some help, especially
in terms of schedules. The Review of International Broadcasting, cited earlier, is a very helpful source of information about broadcast content of Third World stations.
Useful for background information on Third World international
broadcasting are Sydney Head, ed., Broadcasting in Africa;
John Lent, ed., Broadcasting in Asia and the Pacific; and
Douglas Boyd, Broadcasting in the Arab World, all published
by Temple University Press, Philadelphia in 1974, 1978 and
1982 respectively.

Clandestine stations are by their nature elusive, but BBC's
World Broadcasting Information and FRENDX, the monthly publi-
cation of the Association of North American Short Wave
Association (address: 27 Cleveland Avenue, Trenton, New
Jersey 08609, but subject to change) both contain information
on some of their current activities, as does the Review of
International Broadcasting. Clandestine stations operated by
the Communist nations are covered in some of the FBIS, USIA/
USICA and RFE/RL reports mentioned immediately above.
Lawrence Magne's "Broadcasting Stations of Clandestine, etc.
Organizations," How to Listen to the World, Vol. 7 (c. 1973),
pp. 126-155, and "Clandestine Broadcasting 1975," World Radio
TV Handbook 1976, supplement ("Listen to the World"), pp. 55-
70, are both useful for historical detail on clandestine
stations active in the early to mid-1970s. Also helpful is
Kim Andrew Elliott's draft article (1981) "Unofficial Broad-
casting for Politics, Profit and Pleasure".

Religious stations have been the subject of several books, but
almost all of them have been written by people who are uncritical advocates of the stations' missionary work. The
King and Kushner dissertations cited in the footnotes are far
more rigorous as works of scholarship. Reginald Kennedy of
the BBC External Services has written a book about international religious stations, tentatively entitled The Word
Senders, but as of fall 1981 he had not yet found a publisher
for it. The quarterly International Christian Broadcasters'
Bulletin (4440 Saratoga, Downers Grove, Illinois 60515) contains much useful information on these stations.

INDEX

364

ABOUT THE AUTHOR

DONALD R. BROWNE is Professor of Speech-Communication at the University of Minnesota. He served with the U.S. Information Agency in North and West Africa from 1960 to 1963, taught at Boston and Purdue Universities before coming to Minnesota in 1966, and was a visiting professor at the American University of Beirut in 1973-74.

Dr. Browne's articles on the subject of international radio broadcasting have appeared in Journal of Broadcasting, Journalism Quarterly, Rundfunk und Fernsehen, Middle East Journal, Middle East Review and several other scholarly journals, and he has chapters on international broadcasting in books by Head, Lent, and Boyd.

Dr. Browne received his A.B., M.A. and Ph.D. degrees from the University of Michigan. His graduate program combined communication and political science, and he holds an adjunct appointment with the International Relations Program at the University of Minnesota.

Dr. Browne's research for this book was carried out over a 25-year period and included visits to some three dozen stations.